The Innovation Union in Europe

SCIENCE, INNOVATION, TECHNOLOGY AND ENTREPRENEURSHIP

Series editors: Elias G. Carayannis, *Professor of Science, Technology, Innovation and Entrepreneurship, School of Business, George Washington University, USA* and Aris Kaloudis, *NIFU STEP Studies in Innovation, Research and Education, Oslo, Norway*

There is ample and growing evidence that intangible resources such as knowledge, know-how and social capital will prove to be the coal, oil, and diamonds of the twenty-first century for developed, developing, and emerging economies alike. Moreover, there are strong indications and emerging trends that there are qualitative and quantitative differences between the drivers of economic growth in the twentieth and twenty-first centuries.

This new era is punctuated by:

- Development of a service-based economy, with activities demanding intellectual content becoming more pervasive and decisive.
- Increased emphasis on higher education and life-long learning to make effective use of the rapidly expanding knowledge base.
- Massive investments in research and development, training, education, software, branding, marketing, logistics, and similar services.
- Intensification of competition between enterprises and nations based on new product design, marketing methods and organizational forms.
- Continual restructuring of economies to cope with constant change.

This valuable new series concentrates on these important areas by focusing on the key pillars of science, technology, innovation, and entrepreneurship.

Titles in the series include:

Diversity in the Knowledge Economy and Society
Heterogeneity, Innovation and Entrepreneurship
Edited by Elias G. Carayannis, Aris Kaloudis and Åge Mariussen

Crisis, Innovation and Sustainable Development
The Ecological Opportunity
Edited by Blandine Laperche, Nadine Levratto and Dimitri Uzunidis

The Innovation Union in Europe
A Socio-Economic Perspective on EU Integration
Edited by Elias G. Carayannis and George M. Korres

The Innovation Union in Europe

A Socio-Economic Perspective on EU Integration

Edited by

Elias G. Carayannis

Professor of Science, Technology, Innovation and Entrepreneurship, School of Business, George Washington University, USA

George M. Korres

Associate Professor, Department of Geography, University of the Aegean, Greece

SCIENCE, INNOVATION, TECHNOLOGY AND ENTREPRENEURSHIP

Edward Elgar

Cheltenham, UK • Northampton, MA, USA

Published by
Edward Elgar Publishing Limited
The Lypiatts
15 Lansdown Road
Cheltenham
Glos GL50 2JA
UK

Edward Elgar Publishing, Inc.
William Pratt House
9 Dewey Court
Northampton
Massachusetts 01060
USA

A catalogue record for this book
is available from the British Library

Library of Congress Control Number: 2012948844

This book is available electronically in the ElgarOnline.com
Social and Political Science Subject Collection, E-ISBN 978 0 85793 991 3

ISBN 978 0 85793 990 6

Typeset by Servis Filmsetting Ltd, Stockport, Cheshire
Printed and bound in Great Britain by T.J. International Ltd, Padstow

The innovation union in Europe; a socio-economic perspective on EU integration.
Title main entry. Ed. by Elias G. Carayannis and George M. Korres.
(Science, innovation, technology and entrepreneurship)
Edward Elgar Publishing, c2013 194 p. $110.00 (Cloth)

Contents

Contributors

Elias G. Carayannis, Professor of Science, Technology, Innovation and Entrepreneurship, School of Business, George Washington University, Washington, DC, USA.

Urban Gråsjö, University West Trollhättan, Sweden.

Charlie Karlsson, Professor of Economics, Jönköping International Business School, Jönköping, Sweden, Professor of Industrial Economics, Blekinge Institute of Technology, Karlskrona, Sweden, Guest Professor of Economics, University West, Trollhätten, Sweden and President of the European Regional Science Association (ERSA).

Aikaterini Kokkinou, Department of Economics, University of Glasgow, UK.

George M. Korres, Associate Professor, Department of Geography, University of the Aegean, Greece.

Arnoud Lagendijk, Associate Professor, Research Program Governance and Places, Radboud University Nijmegen, the Netherlands.

Alice O. Nakamura, University of Alberta School of Business, Edmonton, Alberta, Canada.

Leonard I. Nakamura, Federal Reserve Bank of Philadelphia, USA.

Masao Nakamura, Professor, Sauder School of Business, The University of British Columbia and Konwakai Japan Research Chair.

Krisztina Varró, Radboud University Nijmegen, the Netherlands.

Peter Warda, Department of Economics, Jönköping International Business School, Jönköping, Sweden.

Preface

Much of the economic and social progress due to technology, along with the growing importance of technological change in world production and employment, has been characteristic of the last four decades. Technological change not only determines growth but also affects international competition and modernization within an economy. Technology has been central to both economic growth and core elements of social welfare that are only partly captured by standard measures of gross domestic product (GDP), including health, education and gender equality.

Technology creation and diffusion are the main components not only of innovation and growth but also of their long-run sustainability, with adoption and diffusion of new technologies affecting economic structure and competitiveness.

The concept of innovation has been frequently used almost as a synonym for technical change. In this case, innovation is seen as a process that has linkages and feedbacks, and connects all the elements of the Schumpeterian triad: invention, innovation and diffusion, together with the more coherent concept of incremental innovation. Within this framework, development is understood as the process of economic transformation brought about by innovation. This concept of development could, therefore, be considered, to a certain degree, as a background for the systems of innovation approach, because this is a core tool for the study of an economy's ability to create and diffuse innovation, and furthermore to 'develop'. The term 'system of innovation' indicates the national technological capabilities, as well as the structure and planning of research and development, with European innovation systems nowadays playing an important role in the economies of EU member states.

One of the most important economic events of recent decades in Europe has been the process of European economic integration. Economic theory, however, is unclear with respect to the effects of economic integration. This book offers such an empirical analysis. It uses the unique example of the EU to analyse whether convergence or divergence occurred among the involved member states. However, this book asserts that convergence and divergence may occur in various ways, mainly affected by national or regional dynamic conditions.

The book argues that national or regional economic development depends mainly on technical change, social and human capital, and knowledge creation and diffusion. The book is intended to provide a basic understanding of the current issues and the problems of the knowledge economy, technical change and innovation activities; it also examines many aspects and consequences of regional integration that are obscure or yet to be explored. In particular, with its wide range of topics, methodologies and perspectives, the book offers stimulating and wide-ranging analyses that will be of interest to students, economic theorists, empirical and social scientists and policy makers, as well as the informed general reader.

The book consists of eight chapters, as follows:

- Chapter 1 focuses on the nature and dynamics of research, education and innovation from a public as well as a private perspective (fractal research, education and innovation ecosystem – FREIE) in the context of the quadruple innovation helix and the Mode 3 knowledge production system architecture.
- Chapter 2 attempts to examine the main models and to review the patterns and the determinants of the diffusion process, and also to analyse the role and the impact of the relationship between adoption, innovation activities, diffusion process and development process.
- Chapter 3 focuses on the innovation initiatives of the EU. It is essential to extend the scope of the initiative to include innovation for financial sector products, processes and regulatory approaches. The authors make this argument using examples of financial sector innovations in the USA following the Great Depression and on the basis of an examination of the 2008 financial crisis.
- Chapter 4 attempts to examine the structure and role of national and regional systems of innovation and their implications for sustainable development and integration and convergence in the EU.
- Chapter 5 attempts, using a theoretical framework, to review the distinction between coding and territorialization. Moreover, a historical account of policy evolution is presented using key documents and evaluations published by EU departments and (funded) organizations dealing with regional innovation policy.
- Chapter 6 focuses on the nature and dynamics of entrepreneurship and innovation as drivers of economic development and their interdependencies and interaction with political regimes in which they exist, with reference to Greece.
- Chapter 7 focuses on one type of externality, namely knowledge spillovers. The empirical studies of the effects of knowledge

spillovers in Europe have normally focused on the localized effects on either total factor productivity or knowledge production measured in terms of patent output. The purpose of this chapter is to quantitatively review the empirical literature on spatial knowledge spillovers within and between European regions by means of meta-analysis to determine the extent to which such spillovers have been empirically documented as well as their spatial reach. In addition, the authors have applied a meta-regression analysis to analyse the determinants of observed heterogeneity across and between publications.

- Chapter 8 attempts to examine the economic role of innovation and efficiency enhancement in economic integration and convergence that is even more important, taking into consideration the slowdown and the effects created by the current financial crisis. Within this framework, the key factors influencing the integration and convergence process are creation and diffusion of innovation, along with productive efficiency enhancement, mainly around three key areas: innovation and research; strengthening networks and clusters; and efficient use of production factors.

We would like to thank the contributors to this volume and also the anonymous reviewer, and, above all, our publisher for encouragement and support.

Elias G. Carayannis
George M. Korres

PART I

Innovation and the Knowledge-Based Economy

1. The innovation ecosystem

Elias G. Carayannis

1. INTRODUCTION

1.1 Specialized Knowledge as Key to Competitive Advantage

Developed and developing economies alike face increased resource scarcity and competitive rivalry. Science and technology increasingly appear as a main source of competitive and sustainable advantage for nations and regions alike. However, the key determinant of their efficacy is the quality and quantity of entrepreneurship-enabled innovation that unlocks and captures the pecuniary benefits of the science enterprise in the form of private, public or hybrid goods. In this context, linking university basic and applied research with the market, via technology transfer and commercialization mechanisms including government–university–industry partnerships and risk capital investments, constitutes the essential trigger mechanism and driving device for sustainable competitive advantage and prosperity. In short, university researchers, properly informed, empowered and supported, are bound to emerge as the architects of a prosperity that rests on a solid foundation of scientific and technological knowledge, experience and expertise, and not in fleeting and conjectural 'financial engineering' schemes. Building on these constituent elements of technology transfer and commercialization, 'open innovation diplomacy' encompasses the concept and practice of bridging distance and other divides (cultural, socio-economic, technological etc.) with focused and properly targeted initiatives to connect ideas and solutions with markets and investors ready to appreciate them and nurture them to their full potential. Chapter 6 develops this in more detail.

The emerging gloCalizing (global/local; Carayannis and von Zedtwitz, 2005; Carayannis and Alexander, 2006) frontier of converging systems, networks and sectors of innovation that is driven by increasingly complex, non-linear and dynamic processes of knowledge creation, diffusion and use confronts us with the need to reconceptualize – if not reinvent – the ways and means that knowledge production, utilization and renewal take place in the context of the knowledge economy and society.

Perspectives from and about different parts of the world and diverse human, socio-economic, technological and cultural contexts are interwoven to produce an emerging new worldview on how specialized knowledge, embedded in a particular socio-technical context, can serve as the unit of reference for stocks and flows of a hybrid, public/private, tacit/codified, tangible/virtual good that represents the building block of the knowledge economy, society and polity.

Thus the major purposes of this chapter could be paraphrased as:

(a) adding to the theories and concepts of knowledge further discursive inputs, such as suggesting a linkage of systems theory and the understanding of knowledge, emphasizing multi-level systems of knowledge and innovation, summarized as the Mode 3 knowledge production systems approach to knowledge creation, diffusion and use that we discuss below;
(b) using this diversified and conceptually pluralized understanding to support practical and application-oriented decision making with regard to knowledge, knowledge optimization and the leveraging of knowledge for other purposes, such as economic performance: knowledge-based decision making has ramifications for knowledge management of firms (global multinational corporations) and universities as well as for public policy (knowledge policy, innovation policy);
(c) exploring, identifying and understanding the key triggers, drivers, catalysts and accelerators of high-quality and -quantity (continuous as well as discontinuous, reinforcing as well as disruptive) innovation and sustainable entrepreneurship (financially and environmentally – see Carayannis and Campbell, 2010) that serve as the foundations of robust competitiveness within the operational framework of open innovation diplomacy (Carayannis and Campbell, 2011) and diaspora entrepreneurship and innovation networks (ibid.) (see also Chapter 6).

1.2 Mode 3 Knowledge Production System

We postulate that one approach to the required reconceptualization is what I call the 'Mode 3' knowledge production system (expanding and extending the 'Mode 1' and 'Mode 2' knowledge production systems), which is at the heart of the fractal research, education and innovation ecosystem (FREIE[1]) ('innovation ecosystem' for short[2]) consisting of 'innovation networks' and 'knowledge clusters' (see definitions below) for knowledge creation, diffusion and use (Carayannis and Campbell, 2006a).

'Mode 3' is a multi-lateral, multi-nodal, multi-modal, and multi-level systems approach to the conceptualization, design, and management of real and virtual, 'knowledge-stock' and 'knowledge-flow', modalities that catalyze, accelerate, and support the creation, diffusion, sharing, absorption, and use of co-specialized knowledge assets. 'Mode 3' is based on a system-theoretic perspective of socio-economic, political, technological, and cultural trends and conditions that shape the co-evolution of knowledge with the 'knowledge-based and knowledge-driven, gloCal economy and society'. (Carayannis and von Zedtwitz, 2005, p. 22).

The Mode 3 knowledge production system is in short the nexus or hub of the emerging twenty-first-century innovation ecosystem, where people,[3] culture[4] and technology[5] (Carayannis and Gonzalez, 2003) meet and interact to catalyze creativity, trigger invention and accelerate innovation across scientific and technological disciplines, public and private sectors (government, university, industry and non-governmental knowledge production, utilization and renewal entities, as well as other civil society entities, institutions and stakeholders) in a top–down, policy-driven as well as bottom–up, entrepreneurship-empowered fashion. One of the basic ideas of this chapter is the coexistence, co-evolution and co-specialization of different knowledge paradigms and different knowledge modes of knowledge production and knowledge use. We can postulate a dominance of knowledge heterogeneity at the systems (national, transnational) level. Only at the subsystem (sub-national) level should we expect homogeneity. We can paraphrase this understanding by the term 'Mode 3' knowledge production system.

1.3 Mode 3 and Systems Theory

Embedding concepts of knowledge creation, diffusion and use in the context of general systems theory could prove mutually beneficial and enriching for systems theory as well as knowledge-related fields of study, as this could:

(a) reveal for systems theory a new and important field of application; and
(b) at the same time, provide a better conceptual framework for understanding knowledge-based and knowledge-driven events and processes in the economy, and hence reveal opportunities for optimizing public sector policies and private sector practices.

To fully leverage the potential of systems (and systems theory) one should demonstrate how a system design can be brought in line with other available concepts, such as innovation networks and knowledge clusters. With regard to clusters, at least three types can be listed:

1. *Geographic (spatial) clusters* Here a cluster represents a certain geographic, spatial configuration, either tied to a location or to a larger region. Geographic, spatial proximity, for example for the exchange of tacit knowledge, is considered crucial. While 'local' clearly represents a sub-national entity, a 'region' could be either sub-national or transnational.
2. *Sectoral clusters* Here different industrial or business sectors develop specific profiles with regard to knowledge production, diffusion and use. One could add that sectoral clusters even support the advancement of particular 'knowledge cultures'. In innovation research, the term 'innovation culture' is now acknowledged (Kuhlmann, 2001, p. 958).
3. *Knowledge clusters* Knowledge clusters are agglomerations of co-specialized, mutually complementary and reinforcing knowledge assets in the form of 'knowledge stocks' and 'knowledge flows' that exhibit self-organizing, learning-driven, dynamically adaptive competences and trends in the context of an open systems perspective. Here, a cluster represents a specific configuration of knowledge, and possibly also of knowledge types. However, in geographic (spatial) and sectoral terms, a knowledge cluster is not predetermined. In fact, a knowledge cluster can cross-cut different geographic locations and sectors, thus operating globally and locally (across a whole multi-level spectrum). It may express an innovative capability, and produce knowledge that excels (knowledge-based) economic performance. A knowledge cluster, furthermore, may include more than one geographic and/or sectoral clusters.

Networks emphasize interaction, connectivity and mutual complementarity, and reinforcement. They can be regarded as the internal configuration that ties together and determines a cluster, and can also express the relationship between different clusters. The concept of networking is important for understanding the dynamics of advanced and knowledge-based societies. Networking links together different modes of knowledge production and knowledge use, and also connects (sub-nationally, nationally, transnationally) different sectors or systems of society. Systems theory, as presented here, is flexible enough for integrating and reconciling systems and networks, thus creating conceptual synergies. Innovation

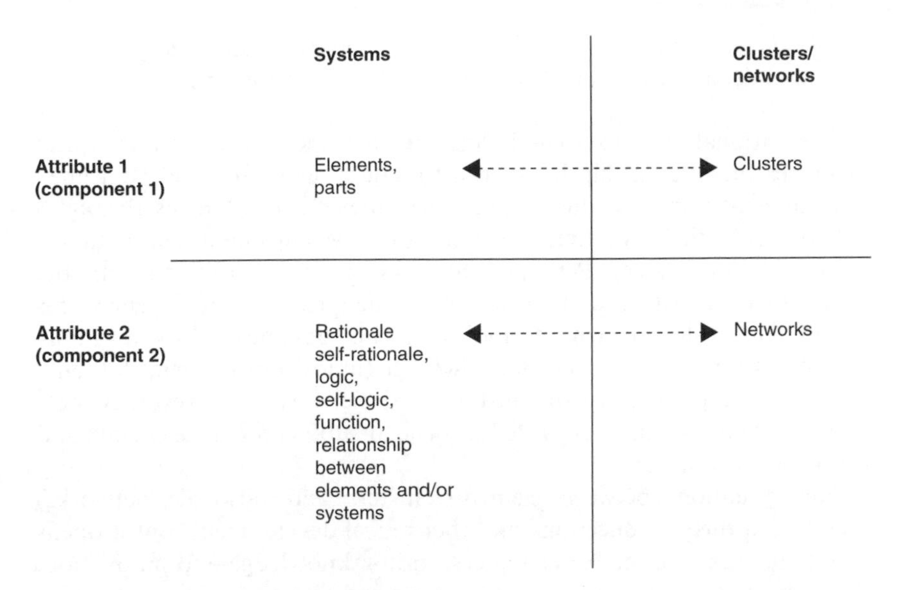

Source: Carayannis and Campbell (2009).

Figure 1.1 Theoretical equivalents between conceptual attributes of systems and clusters/networks

networks are real and virtual infrastructures and infra-technologies that serve to nurture creativity, trigger invention and catalyze innovation in a public and/or private domain context (e.g. government–university–industry public–private research and technology development co-opetitive partnerships) (see Carayannis and Alexander, 1999a, 2004). Innovation networks and knowledge clusters thus resemble a matrix, indicating the interactive complexity of knowledge and innovation. Should the (proposed) conceptual flexibility of systems (and systems theory) be fully leveraged, it appears important to demonstrate how systems relate conceptually to knowledge clusters and innovation networks, as they are key in understanding the nature and dynamics of knowledge stocks and flows. We suggest linking the two basic components (attributes) of systems ('elements/parts' and 'rationale/self-rationale'; Campbell, 2001, p. 426) with clusters and networks (Carayannis and Campbell, 2006a, pp. 9–10). What results is a formation of two pairs of theoretical equivalents (see Figure 1.1).

1. *Elements and clusters* The elements (parts) of a system can be regarded as an equivalent to clusters (knowledge clusters).

2. *Rationale and networks* The rationale (self-rationale) of a system can be understood as equivalent to networks (innovation networks).

The rationale of a system holds together the system elements and expresses the relationship between different systems. It could be argued that, at least partially, this rationale manifests itself ('moves through') networks. At the same time, elements of a system might also manifest themselves as clusters. Perhaps networks could be affiliated with the functions of a system, and clusters with the structures of systems. This would help to show us what to look for. This, obviously, does not imply that structures and functions of knowledge (innovation) systems fall only into the conceptual boxes of 'clusters' and 'networks'. However, clusters and networks should be regarded as crucial subsets for the elements and rationales of systems.

This equation (between elements/clusters and rationales/networks) might need further conceptual and theoretical development. But it opens a convincing route for better understanding knowledge and innovation, through tying together two strong conceptual traditions (systems theory with clusters and knowledge). A further ramification of networks, as we will demonstrate later on, could also imply understanding knowledge strategies as complex network configurations.

1.4 Integrating Different Knowledge Modes

The following presents in greater detail different aspects of advanced knowledge. Crucial for the suggested 'Mode 3' approach is the idea that an advanced knowledge system may integrate different knowledge modes. Some knowledge (innovation) modes will certainly die out. However, what is important for the broader picture is that a co-evolution, co-development and co-specialization of different knowledge modes emerges. This pluralism of knowledge modes should be regarded as essential for advanced knowledge-based societies and economies. This may point to similar features of advanced knowledge and advanced democracy. We could state that the competitiveness and sustainability of the gloCal knowledge economy and society increasingly depend on the elasticity and flexibility of promoting a co-evolution and thereby a cross-integration of different knowledge (innovation) modes. This heterogeneity of knowledge modes should create hybrid synergies.

The 'triple helix' model of knowledge, developed by Henry Etzkowitz and Loet Leydesdorff (2000, pp. 111–12), stresses three 'helices' that intertwine and thereby generate a national innovation system: academia/universities, industry, and state/government. Etzkowitz and Leydesdorff are inclined to speak of 'university–industry–government relations' and networks, also placing a particular emphasis on 'tri-lateral networks and hybrid organizations', where those helices overlap. In extension of the triple helix model we suggest a 'quadruple helix' model (see Figure 1.2), which adds to the above-stated helices a 'fourth helix' that we identify as the 'media-based and culture-based public'. This fourth helix is associated with 'media', 'creative industries', 'culture', 'values', 'lifestyles', and perhaps also the notion of the 'creative class' (a term coined by Richard Florida, 2004). The explanatory potential of such a fourth helix is that culture and values, on the one hand, and the way that 'public reality' is being constructed and communicated by the media, on the other hand, influence every national innovation system. The proper 'innovation culture' is key to promoting an advanced knowledge-based economy. Public discourses, transported through and interpreted by the media, are crucial for a society to assign top priority to innovation and knowledge (research, technology, education).

Figure 1.3 displays from which conceptual perspectives the co-evolution and cross-integration of different knowledge modes could be approached. Mode 3 emphasizes the additionality and surplus effect of a co-evolution of a pluralism of knowledge and innovation modes. The quadruple helix refers to structures and processes of the gloCal knowledge economy and society. Furthermore, innovation ecosystem stresses the importance of a pluralism of a diversity of agents, actors and organizations: universities, small and medium-sized enterprises and major corporations, arranged along the matrix of fluid and heterogeneous innovation networks and knowledge clusters. All this may result in a 'democracy of knowledge', driven by a pluralism of knowledge and innovation and by a pluralism of paradigms for knowledge modes.

In the *Frascati Manual*, the OECD (1994, p. 29) distinguishes between the following categories of research (R&D, research and experimental development): basic research; applied research; and experimental development. Basic research represents a primary competence of university research, whereas business R&D focuses heavily on experimental development. In an empirical assessment of the USA, one of the leading national innovation systems with regard to the financial volume of R&D resources, experimental development ranks first, applied research second and basic research third (see Figure 1.4). What is interesting, however, is the dynamic momentum when observed for a longer period of time. Basic research in the USA grew faster than applied research. In 1981, 13.4 percent of US R&D was devoted to basic research. By 2004, basic research increased its percentage share to 18.7 percent. During the same time period the percentage shares of applied research and experimental development declined

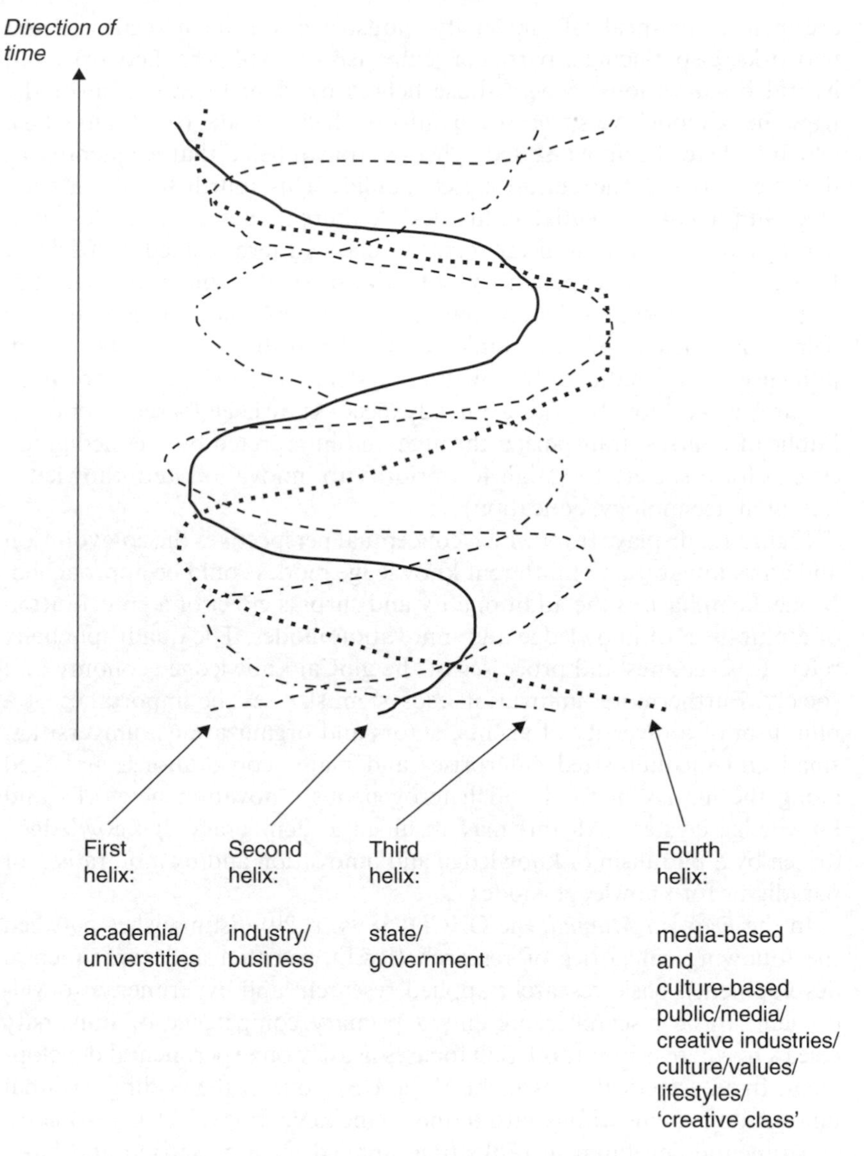

Note: Triple helix: university–industry–government relations (helices); quadruple helix: university–industry–government–media- and culture-based public relations (helices).

Source: Carayannis and Campbell (2009).

Figure 1.2 Conceptualization of the quadruple helix

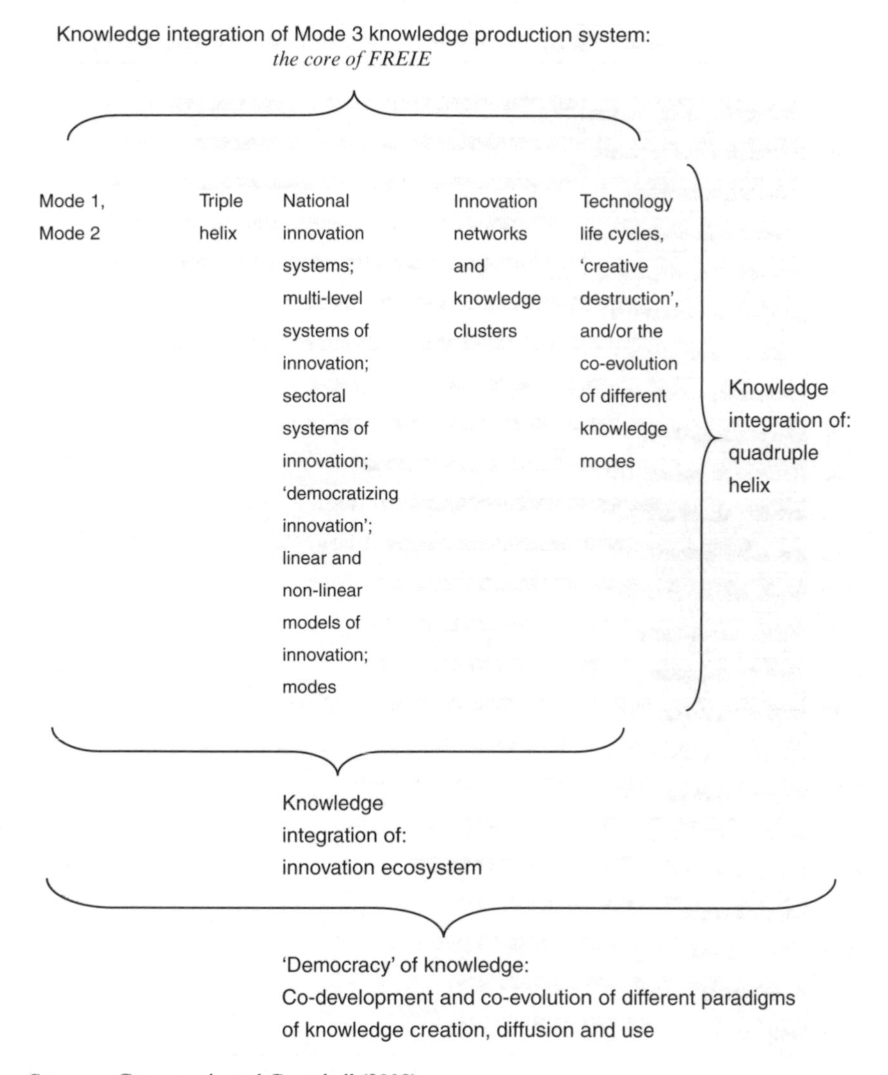

Source: Carayannis and Campbell (2009).

Figure 1.3 Knowledge creation, diffusion and use in a gloCal knowledge economy and society

(Figure 1.5). This links to the question whether we should expect R&D to follow a U-shaped curve for the US innovation system, implying that basic research will further increase its percentage share of overall R&D expenditure. This would go hand in hand with an important gain in basic research.

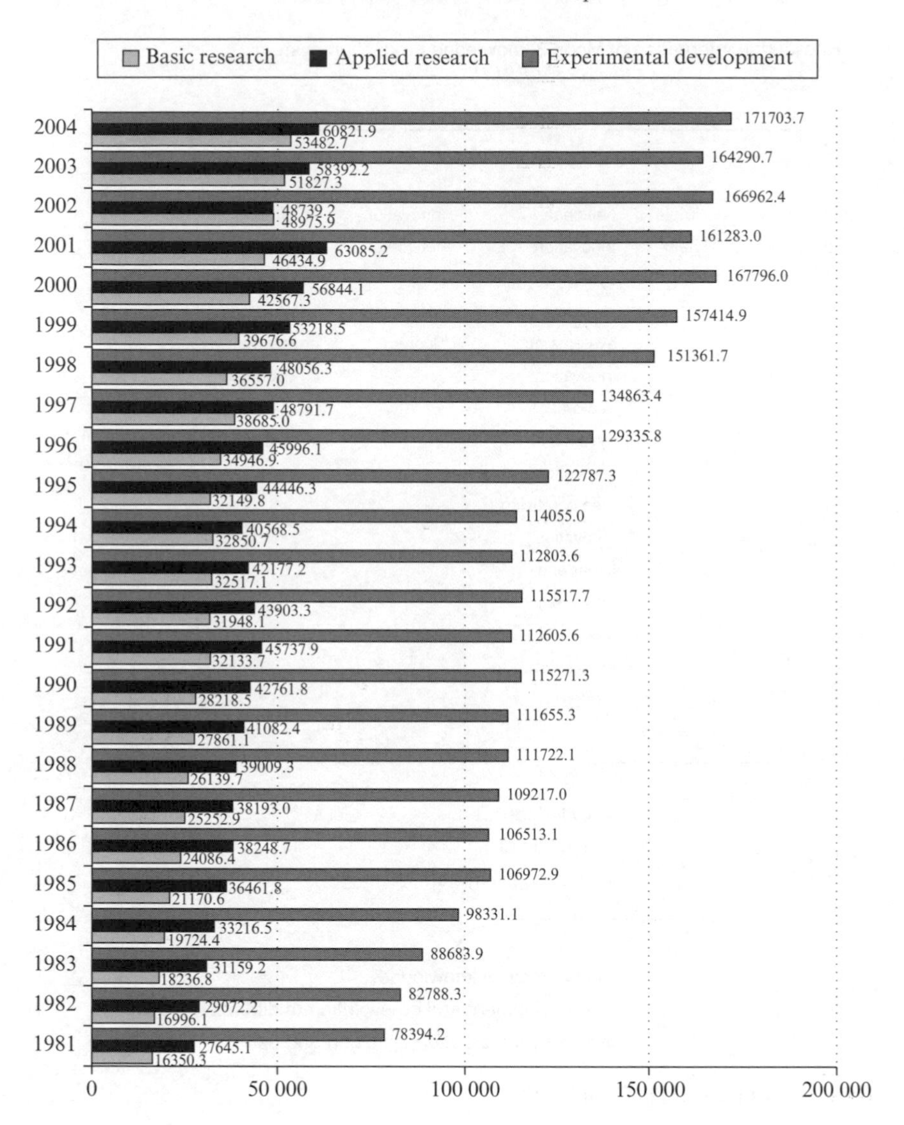

Source: OECD (2006).

Figure 1.4 National R&D performance of the USA according to the 'R&D activities' of basic research, applied research and experimental development (million constant $ 2000 prices and PPPs, 1981–2004)

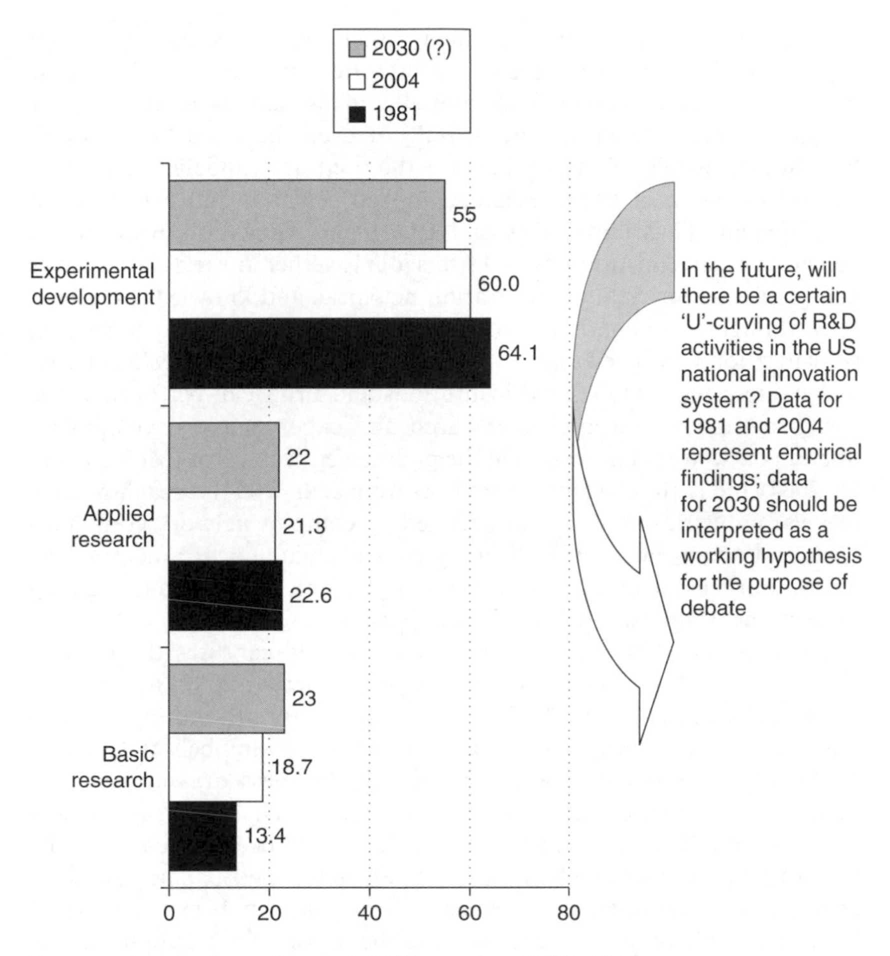

Source: Carayannis and Campbell (2009), based on OECD (2006).

Figure 1.5 National R&D performance of the USA according to the 'R&D activities' of basic research, applied research and experimental development (% of annual R&D activities: 1981, 2004, and a possible projection for 2030)

Furthermore, would such a potential future scenario for the USA also spill over to other national innovation systems?

In a simple interpretation, the linear model of innovation claims that, first, there is basic university research. Later this basic research converts into applied research of intermediary organizations (university-related institutions). Finally, firms pick up, and transform applied research into experimental development, which is then introduced as commercial market applications. This linear view is often attributed to Vannevar Bush (1945), even though Bush himself, in his famous report, neither mentions 'linear model of innovation' nor even the word 'innovation'. Non-linear models of innovation, on the contrary, underscore a more parallel coupling of basic research, applied research and experimental development. Thus universities or HEIs (higher education institutions), university-related institutions and firms join together in variable networks and platforms for creating innovation networks and knowledge clusters. Even though there continues to be a division of labor and a functional specialization of organizations with regard to the type of R&D activity, universities, university-related institutions and firms can perform, at the same time, basic and applied research and experimental development. Surveys on sectoral innovation in the pharmaceutical sector (McKelvey et al., 2004) and in the chemical sector (Cesaroni et al., 2004) reveal how each of these industries may be characterized by complex network configurations and arrangement of a diversity of academic and firm actors. The innovation ecosystem thus represents a model for a simultaneous coupling of 'non-linear innovation modes' (see Figure 1.6).

The concept of the 'entrepreneurial university' captures the need to link more closely university research with the R&D market activities of firms (see, e.g., Etzkowitz, 2003). Just as important as the entrepreneurial university is the concept of the 'academic firm' (Campbell and Güttel, 2005), which represents the complementary business organization and strategy *vis-à-vis* the entrepreneurial university. The interplay of academic firms and entrepreneurial universities should be regarded as crucial for advanced knowledge-based economies and societies. The following characteristics represent the academic firm (ibid., p. 171): 'support of the interfaces between the economy and the universities'; 'support of the paralleling of basic research, applied research and experimental development'; 'incentives for employees to codify knowledge'; 'support of collaborative research and of research networks'; and 'a limited "scientification" of business R&D'. Despite continuing important functional differences between universities and firms, some limited hybrid overlapping may also occur between entrepreneurial universities and academic firms, expressed in the fact that entrepreneurial universities and academic firms can engage more easily in university/business research networks. In an innovation-driven economy, business R&D gains support and excels when it refers to inputs from networking of universities and firms. The academic firm also engages in 'basic business research'. Of course, we must always bear in mind that academic firms and universities are not identical, because academic firms represent commercial units, interested in creating commercial

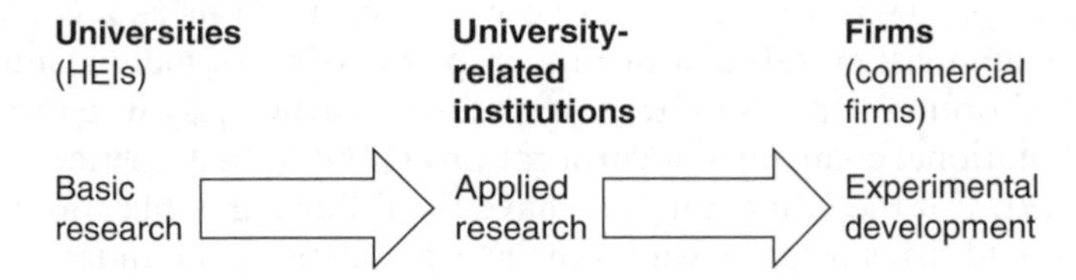

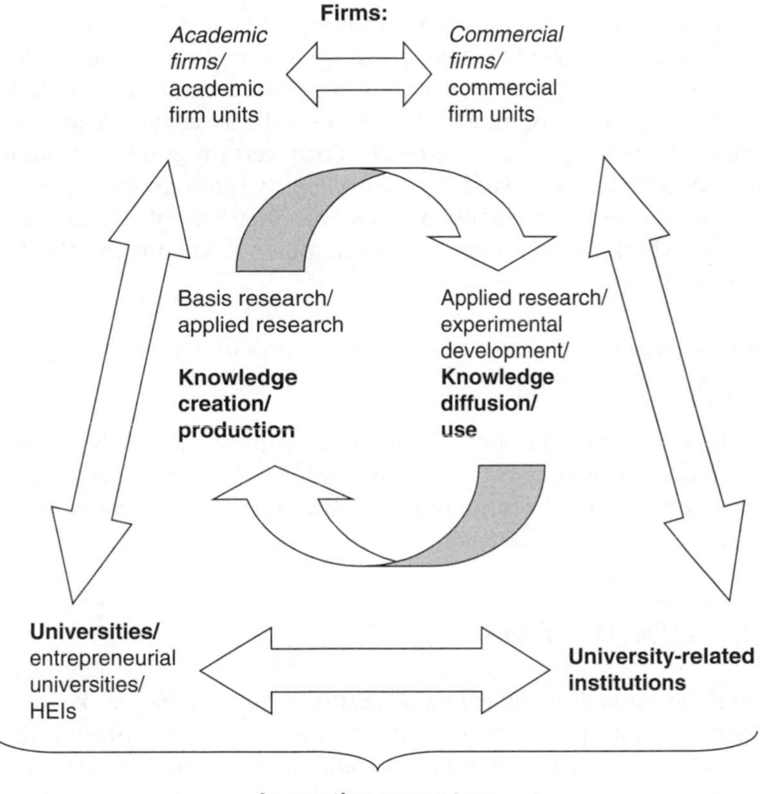

Source: Carayannis and Campbell (2009).

Figure 1.6 Linear and non-linear innovation modes linking universities with commercial and academic firms

revenues and profits. Alternatively, the academic firm could be seen in two ways: (1) as a concept for the whole firm; (2) or as a concept only for a subdivision, sub-unit or branch of the firm. In many contexts, this second option appears to be more realistic, particularly when we analyze multinational companies or corporations (MNCs) that operate in a global context. For the future, this may have the following implication: how can or should firms balance, within their 'organizational boundary', the principle of the academic and of the traditional 'commercial' firm?

The 'technology life cycles' explain why there is always a dynamic in the gloCal knowledge economy and society (Tassey, 2001). The 'saturation tendency' within every technology life cycle demands the creation and launch of new technology life cycles, leading to the market introduction of next-generation technology-based products and services. In reality, different technology life cycles with a varying degree of market maturity will operate in parallel. To a certain extent, technology life cycles are also responsible for the cyclicality (growth phases) of a modern market economy. Perhaps the most succinct way of describing the economic thinking of Joseph A. Schumpeter is to present the following equation:

Entrepreneurship + leveraging opportunities of new technology life cycles = Economic growth

Addressing the cyclicality of capitalist economic life, Schumpeter (1942) used the notion of 'creative destruction'. Mode 3 may open up a route for overcoming or transforming the destructiveness of 'creative destruction' (Carayannis et al., 2007).

2. INNOVATION

Innovation is often linked with creating a sustainable market around the introduction of new and superior product or process. Specifically, in the literature on the management of technology, technological innovation is characterized as the introduction of a new technology-based product into the market:

> *Technological innovation* is defined . . . as a situationally new development through which people extend their control over the environment. Essentially, technology is a tool of some kind that allows an individual to do something new. A technological innovation is basically information organized in a new way. So technology transfer amounts to the communication of information, usually from one organization to another. (Tornazky and Fleischer, 1990)

The broader interpretation of the term refers to an 'idea, practice or material artifact' (Rogers and Shoemaker, 1971, p 19) adopted by a person or organization, where that artifact is 'perceived to be new by the relevant unit of adoption' (Zaltman et al., 1973). Therefore innovation tends to change perceptions and relationships at the organizational level, but its impact is not limited there. Innovation, in its broader socio-technical, economic and political context, can also substantially impact, shape and evolve ways and means people live their lives, businesses form, compete, succeed and fail, and nations prosper or decline.

From a business perspective, an innovation is perceived as the happy ending of the commercialization journey of an invention, when that journey is indeed successful and leads to the creation of a sustainable and flourishing market niche or new market. Therefore a technical discovery or invention (the creation of something new) is not significant to a company unless that new technology can be utilized to add value to the company, through increased revenues, reduced cost and similar improvements in financial results. This has two important consequences for the analysis of any innovation in the context of a business organization.

First, an innovation must be integrated into the operations and strategy of the organization, so that it has a distinct impact on how the organization creates value or on the type of value the organization provides in the market.

Second, an innovation is a social process, since it is only through the intervention and management of people that an organization can realize the benefits of an innovation.

The discussion of innovation clearly leads to the development of a model to understand its evolving nature. Innovation management is concerned with the activities of the firm undertaken to yield solutions to problems of product, process and administration. Innovation involves uncertainty and disequilibrium. Nelson and Winter (1982) propose that almost any change, even trivial, represents innovation. They also suggest, given the uncertainty, that innovation results in the generation of new technologies and changes in the relative weighting of existing technologies (ibid.). This results in the disruptive process of disequilibrium. As an innovation is adopted and diffused, existing technologies may become less useful (reduction in weight factors) or even useless (weighing equivalent to zero) and abandoned altogether. The adoption phase is where uncertainty is introduced. New technologies are not adopted automatically but rather, markets influence the adoption rate (Carayannis and Allbritton, 1997; Rogers et al., 1998). Innovative technologies must propose to solve a market need such as reduced costs or increased utility or increased productivity. The markets, however, are social constructs and subject to non-innovation-related criteria. For example, an invention may be promising, offering a substantial reduction on the cost of a product which normally would influence the market to accept the given innovation; but due to issues like information asymmetry (the lack of knowledge in the market concerning the invention's properties), the invention may not be readily accepted by the markets. Thus the innovation may remain an invention. If, however, the innovation is accepted by the market, the results will bring about change to the existing technologies being replaced, leading to a change in the relative weighting of the existing technology. This is in effect disequilibrium.

Given the uncertainty and change inherent in the innovation process, management must develop skills and understanding of the process, and a method for managing the disruption. The problems of managing the resulting disruption are strategic in nature. The problems may be classified into three groups: engineering, entrepreneurial, and administrative (Drejer, 2002). This grouping correlates to the related types of innovation, namely, product, process and administrative innovation:

- The engineering problem is one of selecting the appropriate technologies for proper operational performance.
- The entrepreneurial problem refers to defining the product/service domain and target markets.
- Administrative problems are concerned with reducing the uncertainty and risk during the previous phases.

In much of the foregoing discussion of innovation, a recurring theme is that of uncertainty, leading to the conclusion that an effective model of innovation must include a multidimensional approach (uncertainty is defined as unknown unknowns whereas risk is defined as known knowns). One model posited as an aid to understanding is the multidimensional model of innovation (MMI) (Cooper, 1998). This model attempts to define innovation by establishing three-dimensional boundaries. The planes are defined as product–process, incremental–radical, and administrative–technical. The product–process boundary concerns itself with the end product and its relationship to the methods employed by firms to produce and distribute the product. Incremental–radical defines the degree of relative strategic change that accompanies the diffusion of an innovation. This is a measure of the disturbance or disequilibrium in the market. Technological–administrative boundaries refer to the relationship of innovation change to the firm's operational core. The use of 'technological' refers to the influences on basic firm output, while the 'administrative' boundary would include innovations affecting associated factors of policy, resources and social aspects of the firm.

		Knowledge	
		yes	*no*
Innovation	*yes*	Knowledge-based innovation or knowledge which, through innovation, is linked with society, economy and politics. Examples: Mode 1 and technology cycles in the long run, Mode 2, triple helix	Innovation, taking place with no (almost no) references to knowledge. Examples: management innovations in businesses, which are not R&D or technology-based
	no	Knowledge, without major references to innovation (and use). Examples: 'pure research', perhaps some components of Mode 1 and of early phases of technology life cycles	*? (Not of primary concern for our conceptual mapping)*

Source: Carayannis and Campbell (2009).

Figure 1.7 A four-fold typology of possible cross-references and interactions between knowledge and innovation

2.1 The Relationship between Knowledge and Innovation

What is the relationship between knowledge and innovation? From our viewpoint it makes sense not to treat knowledge and innovation as interchangeable concepts. The ramifications of this are (see Figure 1.7):

1. There are aspects, areas of knowledge, that can be analyzed without considering innovation (e.g. 'pure basic research' in a linear understanding of innovation).
2. Consequently, there are areas or aspects of innovation that are not (necessarily) tied to knowledge (see various contributions to Shavinina, 2003).
3. However, there are also areas where knowledge and innovation coexist. These we would like to call 'knowledge-based innovation', indicating areas where knowledge and innovation have a mutual interaction.

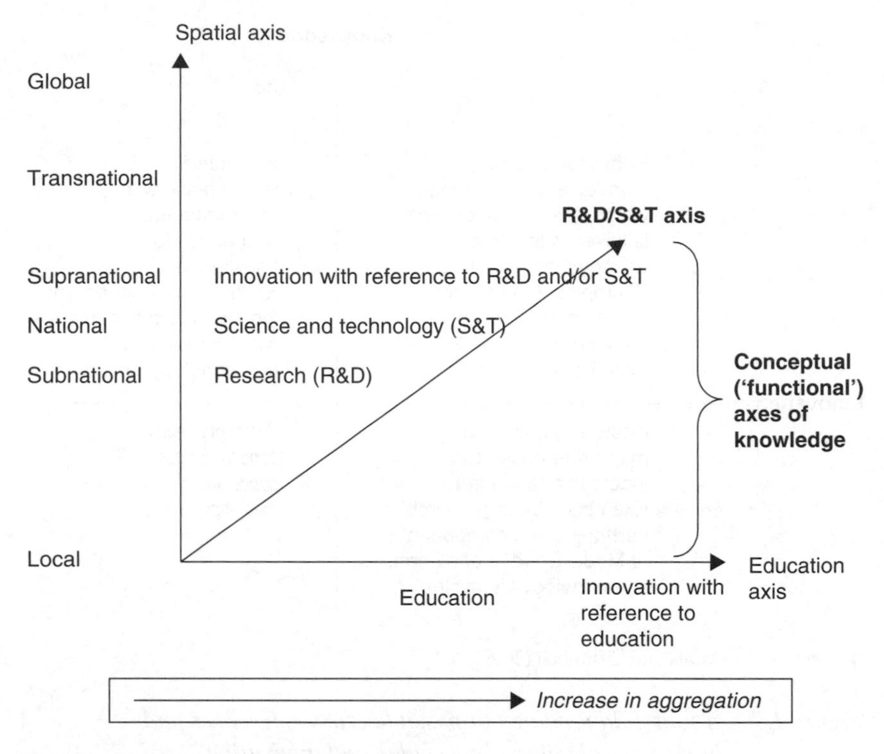

Source: Carayannis and Campbell (2009).

Figure 1.8 A multi-level modeling knowledge

In the case of knowledge-based innovation, we can then speak of innovation that deals with knowledge. Our impression is that in many contexts, when the focus falls on innovation, almost automatically this type of innovation is implied. Even though we will focus on this knowledge-based innovation, it is important to acknowledge the possibilities of a knowledge without innovation, and of innovation independent of knowledge. To further illustrate our point, the notion of the 'national innovation system' or 'national system of innovation' (NSI) conventionally expresses linkages to knowledge (see Lundvall, 1992; Nelson, 1993).

In research on the European Union (EU), references to a 'multi-level architecture' are quite common (see, e.g., Hooghe and Marks, 2001). This 'multi-level' approach is being applied in a diversity of fields, since it supports the understanding of complex processes in a globalizing world. Inspired by this, we suggest using the concept of 'multi-level systems of knowledge' (see Figure 1.8; see also Carayannis and Campbell, 2006a).

One obvious axis, therefore, is the spatial (geographic, spatial–political) axis that expresses different levels of spatial aggregations. The national level, coinciding with the nation state (the currently dominant manifestation of arranging and organizing political and societal affairs), represents one type of spatial aggregation. Sub-national aggregations fall below the nation-state level, and point toward local political entities. Transnational aggregations, for example, can refer to the supranational integration process of the EU. This raises the interesting question whether we should be prepared to expect that in the twenty-first century we will also witness a proliferation of supranational (transnational) integration processes in other world regions, possibly implying a new stage in the evolution of politics, where (small and medium-sized) nation-state structures become absorbed by supranational (transnational) clusters (Campbell, 1994). The highest level of transnational aggregation that we currently know is globalization. Interestingly, the aggregation level of the term 'region(s)' has never been convincingly standardized. In the context and political language of the EU, regions are understood sub-nationally. American scholars, on the other hand, often refer to regions in a state-transcending interpretation (i.e., a region consists of more than one nation state). The term 'gloCal' (explained earlier) underscores the potentials and benefits of a mutual and parallel interconnectedness of different levels.

Despite the importance of this spatial axis, we do not wish to exhaust the concept of multi-level systems of knowledge with spatial–geographic metaphors. We suggest adding on non-spatial axes of aggregation. These we may call conceptual (functional) axes of knowledge. In that context, two axes certainly are pivotal: education and research (R&D, research and experimental development). For research, the level of aggregation can develop accordingly: R&D; S&T (science and technology);[6] and R&D-based innovation, involving a broad spectrum of considerations and aspects. Obviously, every 'axis direction' of further aggregation – as demonstrated here for R&D – depends on a specific conceptual understanding. Should, for example, a different conceptual approach for defining S&T be favored, then the sequence of aggregation might change. (Concerning the education axis, we leave it to the judgment of other scholars what meaningful terms at different levels of aggregation may be.)

How many non-spatial (conceptual) axes of knowledge can there be? We focused on the R&D and education axes, but do not thereby imply that there may not be more than two conceptual axes. Here, at least in principle, a multitude or diversity of conceptual model-building approaches is possible and also appropriate. Perhaps, we could even integrate 'innovation' as an additional conceptual axis, following the aggregation line from local, to national and transnational innovation systems.

We would then have to consider what the relationship is between such an 'extra innovation axis' with the 'innovation' of the research and education axes. 'Regional' innovation could cross-refer to local and transnational innovation systems, implying even gloCal innovation systems and processes that simultaneously link through different aggregation levels.

We have already discussed the conceptual boundary problems between knowledge and innovation. One approach to balancing ambiguities in this context is to acknowledge that a partial conceptual overlap exists between a knowledge-centered and an innovation-centered understanding. Depending on the focus of the preferred analytical view, the same 'element(s)' can be conceptualized as part of a knowledge or of an innovation system. Concerning knowledge, we pointed to some of the characteristics of multi-level systems of knowledge, underscoring the understanding of aggregation of spatial and non-spatial (conceptual) axes. Introducing multi-level systems of knowledge also justifies speaking of multi-level systems of innovation, developing the original concept of the national innovation system (Lundvall, 1992; Nelson, 1993) further. For example, the spatial axis of aggregation of knowledge (Figure 1.8) also applies to innovation. Of course, Lundvall (1992, pp. 1, 3) also explicitly stresses that national innovation systems are permanently challenged (and extended) by regional as well as global innovation systems. But, paraphrasing Kuhlmann (2001, pp. 960–61), as long as nation-state-based political systems exist, it makes sense to acknowledge national innovation systems. In a spatial (or geographic) understanding, the term 'multi-level systems of innovation' is already being used (Kaiser and Prange, 2004, pp. 395, 405–6; Kuhlmann, 2001, pp. 970–71, 973). However, only more recently has it been suggested to extend this multi-level aggregation approach of innovation to the non-spatial axes of innovation (Campbell, 2006a; Carayannis and Campbell, 2006a). Therefore multi-level systems of knowledge as well as multi-level systems of innovation are based on spatial and non-spatial axes. A further advantage of this multi-level systems architecture is that it results in a more accurate and realistic description of processes of globalization and gloCalization. For example, internationalization of R&D cross-cuts these different multi-level layers, links together organizational units of business, academic and political actors at national, transnational and sub-national levels (Von Zedtwitz and Heimann, 2006). One interpretation of R&D internationalization emphasizes how different sub-national regions and clusters cooperate on a global scale, creating even larger transnational knowledge clusters.

The concept of 'sectoral systems of innovation' (SSI) cross-cuts the logic of the multi-level systems of innovation or knowledge. A sector is often understood in terms of industrial sectors. Sectors can perform locally/

regionally, nationally and transnationally. Reviews of SSIs often place particular emphasis on: knowledge and technologies; actors and networks; and institutions. Malerba (2004, p. i) recommends that analyses of sectoral systems of innovation should include 'the factors affecting innovation, the relationship between innovation and industry dynamics, the changing boundaries and the transformation of sectors, and the determinants of the innovation performance of firms and countries in different sectors'.

2.2 Linear versus Non-linear Innovation Models (Modes)

Is the linear model of innovation still valid? In an ideal-typical understanding the linear model states: first there is basic research, carried out in a university context. Later on, this basic research is converted into applied research, and moves from the university to the university-related sectors. Finally, applied research is translated into experimental development, carried out by business (the economy). What results is a first-then relationship, with the universities and/or basic research being responsible for generating the new waves of knowledge creation that are later taken over by business, and where business carries the final responsibility for the commercialization and marketing of R&D. National (multi-level) innovation systems, operating primarily on the premises of this linear innovation model, obviously would be disadvantaged: the time horizon for a whole R&D cycle to reach the markets could be quite extensive (with negative consequences for an economy operating in the context of rapidly intensifying global competition). Furthermore, the linear innovation model exhibits serious weaknesses in communicating user preferences from the market end back to the production of basic research. In addition, how should the tacit knowledge of the users and markets be reconnected to basic research? After 1945, the USA was regarded as a prototype for the linear innovation model system, with a strong university base from where basic research gradually would diffuse to the sectors of a strong private economy, without the intervention of major public innovation policy programs (see Bush, 1945, p. 5). As long as the USA represented the world-leading national economy, this understanding was sufficient. But with the intensification of global competition, the demand for shortening the time horizon from basic research to market implementation of R&D increased (OECD, 1998, pp. 179–81, 185–6). In the 1980s, Japan in particular heavily pressured the USA. In the 2000s, global competition within the triad of the USA, Japan and the EU escalated further, with China and India emerging as new competitors in the global context. In a nutshell, increasing economic competition and intrinsic knowledge demands challenged the linear innovation model.

As a consequence, we can observe a significant proliferation of non-linear innovation models. There are several approaches to non-linear innovation models. The 'chain-linked model' developed by Kline and Rosenberg (1986; cited in Miyata, 2003, p. 716; see also Carayannis and Alexander, 2006), emphasizes the importance of feedback between the different R&D stages. In particular, the coupling of marketing, sales and distribution with research claims to be important. 'Mode 2' (Gibbons et al., 1994, pp. 3–8, 167) underscores the linkage of production and use of knowledge by referring to the following five principles: knowledge produced in the context of application; transdisciplinarity; heterogeneity and organizational diversity; social accountability and reflexivity; and quality control (see also Nowotny et al., 2001, 2003). Metaphorically speaking, the first–then sequence of relationships of different stages within the linear model is replaced by a paralleling of different R&D activities (Campbell, 2000, p. 139–41). Paralleling means: (1) linking together in real time different stages of R&D, for example basic research and experimental development, and/or (2) linking different sectors, such as universities and firms. As mentioned earlier, the 'triple helix' model of Etzkowitz and Leydesdorff (2000, pp. 109, 111) stresses the interaction between academia, state and industry, focusing consequently on 'university–industry–government relations' and 'tri-lateral networks and hybrid organizations'. Carayannis and Laget (2004, pp. 17, 19) emphasize the importance of cross-national and cross-sectoral research collaboration by testing these propositions for transatlantic public–private R&D partnerships. Anbari and Umpleby (2006, pp. 27–9) claim that one rationale for establishing research networks lies in the interest of bringing together knowledge producers, but also practitioners, with 'complementary skills'. Etzkowitz (2003) speaks of the 'entrepreneurial university'. An effective coupling of university research and business R&D demands, furthermore, the complementary establishment of the entrepreneurial university and the 'academic firm' (Campbell and Güttel, 2005, pp. 170–72). Extended ramifications of these discourses also refer to the challenge of designing proper governance regimes for the funding and evaluation of university research (Geuna and Martin, 2003; see also Shapira and Kuhlmann, 2003; Campbell, 1999, 2003). Furthermore, this imposes consequences on structures and performance of universities (Pfeffer, 2006). Interesting also is the concept of 'democratizing innovation', used by Eric von Hippel in his 'user-centric innovation' model, in which 'lead users' represent 'innovating users', who again contribute crucially to the performance of innovation systems. 'Lead users' can be individuals or firms. Users often innovate, because they cannot find in the market what they want or need (Von Hippel, 1995, 2005). Non-proprietor knowledge, such as the 'open source' movement in the software industry (Steinmueller, 2004, p. 240), may be seen as successful examples for gloCally self-organizing 'user communities'.

In summary, one could set up the following hypothesis for discussion: while Mode 1 and perhaps also the concept of 'technology life cycles' (see Cardullo, 1999; Tassey, 2001) appear to be more closely associated with the linear innovation model, the Mode 2 and triple helix knowledge modes have more in common with a non-linear understanding of knowledge and innovation. At the same time we should add that national (multi-level) innovation systems are challenged by the fact that several technology life cycles, at different stages of market maturity (closeness to commercial market introduction), perform in parallel. This parallel, as well as sequentially time-lagged unfolding of technology life cycles, also expresses characteristics of Mode 2 and of non-linear innovation, because organizations (firms and universities) must often must develop strategies of simultaneously cross-linking different technology life cycles. Universities and firms (commercial and academic firms) must balance the non-triviality of a fluid pluralism of technology life cycles.

2.3 From Triple to Quadruple Helix

Knowledge and innovation policies and strategies must acknowledge the important role of the 'public' in achieving goals and objectives. On the one hand, public reality is being constructed and communicated by the media and the media system. On the other hand, the public is also influenced by culture and values. Knowledge and innovation policy should aim to reflect the dynamics of 'media-based democracy', to draft policy strategies. Particularly when we assume that traditional economic policy gradually (partially) converts into innovation policy, leveraging knowledge for economic performance and thus linking the political system with the economy, then innovation policy should communicate its objectives and rationales, via the media, to the public to seek legitimation and justification (see Figure 1.9; see also Carayannis and Campbell, 2006a, p. 18; 2006b, p. 335). Also the PR (public relations) strategies of companies engaged in R&D must reflect on the fact of a 'reality construction' by the media. Culture and values also express a key role. Cultural artifacts, such as movies, can influence public opinion of the public and their willingness to support public R&D investment. Some of the technical and engineering curricula at universities are not gender-symmetric, because a majority of the students are male. Trying to make women more interested in enrolling in technical and engineering studies would also imply changing the 'social images' of technology in society. The sustainable backing and reinforcing of knowledge and innovation in the gloCal knowledge economy and

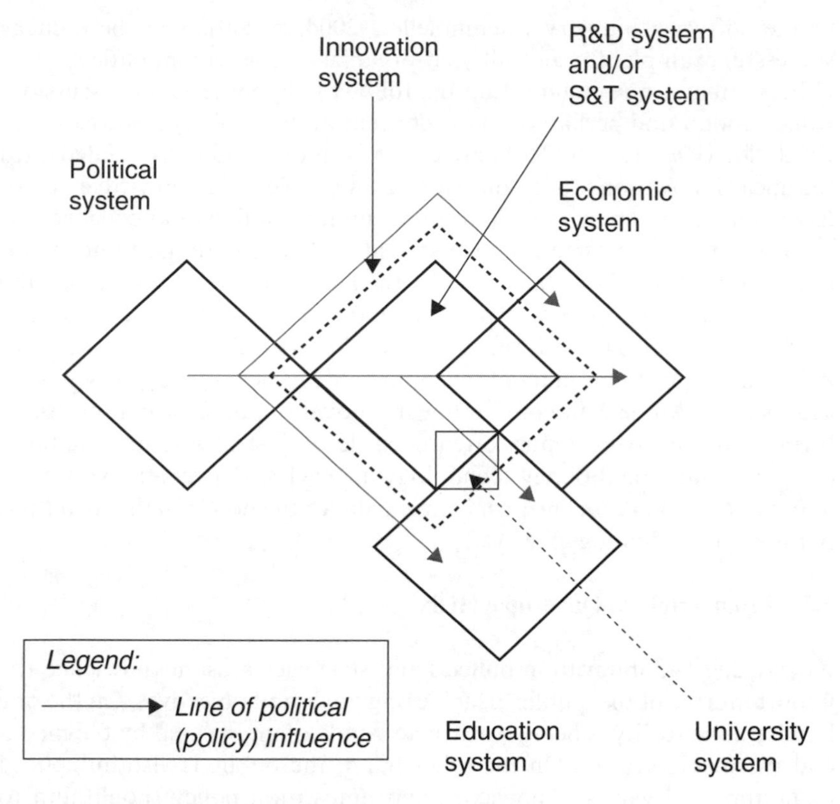

Source: Carayannis and Campbell (2006a).

Figure 1.9 Different societal system: lines of political (policy) influence

society requires substantive support of the development and evolution of 'innovation cultures' (Kuhlmann, 2001, p. 954). Therefore the successful engineering of knowledge and innovation policies and/or strategies leverages the self-logic of the media system and leverages or alters culture and values.

2.4 Coexistence and Co-evolution of Different Knowledge and Innovation Paradigms

Discussing the evolution of scientific theories, Thomas S. Kuhn (1962) introduced the concept of 'paradigms'. Paradigms can be understood as basic fundamentals upon which a theory rests. In that sense paradigms are axiomatic premises that guide a theory but cannot be explained by the theory itself. However, paradigms add to the explanatory power of theories that are interested in explaining the (outside) world. They represent something like beliefs. According to Kuhn, scientific theories evolve following a specific pattern: there are periods of 'normal science', interrupted by intervals of 'revolutionary science' again converting into 'normal science', again challenged by 'revolutionary science', and so on (Carayannis, 1993, 1994, 2000, 2001; see also Umpleby, 2005, pp. 287–8). According to Kuhn, every scientific theory, with its associated paradigm(s), has only a limited capacity for explaining the world. Confronted with phenomena that cannot be explained, a gradual modification of the same theory might be sufficient. However, at one point a revolutionary transformation is necessary, demanding that a whole set of theories/paradigms be replaced by new theories/paradigms. For a while, the new theories/paradigms are adequately advanced. However, in the long run, these cycles of periods of normal science and intervals of revolutionary science represent the dominant pattern.

Kuhn emphasizes this shift of one set of theories and paradigms to a new set, meaning that new theories and paradigms represent not so much an evolutionary offspring, but actually replace the earlier theories and paradigms. While this is certainly often true, particularly in the natural sciences, we want to stress that there also can be a coexistence and co-evolution of paradigms (and theories), implying that paradigms and theories can learn from each other. Particularly in the social sciences this notion of coexistence and co-evolution of paradigms might sometimes be more appropriate than the replacement of paradigms. For the social sciences, and politics in general, we can point to the pattern of a permanent mutual contest between ideas. Umpleby (1997, p. 635), for instance, emphasizes the following aspect of the social sciences: 'Theories of social systems, when acted upon, change social systems.' Not only (social) scientific theories refer to paradigms, also other social contexts or factors can be understood as being based on paradigms: we can speak of ideological paradigms or of policy paradigms (Hall, 1993). Another example would be the long-term competition and fluctuation between the welfare-state and the free-market paradigms (with regard to the metrics of left–right placement of political parties in Europe, see Volkens and Klingemann, 2002, p. 158).

These different modes of innovation and knowledge creation, diffusion and use, which we discussed earlier, can also be understood as linking to knowledge paradigms. Because knowledge and innovation systems clearly relate to the context of a (multi-level) society, the (epistemic) knowledge paradigms can be regarded as belonging to the 'family of social sciences'. Interestingly, Mode 2 addresses 'social accountability and reflexivity' as one of its key characteristics (Gibbons et al., 1994, pp. 7, 167–8). In addition to the possibility that a specific knowledge paradigm is replaced by a new knowledge paradigm, the relationship between different knowledge and innovation modes may often be described as an ongoing and continuous interaction of a dynamic coexistence and (over time) a co-evolution of different knowledge paradigms. This reinforces the understanding that, in the advanced knowledge-based societies and economies, linear and non-linear innovation models can operate in parallel.

2.5 The 'Co-opetitive' Networking of Knowledge Creation, Diffusion and Use

Knowledge systems are highly complex, dynamic and adaptive. To begin with, there exists a conceptual (hybrid) overlapping between multi-level knowledge and multi-level innovation systems. Multi-level systems proceed simultaneously at the global, transnational, national, and sub-national levels, creating gloCal (global and local) challenges. Advanced knowledge systems should demonstrate the flexibility to integrate different knowledge modes – on the one hand, combining linear and non-linear innovation modes; on the other hand, conceptually integrating the modes of Mode 1, Mode 2 and triple helix (for an overview of Mode 1, Mode 2, triple helix, and technology life cycles, see Campbell, 2006a, pp. 71–5). This shows the practical usefulness of an understanding of a coexistence and co-evolution of different knowledge paradigms, and what the qualities of an 'innovation ecosystem' could or even should be. The elastic integration of different modes of knowledge creation, diffusion and use should generate synergistic surplus effects of additionality. Hence for advanced knowledge systems, networks and networking are important (Carayannis and Alexander, 1999b; Carayannis and Campbell, 2006b, pp. 334–9; for a general discussion of networks and complexity, see also Rycroft and Kash, 1999).

How do networks relate to cooperation and competition? 'Co-opetition', as a concept (Brandenburger and Nalebuff, 1997) underscores that there can always exist a complex balance of cooperation and/or competition. Market concepts emphasize a competitive dynamics process between (1) forces of supply and demand, and (2) the need to integrate market-based as well as resource-based views of business activity. To be exact, networks do not replace market dynamics, thus they do not represent an alternative to the market-economy principle of competition. Instead, networks apply a 'co-opetitive' rationale, meaning: internally, networks are based primarily on cooperation, but may also allow a 'within' competition. The relationship between different networks can be guided by a motivation for cooperation. However, in practical terms, competition in knowledge and innovation will often be carried out between different and flexibly configured networks. While a network cooperates internally, it may compete externally. In short, 'co-opetition' should be regarded as a driver for networks, implying that the specific content of cooperation and competition is always decided in a case-specific context.

3. CONCLUSION

The Mode 3 systems approach (the innovation ecosystem) to knowledge creation, diffusion and use emphasizes the following key elements (Carayannis and Campbell, 2006c):

1. *GloCal multi-level knowledge and innovation systems* Because of its comprehensive flexibility and explanatory power, systems theory is regarded as suitable for framing knowledge and innovation in the context of multi-level knowledge and innovation systems (Carayannis and Von Zedtwitz, 2005; Carayannis and Campbell, 2006c; Carayannis and Sipp, 2006). GloCal expresses the simultaneous processing of knowledge and innovation at different levels (e.g. global, national and sub-national; see Gerybadze and Reger, 1999; Von Zedtwitz and Gassmann, 2002), and also refers to stocks and flows of knowledge with local meaning and global reach. Knowledge and innovation systems (and concepts) express a substantial degree of hybrid overlapping, meaning that often the same empirical information or case could be discussed under the headings of knowledge or innovation.
2. *Elements/clusters and rationales/networks* In a theoretical understanding, we pointed to the possibility of linking the elements of a system with clusters and the rationale of a system with networks. Clusters and networks are common and useful terms for the analysis of knowledge.
3. *Knowledge clusters, innovation networks and co-opetition* More specifically, we emphasized the terms knowledge clusters and innovation networks (Carayannis and Sipp, 2006). Clusters, by taking demands of a knowledge-based society and economy seriously for a competitive and effective business performance, should be represented as knowledge configurations. Knowledge clusters, therefore, represent a further evolutionary development of geographical (spatial) and sectoral clusters. Innovation networks, internally driving and operating knowledge clusters or cross-cutting and cross-connecting different knowledge clusters, enhance the dynamics of knowledge

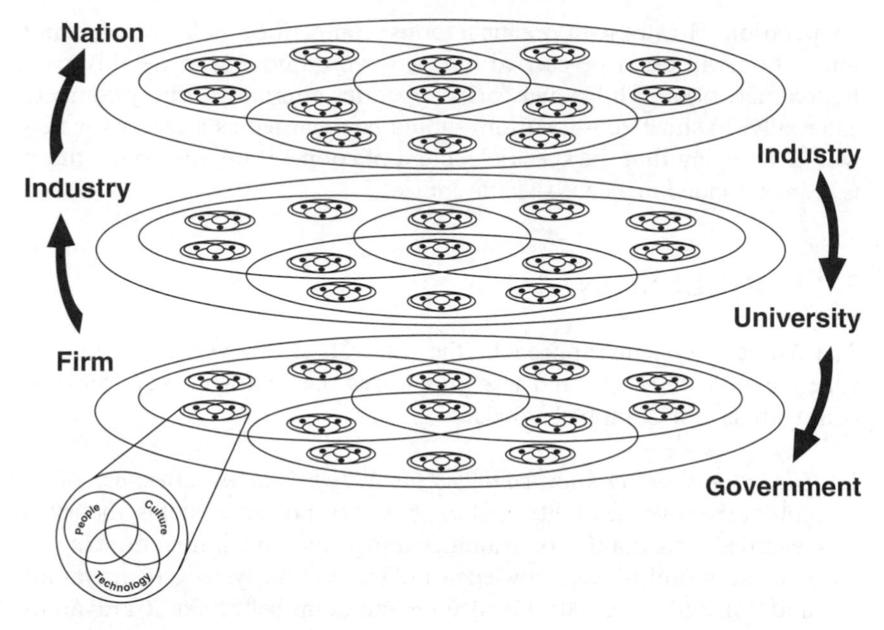

Source: Carayannis (2000–2011).

Figure 1.10 The innovation ecosystem

and innovation systems. Networks always express a pattern of co-opetition, reflecting a specific balance of cooperation and competition. Intra-network and inter-network relations are based on a mix of cooperation and competition, that is co-opetition (Brandenburger and Nalebuff, 1997). When we speak of competition, it will often be a contest between different network configurations.

4. *Knowledge fractals* These emphasize the continuum-like bottom–up and top–down progress of complexity. Each sub-component (sub-element) of a knowledge cluster and innovation network can be seen as a micro-level sub-configuration of knowledge clusters and innovation networks (see Figure 1.10). At the same time, one can also move upward. Every knowledge cluster and innovation network can also be understood as a sub-component (sub-element) of a larger macro-level knowledge cluster or innovation network – in other words, innovation meta-networks and knowledge meta-clusters.
5. *The adaptive integration and co-evolution of different knowledge and innovation modes, the 'quadruple helix'* Mode 3 allows and emphasizes the coexistence and co-evolution of different knowledge and innovation paradigms. A key hypothesis is: The competitiveness and

superiority of a knowledge system is highly determined by its adaptive capacity to combine and integrate different knowledge and innovation modes via co-evolution, co-specialization and co-opetition knowledge stock and flow dynamics (e.g. Mode 1, Mode 2, triple helix, linear and non-linear innovation). The specific context (circumstances, demands, configurations, cases) determines which knowledge and innovation mode (multi-modal), at which level (multi-level), involving what parties or agents (multi-lateral) and with what knowledge nodes or knowledge clusters (multi-nodal) will be appropriate. What results is an emerging fractal knowledge and innovation ecosystem well configured for the knowledge economy and society challenges and opportunities of the twenty-first century by being endowed with mutually complementary and reinforcing as well as dynamically co-evolving, co-specializing and co-opeting, diverse and heterogeneous configurations of knowledge creation, diffusion and use. The intrinsic litmus test of the capacity of such an ecosystem to survive and prosper in the context of continually gloCalizing and intensifying competition represents the ultimate competitiveness benchmark with regard to the robustness and quality of the ecosystem's knowledge and innovation architecture and topology as it manifests itself in the form of a knowledge value-adding chain. The concept of the quadruple helix broadens our understanding because it adds the 'media-based and culture-based public' to the picture.

The societal embeddedness of knowledge represents a theme that Mode 2 and the triple helix explicitly acknowledge. As a last thought for this chapter we want to underscore the potentially beneficial cross-references between democracy and knowledge for a better understanding of knowledge. Democracy could be seen as an interplay of two principles (Campbell, 2005): (1) as a method or procedure based on the application of the rule of the majority (see Schumpeter, 1942). This acknowledges the 'relativity of truth' and 'pluralism' in a society, implying that decisions are carried out, not because they are 'right' (or more right), but because they are backed and legitimized by a majority. Since, over time, these majority preferences normally change, this creates political swings, driving the government/opposition cycles, which crucially add to the viability of a democratic system. (2) Democracy can also be understood as a substance, where understood as an evolutionary manifestation of fundamental rights (O'Donnell, 2004, pp. 26–7, 47, 54–5). Obviously, the method/procedure and the substance approach overlap. Without fundamental rights, the majority rule could neutralize or even destroy itself. On the other hand, the 'real political' implementation of rights also demands a political method, an institutionally set-up procedure. For the purpose of bridging democracy with knowledge and innovation, we highlight the following aspects (see Figure 1.11 for a suggested visualization; see also Godoe, 2007, p. 358; Carayannis and Ziemnowicz, 2007):

1. *Knowledge-based and innovation-based democracy* The future of democracy depends on evolving, enhancing and ideally perfecting the concepts of a knowledge-based and innovation-based democratic polity as the manifestation and operationalization of what one might consider the 'twenty-first-century platonic ideal state':

   > It has been basic United States policy that Government should foster the opening of new frontiers. It opened the seas to clipper ships and furnished land for pioneers. Although these frontiers have more or less disappeared, the frontier of science remains. It is in keeping with the American tradition – one which has made the United States great – that new frontiers shall be made accessible for development by all American citizens. (Bush, 1945, p. 10)

   Knowledge, innovation and democracy interrelate. Advances in democracy and advances in knowledge and innovation express mutual dependencies.[7] The 'quality of democracy' depends on a knowledge base. We see how the gloCal knowledge economy and society and the quality of democracy intertwine. Concepts such as 'democratizing innovation' (Von Hippel, 2005) underscore such aspects. Also the media-based and culture-based public of the quadruple helix emphasizes the overlapping tendencies of democracy and knowledge.[8]
2. *Pluralism of knowledge modes* Democracy's strength lies exactly in its capacity for allowing and balancing different parties, politicians, ideologies, values and policies, an ability discussed by Lindblom (1959) as disjointed incrementalism,[9] as the partisan mutual adjustment process. Just as entrepreneurs and consumers can conduct their buying and selling without anyone attempting to calculate the overall level of prices or outputs for the economy as a whole, Lindblom argued, so in politics. In many conditions adjustments among competing partisans will yield more sensible policies than are likely to be achieved by centralized decision makers relying on analysis (Lindblom, 1959, 1965). This is partly because interaction economizes on precisely the factors on which humans are short, such as time and understanding, while analysis requires their profligate consumption. To put this differently, the lynchpin of Lindblom's thinking was that analysis could be – and should be – 'no more than an adjunct to interaction in political life' (http://www.rpi.edu/~woodhe/docs/redner.724.htm). Similarly, democracy enables the integrating, coexistence and co-evolution of

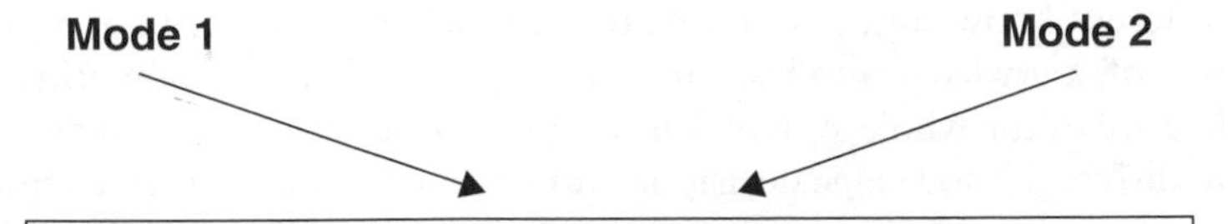

Mode 3

Knowledge-based and innovation-based democracy

Leveraging principles of a democracy style of governance of (sequentially or in parallel) integration of different knowledge and innovation modes

Balancing and integrating different knowledge modes in a multi-level architecture

Triple helix-style governance of Mode 1, Mode 2, linear and non-linear innovation modes

Networking of entrepreneurial universities with commercial and academic firms (firm units)

A 'quadruple helix' framing and extending the the knowledge principles of the triple helix

Gradual conversion of economic policy making to innovation policy making

Democratic mode of strategy development and decision making, socially accountable, and exposed to feedback

Forward-looking, feedback-driven learning

Future-oriented openness

'Knowledge swings'

Source: Carayannis and Campbell (2009).

Figure 1.11 Knowledge, innovation and democracy. GloCal governance styles of the gloCal knowledge economy and society?

different knowledge and innovation modes. We can speak of a pluralism of knowledge modes, and can regard this as a competitiveness feature of the whole system. Different knowledge modes can be linked to different knowledge decisions and knowledge policies, reflecting the communication skills of specific knowledge producers and knowledge users to convince other audiences of decision makers.

3. *Knowledge swings* Through political cycles or *swings* (Campbell, 1992) a democracy ties together different features: (a) decides who currently governs; (b) gives the opposition a chance to come to power in the future; and (c) acknowledges pluralism. Democracy represents a system that always creates and is being driven by an important momentum. For example, the statistical probability of governing parties to lose an upcoming election is higher than to win an election (Müller and Strøm, 2000, p. 589). Similarly, one could paraphrase the momentum of political swings by referring to 'knowledge swings': in certain periods and concrete contexts, a specific set of knowledge modes expresses a 'dominant design' position; however, the pool of non-hegemonic knowledge modes is also necessary for allowing alternative approaches in the long run, adding crucially to the variability of the whole system. Knowledge swings raise at least two issues: (a) What are dominant and non-dominant knowledge modes in a specific context? (b) There is a pluralism of knowledge modes, which exist in parallel, and thus also co-develop and co-evolve. Diversity is necessary to draw a cyclically patterned dominance of knowledge modes.
4. *Forward-looking, feedback-driven learning* Democracy should be regarded as a future-oriented governance system, fostering and relying upon social, economic and technological learning. The 'Mode 3 FREIE' is at its core an open, adaptive, learning-driven knowledge and innovation ecosystem reflecting the philosophy of strategic or active incrementalism (Carayannis, 1993, 1994, 1999, 2000, 2001) and the strategic management of technological learning (Carayannis, 1999; see also De Geus, 1988). In addition, one can postulate that the government/opposition cycle in politics represents a feedback-driven learning and mutual adaptation process. In this context, a democratic system can be perceived as a pendulum with a shifting pivot point reflecting the evolving, adapting dominant worldviews of the polity as they are shaped by the mutually interacting and influencing citizens and the dominant designs of the underlying cultures and technological paradigms (Carayannis, 2001, pp. 26–7).

In conclusion, we have attempted to provide an emerging conceptual framework to serve as the 'creative whiteboard space' of 'knowledge weavers' across disciplines and sectors as they strive to tackle the twenty-first-century challenges and opportunities for socio-economic prosperity and cultural renaissance based on knowledge and innovation.

NOTES

1. The notion of fractals comes from geometry to define objects that are irregular and appear 'broken up': some have a self-similar structure and can describe situations that cannot be explained by classical geometry. In relation to knowledge they help to explain non-linearities (see Carayannis, 2001; Carayannis and Campbell, 2011; Gleick, 1987).
2. See also Milbergs (2005).
3. See discussion on democracy in the conclusion of this chapter.
4. 'Culture is the invisible force behind the tangibles and observables in any organization, a social energy that moves people to act. Culture is to the organization what personality is to the individual – a hidden, yet unifying theme that provides meaning, direction, and mobilization' (Killman, 1985, p. 65–8).
5. Technology is defined as that 'which allows one to engage in a certain activity . . . with consistent quality of output', the 'art of science and the science of art' (Carayannis, 2001, p. 82–3) or '*the science of crafts*' (Braun, 1997, 97–9).
6. In that context also the mutual overlapping between R&D, S&T and ICT (information and communication technology) should be stressed.
7. For attempts to analyze the quality of a democracy, see for example Campbell and Schaller (2002).
8. On 'democratic innovation', see also Saward (2006).
9. Developed by Lindblom (1959, 1965) and Lindblom and Cohen (1979), this approach found several fields of application: 'The Incrementalist approach was one response to the challenge of the 1960s. This is the theory of Charles Lindblom, which he described as "partisan mutual adjustment" or disjointed incrementalism. Developed as an alternative to RCP, this theory claims that public policy is actually accomplished through decentralized bargaining in a free market and a democratic political economy' (http://www3.sympatico.ca/david.macleod/PTHRY.HTM).

REFERENCES

Anbari, Frank T. and Stuart A. Umpleby (2006), 'Productive research teams and knowledge generation', in Elias G. Carayannis and David F.J. Campbell (eds), *Knowledge Creation, Diffusion, and Use in Innovation Networks and Knowledge Clusters. A Comparative Systems Approach across the United States, Europe and Asia*, Westport, CT: Praeger, pp. 26–38.

Brandenburger, Adam M. and Barry J. Nalebuff (1997), *Co-Opetition*, New York: Doubleday.

Braun, C.F. von (1997), *The Innovation War*, Upper Saddle River, NJ: Prentice Hall.

Bush, Vannevar (1945), *Science: The Endless Frontier*, Washington, DC: US Government Printing Office, http://www.nsf.gov/od/lpa/nsf50/vbush1945.htm#transmittal.

Campbell, David F.J. (1992), 'Die Dynamik der politischen Links-Rechts-Schwingungen in Österreich: Die Ergebnisse einer Expertenbefragung', *Österreichische Zeitschrift für Politikwissenschaft*, **21**(2), 165–79.

Campbell, David F.J. (1994), 'European nation-state under pressure: national fragmentation or the evolution of suprastate structures?', *Cybernetics and Systems: An International Journal*, **25**(6), 879–909.

Campbell, David F.J. (1999), 'Evaluation universitärer Forschung. Entwicklungstrends und neue Strategiemuster für wissenschaftsbasierte Gesellschaften', *SWS-Rundschau*, **39**(4), 363–83.

Campbell, David F.J. (2000), 'Forschungspolitische Trends in wissenschaftsbasierten Gesellschaften. Strategiemuster für entwickelte Wirtschaftssysteme', *Wirtschaftspolitische Blätter*, **47**(2), 130–43.

Campbell, David F.J. (2001), 'Politische Steuerung über öffentliche Förderung universitärer Forschung? Systemtheoretische Überlegungen zu Forschungs- und Technologiepolitik', *Österreichische Zeitschrift für Politikwissenschaft*, **30**(4), 425–38.

Campbell, David F.J. (2003), 'The evaluation of university research in the United Kingdom and the Netherlands, Germany and Austria', in Philip Shapira and Stefan Kuhlmann (eds), *Learning from Science and Technology Policy Evaluation: Experiences from the United States and Europe*, Cheltenham, UK and Northampton, MA, USA: Edward Elgar, pp. 98–131.

Campbell, David F.J. (2005), 'Demokratie, Demokratiequalität und Grundrechte: Ein Vergleich der Fiedler- und EU-Verfassung', Vienna: unpublished manuscript.

Campbell, David F. J. (2006a), 'The university/business research networks in science and technology: knowledge production trends in the United States, European Union and Japan', in Elias G. Carayannis and David F.J. Campbell (eds), *Knowledge Creation, Diffusion, and Use in Innovation Networks and Knowledge Clusters. A Comparative Systems Approach across the United States, Europe and Asia*, Westport, CT: Praeger, pp. 67–100.

Campbell, David F.J. (2006b), 'Nationale Forschungssysteme im Vergleich. Strukturen, Herausforderungen und Entwicklungsoptionen', *Österreichische Zeitschrift für Politikwissenschaft*, **35**(1), 25–44, http://www.oezp.at/oezp/online/online.htm.

Campbell, David F.J. and Christian Schaller (eds) (2002), *Demokratiequalität in Österreich. Zustand und Entwicklungsperspektiven*, Opladen: Leske + Budrich, http://www.oegpw.at/sek_agora/publikationen.htm.

Campbell, David F.J. and Wolfgang H. Güttel (2005), 'Knowledge production of firms: research networks and the "scientification" of business R&D', *International Journal of Technology Management*, **31**(1/2), 152–75.

Carayannis, Elias G. (1993), 'Incrementalisme stratégique', *Le Progrès Technique* (no. 2), Paris: France.

Carayannis, Elias G. (1994), 'Gestion stratégique de l'apprentissage technologique', *Le Progrès Technique* (no. 2), Paris: France.

Carayannis, Elias G. (1999), 'Knowledge transfer through technological hyperlearning in five industries', *International Journal of Technovation*, **19**(3), 141–61.

Carayannis, Elias G. (2000), 'Investigation and validation of technological learning versus market performance', *International Journal of Technovation*, **20**(7), 389–400.

Carayannis, Elias G. (2001), *The Strategic Management of Technological Learning*, Boca Raton, FL: CRC Press.

Carayannis, Elias G. and Jeffrey Alexander (1999a), 'Winning by co-opeting in strategic government–university–industry (GUI) Partnerships: the power of complex, dynamic knowledge network', *Journal of Technology Transfer*, **24**(2/3), 197–210.

Carayannis, Elias G. and Jeffrey Alexander (1999b), 'Technology-driven strategic alliances: tools for learning and knowledge exchange in a positive-sum world', in Richard C. Dorf (ed.), *The Technology Management Handbook*, Boca Raton, FL: CRC Press, pp. 1-32–1-41.

Carayannis, Elias G. and M. Allbritton (1997), 'Collaborating in cyberspace: a case study of computer-mediated communication among 100 scholars in 15 countries', Online Journal of Internet Banking and Commerce, http://www.arraydev.com/commerce/jibc/9806-07.htm.

Carayannis, Elias G. and Jeffrey Alexander (2004), 'Strategy, structure and performance issues of pre-competitive R&D consortia: insights and lessons learned', *IEEE Transactions of Engineering Management*, **52**(2), 376–85.

Carayannis, Elias G. and Jeffrey M. Alexander (2006), *Global and Local Knowledge. Glocal Transatlantic Public–Private Partnerships for Research and Technological Development*, Basingstoke: Palgrave Macmillan.

Carayannis, Elias G. and David F.J. Campbell (2006a), '"Mode 3": meaning and implications from a knowledge systems perspective', in Elias G. Carayannis and David F.J. Campbell (eds), *Knowledge Creation, Diffusion, and Use in Innovation Networks and Knowledge Clusters. A Comparative Systems Approach across the United States, Europe and Asia*, Westport, CT: Praeger, pp. 1–25.

Carayannis, Elias G. and David F.J. Campbell (2006b), 'Conclusion: key insights and lessons learned for policy and practice', in Elias G. Carayannis and David F.J. Campbell (eds), *Knowledge Creation, Diffusion, and Use in Innovation Networks and Knowledge Clusters. A Comparative Systems Approach across the United States, Europe and Asia*, Westport, CT: Praeger, pp. 331–41.

Carayannis, Elias G. and David F.J. Campbell (2006c), 'Introduction and chapter summaries', in Elias G. Carayannis and David F.J. Campbell (eds), *Knowledge Creation, Diffusion, and Use in Innovation Networks and Knowledge Clusters. A Comparative Systems Approach across the United States, Europe and Asia*, Westport, CT: Praeger, pp. ix–xxvi.

Carayannis, Elias G. and David F.J. Campbell (2009), '"Mode 3" and "quadruple helix": toward a 21st century fractal innovation ecosystem', *International Journal of Technology Management*, **46**(3/4), 201–34.

Carayannis, Elias G. and David F.J. Campbell (2010), 'Triple helix, quadruple helix and quintuple helix and how do knowledge, innovation and the environment relate to each other? A proposed framework for a trans-disciplinary analysis of sustainable development and social ecology', *International Journal of Social Ecology and Sustainable Development*, **1**(1), 41–69.

Carayannis, Elias G. and David F.J. Campbell (2011), 'Open innovation diplomacy and a 21st century fractal research, education and innovation (FREIE) ecosystem: building on the quadruple and quintuple helix innovation concepts and the "Mode 3" knowledge production system', *Journal of the Knowledge Economy*, **2**(3), 327–72.

Carayannis, Elias G. and Edgar Gonzalez (2003), 'Creativity and innovation = competitiveness? When, how, and why', in Larisa V. Shavinina (ed.), *The International Handbook on Innovation*, vol. 1, Amsterdam: Pergamon, pp. 587–606.

Carayannis, Elias G. and Patrice Laget (2004), 'Transatlantic innovation

infrastructure networks: public–private, EU–US R&D partnerships', *R&D Management*, **34**(1), 17–31.
Carayannis, Elias G. and Caroline Sipp (2006), *E-Development toward the Knowledge Economy: Leveraging Technology, Innovation and Entrepreneurship for 'Smart Development'*, Basingstoke: Palgrave Macmillan.
Carayannis, Elias G. and Maximilian von Zedtwitz (2005), 'Architecting gloCal (global–local), real-virtual incubator networks (G-RVINs) as catalysts and accelerators of entrepreneurship in transitioning and developing economies', *Technovation*, **25**, 95–110.
Carayannis, Elias G. and Christopher Ziemnowicz (eds) (2007), *Rediscovering Schumpeter. Creative Destruction Evolving into 'Mode 3'*, Basingstoke: Palgrave Macmillan.
Carayannis, Elias G. and John E. Spillan and Christopher Ziemnowicz (2007), 'Introduction: why Joseph Schumpeter's creative destruction? Everything has changed', in Elias G. Carayannis and Christopher Ziemnowicz (eds), *Rediscovering Schumpeter. Creative Destruction Evolving into 'Mode 3'*, Basingstoke: Palgrave Macmillan, pp. 1–5.
Cardullo, Mario W. (1999), 'Technology life cycles', in Richard C. Dorf (ed.), *The Technology Management Handbook*, Boca Raton, FL: CRC Press, pp 3-44–3-49.
Cesaroni, Fabrizio, Alfonso Gambardella, Walter Garcia-Fontes and Myriam Mariani (2004), 'The chemical sectoral system: firms, markets, institutions and the processes of knowledge creation and diffusion', in Franco Malerba (ed.), *Sectoral Systems of Innovation. Concepts, Issues and Analyses of Six Major Sectors in Europe*, Cambridge: Cambridge University Press, pp. 121–54.
Cooper, G. (1998), 'Cognitive load theory & instructional design an UNSW', dwb4.unl.edu/Diss/Cooper/UNSW.htm.
De Geus, A. (1988), 'Planning as Learning', *Harvard Business Review*, **66**(2), 70–71.
Drejer, Anders (2002), 'Situation for innovation management: towards a contingency model', *European Journal of Innovation Management*, **5**(1).
Etzkowitz, Henry (2003), 'Research groups as "quasi-firms": the invention of the entrepreneurial university', *Research Policy*, **32**, 109–21.
Etzkowitz, Henry and Loet Leydesdorff (2000), 'The dynamics of innovation: from National Systems and "Mode 2" to a Triple Helix of university–industry–government relations', *Research Policy*, **29**, 109–23.
Florida, Richard (2004), *The Rise of the Creative Class: And How It's Transforming Work, Leisure, Community, and Everyday Life*, Cambridge, MA: Basic Books.
Gerybadze, Alexander and Guido Reger (1999), 'Globalization of R&D: recent changes in the management of innovation in transnational corporations', *Research Policy*, **28**, 251–74.
Geuna, Aldo and Ben R. Martin (2003), 'University research evaluation and funding: an international comparison', *Minerva*, **41**, 277–304.
Gibbons, Michael, Camille Limoges, Helga Nowotny, Simon Schwartzman, Peter Scott and Martin Trow (1994), *The New Production of Knowledge. The Dynamics of Science and Research in Contemporary Societies*, London: Sage.
Gleick, James (1987), *Chaos: Making a New Science*, New York: Viking Press.
Godoe, Helge (2007), 'Doing innovative research: "Mode 3" and methodological challenges in leveraging the best of three worlds', in Elias G. Carayannis and Christopher Ziemnowicz (eds), *Rediscovering Schumpeter. Creative Destruction Evolving into 'Mode 3'*, Basingstoke: Palgrave Macmillan, pp. 344–61.

Hall, Peter A. (1993), 'Policy paradigms, social learning, and the state. The case of economic policymaking in Britain', *Comparative Politics*, April, 257–96.

Hooghe, Liesbet and Gary Marks (2001), *Multi-Level Governance and European Integration*, Lanham, MD: Rowman & Littlefield.

Kaiser, Robert and Heiko Prange (2004), 'The reconfiguration of national innovation systems – the example of German biotechnology', *Research Policy*, **33**, 395–408.

Killman, R. (1985), *Gaining Control of the Corporate Culture*, New York: McGraw-Hill.

Kline, S.J. and N. Rosenberg (1986), 'An overview of innovation', in R. Landau and N. Rosenburg (eds), *The Positive Sum Strategy*, Washington, DC: National Academy Press, p. 283.

Kuhlmann, Stefan (2001), 'Future governance of innovation policy in Europe – three scenarios', *Research Policy*, **30**, 953–76.

Kuhn, Thomas S. (1962), *The Structure of Scientific Revolutions*, Chicago, IL: The University of Chicago Press.

Lindblom, Charles E. (1959), 'The science of muddling through', *Public Administration Review*, **19**, 79–88.

Lindblom, Charles E. (1965), *The Intelligence of Democracy*, New York: The Free Press.

Lindblom, Charles E. and David K. Cohen (1979), *Usable Knowledge: Social Science and Social Problem Solving*, New Haven, CT: Yale University Press.

Lundvall, Bengt-Åke (ed.) (1992), *National Systems of Innovation. Towards a Theory of Innovation and Interactive Learning*, London: Pinter Publishers.

Malerba, Franco (ed.) (2004), *Sectoral Systems of Innovation. Concepts, Issues and Analyses of Six Major Sectors in Europe*, Cambridge: Cambridge University Press.

McKelvey, Maureen, Luigi Orsenigo and Fabio Pammolli (2004), 'Pharmaceuticals analyzed through the lens of a sectoral innovation system', in Franco Malerba (ed.), *Sectoral Systems of Innovation. Concepts, Issues and Analyses of Six Major Sectors in Europe*, Cambridge: Cambridge University Press, pp. 73–120.

Milbergs, Egils (2005), *Innovation Ecosystems and Prosperity*, Center for Accelerating Innovation, http://www.innovationecosystems.com.

Miyata, Yukio (2003), 'An analysis of research and innovative activities of universities in the United States', in Larisa V. Shavinina (ed.), *The International Handbook on Innovation*, Amsterdam: Pergamon, pp. 715–38.

Müller, Wolfgang C. and Kaare Strøm (2000), 'Conclusion: coalition governance in Western Europe', in Wolfgang C. Müller and Kaare Strøm (eds), *Coalition Governments in Western Europe*, pp. 559–92.

Nelson, Richard R. (ed.) (1993), *National Innovation Systems. A Comparative Analysis*, Oxford: Oxford University Press.

Nelson, Richard R. and Sidney G. Winter (1982), *An Evolutionary Theory of Economic Change*, Cambridge, MA: The Belknap Press.

Nowotny, Helga, Peter Scott and Michael Gibbons (2001), *Re-thinking Science. Knowledge and the Public in an Age of Uncertainty*, Cambridge: Polity Press.

Nowotny, Helga, Peter Scott and Michael Gibbons (2003), 'Mode 2 revisited: the new production of knowledge', *Minerva*, **41**, 179–94.

O'Donnell, Guillermo (2004), 'Human development, human rights, and democracy', in Guillermo O'Donnell, Jorge Vargas Cullell and Osvaldo M. Iazzetta (eds), *The Quality of Democracy. Theory and Applications*, Notre Dame, IN: University of Notre Dame Press, pp. 9–92.

OECD (1994), *Frascati Manual. The Measurement of Scientific and Technological Acitivities. Proposed Standard Practice for Surveys of Research and Experimental Development*, Paris: OECD.

OECD (1998), *Science, Technology and Industry Outlook*, Paris: OECD.

OECD (2006), *Research and Development Statistics*, (online database), Paris: OECD.

Pfeffer, Thomas (2006), 'Virtualization of research universities. Raising the right questions to address key functions of the institution', in Elias G. Carayannis and David F. J. Campbell (eds), *Knowledge Creation, Diffusion, and Use in Innovation Networks and Knowledge Clusters. A Comparative Systems Approach across the United States, Europe and Asia*, Westport, CT: Praeger, pp. 307–30.

Rogers, E.M and F.F. Shoemaker (1971), *Communication of Innovations: A Cross-cultural Approach*, New York: Free Press.

Rogers, E.M., E.G. Carayannis, K. Kurihara and M.M. Allbritton (1998), 'Cooperative research and development of agreements (CRADAs) as technology transfer mechanisms', *R&D Management*, **28**, 79–89.

Rycroft, Robert W. and Don E. Kash (1999), *The Complexity Challenge. Technological Innovation for the 21st Century*, London: Pinter.

Saward, Michael (ed.) (2006), *Democratic Innovation: Deliberation, Representation and Association*, London: Routledge.

Schumpeter, Joseph A. (1942), *Capitalism, Socialism and Democracy*, New York: Harper & Brothers.

Shapira, Philip and Stefan Kuhlmann (eds) (2003), *Learning from Science and Technology Policy Evaluation. Experiences from the United States and Europe*, Cheltenham, UK and Northampton, MA, USA: Edward Elgar.

Shavinina, Larisa V. (2003), *The International Handbook on Innovation*, Amsterdam: Pergamon.

Steinmueller, W. Edward (2004), 'The European software sectoral system of innovation', in Franco Malerba (ed.), *Sectoral Systems of Innovation. Concepts, Issues and Analyses of Six Major Sectors in Europe*, Cambridge: Cambridge University Press, pp. 193–242.

Tassey, Gregory (2001), 'R&D policy models and data needs', in Maryann P. Feldman and Albert N. Link (eds), *Innovation Policy in the Knowledge-Based Economy*, Boston, MA: Kluwer Academic Publishers, pp. 37–71.

Tornazky, Louis G. and Mitchell Fleischer (1990), *The Processes of Technological Innovation*, Lexington, MA: DC Heath.

Umpleby, Stuart A. (1997), 'Cybernetics of conceptual systems', *Cybernetics and Systems: An International Journal*, **28**, 635–52.

Umpleby, Stuart A. (2005), 'What I learned from Heinz von Foerster about the Construction of science', *Kybernetes*, **34**(1/2), 278–94.

Volkens, Andrea and Hans-Dieter Klingemann (2002), 'Parties, ideologies, and issues. Stability and change in fifteen European party systems 1945–1998', in Kurt Richard Luther and Ferdinand Müller-Rommel (eds), *Political Parties in the New Europe. Political and Analytical Challenges*, Oxford: Oxford University Press, pp. 143–67.

Von Hippel, Eric (1995), *The Sources of Innovation*, Oxford: Oxford University Press.

Von Hippel, Eric (2005), *Democratizing Innovation*, Cambridge, MA: MIT Press.

Von Zedtwitz, Max and Oliver Gassmann (2002), 'Market versus technology drive in R&D internationalization: four different patterns of managing research and development', *Research Policy*, **31**(4), 569–88.

Von Zedtwitz, Max and Philip Heimann (2006), 'Innovation in clusters and the liability of foreignness of international R&D', in Elias G. Carayannis and David F.J. Campbell (eds), *Knowledge Creation, Diffusion, and Use in Innovation Networks and Knowledge Clusters. A Comparative Systems Approach across the United States, Europe and Asia*, Westport, CT: Praeger, pp. 101–22.

Zaltman, Gerald et al. (1973), *Innovations and Organizations*, New York: John Wiley & Sons.

2. Patterns of innovation and the determinants of the diffusion process in selected EU member states

George M. Korres

1. INTRODUCTION

Technological change is the result of both research and imitation activities. As soon as the information about the advantages provided by the innovation becomes available to the potential adopter, the adoption will take place.

Adoption is the result of a complex process of decision making. Absorption is just the process of diffusion perceived from the perspective of the recipient of the technique. The adoption of a new technology is in fact part of a broader process of technological change. Diffusion, defined as a sequence of adoption lags, is fully explained by the characteristics of the spreading of the information. Much attention has been paid to the identification of the determinants of the diffusion of the demand side and the determinants of the supply side.

Diffusion can be analysed as the process of delayed adoptions and imitations of a given innovation, with fixed economic characteristics, including the performances and the price, occurring because of dynamics on the demand side. The main engine is a well-known epidemic contagion in a population of heterogeneous agents, characterized by information asymmetries, and the eventual decay of information costs for potential adopters, driven by the dissemination of information carried out by all those who have already adopted (Griliches, 1957).

This chapter examines the diffusion process and reviews its patterns and determinants. In addition, it examines and reviews the main models and also investigates the correlation between adoption, innovation activities, the diffusion process and the growth process.

2. ADOPTION AND THE DIFFUSION PROCESS

The distinction between innovation and imitation was first introduced by Joseph Schumpeter (1934) and eventually became a landmark in the economics of innovation and new technology.

A new technology, either a new product or a new process, is first introduced by an innovator and eventually imitated by competitors. Imitators copy the innovation and in so doing enter the market and reduce the excess profits of the innovator. Imitation restores perfect competition. The economics of diffusion addresses relevant questions about the characteristics and the determinants, and the effects of the diffusion process. What is most controversial is why imitation is not instantaneous and all firms do not adopt it at the same time (Stoneman, 1976, 1983, 1986, 2002).

Adoption and innovation are two complementary aspects of a broader process of reaction to the mismatch between expectations and facts, and eventual introduction of technological changes that build upon the creative adoption and recombination of internal and external technological knowledge. The identification of the role of adoption costs paves the way for the distinction between gross and net profitability of adoption. Adoption costs are defined by the broad range of activities necessary to identify an innovation and adapt it to the existing production process. Adoption costs include the costs of search and adaptive research, the costs of scrapping the existing fixed production factors, the restructuring of the production and marketing organizations, the re-skilling of personnel, the actual purchase of the capital good and intermediary input embodying the new knowledge, the purchase of patents and licences and the costs of technical assistance (Amendola and Perrucci, 1985, 1986).

Net profitability of adoption is the result of the algebraic sum of the gross profitability engendered by the adoption of an innovation and the costs that it is necessary to incur in order to identify, select and finally adapt the new technology to the existing production conditions (Antonelli, 1990).

Figure 2.1 illustrates that the positive and constant slope of adoption costs is associated with the number of adopters and the positive, but decreasing, slope of the gross profitability of adoption is also associated with the number of adopters, the net profitability. The rate of diffusion will be influenced by the adoption costs and gross profitability of adoption, and also by the dynamics of technological change (Korres, 2011).

The distinction between diffusion within final consumers and diffusion within firms makes it possible to stress the related distinction between gross and net profitability of adoption and the identification of its costs. The distinction between net and gross profitability together with an

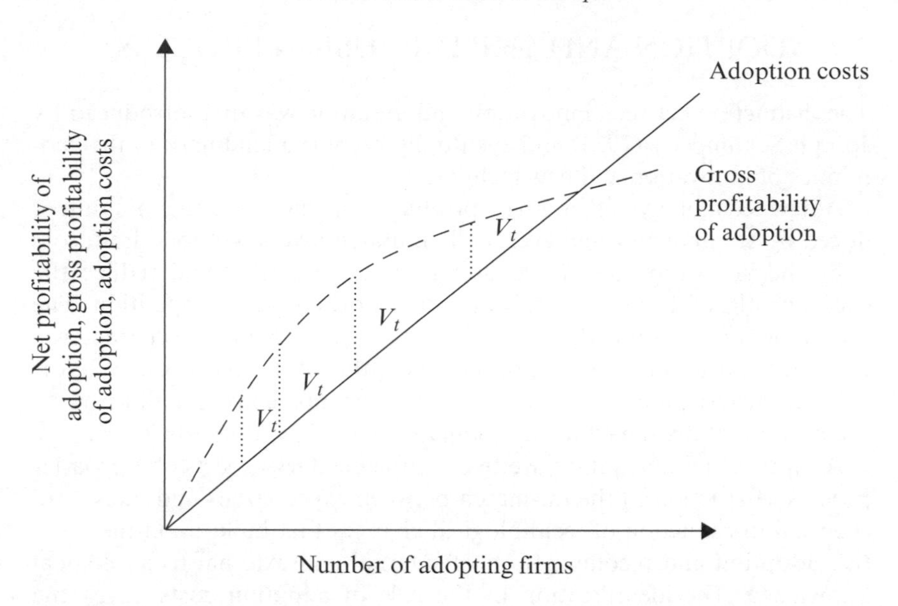

Figure 2.1 Adoption costs, gross net profitability of adoption and diffusion process

understanding of their dynamics, including the effects of the stocks of adoption on the evolution of the net profitability of adoption, provides an analytical probe that combines the demand and supply tradition of analysis of diffusion and shows the complementarity between innovation and adoption within the context of the economics of technological change (Korres, 2011).

3. THE DETERMINANTS AND THE PATTERNS OF DIFFUSION MODELS

The literature on diffusion of technology incorporates the best-known 'inter-industry innovation approach' pioneered by Mansfield (1961, 1988). This approach attempts to study diffusion as one or more innovations in a number of industries, and tries to explain empirically the variance of the speed of diffusion in terms of differences in the attributes of the industries and innovations concerned. Box 2.1 illustrates the main determinants of the demand and supply sides of innovation diffusion.

According to Schumpeter (1934), the diffusion process of major innovations is the driving force behind the trade cycle (the long-term Kondratieff cycle). However, the forces driving the diffusion process *per se* are not

BOX 2.1 DETERMINANTS OF INNOVATION DIFFUSION

Demand side:

- Investment in human capital (increases ability to adopt innovations)
- Investment in R&D (increases ability to adopt innovations)
- The level of prior related knowledge owned by the firm adopting the innovation
- The balance between specialization and diversity in order to absorb external knowledge
- Organizational innovation, ability of users to make organizational changes, kind of organizational structure
- The size of the firms
- Market characteristics of potential users; share of the market; market dynamism; demand growth; number of previous adopters in the market

Supply side:

- R&D and innovation capacity of new-technology suppliers
- The financial means (advertising costs, users' guide etc.)
- Interaction between users and suppliers
- Exchanges of tangible and intangible assets, i.e. trade, FDI, face-to-face contacts, labour mobility etc.
- ICT facilitates awareness about the new technology
- Market structure: horizontal integration favours flows of tangible and intangible assets
- Geographical concentration facilitates awareness of the new technology
- Role played by the standardization procedures
- Insurance system
- IPRs (intellectual property rights)
- Competition
- Integration of the economies

Source: Suriñach et al. (2009).

made explicit. The idea is that the entrepreneur innovates and the attractiveness of attaining a similarly increased profit and similar cost reduction encourages others to imitate; this imitation represents a diffusion process.

The Schumpeterian approach investigated and tried to explain long waves in economic activity (the Kondratieff cycle). The Schumpeterian hypothesis is concerned with the implications of new technology on the economy. In Schumpeterian theory, the entrepreneur introduces innovations and the resulting profits give the signal for imitation by other entrepreneurs. The introduction of new technologies results in the reduction of factor and product prices. The change of prices will induce non-adopters to use the new technology (Korres et al., 2003).

Diffusion of technology can be defined as the process by which the use of an innovation spreads and grows. Diffusion is very important for the process of technological change. On the one hand, it narrows the technological gap between the economic units of an industry, and thus the rate of diffusion determines to a large extent the rate of technological change measured as the effect of an innovation on productivity increase in an industry. On the other hand, diffusion plays an important part in the competitiveness process in the sense that it blunts the competitive edge maintained by the originator of successful innovations. Schumpeter has classified technological change in the following steps (Korres, 2011):

(a) invention;
(b) innovation; and
(c) diffusion.

Diffusion is the last step in the economic impact of a new product or process. It is the stage in which a new product or process comes into widespread use. Figure 2.2 illustrates the importance of diffusion in the process of technological change (Chen, 1983; Korres, 2011). Most literature on diffusion is focused on the theoretical arguments underlying the traditional S-shaped epidemic diffusion curve (Korres, 2011).

4. REVIEW OF THEORY AND EVIDENCE

4.1 The Epidemic Model and the Logistic Curve

Many diffusion models (e.g. Davies, 1979; Stoneman, 1987) are based on the approach of the theory of epidemics. Epidemic models can be used to explain how innovation spreads from one unit to others, at what speed and what can stop it. The epidemic approach starts with the assumption that

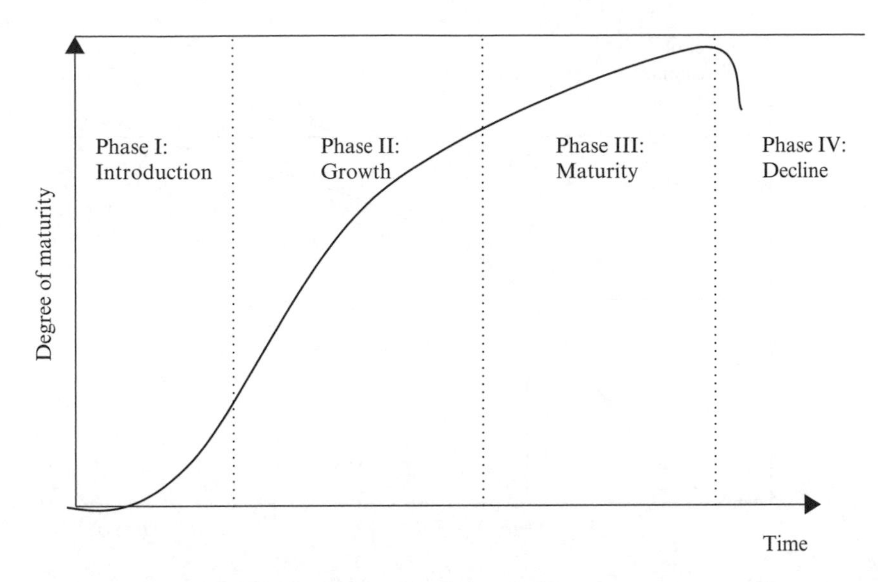

Figure 2.2 The S-shaped curve: the diffusion and growth process

the diffusion process is similar to the spread of a disease among a given population. The basic epidemic model is based on three assumptions:

- the potential number of adopters may not be in each case the whole population under consideration;
- the way in which information is spread may not be uniform and homogeneous;
- the probability of optimizing innovation once informed is not independent of economic considerations, such as profitability and market perspectives.

The epidemic model is based on the idea that the spread of information about a new technology is the key to explaining diffusion. Epidemic models hypothesize that some firms adopt later than others because they do not have sufficient information about the new technology. According to this theory, potential adopters initially have little or no information about the new technology and are therefore unable or disinclined to adopt it. However, as diffusion proceeds, non-adopters glean technical information from adopters via day-to-day interactions, just as one may contract a disease by casual contact with an infected person. As a result, as the number of adopters grows, the dissemination of information accelerates, and the speed of diffusion increases.

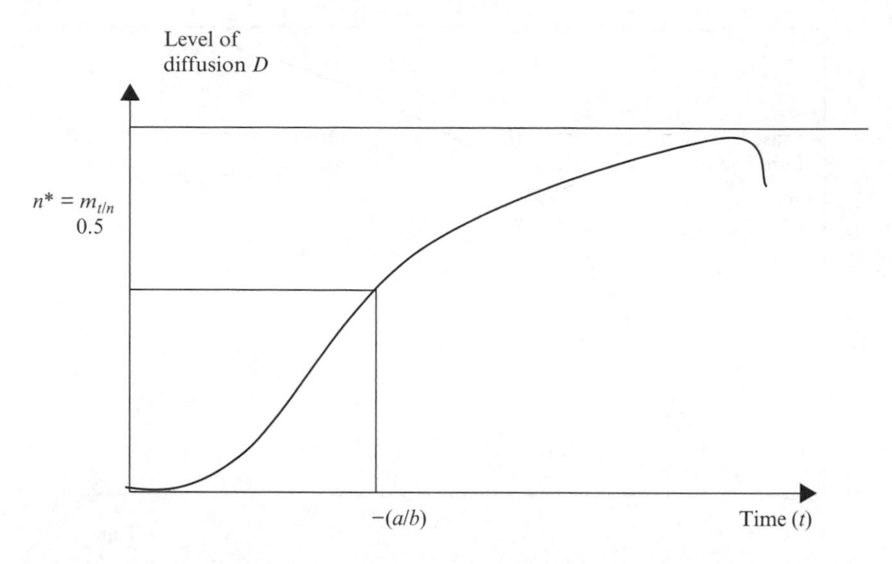

Notes: (a/b) = spread of new technology; D = level of diffusion; n = total firms in a population; m_t = number of adopters in a population; $n-m_t$ = number of potential adopters in a population.

Figure 2.3 The logistic epidemic curve

The spread of new technology among a fixed number of identical firms can be represented as follows. Let us assume that the level of diffusion is D, which corresponds to m_t number of firms in a fixed population of n which have adopted the new innovation at time t and to $(n-m_t)$ firms that remain as the potential adopters. Figure 2.3 illustrates the logistic epidemic curve. There is a huge literature on the law of logistic growth, which must be measured in appropriate units. Different studies on plants and animals were found to follow the logistic law, even though these two variables cannot be subject to the same distribution. Population theory relies on logistic extrapolations. The only trouble with this theory is that not only the logistic distribution but also the normal, the Cauchy, and other distributions can be fitted to the same material with the same or better goodness of fit. Examining the logistic curve, we can summarize the following disadvantages:

- the infectiousness of the disease must remain constant over time for all individuals; this means that b must be constant; however, in the case of a reduction in the contagiousness of the disease, b falls over time;
- all individuals must have an equal chance of catching the disease.

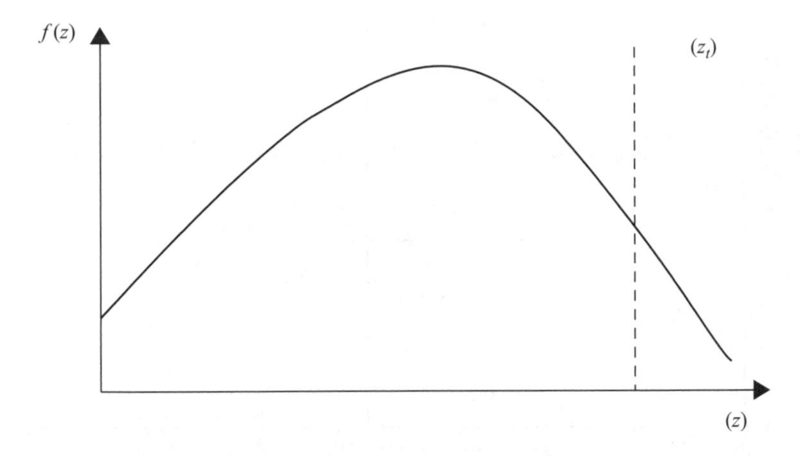

Figure 2.4 The cumulative distribution

4.2 The Probit Models

Probit analysis is a well-established technique in the study of diffusion of new products between individuals. This approach concentrates on the characteristics of individuals in a sector and is suitable not only to generate a diffusion curve, but also to give some indication of which firms will be early adopters and which late. Given the difficulties associated with the linear probability model, it is natural to transform the original model in such a way that predictions will lie between the (0,1) interval for all X. These requirements suggest the use of a cumulative probability function (F) in order to be able to explain a dichotomous dependent variable (the range of the cumulative probability function is the (0,1) interval, since all probabilities lie between 0 and 1).

The probit probability model is associated with the cumulative normal probability function. The central assumption underlying the probit model is that an individual consumer (or a firm/country) will be found to own the new product (or to adopt the new innovation) at a particular time when the income (or the size) exceeds some critical level. Let us assume that the potential adopters of technology differ according to some specified characteristic, z, that is distributed across the population as $f(z)$ with a cumulative distribution $F(z)$, as Figure 2.4 illustrates. The advantage of the probit diffusion models is that they relate to the possibility of introducing behavioural assumptions concerning the individual firm (firms). The probit model also offers interesting insights into the slowness of the technological diffusion process.

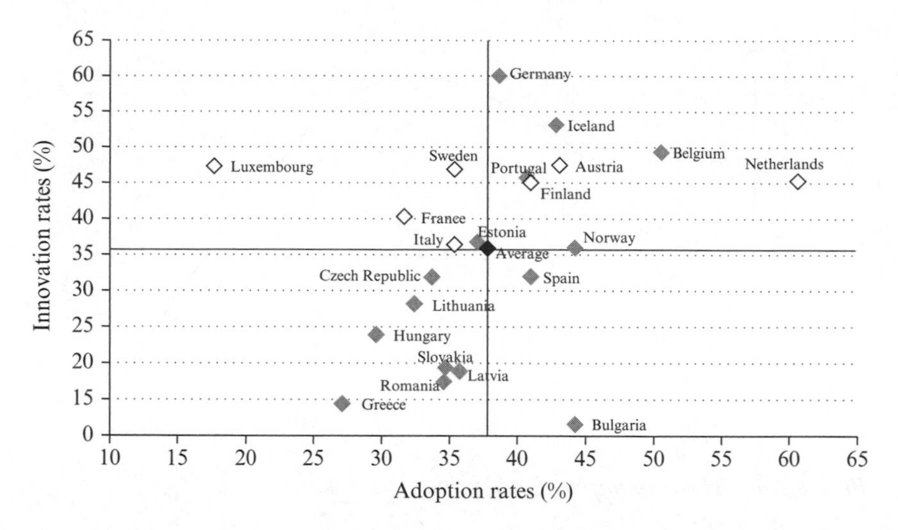

Note: The average adoption rate given in the figure (and in the following figures) is computed as an average of the country rates and not as a global rate computed from the country and industry database.

Source: Suriñach et al. (2009).

Figure 2.5 Innovation and adoption rates by selected member states

Furthermore, a number of economists (such as Mansfield, 1961; Sahal, 1977) consider diffusion as a disequilibrium phenomenon. Usually, when a new technology or a new method is introduced, it is less developed than the older method with which it competes. Therefore it is likely to have greater potential for improvement and for reduction in cost. The introduction of a new product or process broadens the range of choice of producers and consumers, and the equilibrium is altered. In the real world, there is only a gradual adjustment over the course of time to the new equilibrium level.

4.3 Diffusion and Adoption Process: Evidence from European Member States

The performance of innovation adoption for European member states seems to be more important for process innovations than for product innovations. Cooperation activities drive innovation adoption at the EU level while the acquisition of innovations from external innovators is a less important source of adoption of innovation (both process and product). Figures 2.5–2.7 illustrate the innovation and adoption rates by

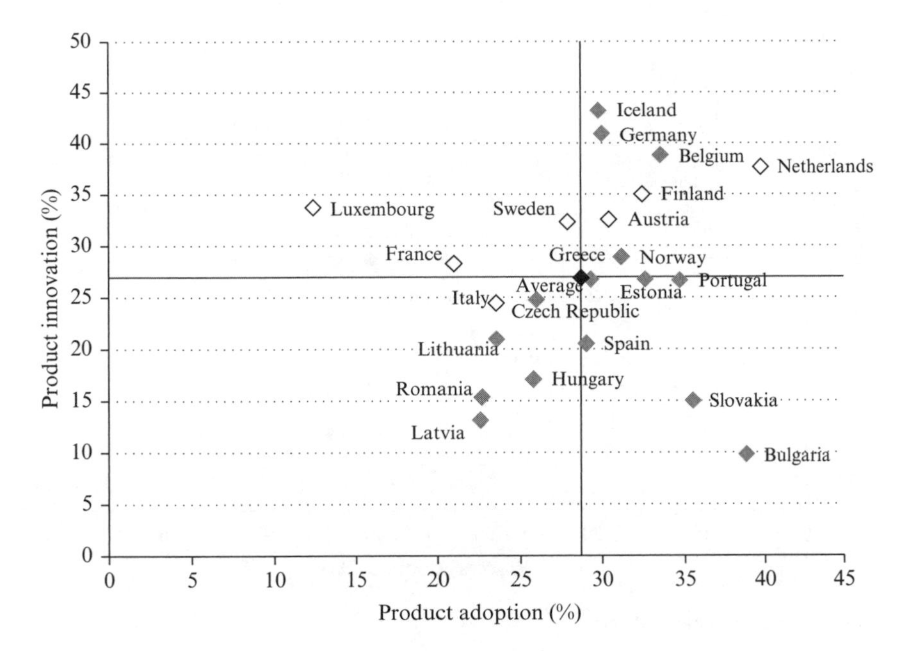

Source: Suriñach et al. (2009).

Figure 2.6 Product innovation and product adoption by member states

member states, product innovation and the product adoption by member states, and process innovation and process adoption by member states, respectively.

The most important features of the diffusion process of innovation activities are, according to Suriñach et al. (2009):

- For all European states, the adoption rate is higher in the case of process innovation (41 per cent) than product innovation (28 per cent). So, innovation adoption is more process oriented (even if innovation on its own is more product-oriented, 24 per cent of EU firms make process innovations versus 28 per cent that perform product innovations).
- Innovation adoption rates vary substantially across EU member states. The highly innovative countries seem also to be those that are more engaged in adoption activities. Luxembourg has a high rate of innovation but the adoption rate is very low. This feature can also be observed for France and Sweden but to a lesser extent. Bulgaria has a very low innovation rate but an important adoption rate.

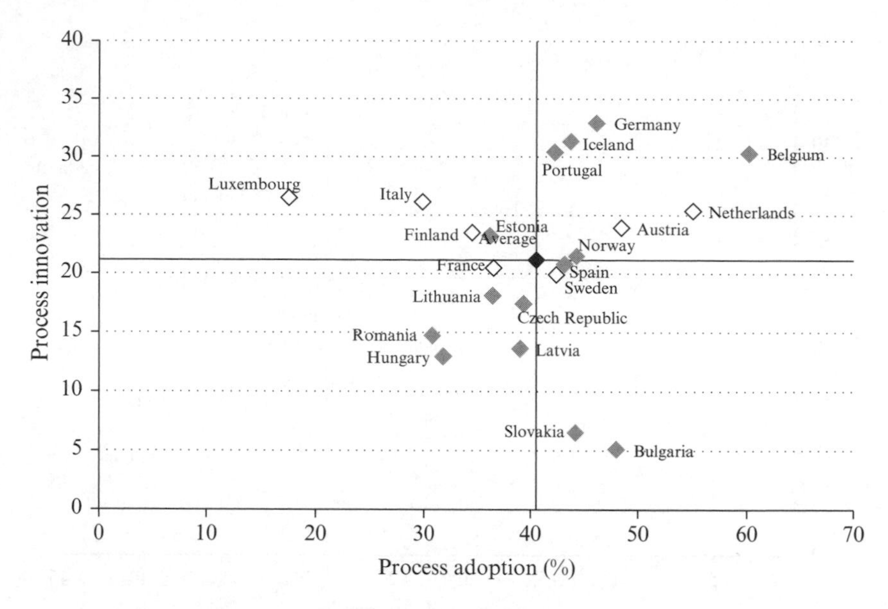

Source: Suriñach et al. (2009).

Figure 2.7 Process innovation and process adoption by selected member states

- The average percentage of adoptive firms is equal to 39 per cent; this rate varies a great deal according to countries. The maximum value is observed for the Netherlands with 61 per cent, then for Belgium with 51 per cent. On the contrary, the minimum value is observed for Luxembourg with 18 per cent. This percentage is low if compared to other countries since all other values are between 27 per cent and 44 per cent.
- The member states with low innovation rate also record a low adoption rate. This applies to Greece and to the majority of Eastern Europe countries (Romania, Latvia, Slovakia and Hungary). On the contrary, countries with high innovation rates have higher adoption rates (such as Belgium, the Netherlands, Iceland, Germany and Austria).
- European member states with higher rates of product innovation also experience higher rates of product adoption (apart from the specific cases of Bulgaria and Luxembourg). The same is true for process innovation activities; those countries innovating more on process are also those that seem to benefit from process innovation adoption.

Source: Suriñach et al. (2009).

Figure 2.8 Geographical pattern of EU states according to their adoption and innovation levels

Figure 2.8 illustrates the geographical pattern of EU states according to their adoption and innovation levels. According to these results, groups 1 and 2 face high adoption rates while, on the contrary, groups 5 and 6, which differ in their innovative and general economic features, register low adoption rates.

Figures 2.9–2.11 illustrate the share of sales due to adoption, the share of both product and process adopting firms by sector and also the innovation adoption rates in the EU, respectively. Regarding the adoption behaviour in the sectoral case, we can state the following facts (Suriñachi et al. 2009):

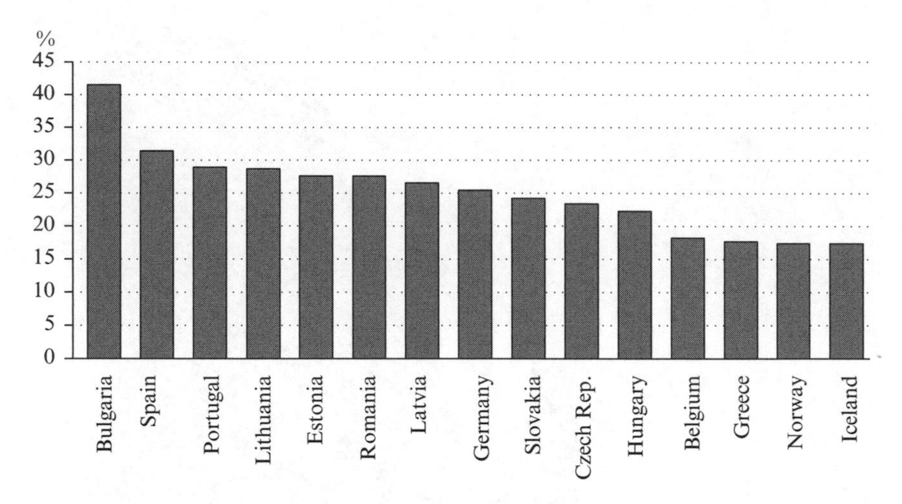

Source: Eurostat.

Figure 2.9 Share of sales due to adoption (based on 'new to the firm' definition of adoption)

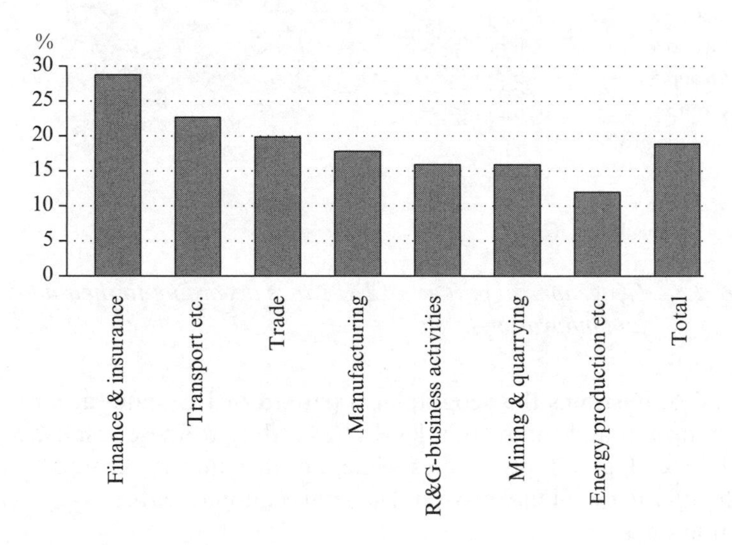

Source: Eurostat.

Figure 2.10 Share of both product and process adopting firms over total adopting firms by sector

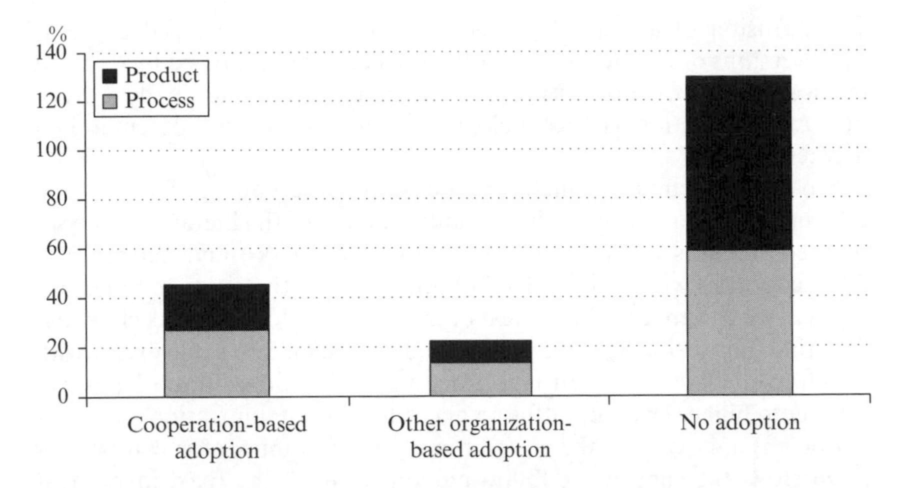

Source: Eurostat.

Figure 2.11 Innovation adoption rates in the EU

- For both product and process innovations, cooperation rates are particularly high for wholesale trade, financial activities and transport and communication (and energy only for process innovation adoption). On the contrary, manufacturing and extractive industry record the lowest rates.
- Whatever the sector and the nature of innovation (product or process), cooperation is more frequent than outsourcing to other organizations.
- The adoption is more cooperation-based for process innovation than product innovation, whatever the sector.

5. SUMMARY

New technologies imply some micro effects (on firms and organizations) and some macro effects (on industrial sectors) for the whole economy. In addition, new technologies play an important role in the productivity and competitiveness of a country. For instance, the faster the technological progress, the faster should the factor productivity rise and the less should 'cost-push' exert upward pressure on the price level. The principal effects for technological policy can be distinguished on the demand and supply sides.

Diffusion is the spread of a technology through a society or industry.

The diffusion of a technology generally follows an S-shaped curve as early versions of technology are rather unsuccessful, followed by a period of successful innovation with high levels of adoption, and finally a dropping off in adoption as a technology reaches its maximum potential in a market.

Most of the empirical literature focuses on the impact of innovation diffusion on economic growth. In addition, most of the literature analyses the determinants of innovation adoption, both micro and macro level. Also, countries with a higher level of innovative activities seem to be also those more dynamic in the context of innovation adoption. It is clear that fostering innovation activities may also be associated to some extent with spillover effects (which can take place through 'adoption mechanisms') leading to higher levels of diffusion and adoption of innovation.

For any innovation, the costs of entry for the innovator can be represented as the sum of the following components: the fixed investment cost in plant and equipment; the cost incurred by the innovator in acquiring scientific and technical knowledge not possessed by the firm at the beginning of innovation process; the cost incurred by the innovator in acquiring the relevant experience (know-how in organization, management, marketing or other areas) required to carry the innovation through; and the cost borne by the innovator to compensate for whatever relevant externalities are not provided by the environment in which the firm operates. Imitators will compare the cost of buying the technology with the cost of developing it themselves, if they can. However, the imitators' knowledge related to the entry costs will depend crucially on their own initial scientific and technical knowledge base in the relevant areas. Consequently, the entry costs may be much higher or much lower than the innovators, depending on their relative starting positions in the knowledge level of the firm. Furthermore, government regulations, taxes, tariffs and other relevant policies will strongly affect environmental and actual costs for an innovator. Specifically, the difficulty of catching up for industries/firms in the developing countries exists because scientific and technical knowledge, practical experience and locational advantages may be lower than in the more advanced countries, while those of technology may be higher.

REFERENCES

Amendola, G. and Perrucci, A. (1985), 'The diffusion of an organizational innovation: international data telecommunications and multinational industrial firms', *International Journal of Industrial Organisation*, **3**: 109–18.

Amendola, G. and Perrucci, A. (1986), 'The international diffusion of new information technologies', *Research Policy*, **15**: 139–47.
Antonelli, C. (1990), 'Induced adoption and externalities in the regional diffusion of new information technology', *Regional Studies*, **24**: 31–40.
Chen, E. (1983), 'The diffusion of technology', in *Multinational Corporations, Technology and Employment*, Basingstoke: Palgrave Macmillan, ch. 4.
Davies, S. (1979), *The Diffusion of Process Innovations*, Cambridge: Cambridge University Press.
Griliches, Z. (1957), 'Hybrid corn: an exploration in the economics of technological change', *Econometrica*, **25**: 501–22.
Korres, G. (2011), *Handbook of Innovation Economics*, New York: Nova Publishers.
Korres, G., Lionaki, I. and Polychronopoulos, G. (2003), 'The role of technical change and diffusion in the Schumpeterian lines', in Jürgen Backhaus (ed.), *Joseph Alois Schumpeter: Entrepreneurship – Style and Vision*, New York: Kluwer Academic Publishers, pp. 293–312.
Mansfield, E. (1961), 'Technical change and the rate of imitation', *Econometrica*, **29**: 741–65.
Mansfield, E. (1988), 'The speed and cost of industrial innovation in Japan and the United States: external vs. internal technology', *Management Science*, **34**(10): 1157–68.
Sahal, D. (1977), 'Substitution of mechanical corn pickers by field shelling technology – an econometric analysis', *Technological Forecasting & Social Change*, **10**: 53–60.
Schumpeter, Joseph A. (1934), *The Theory of Economic Development*, Cambridge, MA: Harvard Economic Studies.
Stoneman, P. (1976), *Technological Diffusion and the Computer Revolution*, Cambridge: Cambridge University Press.
Stoneman, P. (1983), *The Economic Analysis of Technological Change*, Oxford: Oxford University Press.
Stoneman, P. (1986), 'Technological diffusion: the viewpoint of economic theory', *Richerche Economiche*, **XL**(4): 585–606.
Stoneman, P. (1987), *The Economic Analysis of Technology Policy*, Oxford: Oxford University Press.
Stoneman, P. (2002), *The Economics of Technological Diffusion*, Oxford: Blackwell.
Suriñach, Jordi, Autant-Bernard, Corinne, Manca, Fabio, Massard, Nadine and Moreno, Rosina (2009), 'The diffusion/adoption of innovation in the internal market', Economic Papers No. 384, September, Directorate-General Economic and Financial Affairs.

3. Building the innovation union: lessons from the 2008 financial crisis

Alice O. Nakamura, Leonard I. Nakamura and Masao Nakamura[1]

1. INTRODUCTION

The focus of the Innovation Union initiative of the European Union (EU) is on product and process innovation for tangible goods. We argue that it is essential to extend the scope of the initiative to include innovation for financial sector products, processes and regulatory approaches. We make this argument using examples of financial sector innovations in the USA following the Great Depression and on the basis of an examination of the 2008 financial crisis.

2. THE INNOVATION UNION IN BRIEF

The website for the Competitiveness and Innovation Framework Programme of the European Commission (2010) states:

> Innovation is the only means of tackling the major societal challenges such as climate change, scarce natural resources and an aging society, while fostering jobs and growth.

The Europe 2020 strategy and its flagship Innovation Union initiative are based on this perspective. The aim is to spur growth of the EU economy and jobs via enhanced innovation activity. The ultimate goal is to harness innovation in the service of raising EU living standards now and for generations to come (European Commission, 2011a).

There are plans to offer researchers more attractive careers and to remove obstacles to the mobility of researchers across sectors and EU countries. Reforms have been agreed on too for modernizing higher education, including increases in graduate student numbers. Other measures include helping EU students and trainees study abroad and making

Europe's universities more attractive destinations for talent from other nations (European Commission, 2011b).

The Europe 2020 strategy includes multiple programs as well for making the EU a more welcoming region for businesses interested in developing innovative products and processes. For example, intellectual property rights protections are being strengthened and the costs of patenting in Europe are being reduced. Other efforts under way have the goal of improving business access to financing. Especially for young companies, finding suitable investors can be a crucial step towards business expansion and survival. Taken as a share of GDP, venture capital investment in the USA is four times higher than in the EU. The Commission has appointed the Chairman of the British Business Angels Association to head an expert group tasked with formulating recommendations on how to improve the cross-border matching of innovative firms with investors. The expert group findings were presented in 2012 (European Commission, 2011b).

3. SETBACKS ATTRIBUTED TO THE 2008 FINANCIAL CRISIS

The Europe 2020 and Innovative Union programs and plans and objectives make sense, but the lingering effects of the 2008 financial crisis represent an overarching feasibility question mark. In the program documents, it is noted that the EU economy is slowly emerging from the deepest recession in decades and that the economic crisis has resulted in large losses in economic activity in the EU. Millions of jobs have been lost (European Commission, 2011e).

By the end of 2012, it is anticipated that the economies of a large share of the member states will still be operating at output and employment levels below those preceding the crisis. The incidence of people unemployed for more than one year has increased steeply across the EU and youth unemployment exceeds 20 percent in more than half the EU member states.

The financial crisis impact on public finances has been very negative. Government debt-to-GDP ratios have risen sharply in most member states, reflecting both a decline in tax revenues and increased pressures on government expenditure for income support and fiscal stimulus. The crisis has further reduced potential growth via a fall in the investment rate. Business R&D investments have been hit especially hard (European Commission, 2011c).

The profitability outlook for the EU area banks is especially uncertain due to the sluggish recovery, heavy exposure to the real-estate sector, and tensions in the sovereign debt market. The negative feedback from the real economy to the financial sector has been reinforced in some member states by high household and non-financial corporate sector indebtedness, with the prevalence of non-performing loans increasing considerably.

The EU has established new rules and agencies to try to ensure that all financial players are properly regulated in years to come (European Commission, 2011d). Efforts are under way, in particular, to ensure that EU banks have sufficient capital reserves to withstand future shocks to the financial system while continuing to function and to provide credit to households and businesses. However, stricter leverage rules mean that EU banks will be more constrained in their lending even when more favorable economic growth conditions have been restored.

One way to minimize the impact of the heightened regulatory policies is to improve the ability of financial regulators to monitor financial institutions and instruments, as well as the ability of financial intermediaries to measure and limit their own risks. Indeed, in the USA the Dodd–Frank Act included an Office of Financial Research to specifically accomplish these ends. Part of the charge of the Office of Financial Research is to establish data infrastructure for the study of financial instruments and institutions, and to improve the monitoring capabilities of financial regulators and the financial industry. Nakamura (2011) discusses the value of such a data infrastructure and suggests one framework for it.

The Europe 2020 and the Innovation Union programs and stated goals pertain mostly to boosting R&D for products that are tangible and processes for producing tangible products. There is little mention of basic research aimed at achieving a deeper understanding of the causes of the 2008 financial crisis or that seeks to discover and develop new financial sector products, institutions and regulatory approaches that could help address the post-crisis problems and needs. This state of affairs represents a contrast to US financial innovation activities in the wake of the Great Depression, as explained below, those innovations included new financial products and institutions.

Some see the 2008 financial crisis as a continuation of a pattern documented by Kindleberger and Aliber (2005), who argue that financial crises keep happening because of a recurrent pattern. The authors find that sustained increases in the price level for some asset lead investors to become increasingly optimistic and more eager to pursue speculative profit opportunities while the lenders become less risk-averse. The profit opportunities often arrive as a consequence of the 'widespread adoption of an invention with pervasive effects – canals, railroads, the automobile – some political event or surprising financial success' (p. 18). An increasingly large share of asset purchases is undertaken in anticipation of short-term capital gains and a large and growing share of these purchases are financed with credit.

There is a pervasive sense, they argue, that it is 'time to get on the train before it leaves the station' and the exceptionally profitable opportunities disappear. Asset prices increase further, fuelled by increasing speculative activity.

Eventually, Kindleberger and Aliber observe, the asset price bubble bursts, and speculators rush to unload their asset holdings, which pushes the asset prices down further. John Geanokoplos (2010) has nicely discussed how a key aspect of these repetitive price increases and declines may be differences in opinion – the optimists hold and increase their asset holdings while the price is rising, because the increase in the value of the assets increases the wealth of the optimists. When the price turns, the optimists lose wealth and must divest. Speculators who made their purchases largely using borrowed funds end up owing more on their loans than the assets can be sold for. Kindleberger and Aliber document repeated historical episodes that follow this pattern: a pattern that fits what happened in the 2008 financial crisis in multiple respects. Nevertheless, we feel that the 2008 financial crisis also involved specific financial products and regulatory problems that require specific attention.

4. THE US FINANCIAL SECTOR

4.1 Financial Institutions Created in the Wake of the Great Depression

Americans were bitter toward and fearful of bankers in the wake of the Great Depression, and the institutions established and rules enacted then reflect those feelings. The 1933 McFadden Act prohibited banks from having branches in more than one state. The 1933 Glass–Steagall Act prohibited depository banks from creating and selling securities. That Act also created the Federal Deposit Insurance Corporation (FDIC), which insures bank deposits. In 1934, the Securities and Exchange Commission (SEC) was established to regulate the nation's stock and options exchanges and to help prevent corporate abuses in reporting and in the sale of securities.

Also in 1934, Congress created the Federal Housing Administration (FHA)[2] to help rebuild the US home construction and housing markets by providing insurance on mortgages originated by FHA-approved lenders. Soon after the FHA was established in 1934, the agency moved to create a new sort of mortgage instrument for Americans: a 30-year mortgage with the rate of interest fixed over the full mortgage term, and with the mortgage being prepayable at any time without penalty. As Woodward and Hall (2009) explain, this American mortgage greatly reduced homeowner risks and was instantly popular with homeowners. However, it exposes any institution that originates and holds mortgages to two sorts of serious risks. Future expected revenue from profits on mortgages already originated can suddenly vanish if interest rates fall and homeowners refinance. Alternatively, if interest rates rise, lenders can end up facing higher rates on short-term funds borrowed to finance the portfolios they are carrying than the rates being paid by homeowners on their mortgages.

On the institutional front, US financial innovations following the Great Depression also included the creation in 1938 of Fannie Mae. Fannie's initial mandate was to borrow funds and then to buy up US government-insured mortgages from private sector mortgage originators (i.e. mortgage lenders). This replenished the funds of the lenders so they could then originate more mortgages. Originally, Fannie held the mortgages purchased in the corporation's portfolio and received income as borrowers repaid the interest and principle. Back then, Fannie's debt from those purchases was fully backed by the US government.

However, governments, like private businesses, often look for accounting and organizational expediencies that can legitimize operation with greater leverage. Thus, in 1954, government backing for Fannie's borrowings was rescinded,[3] and in 1968, Fannie's mortgage portfolio was taken off the federal balance sheet entirely. The original Fannie Mae was split in two. One part was renamed and became a new government corporation called Ginnie Mae. Ginnie was given the mission of selling US government-insured mortgages. The other part retained the name of Fannie Mae and became a 100 percent stockholder-owned enterprise. Soon thereafter, in 1970, Freddie Mac was also created by the US government as a 100 percent shareholder-owned enterprise. However, investors clearly continued to believe there was government backing for Fannie and Freddie's debt, and were encouraged in this belief by special privileges accorded to Fannie and Freddie by the US government and special demands that were placed on Fannie and Freddie to help meet national affordable housing objectives.

4.2 The Invention of Mortgage-Backed Securities (MBS) and Securitization

Mortgages have always been hard to sell to investors. Hence the US government department of Housing and Urban Development (HUD) designed a mortgage-backed security (MBS).[4] An MBS, in its simplest form, is a bond backed by a pool of mortgages on which homeowners are contractually obligated to make regular monthly payments. Those payments are collected monthly and then passed through to the MBS holders.

Soon Ginnie Mae, Fannie Mae and Freddie Mac were all packaging mortgages into pools and then selling MBSs that were enhanced by agency guarantees against the financial risk of losses due to default. Indeed, investors were guaranteed not just full repayment, but *timely* repayment, though only the guarantees of Ginnie Mae were, in fact, legally backed by the US government.

The private sector took years to develop a competing product that could match the popularity of the MBS that Ginnie, Fannie and Freddie sold. Thus Ginnie, Fannie and Freddie were able to dominate the MBS market through the 1990s. However, by 2001, another financial product innovation called a collateralized debt obligation (CDO) finally made it possible for private firms to compete with the Ginnie–Fannie–Freddie MBS. A CDO consists of a collection of bonds called tranches that are backed by a pool of debt assets which usually includes mortgages, and often also other debt assets such as car loans and credit card accounts.[5] The payments from the pool flow to the different tranches in order of their seniority.

The most senior tranche, sometimes called super senior, has the highest-priority claim on the mortgage pool cash flows. Once that tranche has been taken care of, then cash is sequentially allocated to fill each of the remaining tranches, in their seniority priority order. The so-called equity investors are those holding the most junior MBS tranches with the lowest cash flow priority and hence the highest risk of losses. However, the equity investors also get the highest rate of return when a CDO does well over time. Investment bank hedge funds turned out to be among the largest of the CDO equity investors.

On 8 April 2005, in his address to the Federal Reserve System's Fourth Annual Community Affairs Research Conference, then Fed Chairman Alan Greenspan declared:

> Innovation has brought about a multitude of new products, such as subprime loans and niche credit programs for immigrants . . . With these advances in technology, lenders have taken advantage of credit-scoring models and other techniques for efficiently extending credit to a broader spectrum of consumers . . . The mortgage-backed security helped create a national and even an international market for mortgages, and market support for a wider variety of home mortgage loan products became commonplace. This led to securitization of a variety of other consumer loan products, such as auto and credit card loans.[6]

In this statement, Greenspan is celebrating the financial product innovations of the USA, and especially the development of MBS and CDO. Although some of these products were inadequately regulated and subsequently caused great losses not only in the USA but also in the EU and elsewhere, many of the innovations themselves are clearly success stories.

4.3 Special Investment Vehicles (SIV)

A special investment vehicle (SIV), also referred to by a variety of other names including a special purpose vehicle and a special purpose entity, is a corporate legal entity created by a sponsoring organization to segregate specific activities (risks). By isolating high-risk projects from a parent organization and by allowing new investors to take a share of the very specific segregated risks held by the SIV, it can be easier to attract increased investor participation. An SIV often consists simply of a set of legal documents and has no offices, management or employees. It is also usually 'bankruptcy remote', meaning that if the sponsoring organization has financial problems, its creditors cannot seize the assets of the SIV.

A firm can use SIV to finance large R&D and other sorts of risky projects so that these can be pursued without putting the entire firm at risk. This usage of SIV can help increase investor participation in R&D: an EU objective. In addition, however, SIV can be used by firms to avoid future taxes on the returns from R&D and many other sorts of projects that were, in fact, mostly carried out with personnel and other resources located in countries other than where the SIV are located.

Prior to the 2008 financial crisis, SIV had come to be widely used in the creation and sale of asset-backed securities including CDO. In creating a CDO, an SIV is usually created first. The SIV is often established in a tax haven. The SIV issues bonds to investors in exchange for cash, which is then used to purchase the portfolio of assets which will be used for the CDO. The bonds, called tranches, are issued in layers with different risk characteristics, as noted above.

4.4 The US Nationally Recognized Statistical Rating Organizations (NRSRO)

Perhaps because of being especially reliant on capital market funding for many purposes including mortgage funding, the USA has developed the world's most known and used rating companies for assessing the riskiness of securities traded on financial markets, including debt securities like CDO. A small number of these rating agencies have essentially become part of the US financial sector regulatory system. These are called nationally recognized statistical rating organizations (NRSRO).

The NRSRO first came to be designated this way in 1973. Back then, the US Securities and Exchange Commission (SEC) decided to tie the capital requirements for broker–dealers to ratings for the securities they held. In designing these new regulatory capital requirements, the SEC worried that if they were designated as NRSRO, some of the many agencies then producing ratings for securities might start essentially selling favorable ratings. Thus the SEC designated just a short list of the established agencies in the securities rating business as NRSRO, and decreed that only the ratings of those agencies could be used for satisfying SEC regulatory capital requirements.[7]

Soon NRSRO ratings began to be incorporated into other rules and regulatory procedures, including the leverage regulations for money market funds, pension funds and insurance companies. In the early 1980s, there were seven NRSROs. In the 1990s, mergers reduced the number to three: Standard & Poor's (S&P), Moody's and the Fitch Group Inc. (Fitch). Those three continue to dominate the NRSRO ratings business, although the number of NRSROs was subsequently increased again by the SEC.

Corporations (including municipalities) that issue securities want NRSRO triple A ratings for their securities because this allows those corporations to raise funds at lower cost. And financial institutions, including banks and funds, have wanted to invest in triple A securities because the regulators for financial institutions in many countries have permitted them to operate with lower capital reserves if they were holding triple A rated securities.[8] In good times, holding less regulatory capital lets financial institutions achieve higher profit rates.

Soon international guidelines for financial institutions also began to build in NRSRO ratings. Of special importance, in 1988, the Basel Committee on Banking Supervision, an international body made up of representatives from the major central banks, produced the Basel Accord, which went into effect in 1992 in the EU and many other participating countries. The original Basel Accords were superseded in 2004 by Basel II, which was intended to create an international standard for banking regulators to control how much capital banks needed to hold in reserve to guard against financial risks.[9]

From the perspective of a lender, experience suggests that the safest direct loans are home mortgage loans to borrowers with excellent credit and loan amounts that are 80 percent or less of their property values. These loans to 'prime' borrowers had a risk weighting of 35 percent under Basel II. However, when loans of that sort were packaged into a mortgage-backed security rated triple A, the risk weighting under Basel II was only 20 percent! In this way, Basel II reduced the amount of capital a bank had to keep in reserve to back up loans, and thereby increased bank profits so long, of course, as the bank did not end up facing solvency challenges. Thus banks had a strong incentive to sell the mortgage and other consumer loan accounts they originated and to replace holdings of those sorts of debt assets with triple A debt asset-backed securities. Thus EU area banks loaded up on triple A rated MBS and CDO tranches.[10]

The NRSRO credit ratings for securities backed by consumer debt assets are arrived at using the credit rating information for the borrowers for the pooled debt assets.[11] Empirical evidence collected in recent years had shown that people with steady track records of paying all their bills on time almost never defaulted on mortgage loans, and this empirical 'fact' was built into the CDO rating processes of the NRSRO. By now, however, it was recognized that there is one condition under which mortgage default becomes considerably more likely even for homeowners who, previously, had been regularly paying all their bills on time. This is the situation in which the market value of a home falls below the value of the mortgage: the underwater homeowner case. The NRSRO, along with much of the rest of the finance industry, ended up greatly underestimating the likelihood of default for subprime, and also for prime, mortgages in the underwater case.

4.5 The Use of Credit Default Swaps to Upgrade Mortgage-Backed Securities

Credit default swaps (CDS) are an insurance or a gambling product, depending on how they are used. CDS were invented by a team led by Blythe Masters of JPMorgan in 1997 as a tool for hedging default risk on loans. The cost of a freely traded CDS could potentially provide a better estimate of the risk on a debt instrument than the opinion, say, of a credit rating agency expressed in the form of a credit rating.[12]

With a CDS, the buyer makes a series of payments to the seller and is then entitled to a payment if a specified 'credit event' happens, such as a loss of value for the 'reference entity' named in the CDS purchased. CDS increasingly were used by those packaging and selling CDO tranches for the purpose of obtaining ratings upgrades for lower-quality securities such as subprime debt assets. Buyers of CDO were especially reassured by CDS sold by companies with triple A ratings from an NRSRO like the American Insurance Group (AIG), the world's largest insurance company, or a monoline insurance company like Ambac.[13]

The triple A claims-paying record of AIG had been built up over years of selling types of insurance like life insurance with little potential for systemic risk. And the triple A rated monolines had built up their good credit-paying records over the years by just insuring municipal bonds, for which defaults had been rare (Madigan, 2008). It turned out, therefore, that the companies that sold most of the CDS had earned their triple A ratings from the NRSRO for business activities in prior years that were quite different from the business of insuring CDO. Moreover, AIG was able to avoid holding reserves against the risk of writing the CDS because it argued that the purpose of the CDS was not insurance but simply regulatory arbitrage.

The explosion in the use of CDS to shore up the ratings of CDO backed by mortgages of increasingly dubious quality seems to have been driven by the role that triple A rated securities could play for financial institutions in meeting regulatory capital requirements. In the years prior to 2008, European banks reportedly acquired mortgage and other debt asset-backed securities that were accompanied by more than US$426 billion in AIG credit default swaps. When AIG's rating fell in September 2008, causing downgrades for all securities for which the rating had been enhanced via a CDS sold by AIG, this left large numbers of European banks holding less than the required levels of capital.

4.6 Synthetic CDO: The Key to Creation of Vastly More Triple A Securities

Increasingly in the years leading up to 2008, CDS were also purchased for purely speculative purposes by buyers without any insurable interest whatsoever in the named credit events for the CDS. These CDS are referred to as naked. A speculator who bought a naked CDS was betting the reference entity written into the CDS would suffer a credit event. Sales of naked CDS to speculators had come to dominate the CDS market by 2008.

Although they had been used for decades to hedge risks, CDS sales had remained limited in earlier years. One reason for this is that, to be useful for regulatory capital purposes, a CDS had to be combined with an asset. For example, a CDS might be used to enhance the rating of a security like a CDO so that it could be held as regulatory capital by a bank. But pools of mortgages were needed to create regular CDO, and the supply of suitable mortgages available for purchase that met the specifications needed for the creation of CDO tranches that could be highly rated if combined with a CDS was limited. However, that limitation was removed with the creation of synthetic CDO.

A synthetic CDO combines newly created CDS with fixed income securities. The latter could be one or more already existing CDO, say. Tranches of synthetic CDO are securities that can be rated, and the highly rated tranches could then be used to satisfy regulatory capital requirements. The term 'synthetic CDO' arises because the cash flows from the premiums (via the included CDS) are analogous in some ways to the 'fixed income' cash flows arising from the mortgage or other debt obligations in the pools backing up regular CDO. However, if a credit event occurs in the fixed income portfolio part of a synthetic CDO, then the synthetic CDO investors become responsible for the losses, starting from the lowest-rated tranches of the synthetic CDO and working up. With a synthetic CDO, credit losses hurt the investors in the synthetic CDO and benefit the writers of the embedded CDS.

A buyer of a synthetic CDO is taking the 'long' position, meaning they are betting that the referenced fixed income securities will perform well. The seller of a synthetic CDO pays premiums to the buyer so long as there has not been a credit event for the referenced entity. This party is taking the 'short' position, meaning they are betting the referenced securities will default. The seller receives a large payout from the synthetic CDO buyer if the referenced entities have a credit event. While the supply of synthetic CDO was primarily driven by the intense demand for assets with the risk–return characteristics of CDO, the sellers also stood to gain in the event of poor mortgage performance.

4.7 Innovative Changes that Resulted in Increasing Maturity Mismatch

The market for debt securities with a maturity of 13 months or less is generally referred to as the money market. Money market mutual funds have traditionally invested in short-term, low-risk instruments such as government securities, commercial paper, certificates of deposit, repurchase agreements and discount notes. These funds often offer immediate and full redemption of shares to members, but they fund assets that have longer terms and may be costly to liquidate. This innate fragility of money market funds can cause problems for other financial firms and the broader economy because of the size of the money fund industry and its prominence in short-term financing for other financial institutions.

The wholesale money market intermediates cash balances predominantly for institutional investors. These funds are usually raised on a short-term rollover basis (see Pozsar et al., 2010). Maturity transformation refers to the use of funding that is shorter term than the assets being financed. By definition, a financial institution engaging in maturity transformation cannot honor a sudden request for full withdrawals. As the maturity mismatch between a financial institution's debt assets and liabilities grows, the required maturity transformation and associated risks grow too.

Date and Konczal (2010) note that the traditional assets of US commercial banks were relatively illiquid commercial and consumer loans and the traditional funding source for these banks were deposits. Because deposit funding in the USA enjoys some measure of FDIC insurance and is provided by independent, atomized depositors, these funds are not usually withdrawn en masse in response to shocks to the economy or to a financial institution. This source of funding fits well with the inherently illiquid nature of most consumer and many commercial loans.

In contrast, the US investment banks have traditionally favored inexpensive, short-term funding in the wholesale money markets. This funding derives from relatively few institutional sources. Moreover, over time, the US investment banks increased their exposure to long-term, illiquid assets, while becoming increasingly dependent on the wholesale money market for funding. The maturity of their liabilities declined to as short as a day. Hedge funds, which basically are unregistered investment banks that serve high net worth or institutional investors, became similarly vulnerable. In addition, over time some of the US commercial banks began to also rely heavily on short-term, wholesale money market funding (Huang and Ratnovski, 2011).

Even though Canadian commercial banks have been allowed all along to carry out investment bank activities, Ratnovski and Huang (2009) point out that the Canadian banks have consistently depended less on wholesale funding, and much more on depository funding from households, than many US depository banks. As Bordo et al. (2010) also explain, when Canadian banks do use short-term wholesale funding, they are required to maintain stocks of highly liquid assets appropriate for their cash flow and funding profiles. Banks with more than 10 percent of funding coming from wholesale money market sources have been required in Canada to put in place internal limits on short-term funding requirements.

4.8 Off-Book Budget Items

Off-budget items are part of a broader problem of missing information that the decision makers running private financial firms and the public sector regulators need to be able to effectively do their jobs. The consequences of missing and wrong information are illustrated, for example, in a now public Lehman study completed in the fall of 2007 by company analysts Shilpiekandula and Gorodetsky. Amazingly, these analysts found little cause for concern except for the monolines that had sold large volumes of CDS that had been used to upgrade the ratings of CDO. Beyond that, however, these analysts were mostly clueless about the developing financial market conditions that would soon destroy their company.[14]

The Commodity Futures Modernization Act (CFMA), passed on 20 December 2000, exempted derivative transactions, including CDO and CDS sales, from all requirements of exchange trading and clearing. This meant that there were no comprehensive, real-time sources of data about the volumes of CDO and CDS that had been sold (Greenberger, 2010).

Also, Partnoy and Turner (2010) explain that, historically, US accounting rules required corporations to consolidate on their balance sheets any special investment vehicles they used to finance assets. During the 1970s, if a transaction was a financing, both the assets being financed and the financing had to be on the balance sheet. However, over the following decades, those rules were modified so that a corporation only had to include the assets and liabilities of another corporate entity in its financial statements if it had a 'controlling interest' in that entity. Accounting standards like this that enable the growth of off-book business activities mess up the economic data used not only for regulation of financial institutions, but also for economic planning.

5. BREAKING THE FINANCIAL CRISIS OF 2008 INTO A CHAIN OF FOUR COMPONENT CRISES

We see the financial crisis of 2008 as a chain reaction of component crises. Recognizing these components may make it easer to understand why extensive financial sector expertise and research are needed as a defense against follow-up financial crises of a similar nature. Poor financial sector outcomes undermine the means of paying for R&D in other sectors.

5.1 Crisis 1: Rising Mortgage Defaults

Mortgage defaults were the trigger for the 2008 crisis. In turn, the waves of mortgage defaults were triggered by the change from rising to falling in the USA of average home prices. Although many argue now that change in the direction of the US home price trend should have been anticipated, the timing of that change clearly came as a surprise to many. It was the change in the direction of the home price trend beginning in 2006 that triggered the mortgage defaults, and those defaults contributed to further and deeper declines in home prices, leading to more defaults. It is understood by now that owners of homes for which the market values have fallen below the values of their mortgages ('underwater' homeowners) are likely to default on their mortgages even if those mortgages are classified as prime.[15]

The extent of the boom–bust cycle in housing was exacerbated during the boom phase as well, as rising house prices directly lowered the risk of home lending. Borrowers who lack the funds to make their mortgage payments could either borrow additional sums against their increased home equity or sell their homes. This reduction in risk then apparently led to additional reductions in the credit standards of lenders, allowing new borrowers to raise home demand further in a boom cycle, as described by Brueckner et al. (2012). That is, in addition to failing to foresee when the US average home price would stop rising, the US consumer credit scoring agencies[16] failed to properly take account of the likelihood of loan defaults for underwater homeowners, and this contributed to the US practice of giving mortgages without requiring significant down-payments.

5.2 Crisis 2: The Ratings Downgrades and Value Slides for Mortgage-Backed Securities

The volume of mortgage-backed CDO grew rapidly between 2000 and 2006, and then went into decline once mortgage defaults began to rise. The credit ratings for mortgage-backed securities, including CDO, began to be downgraded by the ratings agencies once the default rate began to rise. Mortgage-backed CDO performed far worse than other types of CDO issued over the years of 1999–2007.[17] Published in January 2007, Moody's report on structured finance ratings over the period of 1983–2006[18] notes that the slowing US housing market and rising interest rates had very negative effects on the ratings of US mortgage-backed securities.

Without a triple A credit rating, a CDO was no longer useful for reducing the regulatory capital requirements for a bank or fund. Financial institutions thus began selling large volumes of their downgraded CDO securities, pushing CDO market values and ratings down further. As CDO prices fell, the trading of CDO became increasingly difficult. This liquidity failure was aggravated by rising margin requirements, which limited the freedom of action for speculative investors and many of them also began trying to unload their CDO holdings. The regulators for financial institutions failed to foresee and guard against the chain reaction of ratings downgrades that ensued (see Benmelech and Dlugosz, 2009; Bartlett, 2010).

5.3 Crisis 3: Downgrades for Credit Default Swap Sellers

When homeowners began to default on their mortgages in record numbers, the owners of CDO who had hedged their risk by CDS, and also the speculators who had placed bets that there would be widespread mortgage defaults by buying naked CDS naming downgrades of mortgage-backed CDO as the named credit events, began to be entitled to collect payouts. However, the sellers of the CDS had not held sufficient capital reserves to deal with large numbers of claims.

In 2008, the financial press was filled with dire news about the CDS sellers. The monolines were the focus of worries back then. It was widely recognized that they had sold more CDS than they were in a position to back up. The news reports explained that if one or more of the main triple A monolines were downgraded by the rating agencies, a wide range of other financial institutions would also be in trouble.[19]

In addition to selling CDS to shore up CDO, the monolines had also collectively guaranteed about $2.4 trillion worth of municipal bonds. Those CDS guarantees had allowed municipalities to borrow more cheaply. Downgrades for the monolines meant downgrades too for the municipal bonds guaranteed by the monolines. The perceived likelihood of monoline ratings downgrades rose steadily beginning in the summer of 2007.

In January 2008, the credit rating was reduced from triple to double A for Ambac, the largest of the monolines. This caused immediate downgrades of thousands and thousands of municipal bonds, and there were resulting downgrades as well of CDO held by financial institutions. As the major rating agencies began to downgrade other monoline insurers too during 2008, vast numbers of additional municipal bonds, CDO and other securities insured by those companies were downgraded as well. In addition, AIG had also sold far more CDS than the company was in a position to pay out claims on. Thus the CDS crisis rapidly worsened in 2008.

The CDS sellers in the USA should have been regulated under both insurance and bucket shop (i.e. gambling) laws. Unfortunately, the USA explicitly exempted CDS from both those sorts of regulation (Greenberger, 2010). Europe needs to be in a position to notice a US regulatory lapse like this and to take defensive measures.

5.4 Crisis 4: The Collapse of Investment and Some Commercial Banks and Fannie and Freddie

The mortgage defaults, falling CDO values, and downgrades and payout failures of CDS sellers caused the failure of all the main US investment banks. This was the most spectacular manifestation of the 2008 financial crisis. Bear Stearns was the first to fail. On 17 March 2008, the Fed opened a line of credit that enabled JPMorgan to buy Bear for just $2 a share.[20] On 15 September, Lehman Brothers declared bankruptcy. Also on 15 September, Merrill Lynch was purchased by the Bank of America in an emergency deal. Back then, Merrill was the largest US brokerage firm. In addition, on 21 September, the Fed agreed to let Morgan Stanley and Goldman Sachs become bank holding companies, making them eligible for federal aid.[21]

Many other financial giants failed as well that year. For example, in

November, the nation's largest bank holding company, Citigroup, had to be rescued with taxpayer money. The nation's largest mortgage lender, Countrywide Financial, was acquired by Bank of America in a distressed sale, and Bank of America then had to be rescued by the Fed, due in part at least to problem assets acquired along with Merrill Lynch.

Based on a study of 72 large banks and bank holding companies in the OECD, Huang and Ratnovski (2011) conclude that greater reliance on wholesale money market rather than retail depository funding was a key determinant of which banks fared badly in the 2008 financial crisis. The study revealed that many of the US investment and depository banks that got into trouble in the crisis relied heavily on wholesale (and other sorts of) funding that could be withdrawn quickly.[22]

Concerns arose as well in 2008 regarding the leverage of Fannie and Freddie and their ability to make good on their guarantees for the MBS those corporations had sold. As part of their capital reserves, they held large portfolios of private label CDO that had lost their original triple A ratings and much of their original market value over the summer of 2008. On 7 September 2008, the federal regulator for Fannie and Freddie put them into conservatorship.[23]

Many money market funds had purchased MBS under binding buy-back agreements that were conditional on continued triple A ratings for those assets. Hence a sudden loss of triple A status for large volumes of MBS put those funds at imminent risk too. Risk assessments rose for CDO and MBS. A large portion of these securities were held in various special investment vehicles that relied on asset-backed commercial paper for financing. Doubts on the part of money market fund managers regarding the securities those SIV held led to a market liquidity collapse for asset-backed commercial paper. Banks hoarded liquidity in order to provide sufficient funding for their SIV and drastically reduced their lending.

Following the bankruptcy of Lehman Brothers in 2008, Mora (2010) explains that money market funds were hit by massive redemptions, as were hedge funds, which led to forced asset sales that intensified the downward spiral in asset prices. Instead of offering liquid funds to banks, money market funds began competing with banks for financing. Also, a large number of creditors, including some major hedge funds, had their assets frozen in the Lehman bankruptcy, and were forced to find alternative funds, adding to the selling pressure in equity markets.

The USA allowed its financial system to become very vulnerable to disruptions in the availability of wholesale money market funds. Europe needs to be in a position to notice financial market problems like this and to have ways of limiting EU area contagion.

6. LESSONS FOR THE INNOVATION UNION FROM THE 2008 FINANCIAL CRISIS

The reality of the 2008 financial crisis is that inadequately regulated new financial sector products and practices undermined the financial support for R&D and new product and product market developments in virtually all other sectors of not just the US economy, where both the financial sector innovation and the 2008 financial crisis were rooted, but also the EU economy. A wide slowdown in R&D and in getting new innovative products to market is a perennial consequence of financial crises, regardless of their causes. Public and private sector R&D and the commercial development of new products all predictably diminish in the wake of a large financial crisis because the funding sources dry up. The lesson we draw from this reality is that basic research on financial markets, products and regulation should also be an Innovation Union focus since financial market stability is essential for sustained innovation.

If the EU were playing more of a leadership role in financial sector innovation, this could also increase its weight in international negotiations on financial sector regulation. The US-certified NRSRO provide selective discipline for the financial activities of banks, other companies and even nations in the EU. However, the EU does not seem to have had effective ways of modifying US financial sector activities even when those activities threatened to, or did, have bad consequences for the EU.[24] Nor did the EU take effective defensive actions to lessen the impact on the EU of the errors of the US rating agencies and regulators.

7. A RELATED NEED FOR INCLUDING TAX POLICY RESEARCH IN THE INNOVATION UNION AGENDA

R&D expenditure figures play a key role in the performance metrics built into the Innovation Union initiative and the Europe 2020 strategy. Yet the results in a 2010 article by Robert E. Lipsey raise concerns about what is being captured by the national R&D expenditure data being compiled by the EU official statistics system. A related concern is that the hoped-for benefits of the Innovation Union initiative include the projected tax revenues from resulting product sales. Lipsey's results raise concerns about those benefit projections too.

Intangible productive assets often lack clear geographical locations. The firm that owns such assets, if it is a multinational firm, can move them from one member of the multinational group to another, changing the nominal geographical location without changing the geographical location of the use or the control of the asset. The effect of such a transaction is to shift the apparent location of the production based on that asset. In the process, the firm may change what had been recorded as production in a location into imports to that location.

The geographical assignments by the firm then determine where production based on some assets is reported to take place, and hence the distribution of production across countries, and which sales are measured as exports or imports. As production comes to depend more and more on intangible assets such as patents, copyrights, technological and scientific knowledge, and techniques of management, the location of production by multinational firms will become more and more ambiguous. Yet this is precisely the direction in which the Innovation Union initiative is trying to move EU production, and in which EU and other developed economies are believed to be moving anyway.

Lipsey provides strong empirical evidence that many firms choose the locations of production for intangible productive assets so as to minimize taxes, and that they operate to reduce their measured output in countries with higher tax rates on business income. Lipsey shows that these reporting practices also exaggerate the imports of high-tax countries and understate their exports. The problem in trade data is probably worse for trade in services than for trade in goods, but it exists also for trade in goods, especially of types for which much of the value comes from intangible assets. Lipsey singles out insurance as one of the industries that takes advantage of these opportunities for tax minimization.

Moreover, many of the same problems arise with the location of production based on financial assets of a multinational firm, although the valuations of the assets are more easily defined at least. With a transfer of assets from a parent to an affiliate, or among affiliates, production appears to have shifted its location, but all the other inputs into production may have remained in the former locations.

One sign of distorted measures of output by location is the reporting of high levels of output and profits in locations where there is little labor or tangible capital. Another is the reporting of ratios of output and profits to tangible inputs that differ to an extreme extent from worldwide norms. The inputs for which location is most reliably measured and least likely to be manipulated are of labor and of physical capital in the form of plant and equipment.

For 2004, Lipsey (2010) estimated the exaggeration of the value added, or output, and of sales of US affiliates in eight tax havens. The exaggeration of value added in 2004, estimated from its relation to fixed capital and labor compensation, was $33 billion, which is about 4 percent of the worldwide total of affiliate value added. The estimated exaggeration in the sales of these affiliates in that year was almost $360 billion, which was more than 10 percent of worldwide sales! Since the tax havens examined are relatively small countries, most of the reported sales must have been exports, suggesting an even larger impact on measured exports and imports and the balances of payments.

Hines (2005) claims that much of reported tax haven income consists of financial flows from foreign affiliates that parent companies own indirectly through their tax haven affiliates. He notes that firms in other countries that largely exempt their firms' foreign income from taxation, such as Germany and the Netherlands, have especially strong incentives to locate investment and income production in tax havens (p. 79).

The European Commission has been discussing proposals for a uniform method of allocating income among the countries in which a multinational operates. A paper by Fuest et al. (2007), based on the Deutsche Bundesbank's database on German multinationals' foreign operations and a matched database on the firms' domestic operations, calculated what firms' distributions of taxable income across countries would be under a hypothetical allocation of income based on sales, employment and assets, including tangible and intangible assets. The paper shows large discrepancies between the hypothetical allocated income distribution and the reported one. We see this as an important topic area for research, and institutional and regulatory as well as product innovation. Without progress on this front, much of the hoped-for economic benefits of the Innovation Union could end up being lost as a side effect of the economic conditions that result from financial crises, or could end up mostly benefiting tax havens rather than EU member nations.

8. CONCLUDING REMARKS

Kindleberger studied hundreds of financial crises around the world. The discouraging conclusion he (1993) draws is that most of the rules for sound banking were already incorporated in financial sector regulations long ago, either explicitly or implicitly in the form of financial sector traditions. He asserts that financial crises happen because whatever rules are instituted following each new financial crisis, these soon come to be selectively ignored by financial institutions, regulators and politicians as the expansion phase of the next credit cycle takes hold.

There are signs of what Kindleberger describes as the seeds of the next financial crisis in the making in some aspects of how the Dodd–Frank Act is, and is not, being implemented. On 21 July 2010, President Barack

Obama signed the Dodd–Frank Wall Street Reform and Consumer Protection Act ('Dodd–Frank Act') into law. However, Wall Street lobbyists ensured that even under the Dodd–Frank Act, banks are permitted to exclude their full exposure to swaps from their financial statements, and instead report only the 'fair value' changes in those swaps over time. Such reporting, Greenberger (2011) argues, is like an individual reporting only the change in their debt balances, instead of the reporting the debts themselves. Yet he also feels that 'The Act has the potential to effectively regulate the derivatives markets, if regulators make the most of the tools made available to them by Dodd–Frank.'

The crisis that engulfed the financial system of the USA and many of the EU area economies in 2008 has had severe and widespread negative consequences. The R&D activities that the Innovation Union seeks to enhance have been especially hard hit. We argue, therefore, for including in the Innovation Union research aimed at increasing financial sector stability while protecting economic growth. In designing this program of research, it might make sense to examine the Canadian experience and regulatory methods much more carefully (Leblond, 2011). Canada is a nation that has had sustained economic growth and that has a slightly higher proportion of households living in owned housing than the USA, but that has not been vulnerable to banking and other financial sector instability like the USA, going back at least as far as the Great Depression.

NOTES

1. Thanks are due to Karl R. Kopecky of the University of Alberta and a long-time successful investor in financial markets for his help with multiple parts of this chapter, and to Ivan Fellegi, Dennis Fixler, Michael Greenberger and Randall Morck and other participants in a 4 June session of the 2011 meeting of the Canadian Economics Association for comments on an earlier version of the chapter (under a different title). Funding from the Social Sciences and Humanities Research Council of Canada is also gratefully acknowledged. The authors are solely responsible for the opinions expressed and for any errors of fact or interpretation; our views do not necessarily reflect those of the Federal Reserve Bank of Philadelphia or the US Federal Reserve System.
2. http://portal.hud.gov/hudportal/HUD?src=/program_offices/housing/fhahistory.
3. This happened with the passage of the Charter Act of 1954.
4. The first mortgage-backed securities (then called 'passthroughs') were guaranteed and issued by Fannie Mae and Freddie Mac over the years 1968–71.
5. CDO backed as well by other types of debt assets besides mortgages are often referred to as a type of asset-backed security (ABS). CDO backed only by mortgages are also a type of MBS.
6. Alan Greenspan, Consumer Finance, Remarks at the Federal Reserve System's Fourth Annual Community Affairs Research Conference, Washington, DC, 8 April 2005, at www.federalreserve.gov/BoardDocs/speeches/2005/20050408/default.htm.
7. http://www.sec.gov/answers/nrsro.htm.

8. Moody's denotes its top rating by Aaa. AAA is the top rating for Standard and Poor's. We use the term 'triple A' throughout to denote the top rating.
9. For more on the Basel processes and accords, see http://en.wikipedia.org/wiki/Basel_Committee_on_Banking_Supervision.
10. Basel III represents an attempt to overcome some of these problems. http://www.moodysanalytics.com/Contact-Us/ERM/Contact-Form-Basel-III-Implementation/~/media/Insight/Regulatory/Basel-III/Thought-Leadership/2011/11-01-09-Implementing-Basel-III-Whitepaper.ashx.
11. Witt (2010) explains several different methods that were used to rate CDO. He was an analyst, and then a managing director in the US derivatives group at Moody's over 2000–2005.
12. The risk-related meaning of a triple A versus, say, a double B rating for a security is hard to quantify. In contrast, a CDS priced at, say, 1.08 percent on an 8 percent bond can be valued using standard financial methods as the equivalent of a risk-free 6.92 percent bond.
13. These are the monoline insurance companies, denoted there by MI, that the internal Lehman 2007 risk analysis report of Shilpickandula and Gorodetsky singled out as being at risk. As of December 2007, it was estimated that the monoline insurers – 11 monoline insurers, all based in New York and regulated by that state's insurance regulator – had given their insurance guarantee to enable the triple A rated securitization of over $2.4 trillion worth of asset-backed securities. On the official website of the monoline trade association, The Association of Financial Guaranty Insurers, it states that a security insured by an AFGI member has the 'unconditional and irrevocable guarantee that interest and principal will be paid on time and in full in the event of a default': www.afgi.org/who-fact.htm. See Acharya et al. (2009) for more on how inadequacies of insurance regulation in the USA contributed to the 2008 financial crisis.
14. See the Report of the Examiner in the bankruptcy proceedings of Lehman. http://lehmanreport.jenner.com/VOLUME%203.pdf.
15. The main role played by relaxed lending seems to have been that the large volume of subprime mortgages originated with little or no money down created a pool of homeowners who quickly were underwater once the upward trend in home prices had turned. Their defaults then contributed to further home price declines. See Mian and Sufi (2008, 2009) and Calabria (2011) for more on this. And by 2007 and 2008, more than half the foreclosures in Massachusetts involved prime loans to homeowners whose homes had mortgages that were larger than the market values of their homes (Gerardi et al., 2007).
16. Note that these are different from the credit rating companies for securities.
17. This includes CDO backed by emerging market bonds, investment-grade bonds, and high-yield bonds, all of which did significantly better. See Newman et al. (2008).
18. http://fcic-static.law.stanford.edu/cdn_media/fcic-docs/2007-01-00%20Moody's%20Structured%20Finance%20Rating%20Transitions%20-%201983-2006%20(Moody's%20Special%20Comment).pdf.
19. See, for example, Madigan (2008).
20. http://www.nytimes.com/2008/03/17/business/17bear.html.
21. http://www.bloomberg.com/news/2011-03-31/morgan-stanley-got-6-9-billion-from-fed-window-in-october-2008.html.
22. In an EU context, Poghosyan and Čihák (2009) also find that wholesale financing reliance distinguishes vulnerable banks from sound banks.
23. Also, as a result of the financial crisis, 25 US commercial banks became insolvent and were taken over by the FDIC in 2008, including Washington Mutual. A total of 140 more failed in 2009, and 157 failed in 2010. Those bank failures seriously depleted the FDIC funds.
24. For example, in the Greek debt crisis, the story behind the headlines is that, in 2001, Goldman Sachs helped the Greek government borrow billions, with this showing on the government books as a currency trade rather than as debt. That deal gave Greece cash upfront in return for pledging future landing fees for the country's airports. This and

subsequent other deals of a similar nature initially duped the regulators of the European Monetary Union (EMU) into agreeing that Greece met the standards for admission to the EMU (Mitsopoulos and Pelagidis, 2011). Most Greek voters were probably unaware of how their government services were being paid for.

REFERENCES

Acharya, Viral V., John Biggs, Matthew Richardson and Stephen Ryan (2009), 'On the financial regulation of insurance companies', NYU Stern School of Business. http://w4.stern.nyu.edu/salomon/docs/whitepaper.pdf.

Bartlett, Robert P. III (2010), 'Inefficiencies in the information thicket: a case study of derivative disclosures during the financial crisis', http://www.law.illinois.edu/_shared/pdfs/Inefficiencies%20in%20the%20Information%20Thicket_0926.pdf.

Benmelech, E. and J. Dlugosz (2009), 'The alchemy of CDO credit ratings', *Journal of Monetary Economics*, **56**, 617–34.

Bordo, M.D., A. Redish and H. Rockoff (2010), 'Why didn't Canada have a banking crisis in 2008 (or in 1930, or 1907, or 1893)?', paper prepared for the Economic History Association (EHA) conference, Evanston, September, http://www.eh.net/eha/system/files/Bordo.pdf.

Brueckner, Jan K., Paul S. Calem and Leonard I. Nakamura (2012), 'Subprime mortgages and the housing bubble', *Journal of Urban Economics*, **71**, 230–43.

Calabria, M. (2011), 'Fannie, Freddie, and the subprime mortgage market', Report No. 120, 7 March, Cato Institute.

Date, Raj and Michael Konczal (2010), 'Out of the shadows: creating a 21st century Glass Steagall', in Johnson and Payne (2010), 61–72.

European Commission (2010), 'Competitiveness and Innovation Framework Programme (CIP)', http://ec.europa.eu/cip/eip/innovation/index_en.htm.

European Commission (2011a), 'Innovation Union Competitiveness report 2011', http://ec.europa.eu/research/innovation-union/pdf/competitiveness-report/2011/executive_summary.pdf#view=fit&pagemode=none.

European Commission (2011b), 'Report from the Commission to the European Parliament, the Council, the European Economic and Social Committee and the Committee of the Regions', COM(2011) 849 final, http://ec.europa.eu/research/innovation-union/pdf/state-of-the union/2011/state_of_the_innovation_union_2011_en.pdf#view=fit&pagemode=none.

European Commission (2011c), 'Innovation Union Competitiveness report 2011: executive summary', http://ec.europa.eu/research/innovation-union/pdf/competitiveness-report/2011/executive_summary.pdf#view=fit&pagemode=none.

European Commission (2011d), 'Europe 2020: economic governance', http://ec.europa.eu/europe2020/priorities/economic-governance/index_en.htm.

European Commission (2011e), 'Annual growth survey: Annex 2 – macroeconomic report', COM(2011) 11 final, http://ec.europa.eu/europe2020/pdf/2_en_annexe_part1.pdf.

Fuest, Clemens, Thomas Hemmelgarn and Fred Ramb (2007), 'How would the introduction of an EU-wide formula apportionment affect the distribution and size of the corporate tax base? An analysis based on German multinationals', *International Tax and Public Finance*, **14**(5), 605–26.

Geanokoplos, John (2010), 'The leverage cycle', in D. Acemoglu, K. Rogoff and M. Woodford (eds), *NBER Macroeconomic Annual 2009*, vol. 24, Chicago, IL: University of Chicago Press, pp. 1–65.
Gerardi, Kristopher, Adam Hale Shapiro and Paul S. Willen (2007), 'Subprime outcomes: risky mortgages, homeownership experiences and foreclosures', Federal Reserve Bank of Boston Working Paper 07-15.
Greenberger, M. (2010), 'Out of the black hole: regulatory reform of the over-the-counter derivatives market', in R. Johnson and E. Payne (2010), 99–115. http://www.rooseveltinstitute.org/sites/all/files/OTC%20Derivatives.pdf. See also http://www.rooseveltinstitute.org/policy-and-ideas/ideas-database/out-black-hole-regulatory-reform-over-counter-derivatives-market.
Greenberger, Michael (2011), 'Overwhelming a financial regulatory black hole with legislative sunlight', *Journal of Business and Technology Law*, **6**(1), 127.
Hines, James R., Jr (2005), 'Do tax havens flourish?', in James M. Poterba (ed.), *Tax Policy and the Economy* 19, Cambridge, MA: MIT Press, pp. 65–99.
Huang, R. and L. Ratnovski (2011), 'The dark side of bank wholesale funding', *Journal of Financial Intermediation*, **20**(2), 248–63.
Johnson, R. and E. Payne (2010), *Make Markets Be Markets*, http://www.rooseveltinstitute.org/sites/all/files/MMBM%20FINAL%20March%208.pdf.
Kindleberger, C.P. (1993), *A Financial History of Western Europe*, 2nd edn, Oxford: Oxford University Press.
Kindleberger, Charles P. and Robert Z. Aliber (2005), *Manias, Panics, and Crashes: A History of Financial Crises*, 5th edn, New York: John Wiley & Sons.
Leblond, P. (2011), 'A Canadian perspective on the EU's financial architecture and the crisis', in K. Hübner (ed.), *Europe, Canada and the Comprehensive Economic Partnership*, London: Routledge, pp. 165–79.
Lipsey, Robert E. (2010), 'Measuring the location of production in a world of intangible productive assets, FDI and intrafirm trade', *Review of Income and Wealth*, **56**(s1), S99–110, http://onlinelibrary.wiley.com/doi/10.1111/j.1475-4991.2010.00385.x/abstract.
Madigan, Peter (2008), 'JP Morgan CDS exposure may top $10trn notional', *Risk magazine*, 1 April, http://www.risk.net/risk-magazine/news/1506245/jp-morgan-cds-exposure-usd10trn-notional.
Mian, A. and A. Sufi (2008), 'The consequences of mortgage credit expansion: evidence from the U.S. mortgage default crisis', Working Paper.
Mian, A. and A. Sufi (2009), 'House prices, home equity-based borrowing, and the U.S. household leverage crisis', Working Paper.
Mitsopoulos, M. and T. Pelagidis (2011), *Understanding the Crisis in Greece: From Boom to Bust*, Basingstoke: Palgrave Macmillan.
Mora, Nada (2010), 'Can banks provide liquidity in a financial crisis?', Report, Federal Reserve Bank of Kansas City, http://www.kc.frb.org/publicat/econrev/pdf/10q3Mora.pdf.
Nakamura, Leonard (2011), 'Durable financial regulation: monitoring financial instruments as counterpart to the regulation of financial institutions', NBER Working Paper 17006, May.
Newman, Daniel, Frank J. Fabozzi, Douglas J. Lucas and Laurie S. Goodman (2008), 'Empirical evidence on CDO performance', *Journal of Fixed Income*, **18**(2), 32–40.
Partnoy, Frank and Lynn E. Turner (2010), 'Bring transparency to off-balance sheet accounting', in Johnson and Payne (2010), 85–98.

Poghosyan, Tigran and Martin Čihák (2009), 'Distress in European banks: an analysis based on a new data set', IMF Working Paper WP/09/9.
Pozsar, Zoltan, Tobias Adrian, Adam Ashcraft and Hayley Boesky (2010), 'Shadow banking', Staff Report No. 458, Federal Reserve Bank of New York, July, http://www.newyorkfed.org/research/staff_reports/sr458.pdf.
Ratnovski, L. and R. Huang (2009), 'Why are Canadian banks more resilient?', IMF Working Paper 09/152.
Shilpiekandula, Vikas and Olga Gorodetski (2007), 'Who owns residential credit risk?', Lehman Brothers, Fixed Income Research, US Securitized Products Research, 7 September.
Witt, Gary (2010), 'Statement of Gary Witt, Former Managing Director, Moody's Investors Service, submitted by request to the Financial Crisis Inquiry Commission', 2 June, http://fcic-static.law.stanford.edu/cdn_media/fcic-testimony/2010-0602-Witt.pdf.
Woodward, Susan and Robert Hall (2009), 'What to do about Fannie Mae and Freddie Mac', http://woodwardhall.wordpress.com/2009/01/28/what-to-do-about-fannie-mae-and-freddie-mac/.

PART II

National and Regional Systems of Innovation

4. The European national and regional systems of innovation

George M. Korres

1. INTRODUCTION

Innovation has been recognized as a major source of competitiveness of firms and regions. It is recognized as highly relevant to economic performance and sustainability and thus it has been gaining increased support and attention. Public policies in new technologies aim exactly to reinforce technological capabilities in order to enhance productivity, competitiveness and economic growth. Public support is usually given in the form of 'direct and indirect measures', namely grants, loans, tax concessions and equity capital. Regional differences remain the prime source of competitive advantage. A long-term approach to development of regional knowledge economies must therefore combine local (regional) bottom–up approaches with global or European top–down approaches.

This chapter attempts to examine the structure and role of national and regional systems of innovation and their implications for sustainable development and integration and convergence in the EU.

2. NATIONAL AND REGIONAL SYSTEMS OF INNOVATION

The interaction between technological innovation, social learning and economic development is crucial for the survival and growth of the systems of innovation, at national or regional level. Technological policies aim to support and promote the new technologies through different 'direct and indirect measures'. 'Direct measures' usually include different subsidies, or different favourable tax treatments for research and technological activities. 'Indirect measures' are carried out in the pursuit of other policy objectives (e.g. competition policy, monetary, fiscal policies etc.), and, consequently, affect different research and technological activities. The interactive model demonstrates the main interconnections between three systems: society, technology and economy (Mahdjoubi, 1998). Innovation, as a socio-technical comprises system, two main divisions (Korres, 2012):

- Social innovation (social structures, human resource development).
- Technological innovation (technical development).

These two structures foster the development process.

Freeman and the 'Aalborg version' of the national innovation system approach (Freeman, 1987; Freeman and Lundvall, 1988) aim at understanding 'the innovation system in the broad sense'. The definition of 'innovation' is broader. Innovation is seen as a continuous cumulative process involving not only radical and incremental innovation but also the diffusion, absorption and use of innovation and a wider set of sources of innovation is taken into account. In this respect, innovation is seen as reflecting, besides science and R&D, interactive learning taking place in connection with ongoing activities in procurement, production and sales. A wide definition of innovation should be used, including product innovations (both material goods and intangible services) as well as process innovations (both technological and organizational ones).

While there are competing conceptions regarding what constitutes the core elements of an innovation system, it might still be useful to see what the different definitions have in common.

- One common characteristic is the assumption that national systems differ in terms of specialization in production, trade and knowledge (Archibugi and Pianta, 1992). The focus is on the co-evolution between what countries do and what people and firms in these countries know how to do well. This implies that both the production structure and the knowledge structure will change only slowly and that such change involves learning as well as structural change.
- A common assumption behind the innovation system perspective is that knowledge is something more than information and includes tacit elements (Polanyi, 1966). Important elements of knowledge are embodied in the minds and bodies of agents, in routines of firms and not least in relationships between people and organizations (Dosi, 1999).
- Another feature of the idea of innovation systems is a focus on interactions and relationships. The relationships may be seen as carriers of knowledge and interaction as processes where new knowledge is produced and learnt (Johnson, 1992; Edquist and Johnson, 1997).
- A final common assumption behind the different approaches to innovation systems is that elements of knowledge important for

economic performance are localized and not easily moved from one place to another.

We can use the term 'innovation' rather broadly in order to include processes through which firms master and practise product designs and manufacturing processes that are new to them. The term indicates a set of institutions whose interactions determine innovative performance. The term 'system' refers to a set of institutional actors who play a major role in influencing the innovative performance. We use the term 'national systems of innovation' to indicate policies that are related to research and technological activities planning (from both a macro- and microeconomic view) in a country (Korres, 2012).

Systems of innovation may be delimited in different ways; spatially/geographically or sectorally, accordingly to the breadth of activities they consider.

- Geographically defined innovation systems may be local, regional, national or supranational. This type of delimitation presumes that the area in question has a reasonable degree of 'coherence' or 'inward orientation' with regard to innovation processes.
- Sectorally delimited systems of innovation include only a part of a regional, national or international system. They are limited to specific technological fields (generic technologies) or product areas. They can be, but are not necessarily, restricted to one sector of production. Both 'technological systems' (Carlsson and Stankiewicz, 1995) and 'sectoral innovation systems' (Breschi and Malerba, 1997) belong to this category. Whether a system of innovation should be spatially or sectorally delimited – or both – depends on the object of study.

The system of innovation approach is also associated with problems and weaknesses. One example is the term 'institution', which is used in different senses by different authors – some refer to social norms, such as trust, while others refer to types of organizations, such as universities.

Another important point is that there is no agreement among scholars regarding what should be included in and what should be excluded from a 'system of innovation'. It should also be pointed out that 'systems of innovation' is not a formal theory, in the sense of providing propositions regarding established and stable relations between well-defined quantitative variables. According to the World Bank (2002, p. 8), institutions have three main objectives: they channel information about market conditions, goods and participants; they define and enforce property rights and

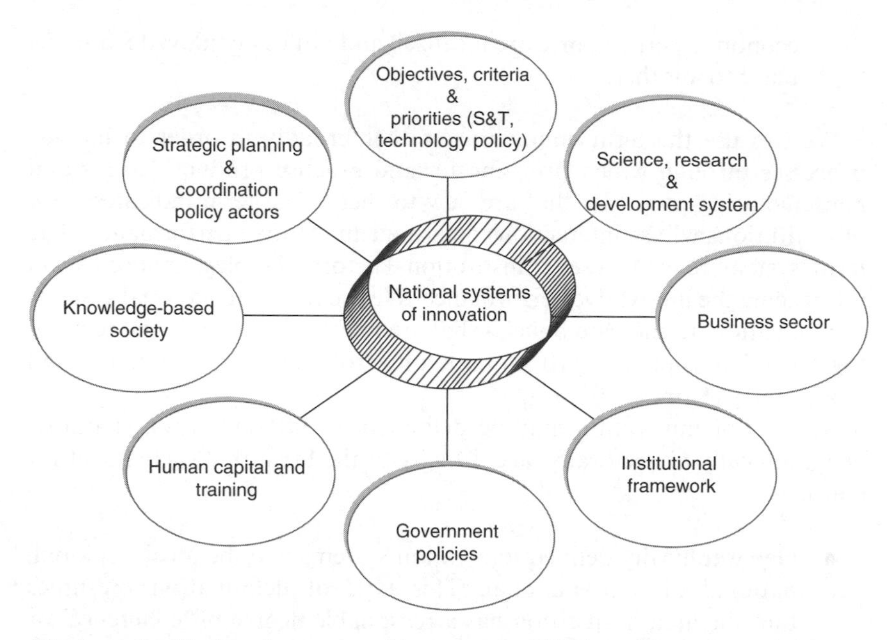

Figure 4.1 National systems of innovation (NSI)

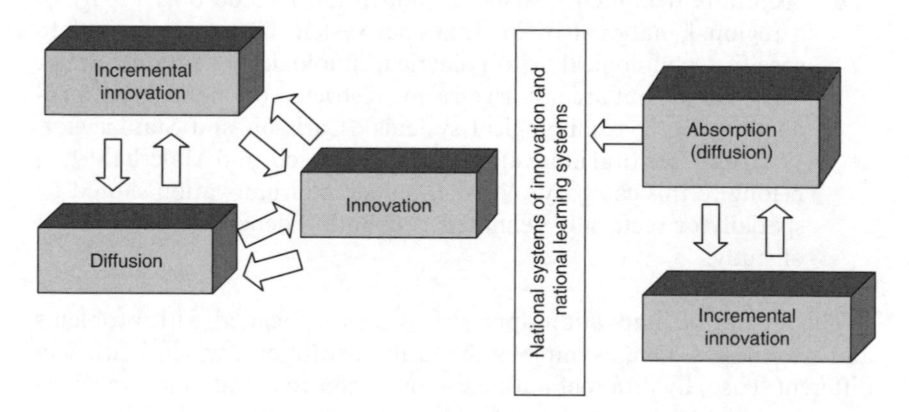

Figure 4.2 National systems of technical change

contracts; and they regulate competition. The overall structure of the functionality of national systems of innovation (NSI) is shown in Figure 4.1.

Figure 4.2 illustrates national and regional systems of innovation and technical change. Regions are considered to play a crucial role in the European Research Area, because they bring policy measures close to the citizen, thereby following the subsidiarity principle, and because they bridge the EU level and the local level (CEC, 2001). Regions can differ substantially with respect to their industrial specialization, their connections at the national and global level and, in particular, with respect to their potential to face national and global competition. Therefore policy measures are best adapted to the region at hand. It makes sense to regionalize innovation policy for the following four reasons (Korres, 2012):

- Innovation processes take place unevenly in geographic space.
- Innovation networks function differently in various regions.
- Innovation activity is crucial for economic development and growth on the regional as well as on the national level.
- Using various policy approaches in different regions enables countries to gain much more varied experiences, thereby enabling regions to learn from one another.

Recently, academics and policy makers have begun to refine the idea of national innovation systems, considering the utility of 'regional innovation systems' as both a theoretical concept and a policy objective (Cooke et al., 1997). Whilst the regional innovation systems perspective is clearly a development of the innovation systems literature, it can also be considered part of the 'new regionalism'.

The concept of regional innovation systems has been gaining much attention from policy makers and academic researchers since the early 1990s. The approach has been seen as a promising analytical framework for advancing our understanding of the innovation process in the regional economy (Asheim et al., 2003; Cooke and Memedovic, 2002). The popularity of the concept of regional innovation systems is closely related to the emergence of regionally identifiable nodes or clusters of industrial activity as well as the surge in regional innovation policies where the region is deemed as the most appropriate scale at which to sustain innovation-based learning economies (Asheim and Isaksen, 1997).

Most of the new contributions in regional economics are clearly indebted to the pioneering works and intuitions of Marshall, who stressed the importance of local externalities in favoring the geographical concentration of economic and innovative activities. 'Regional innovation systems' has no commonly accepted definition, but is usually understood as a set of interacting private and public interests, formal institutions and other organizations that function according to organizational and institutional arrangements and relationships conducive to the generation, use and dissemination of knowledge (Doloreux, 2003). The basic argument is that this set of actors produces pervasive and systemic effects that encourage firms within the region to develop specific forms of capital derived from social relations, norms, values and interaction within the community in order to reinforce regional innovative capability and competitiveness (Gertler et al., 2000).

As Asheim and Gertler (2005) point out, regional innovation systems are not sufficient on their own to remain competitive in a globalized economy and production systems seem to be rather important to innovation systems at the regional level. Moreover, as these authors assent, local firms must also have access to national and supranational innovation systems, as well as to corporate innovation systems. This line of reasoning is followed to a point where the regional innovation system expands beyond its own boundaries through a process of economic integration and globalization.

Many elements characterizing a national system could be, in principle, transferred to a smaller territorial scale and used also to define the regional system of innovation, including Korres (2012):

- the internal organization of firms
- interfirm relationships
- role of the public sector and public policy
- institutional set-up of the financial sector
- R&D intensity and organization
- institutional framework, for instance regional governance structure, political, legal, fiscal, financial and educational arrangements etc.
- production system (including the competition and collaboration faced by firms, market structure, the division of labor and sectoral specialization)
- degree of openness and the capacity to attract the external resources and core hierarchical forces taking into account the peculiarities of different geographical scale.

Many studies of regional innovation systems are motivated by the relation between technical advances and regional growth, depending on the amount of technological knowledge in a region. The concept of regional systems of innovation (RSI) is distinctly different from that of national systems of innovation (NSI). A schematic illustration of the structuring of RSIs is shown in Figure 4.3, which distinguishes between the two subsystems that constitute the main building blocks of RSIs. These are the knowledge application and exploitation subsystem and the knowledge generation and diffusion subsystem. (The main external influences on RSIs take the form of NSI institutions and policy instruments, other RSIs, and international institutions and policy instruments.)

The first subsystem consists mainly, but not exclusively, of industrial companies, while the second comprises various (mostly public sector)

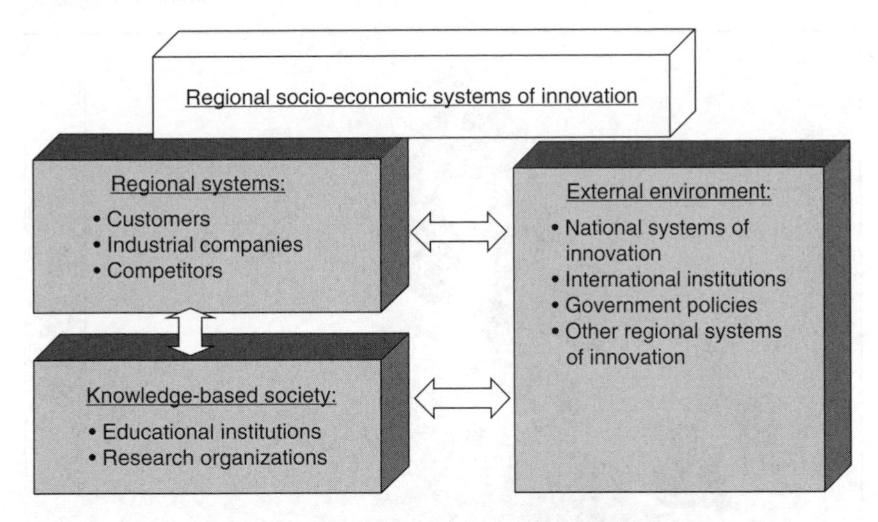

Figure 4.3 The structuring of regional systems of innovation

institutions involved in knowledge creation and diffusion. The distinction between these two subsystems largely corresponds to the division between public and private sectors and between non-commercial and commercial activities.

3. THE EUROPEAN REGIONAL SYSTEMS OF INNOVATION

The EU is one of the most prosperous economic areas in the world but the disparities between its member states are striking, especially if we look at the EU's 250 regions. To assess these disparities, we must first measure and compare the levels of wealth generated by each country, as determined by gross domestic product (GDP). For instance, in Greece, Portugal and Spain, average per capita GDP is only 80 percent of the Community average. Luxembourg exceeds this average by over 60 percentage points. The ten most dynamic regions in the EU have a GDP almost three times higher than the ten least developed regions. Figure 4.4 illustrates the European regional innovation performance groups. We can summarize some of the main results (INNO-Metrics, 2009):

- There is considerable diversity in regional innovation performance. The results show that all countries have regions at different levels of performance. The most heterogeneous countries are Spain, Italy

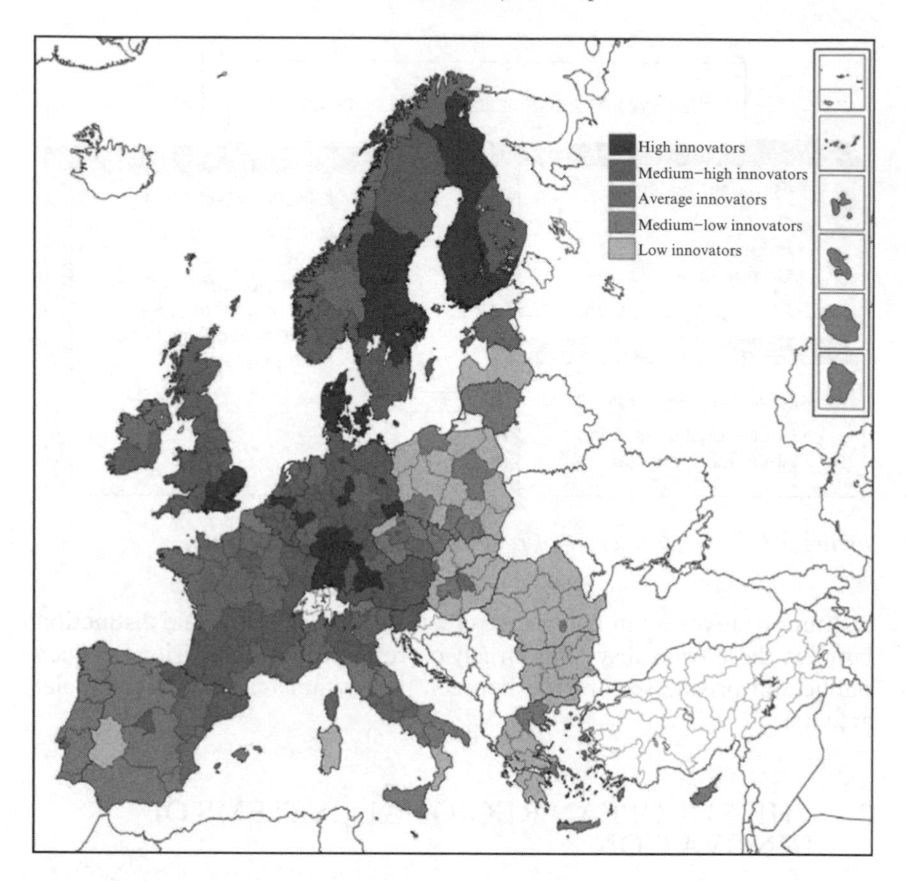

Source: European Commission (2010).

Figure 4.4 European regional innovation performance groups

and the Czech Republic, where innovation performance varies from low to medium-high.

- The most innovative regions are typically in the most innovative countries. North Brabant in the Netherlands is a highly innovative region located in an innovation follower country. Prague (Czech Republic), Basque Country, Navarre, Madrid and Catalonia in Spain, Lombardy and Emilia-Romagna in Italy, Oslo and Akershus, Agder and Rogaland, and Western Norway are all medium to highly innovating regions from moderate innovators. The capital region in Romania, Bucharest–Ilfov, is a medium–low innovating region in a catching-up country.

- Regions have different strengths and weaknesses. There are no straightforward relationships between the level of performance and relative strengths; many of the 'low innovators' have relative weaknesses in the dimension of innovation enablers, including human resources.
- Regional performance appears relatively stable since 2004. Most of the changes are positive and relate to Catalonia, Valencia, the Balearic Islands and Ceuta (Spain), Paris Basin, East and South-west France, Lower Franconia (Germany), Közep- Dunántúl (Hungary), the Algarve (Portugal) and Hedmark and Oppland (Norway).
- In terms of scientific publications, Europe's strong growth seems to have halted. Actual numbers are still rising, but the EU share of world publications is declining, whereas the US share is recovering.
- Regarding per capita shares, the EU generates fewer patents with high economic value than the USA or Japan.
- The EU is lagging behind the USA in its share of patents in biotechnology and information and communications technology.
- There has been a slight increase in the EU share of global exports of high-tech products in value terms between 1996 and 2001. Japan's share fell sharply in 2001, hit by falling sales of electronic goods.
- Since the middle of the 1990s, the EU has stopped catching up with the USA in terms of labor productivity.
- Large disparities persist among EU countries in high-tech manufacturing. Japan outperforms the EU in high-tech manufacturing indicators while the Central European countries perform better than the EU average.
- The production of scientific research and technological know-how increasingly depends on research conducted in other countries. Indicators of cross-border co-authorship of scientific articles and co-invention of patents seek to shed light on this trend.
- Scientific collaboration with advanced countries is generally much more widespread than with smaller ones. Researchers in 160 countries co-authored at least 1 percent of their internationally co-authored papers with US researchers. The UK, France and Germany also play a leading role in international scientific collaboration.
- By the late 1990s, about 6 percent of patents were the result of international collaborative research. Several factors may affect the degree of a country's internationalization in science and technology: size, technological endowment, geographical proximity to regions with high research activity, language, industrial specialization, existence of foreign affiliates and so on.

- Internationalization tends to be higher in smaller European countries. For example, 56 percent of Luxembourg's patents have foreign co-inventors compared with 30 percent of Iceland's and Belgium's. International cooperation in science and technology is also relatively high in Poland, the Czech Republic and the Slovak Republic.
- International collaboration in patenting is lower in the EU than in the USA. In Japan, international cooperation in science and technology is rather limited.

'Europe Strategy 2020' is a ten-year growth strategy proposed by the European Commission in March 2010 for reviving the economy of the EU to become a smart, sustainable and inclusive economy.

The EU identifies three key drivers for growth, to be implemented through concrete actions at EU and national levels (Korres, 2012):

- smart growth (fostering knowledge, innovation, education and digital society);
- sustainable growth (making production more resource efficient while boosting competitiveness); and
- inclusive growth (raising participation in the labor market, the acquisition of skills and the fight against poverty).

Table 4.1 illustrates the objectives of the European regional innovation strategy for the period 2010–13. The EU strategy towards regional innovation policy emphasizes the following points:

- enhance the scientific and innovation framework and the related structural changes;
- encourage and expand the creation and growth of innovative enterprises; and
- improve the key interfaces in the innovation system.

The main objectives of technological policy may be summarized under five headings:

- improve the efficiency of the transfer of technology from foreign suppliers to local users;
- increase the efficiency of operation of technology;
- strengthen the industrial base;
- develop the indigenous technological capability; and
- smooth adjustment forced by new technologies.

Table 4.1 Objectives of the European regional innovation strategy, 2010–13

General objective: increase of innovation and competitiveness of the regions		
Pillars		
I	II	III
Economy based on knowledge	**Innovation culture**	**Innovative management**
Objective: Transition of the regions into the region based on knowledge and the center for innovation	*Objective:* Improvement of intangible environment supporting innovations (culture, attitudes, norms and behavior patterns, human capital) and the increase of the susceptibility of local authorities and society to innovations	*Objective:* Higher efficiency and innovativeness in the development process support
Priorities		
• Increased financial support, especially from the state, on R&D • Enhancing regional R&D potential and the effectiveness of the R&D institutions • Support to development of high technology industries • Transition of traditional industries into the more scientific-based • Development of information society and knowledge-based economy services	• Promotion of innovation and entrepreneurship • Education for innovation	• Durable partnership • Anticipating the future • Effective mechanisms of implementation

Source: ec.europa.eu/regional_policy/conferences/od2006/doc.

In addition, science and research policies should be oriented towards two main objectives:

- to assess the possibilities and needs of private and public enterprises with respect to research and technological activities;
- to choose those priority objectives that can delineate government technological action.

Small countries are likely to need a more comprehensive and targeted policy of cooperative innovative effort in order to develop their future capabilities and make the necessary choices for technological priorities. The participation of member states in the EU research and technological programmes can increase the opportunities for promotion and improvement of research activities, creation of new research institutions so as to support innovation and diffusion of new technologies and, therefore, to improve the level of economic and regional growth and induce social development.

4. CONCLUSIONS

New technologies imply some direct and indirect effects or, more specifically, some micro effects (such as firms or organizations) and macro effects (such as inter- and intra-industrial and regional effects) for the whole economy. New technologies play an important role in sectoral productivity, overall growth, employment, modernization, industrialization, socio-economic infrastructure and competitiveness of a country.

The Community's research programmes also attempt to establish cooperation between theoretical research through the different research bodies of the public sector (such as research institutes and universities) and industrial research through private enterprises.

We can summarize the main conclusions and policy implications as follows: technology policy has been heavily concerned with the external gap of the EU *vis-à-vis* Japan and the USA. However, the same size of gap also exists among EU countries. It is true that technological competition among Japan, the USA and the EU is intense. Moreover, one tends to find most of the European countries in a position of catching up from relatively low levels of S&T output. Although there are some noticeable encouraging tendencies in several European countries, one can expect that with the enlargement of the EU the 'European paradox' will be, at least temporarily, further accentuated. In other words, in relation to its enlarged population, the EU-27's strong performance in science will contrast increasingly with its weaker development and commercialization of technology.

REFERENCES

Archibugi, D. and Pianta, M. (1992), *The Technological Specialization of Advanced Countries*, Dordrecht: Kluwer Academic Publishers.

Asheim, B.T. and Gertler, M. (2005), 'The geography of innovation: regional innovation systems', in J. Fagerberg, D. Mowery and R. Nelson (eds), *The Oxford Handbook of Innovation*, Oxford: Oxford University Press, pp. 291–317.

Asheim, B.T. and Isaksen, A. (1997), 'Regional innovation systems: the integration of local "sticky" and global "ubiquitous" knowledge', *Journal of Technology Transfer*, **27**(1), 77–86.

Asheim, B., Isaksen, A., Nauwelaers, C. and Tödtling, F. (2003) *Regional Innovation Policy for Small–Medium Enterprises*, Cheltenham, UK and Northampton, MA, USA: Edward Elgar.

Breschi, S. and Malerba, F. (1997), 'Sectoral innovation systems–technological regimes, Schumpeterian dynamics and spatial boundaries', in C. Edquist (ed.), *Systems of Innovation: Technologies, Institutions and Organizations*, London: Pinter Publishers/Cassell Academic, pp. 130–56.

Carlsson, B. and Stankiewicz, R. (1995), 'On the nature, function and composition of technological systems', in B. Carlsson (ed.), *Technological Systems and Economic Performance. The Case of Factory Automation*, Dordrecht: Kluwer, pp. 21–56.

Commission of the European Communities (CEC) (2001), 'The regional dimension of the European research area', mimeo: Commission of the European Communities, Brussels, October.

Cooke, P. and Memedovic, O. (2002), *Strategies for Regional Innovation Systems: Learning Transfer and Applications*, Vienna, Austria: United Nations Industrial Development Organization.

Cooke, P., Uranga, M.G. and Etxebarria, G. (1997), 'Regional innovation systems: institutional and organizational dimensions', *Research Policy*, **26**(4/5), 475–91.

Doloreux, D. (2003), 'Regional innovation systems in the periphery: the case of Québec (Canada)', *International Journal of Innovation Management*, **7**(1), 67–94.

Dosi, G. (1999), 'Some notes on national systems of innovation and production, and their implications for economic analysis', in Daniele Archibugi, Jeremy Howells and Jonathan Michie (eds), *Innovation Policy in a Global Economy*, Cambridge: Cambridge University Press, pp. 35–48

Edquist, C. and Johnson, B. (1997), 'Institutions and organizations in systems of innovation', in C. Edquist (ed.) *Systems of Innovation: Technologies, Institutions and Organizations*, London: Pinter Publishers/Cassell Academic, pp. 41–63.

European Commission (2010), *European Innovation Scoreboard 2009: Comparative Analysis of innovation Performance*, Brussels: CEC.

Freeman, C. (1987), *Technology Policy and Economic Performance: Lessons from Japan*, London: Pinter Publishers.

Freeman, C. and Lundvall, B.-Å. (eds) (1988), *Small Countries Facing the Technological Revolution*, London: Pinter Publishers.

Gertler, M., Wolfe, D. and Garkut, D. (2000), 'No place like home? The embeddedness of innovation in a regional economy', *Review of International Political Economy*, **7**(4), 688–718.
INNO-Metrics (2009), *Regional Innovation Scoreboard*, Hugo Hollanders (MERIT), Stefano Taranto la and Alexander Loschky (JRC).
Johnson, B. (1992), 'Institutional learning', in Bengt-Åke Lundvall (ed.), *National Innovation Systems: Towards a Theory of Innovation and Interactive Learning*, London: Pinter Publishers, pp. 23–46.
Korres, G.M. (2012), *Handbook of Innovation Economics*, New York: Nova Publishers.
Mahdjoubi, D. (1998), 'Mapping the regional innovation systems', Working Paper, University of Austin, TX.
Monfort, P. (2009), 'Regional convergence, growth and interpersonal inequalities across EU', Working Paper, Directorate General Regional Policy European Commission.
Polanyi, M. (1966), *The Tacit Dimension*, London: Routledge & Kegan Paul.
World Bank (2002), *World Development Report 2002: Building Institutions for Markets*, New York: Oxford University Press.

5. European innovation policies from RIS to smart specialization: a policy assemblage perspective

Arnoud Lagendijk and Krisztina Varró

1. INTRODUCTION

Policy initiatives such as regional innovation strategies are strategically and selectively infused by rationales and imaginaries that resonate with major political and societal shifts. A core example is how the transition from spatial Keynesianism to neoliberal thinking has been accompanied by a discourse of the 'knowledge-based economy', overpowering the more socially oriented notion of the 'information society'. Using the notion of policy assemblage, this chapter advocates a more complex and political reading of the role of rationales and imaginaries. Undertaking an analysis of four decades of regional innovation policy in Europe, we show how a variety of concerns, notably around competitiveness, sustainability and cohesion, have all made their inroads into the substantiation and legitimization of innovation policies. In doing so, we pay attention to the way innovation policies have been shaped by the continuous (re)imagination of European, national and regional spaces in terms of developmental ambitions.

The last four decades have witnessed the rise, peak and modification of regional innovation policy. This is especially noteworthy in Europe, where the EU has taken a leading role in the development and proliferation of innovation-oriented policy ideas and practices. The evolution of EU regional innovation policy has been marked by a number of major trends and shifts. Underlying development perspectives have moved from Keynesian to neoliberal approaches; policy perspectives took on board academic notions of learning and the building of institutional capacity; in terms of governance, a direct nexus was created between the EU and the regional level.

This chapter will discuss this process of evolution by applying a policy assemblage perspective. The concept of assemblage draws on French post-structural thinking (Anderson and Harrison, 2010; McFarlane, 2009), and has recently been interpreted from a more realist stance by DeLanda (2006). A key point in assemblage theory is that, as a whole, assemblages have capacities that are more than the sum of the capacities of their components. In turn, in becoming part of an assemblage, the components – resources, agents, ideas and so on – retain a spectrum of potentialities and capacities that transcend their specific role in the assemblage. In other words, they continue to present an (often unexpected) source of development as well as change. In assemblage theory, social phenomena do not fall into place according to some predestined design or principle, but they result from hard work invested in producing a more or less coherent whole.

The assemblage perspective is particularly helpful in accounting for the performativity of core concepts and ideas, as well as for shedding light on the complexities of creating effective and legitimate forms of policy practice. Policies consist, on the one hand, of tangible components, that is, concrete measures, budget and resources, domains, rules and procedures, demarcated times and places of action and so on. On the other hand, policies tend to be infused and justified on the basis of less tangible, more fluid aspects, such as prominent ideas and discourses, images and expectations. By thinking in terms of 'policy assemblages' we can observe how policies emerge and become effective through the assembly and aligning of a heterogeneous set of components, of material as well as of expressive kinds. The use of the assemblage perspective allows us also to deal with the ambivalences, frictions and dilemmas stemming from the compound nature of policy making, drawing on notions of policy discourse as well as policy practice. It helps us, moreover, to account for the more technical and political aspects of policy making (Prince, 2010), at different levels.

The chapter is structured as follows. First, a theoretical framework is presented drawing from assemblage theory, notably its distinction between coding and territorialization. Subsequently, a historical account of policy evolution is presented using key documents and evaluations published by EU departments and (funded) organizations dealing with regional innovation policy.

2. POLICY ASSEMBLAGES

This section sets out our basic conceptual framework. To account for the semiotic and practical sides of policy making, and their intertwinement, we will start with what are generally considered as two core dimensions of assemblages: coding and territorialization. Coding, which covers the semiotic (discursive) aspects of policy making, can be divided into two major policy processes: framing and scripting. Territorialization, in turn, deals with the realm of policy practice. Territorialization serves an important aim in dealing with the multi-level, multi-actor and multi-issue characteristics of policy making. In line with our approach, it should be added that we do not suggest that these concepts represent essential aspects of policy making; they are considered primarily useful analytical tools to study policy dynamics. Above all, their significance is epistemological, not ontological.

Coding

The first dimension, coding, deals with the expressive dimension of assemblage (DeLanda, 2006), more specifically the formative–strategic aspect of policy assemblages (Prince, 2010), that is, the development and adoption of discourses to mark out, characterize and legitimize a particular policy. In coding, an important role is played by key signifiers, and the semantic webs woven between and around them, in the form of 'chains of significance'. In our case, innovation is associated with the regional level, and also with notions of economic, social and environmental sustainability. These discursive practices result in the development and institutionalization of what Collier and Ong (2005, p. 11) label 'global forms', phenomena that 'have a distinctive capacity for decontextualisation and recontextualisation, abstractability and movement, across diverse social and cultural situations and spheres of life'.

The coding of policy assemblages comprises two major discursive practices: framing and scripting. This division corresponds with Torfing's observation (2011, p. 1881) that discursive practices 'are not only *staging* the choice and interaction of the relevant policy actors, but also seem to be *scripting* their actions'. Framing starts with associating a policy with selected key signifiers and their chains of signification, thus relating to the 'grand' or meta-stories about societal and economic prospects and development, as well as about what constitutes legitimate and effective policy making. Building on this semantic position, particular policy frames or rationales are developed and invoked that connect specific 'policy problems' to specific sets of solutions, where especially the latter are prone to evolve into 'global forms'. So to address the gap between advantaged and disadvantaged regions, the latter should implement regional innovation and clustering strategies, approaches that have developed and circulated across the globe. Framing also plays an important role in legitimizing a policy by grafting policy rationales onto what are called 'derived theoretical rationales' (Laranja et al., 2008). Policies are deemed to be prudent because they are underwritten, and refined, by academic 'evidence'.

The other face of policy coding is scripting. Scripting assigns particular roles and tasks to policy actors, thus enabling as well as constraining the processes of subject and strategy formation. More specifically, scripting details how the chain of agents and organizations extending from the initiating 'policy makers' to the final 'policy takers' is organized. How are agents expected to be linked in terms of strategic, programmatic and evaluative activities? How is the interaction with stakeholders envisaged? How do chains of legitimacy and accountability take shape? What role is assigned to different levels of administration? Summarizing, where framing explains the 'what' and 'why' of policy making – which solution addresses which problem, on the basis of which policy and derived theoretical rationales – scripting details the 'how' and 'who' – which steps to take and which roles to play by which organization. The latter helps, to quote Shore and Wright (1997, p. 35), to understand 'how policies work as instruments of governance, as ideological vehicles, and as agents for constructing subjectivities and organizing people within systems of power and authority'.

Territorialization

Now we turn to the second dimension of policy assemblage, territorialization. This concerns practical–organizational aspects of assemblages in material and institutional terms. The crux of territorialization is not so much the aspect of spatial demarcation (although this also plays a certain role), but the setting in place and linking together of all kinds of resources, creating what can be seen considered as a marking and creation of an 'organizational space'. Territorialization involves the building of actor networks and their stabilization and marking in the wider space of policy making (Latour, 2005). Territorialization entails, in other words, the 'everyday' practice of policy making and implementation, involving the creation and bringing together of a variety of organizational–logistical resources and mechanisms. In relation to coding, territorialization thus presents acts of concretizing and contextualization, of overcoming the many hurdles confronted by policies when they are put 'in practice'.

However, territorialization does not just follow coding. On the contrary, in many cases coding entails the capturing of an emerging, apparently successful, policy practice, turning it into a decontextualized, expressive form (DeLanda, 2006). While certain details of policy making may be premeditated on the basis of abstract thinking, global policy forms generally originate from concrete practices, in which the latter often come to feature as 'success stories'. In the case of regional innovation and cluster policies, examples of such 'success stories' are Silicon Valley, Baden-Württemberg, Rhône-Alpes, among others. Decontextualization and coding allow frames and scripts to travel and engender policy making elsewhere, thus contributing to the strength and proliferation of a global policy form. What emerges is thus not only a policy form but also a policy geography. The latter consists of policy locales, each manifesting its own forms of coding and territorialization, as well as diffusion channels and relay networks connecting the locales at higher scales.

The geographical dimension, including a notion of scale, greatly adds to the complexity of policy-making processes. The channels of policy transfer present, in terms of Latour (2005), mediators rather than 'simple' intermediaries. As mediators they play an important role in modifying global forms and geography of policy making (Lagendijk and Cornford, 2000). Such mediators consist of a wide variety of actors, networks and circuits, including leading policy entrepreneurs, gurus, thinks tanks and policy research centres (Thrift, 1997), and international policy networks, as well as broader social and media networks that support what Thrift and Olds (1996) have aptly labelled the 'cultural circuit of capital'. These mediators all present assemblages themselves, with different kinds and degrees of territorialization that help ideas, scripts and resources to travel.

What thus emerges, in geographical terms, is a topology of nested assemblages. A basic distinction can be made between two levels. First, policy locales constitute the centres of policy making and implementation, such as regions in the case of regional policy making. Here, policy assemblages serve to put policies into practice, mustering knowledge and resources, building institutional capacities, engaging with stakeholders, and measuring and communicating impact. Second, policy transfer networks and organizations engage in the circulation and mediation of codings – frames and scripts – abstracted from, as well as infusing, policy locales. In turn, the mediation at the policy transfer level is also coded, by providing a language to assess, compare and steer policy practices at the level of locales. This coding contains the understanding of policy making in terms of, for instance, 'best practices' or 'how-to' manuals of policy implementation (Prince, 2010), learning protocols, funding criteria, calculative techniques such as benchmarking, impact assessments and, through aggregation and interpretation, reviews and foresight. Such understanding is often advanced, moreover, by charismatic experts and successful international consultants. Coding is, in turn, substantiated and justified through the building of chains of signification with core political ambitions (often masquerading as 'societal' ambitions) such as competitiveness, cohesion and sustainability.

Such alignment presents a process of 'overcoding', that is, the homogenizing of a population through a common set of empty or floating signifiers (Colebrook, 2002). Overcoding ensures that the frames and scripts articulated at the level of policy locales are brought in line and resonate with prevailing political perspectives and ambitions. How this works will be the topic of the next section.

(Neoliberal) Overcoding

In the orchestration of policy transfer and overcoding, a crucial role is played by 'central' agents – state and non-state – and the core discourses adopted, articulated and circulated by them. Such agents include national bodies, as well as international organizations to which certain policy responsibilities have been delegated, such as the EU, the OECD and the World Bank, as well as a wide range of think tanks and influential 'experts'. While, as explained before, many agents are involved in policy transfer, public bodies play a fundamental role in providing the main institutional infrastructure for mediation and support, as well as the main policy discourses feeding into overcoding. Dominant trends, such as the upsurge of neoliberal thinking, make inroads through the coordinating and controlling activities of the state and other central agents (Cumbers et al., 2003).

In 'making inroads', however, overcoding does not imply a simple route from dominant ways of thinking to policy practices. On the contrary, overcoding involves intricate discursive practices, in which policy performances are measured up to certain standards following scripts of monitoring and assessment, and codes of articulation. Such standards correspond to core signifiers – for example innovation, competitiveness, cohesion, sustainability – as well as to prevailing policy conventions, for example on financing, project development and management, accountability and evaluation. In other words, not only does territorialization not just follow coding; coding does not simply follow overcoding. As Prince (2010) and Arts and Lagendijk (2009), among others, claim, one should always take account of the 'hard' work of policy making 'on the ground', and the impact of the mediators involved in processes of policy transfer, implementation and monitoring. While policy making is globally integrated through 'neoliberal' practices of policy transfer and 'neoliberal' overcoding, each site will manifest its own form of what Brenner and Theodore (2002) call 'actually existing neoliberalism'.

In assemblage terms, the way in which policy locales are brought in line with policy overcodes depends on two factors. First, it depends on how strongly local assemblages have become coded, and can be adapted through (re)coding (which is, in turn, a function of their local territorialization). Second, an important role is played by the territorialization of policy transfer, and its capacity to homogenize local codings through the practical work of overcoding. Neoliberal overcodes have been transferred, in particular, by the imposition of specific modes and techniques of accountability, and the accompanying 'control' versions of legitimacy. Such discursive practices have had a great impact on the territorialization of local policy making, for instance through the use of 'objective' input, throughput and output indicators, resulting in what has been characterized as 'technocratization' (Gertler, 2001). If executed successfully, such technocratization greatly enhances the grip of central agents on policy locales. Yet one cannot consider trends towards homogenization as given or self-evident. They can only result from continuous hard work from the centre as well as from all intermediary agents. To what extent this really materializes is a matter, of empirical fact, not a matter of principle.

By charting the conceptual and practical intricacies of overcoding, both top–down and bottom–up, we can also shed light on the political nature of policy making. A first association is that of the political with politics, which would mean with the expressive (interpretive, strategic) side of assemblages. In his account of policy assemblages, Prince (2010) locates the political largely at the level of the formative–strategic aspects of assemblages, that is the realms of 'coding' and 'overcoding'. Coding is political through the way it selects certain ideas, prioritizes certain forms of action and strategies, draws on certain forms of knowledge, and privileges certain actors while excluding others. Frames and scripts, accordingly, are political entities based on closure.

However, in addition to articulating such choices, the political also manifests itself through terms of reference in which such choices are couched, and the techniques through which they are given organizational and material form. This even applies when these terms and techniques appear to be free from contestation and considered self-evident. As argued by Varró (2010b), any vocabulary always comprises a necessarily political view of how a particular issue, such as regional development, relates to particular general interests (however defined). Consensus and self-evidentiality are not givens, but stem from the fact that political discussions generally do not question universalizing notions of the social. Consensus is reached by silencing possible alternative views, while self-evidentiality is achieved by turning policy and derived theoretical rationales into mantra-like narratives (Hillier, 2000). An example is how, in neoliberal thinking, economic 'imperatives' are invoked to promote the 'learning economy', with emphasis on place-based innovation and competitiveness. Such localized, supply-side orientations obscure the ways cities and regions may have to meet other 'imperatives' – such as the financial crisis through strategies of 'resilience' – as well as the fact that other regional responses may be possible (Ward and Jonas, 2004). Hence the terms of reference required for any political debate to take place, for any politics to be territorialized and coded, can never be self-evident. They always present political forms of closure and silencing.

The political significance of 'technical' aspects, moreover, goes beyond mere instrumentalization (scripting and territorialization) of codings. Certain 'technical' choices, such as the use of particular policy standards or methods, or the enrolment of certain capacities, may be informed by specific political ambitions. Such practices may serve to invest a policy with a particular positionality and identity, and to mark out a specific domain for a policy to cover. In the EU, for instance, the ways legitimacy and accountability are understood and practised have a decisive impact on the shaping of European policies regardless of the policy field. So overcoding is supported here through universalizing repertoires of practice and technologies (van Heur, 2008).

A final point is that, given their discursive nature, forms of overcoding are never complete, and always temporary. Indeed, under the surface of consensual languages and universalizing practices, the meanings of the social, spatial and technical continue to be negotiated and contested, even if only at the very margin. One of the key research challenges, therefore, is to detect the rise of alternative forms of territorialization and alternative codings, and see to what extent they assemble the power and acquire the clout to defy and overturn current overcodes. Another possibility is that new overcodes emerge that provide an alternative reading, and hence meaning, of existing practices. Although the latter may simply be a manifestation of 'old wine in new bottles', when such alternative readings gain sufficient appeal they may also provoke a kind of 'paradigm shift'. Both such cases will be examined for the case of regional innovation policy below.

3. REGIONAL INNOVATION POLICY: EMERGENCE AND CODING

As referred to above, regional innovation policy originates basically from two types of state policies, namely national technology policy and regional (or spatial–economic) policy. In the postwar period, these policies initially evolved as separate fields. This changed when technology policy extended its scope from 'pure' technology production and circulation to innovation, and when regional policies broadened out from Keynesian redistribution and investment subsidies to business support. One frontier country was France, where these recodings supported the development of a new possible assemblage around the notion of the 'growth pole'. The promotion of state technology development in the periphery (i.e. out of Paris) was combined with a strategy of innovation-oriented business support. Similar initiatives followed in the UK and West Germany (Cooke, 1985). In terms of derived theoretical rationales, an important source of inspiration was the system approach to innovation, as well as the debate on the important seedbed role of SMEs. This was translated in to a 'self-help' policy rationale in which limited resources would serve to boost certain targeted segments of the local economy.

The recoding of the policy form not only affected its substance, but also its institutional and organizational aspects. Zooming in on the performances of local businesses, research institutes and their interaction, the old policy assemblages, with a singular, top–down form of territorialization, became increasingly impractical. Because of regional specificities and complexities, it became clear that detailed national scripts and practices would not work and that innovation policies needed to be shaped at the regional level itself. According to Cooke (1985, p. 259), 'There has to be a regional-level policy development with national government playing coordinative and supportive roles'. This shift downwards started with policy implementation, through providing scope for the practical adaptation of national R&D policies and instruments, focusing on technology development and absorption. Gradually, decentralization also started to cover policy formulation, promoting more decentralized forms of innovation and economic development policy (Ewers and Wettmann, 1980), calling for more 'bespoke' policy approaches (cf. Howells, 2005; Todlting and Trippl, 2005). In addition, the focus on technological innovation was complemented with an interest in management practices, the provision of joint services and sector studies (Bachtler et al., 2003; Molle, 1983). Both the coding and territorialization of innovation policy thus became organized at a regional level, set in a national framework in what can be described as a nested policy assemblage.

The shift to a more 'bottom–up' approach has been justified on the basis of policy rationales supporting collective, strategic forms of regional governance featuring close involvement of the business community. Regional governance should foster public–private collaboration, and invest in a 'soft infrastructure' nurturing networking and trust-building (MacLeod, 2001; IRE, 2008). Rather than the singular focus on large companies, these practices were now targeting other business segments, notably

SMEs. Such regionalized business support and governance modes were underwritten by well-known derived theoretical rationalities combining economic–geographical work on the region (labelled as 'TIM' approaches) and insights into cognitive and interactive aspects of innovation (Loasby, 1998; Boschma, 2005).

4. EU REGIONAL INNOVATION POLICY: ASSEMBLAGE OF RIS/RITTS

Next, enter the EU (then called the European Community). The recoding and reterritorialization of innovation policy highly appealed to the Community, specifically to the directorates responsible for regional and industrial development (now known as DG-Regio and DG-Industry). The coding of 'regional-level policy development' with a supply-side orientation, with central government 'playing coordinative and supportive roles' matched Europe's neoliberal programme of market integration and supply-side-led growth. More specifically, it addressed a major conundrum faced by the Community. For both economic and political reasons, it was paramount that spatial inequalities across Europe be reduced. But how to accomplish this without weakening economic growth, or, even worse, distorting the operation of the free market? How to accomplish, to use Europe's own codings, 'balanced development'? One solution has been to create a highly regimented system of regional policy, geared towards investments in physical infrastructure, notably through overcoding in the form of detailed scripts of resource allocation and usage.

In the case of regional innovation policy, a specific approach was followed. Lured by the 'self-help' rationale and the nested model of policy organization, the Community was able to set apart a small chunk of its regional policy budget under a special arrangement (Article 10 of the European Regional Development Fund). This money was used to fund the drafting and, in part, implementation of regional innovation strategies (initially framed as 'technology plans'). What made this assemblage unique was that it was able to largely bypass, apart from financial–administrative issues, the national level. This allowed the Community to engage in overcoding not only through scripting, but also through framing. The Community thus became a key promoter of framing regions as engines for learning, innovation and 'place-based' economic growth. By supporting regions, and thus business environments rather than individual businesses, the approach could be coded and legitimized as market reform. From a more political stance, what counts for the Community is that policies conform to the (neo)liberal idea that intervention is only warranted in two cases, namely (1) in the case of market failure and (2) when welfare distribution is found wanting (as in the case of spatial inequalities). Place-based forms of nurturing knowledge development and circulation, targeting SMEs, meet both these conditions (PRO INNO, 2009).

In practical terms, DG-Regio and DG-Industry set up a joint programme supporting regional innovation based on Article 10 and the Community's Innovation Programme. In 1993, corresponding to the two directorates involved, two schemes were launched:

1. Regional Technology Plans (RTP), followed by Regional Innovation Strategies (RIS), destined for less favoured regions (ERDF-assisted NUTS-2 areas, later the 'cohesion regions'), and
2. Regional Innovation and Technology Transfer Strategies (RITTS), open to all (kinds of) regions, with explicit focus on innovation support structures (now known as 'competitiveness regions').

Delivering a small amount of seed money (around €0.5 million, with 50 per cent European support), these schemes funded the establishment of regional structures to initiate and try out regional innovation practices. In line with the Community's policy rationale of 'mainstreaming', that is, the idea that any Community-supported project should result in encoded forms of policy making that can be applied more widely, important aspects of the programme were learning and dissemination. Learning was brought about by scripting a requirement for drawing policy lessons in the RIS/RITTS policy manuals (European Commission, 1996). Dissemination was facilitated by the establishment of a variety of platforms and networks dedicated to interregional learning. This included, in particular, the IRE (Innovating Regions in Europe) network and its Mutual Learning Platform (IRE, 2006). IRE has played a pivotal role in diffusing and advocating the 'RIS/RITTS methodology', framing it as a holistic, system-based approach to regional development.

Documentation from the Innovating Regions in Europe network sheds an interesting light on the coding and territorialization of regional innovation policy in the RIS/RITTS era. The key policy rationale is couched in terms of achieving regional 'excellence' by accumulating strategic intelligence (through foresight and benchmarking scripts) and the exchange of 'good' or 'best practices' for regional knowledge creation and valorization (IRE, 2006; EC, 2008). This approach is underwritten by two derived theoretical rationales. First, the notion of the knowledge economy, drawing from theoretical work on the fundamental role of knowledge in the economy (Jessop, 2009), combined with strategic management thinking (accompanied by SWOT scripts) (Lagendijk, 2007). In theoretical terms, a fundamental issue here is the shift from a relative to an absolute conceptualization of 'competitiveness' (cf. Porter, 2000). In an absolute view, regional wealth is not based on the relative disposition of resources and levels of productivity, but on knowledge-based distinctiveness. Second, regional excellence and strategic intelligence are shaped by forms of regional governance grafted on to the notion of the 'associational economy' (Cooke and Morgan, 1998). The core claim of the associational economy perspective is that local state, business, educational and support organizations should join forces to develop and implement sector- and innovation-oriented strategies. Such ideas have been elaborated particularly in the context of cluster approaches, featuring cluster mapping, networking strategies, collaborative innovation and institutional capacity-building aiming at (re)orienting a region's sectoral or 'cluster' profile (cf. CLOE, 2007).

In addition to the close links in codings with the academic debate, what has made European regional policy particularly successful is its territorialization. Within the highly complex, politicized, volatile context of the European Community/Union, RIS/RITTS managed to carve out its own organizational space, with its own boundaries. At the Community level, it managed to do this by promoting the political and administrative proliferation of regional and cohesion policies, coupling a 'strong' story – innovation, balanced development, self-help – with a small budget and lean organization. As explained, its special position allowed it to largely bypass the national level, so that central coding (like the RIS/RITTS scripts) could be applied directly to the regional level. At the latter level, moreover, territorialization occurred by the setting up of dedicated organizational units engaged in the drafting, submitting and implementing of regional plans. In many cases entire regional governance structures were established to grasp the expanding opportunities offered by European regional policy. Finally, across Europe, a wide range of actors, including politicians at different governance levels, academics, research centres and business representatives jumped on to the bandwagon of regional innovation policy, facilitating the build-up of resources and further infusing and disseminating the concept and practice.

5. EUROPEAN REGIONAL INNOVATION POLICY UNDER CHALLENGE

While successful, the coding and territorialization of RIS has been contested on various fronts. What makes the chains of significance intriguing is how they connect absolute competitiveness – based on producing and using distinctive knowledge – and collaboration – through the exchange of knowledge. From a broader policy perspective, this raises a critical issue of how policy makers, notably at the local level, are motivated to serve the general interest. To put it bluntly, if regional agents realize that a certain practice proves to be effective, would they then not be tempted to protect this form of knowledge, rather than 'mainstreaming' it? IRE and other bodies involved in regional policy have been addressing this issue to some extent, by discussing the role and meaning of knowledge and by discussing and scripting the build-up and exchange of 'best practice' (IRE, 2008). More generally, policy makers and students have stressed that there is no magic bullet, that each practice requires local adaptation and implementation and monitoring. Best practice is thus about learning, not copying (IRE, 2006, 2008). In recent debates on the evaluation of regional and cohesion policies, a call has been made for moving away from success stories to learning from both success and failure (Reid, 2008). Yet pregnant questions remain. If achieving distinctiveness in the knowledge economy is so paramount, to what extent can the circulation of 'best practices' among regions really make a difference?

Even if 'best practices' circulate, the question arises to what extent they can infuse the catching up of laggard regions. According to Oughton et al. (2002), catching up may be inhibited by what they call the 'innovation paradox'. The policy rationale of 'self-help' is based on the idea that subsidies and assistance given to laggard regions will help them to substantially increase their learning and innovation capacities. Yet the extent to which this takes place depends on the region's absorptive capacity for turning external resources into effective plans, projects and measures. As Oughton et al. (2002) observe, this capacity is often lacking, thus undermining the very idea of 'self-help'. Moreover, even when basic capacities are present, it takes a long time from building up a local governance structure and 'soft infrastructure' to producing world-class excellence and distinctiveness. In general, many regional plans and initiatives pursue the same dreams of becoming the next hot-spot in biotech, ICT or business services. From a political perspective, what is at stake here is the modernist view in which places, although with differences in time, all march along the same path towards an envisaged optimum level of wealth (Massey, 2005).

Another fundamental issue is the understanding of the region. In the 1990s, the coding of regional significance reached such a prominence that it presented a high degree of closure. The result was that in both academic and policy circles, the region became the focal point of the debate. Alternative views thus had to start with challenging the dominance of the region. In line with the competition–collaboration conundrum explained above, this started with refuting the idea that lagging areas and poorer communities would benefit from an approach pitting regions against each other in their search for 'excellence' (Amin and Thrift, 1993). Not only was this model considered flawed from a political stance, it was also criticized for universalizing an exceptional model of spatial–economic development, that of the archetypal Marshallian district or high-tech agglomeration. This prompted a call for considering the 'non-local' aspects of regional development, and, in a more sophisticated way, the understanding of the region in 'relational' terms. The latter seeks to avoid what Sassen (2006), in her usage of assemblage, calls the 'endogeneity trap'. Rather than seeing the region as a bounded entity primarily constituted through internal mechanisms, the region is considered as a fragment, with potentially some degree of coherence, in a world in which most entities and processes are organized at other scales and in other settings. On reflection, it may be striking how much hard work the debate has been investing in loosening the regional straitjacket, in view of the widespread evidence for and recognition of other spatialities (Varró, 2010a). In our view, the effort it takes to unlock the debate vindicates the significance of closure and the political nature of understanding spatialities.

The policy side, on the other hand, has manifested similar trends of zooming out and connecting to other scales. An important moment was the EU's Lisbon Strategy, in which innovation became the core aspiration for a much wider set of EU policies, and which led to three major trends of policy integration. First, cohesion policies and Community programmes such as Interreg had to commit much larger budgets to innovation-oriented programmes (EC, 2006). Second, industrial and regional policies were more intertwined through the elaboration of 'place-based' cluster approaches (Barca, 2009). Third, an idea was launched to connect research policy (including the European Research Area) to 'place-based' innovation approaches (Soete, 2009). These moves presented a wish to build a stronger alignment of regional policy, industrial policy and research policy, in view of the Lisbon Agenda's main ambitions to strengthen the Union's competitiveness and cohesion (Tewdwr-Jones and Morais Mourato, 2005).

6. TOWARDS 'SMART SPECIALIZATION'

As a result of these various changes, regional innovation policy has turned from a hotchpotch of local projects to an embedding of initiatives in a broader multi-level and multi-sector governance context, with a completely different form of territorialization. Also in response to the eastwards expansion, after 2000 the RIS programme focused on the accession countries, promoting learning between regions from 'old' and 'new' member states. A final round of RIS was launched in 2005, and the IRE network shut down in 2008. The learning and knowledge exchange approach was embedded within the new programme of DG-Regio, 'Regions for Economic Change' (RfEC) (EC, 2006). By sharing excellence, RfEC seeks to contribute to internal 'balanced development' and the Union's overall competitiveness, in line with the RIS-RITTS programme. Other RIS-RITTS elements, such as the support for networking, have been continued in the context of the PRO INNO innovation policy initiative of DG Enterprise & Industry (PRO INNO, 2009).

Compared with the hard work needed in the academic debate to move away from a regional straitjacket, policy recoding and reterritorialization has occurred more smoothly. This can be attributed to the fact that, as described above, regional innovation policy has always been part of a nested configuration of policy assemblages. As explained above, the relative autonomy that EU regional innovation policy enjoyed in the 1990s was more a matter of territorialization than of coding, more a matter of practice than of principle. Policy rationales such as streamlining (i.e. focusing on the core aims of competitiveness and cohesion) and policy integration (aligning different domains) served to justify a transition to another policy form. A concrete reason for recoding reterritorialization and overhaul of regional and cohesion policy, moreover, was the massive eastwards expansion undertaken in 2000, which radically changed the inequality map of the Union (Bachtler et al., 2003; Bachtler et al., 2007).

In addition to these territorial aspects, recoding has also been accompanied by changing political views on the regional problem. Although the debates on the issues are still ongoing, two developments are particularly noteworthy. The first concerns a move towards a more differentiated view on regional 'opportunities'. In part inspired by debates on the spatial concentration of core economic activities within major agglomeration and along major axes, a differentiated view starts with an acceptance that only a limited number of regions can be at the frontier of research and innovation. Accordingly, non-core regions need to find alternative routes to position themselves in the knowledge economy. Adopting an evolutionary approach, Foray (2006) and Soete (2009) thus make a case for 'smart specialization'. Rather than targeting similar clusters or technology segments, regions should explore individually how promising technologies can be applied to views of local capabilities and scope for enduring market potential. Differentiation entails a basic distinction between 'leading' regions that primarily engage in the valorization of new, frontier technology, and 'follower' regions searching for specific combinations and applications meeting market opportunities. This should be accompanied by an 'unbounded' view of the regional economy, taking into account the critical role played by external economic and research linkages, and the position of regions in 'global' value chains.

Such 'unboundedness' not only bears on the economic but also the governance dimension. A second move concerns the position of the region in spatial governance structures. This debate focuses on the question to what extent one should move from the existing division of responsibilities between spatial levels to a division and alignment of tasks (Soete, 2009). Breaking with the principle of keeping a strict separation of political and administrative responsibilities, as implied by the EU principle of subsidiarity, a task-based model is based on a process of mutual recognition and blending of strengths and opportunities at different levels. If such a flexible model of vertical coordination and collaboration is applied to regional innovation policy, the latter is recoded and reterritorialized in quite fundamental ways. Regions should no longer be considered as generic laboratories producing 'best practices' to be mainstreamed to the community at large. Instead, regional innovation practices should become strategically tied to specific (combinatory) research and innovation networks and programmes at (inter)national levels. Smart specialization in research networks and value chains, in other words, should be accompanied by smart specialization in a multi-level governance approach to innovation. Instead of focusing on 'best practices', policy should focus on an assessment of missing strategic connections and other development constraints (Soete, 2009).

From an assemblage perspective, such a move will encounter major points of resistance. A first sensitive issue, as already mentioned, is that it will require a decoding of the subsidiarity principle, which presents one of the pillars of the EU's multi-level governance structure at present. In addition, a more flexible approach will not be easy to match with the neoliberal overcodes ruling much of the EU's governance practices. As referred to above, EU policies have become more and more dominated by top–down goal-setting, managerial and financial control, project tendering and evaluation. In terms of accountability and legitimacy politics, this reflects neoliberal preferences for limited state intervention, competition-based forms of governance, financial accountability and performance assessment. The result is a procedural, technocratic relationship between programmes at the EU level and projects at the local level. Multi-level governance, in contrast, requires more long-term vision and strategy making at a central level of policy making, and thus calls for a move towards a more programmatic and longer-term policy approach. Moreover, rather than being imposed solely in a top–down way, such a strategy should be articulated and attuned with visionary as well as practical developments 'on the ground' (Howells, 2005). A key question is thus whether 'smart specialization' as discussed here can be territorialized under neoliberal overcodes.

7. CONCLUSION

This chapter started from the acknowledgement that policy design and transfer exhibit a complex, evolutionary pattern of development. To come to terms with this complexity, an approach is required that accounts for both the expressive and material–organizational aspects of policy making, as well as for the critical roles of agency and institutional forms. For this purpose, this chapter has adopted the neo-realist approach of assemblage theory. The evolution of European innovation policy over the last four decades has been disentangled and put in context using the notions of (over)coding and territorialization.

Assemblage theory serves to identify core operators in the construction of social phenomena, without resorting to pre-given theoretical concepts. Significantly, it pays attention to how a phenomenon creates its own space and processes of structuration. European regional innovation policy could emerge and proliferate because of the relative autonomy it managed to enjoy in the 1990s, benefiting from and contributing to a booming academic discourse and policy interest. The combination of the latter helped to dramatically raise the significance of the region in innovation and economic growth. It thus generated the capacity to muster considerable support across Europe, and to forge effective networks of exchange. Yet, in terms of both coding and territorialization, the policy encountered major obstacles. In particular, the regional lens on innovation proved too narrow, and changes of and within the EU's governance structure, as well as political shifts, called for a stronger integration of innovation policies within the broader policy framework of the Union.

The most fundamental change has been a reversal in the roles of innovation and cohesion. In the past, innovation was a seen as a tool for boosting regional development and, in particular, the catching up of laggard regions. Now, cohesion, as well as other policies (research policy, industrial policy), are seen as deliverables for the Lisbon Agenda and its follow-up, Europe 2020. In other words, they are the servants of innovation. Policy integration means that, more than ever before, the chain of signification is now pulled by a single force. And that force is the need for innovation. In our vocabulary, policies, programmes and projects need to be overcoded primarily in terms of innovation, with other ambitions (sustainability, cohesion) coming in second or third position. This has opened the door for a less critical stance towards spatial inequality, for an acceptance of the 'forces' of agglomeration and concentration that 'inevitably' accompany the rise of centres of global 'expertise' and 'competitiveness'. It is this pivotal issue that drives the current debates on 'smart specialization' and the reform of cohesion policy.

Besides this empirical account, the theoretical contribution of this chapter lies in the conceptualization of the political in policy making. An important political issue is the distribution of wealth across Europe, and specifically the extent to which concentrations of wealth are deemed acceptable or even desirable. Moreover, and in contrast to many policy studies, we locate the political beyond the realm of the expressive. Decisive political aspects may actually be contained within institutional forms, methods of policy practice and in routine forms of action. Tracing these links serves to shed light on the performativity of policy ideas and approaches in a way that considers policy development not just as an evolutionary process based on successful assembly, but as something deeply penetrated by the way political views on what is tolerable and desirable work their way through the machinations of policy making and implementation, in terms of core imaginations and ambitions ('a competitive European space economy'), as well as the measures employed.

Through its fundamentally empirical orientation, in which no *a priori* significance is placed on policy discourse, policy practice or ideologies, the policy assemblage approach presents a fundamentally open perspective. As a result, the policy assemblage perspective may provide a fruitful alternative to more deterministic approaches, such as 'state restructuring' perspectives and structural scalar narratives (Brenner, 2004; Jessop, 2004; Uitermark, 2003). The separation of the material–organizational and the expressive, coding and overcoding, the identification of nested structures of policy making, and the conceptualization of state impact 'at a distance' produces a more subtle empirically grounded approach sensitive to context and contingency. This comes with a risk, however. Without *a priori* ideas of where to look for important phenomena, a researcher may be tempted to select those items that, at face value, appear to be most fitting to explain policy dynamics. Rather than revealing the complex political nature of policy making, this may then lead to a somewhat crude social–evolutionary form of explanation, in which social phenomena are explained primarily in terms of fitting, well-packaged forms of coding and territorialization. There is a pressing need, accordingly, to further elaborate this approach to make it truly stand up to its promises.

REFERENCES

Amin, A. and Thrift, N. (1993), 'Globalization, institutional thickness and local prospects', *Revue d'Économie Régionale et Urbaine*, 405–27.

Anderson, B. and Harrison, P. (2010), 'The promise of non-representational theories', in B. Anderson and P. Harrison (eds), *Taking-place: Non-Representational Theories and Geography*, Farnham, UK: Ashgate, pp. 1–34.

Arts, B. and Lagendijk, A. (2009), 'The disoriented state', in B. Arts, A. Lagendijk and H. van Houtum (eds), *The Disoriented State: Shifts in Governmentality, Territoriality and Governance*, Dordrecht: Springer, pp. 231–47.

Bachtler, J., Wishlade, F. and Mendez, C. (2007), 'New budget, new regulations, new strategies: The 2006 reform of EU Cohesion Policy', Glasgow, European Policies Research Centre, University of Strathclyde.

Bachtler, J., Wishlade, F. and Yuill, D. (2003), 'Regional policies after 2006: complementarity or conflict?', Glasgow, European Policies Research Centre, University of Strathclyde.

Barca, F. (2009) 'An agenda for a reformed cohesion policy. A place-based approach to meeting European Union challenges and expectations. Independent Report prepared at the request of Danuta Hübner, Commissioner for Regional Policy', Brussels: Commission of the European Communities.

Boschma, R.A. (2005), 'Proximity and innovation: a critical assessment', *Regional Studies*, **39**, 61–74.

Brenner, N. (2004), *New State Spaces: Urban Governance and the Rescaling of Statehood*, Oxford: Oxford University Press.

Brenner, N. and Theodore, N. (2002), 'Cities and the geographies of "actually existing neoliberalism"', *Antipode*, **34**, 349–79.

CLOE (2007), *Cluster Management Guide – Guidelines for the Development and Management of Cluster Initiatives*, Karlsruhe: Clusters Linked Over Europe.

Colebrook, C. (2002), *Gilles Deleuze*, London: Routledge.

Collier, S.J. and Ong, A. (eds) (2005), *Global Assemblages: Technology, Politics, and Ethics as Anthropological Problems*, Oxford: Blackwell.

Cooke, P. (1985), 'Regional innovation policy – problems and strategies in Britain and France', *Environment and Planning C – Government and Policy*, **3**, 253–67.

Cooke, P. and Morgan, K. (1998), *The Associational Economy: Firms, Regions and Innovation*, Oxford: Oxford University Press.

Cumbers, A., Mackinnon, D. and McMaster, R. (2003), 'Institutions, power and space – assessing the limits to institutionalism in economic geography', *European Urban and Regional Studies*, **10**, 325–42.

DeLanda, M. (2006), *A New Philosophy of Society: Assemblage Theory and Social Complexity*, London and New York: Continuum.

EC (2006), *Communication from the Commission. Regions for Economic Change*, Brussels: Commission of the European Communities, Directorate-General for Regional Policy.

EC (2008), *Good Practice in the Field of Regional Policy and Obstacles to the Use of the Structural Funds*, Brussels: Commission of the European Communities, Directorate-General for Regional Policy, Policy Department Structural and Cohesion Policies.

European Commission (1996), *Practical Guide to Region Innovation Actions. Regional Innovation Strategies (RIS). Regional Innovation and Technology*

Transfer Strategies (RITTS), Luxembourg: Office for Official Publications of the European Communities.
Ewers, H.J. and Wettmann, R.W. (1980), 'Innovation-oriented regional policy', *Regional Studies*, **14**, 161–79.
Foray, D. (2006), *Globalization of R&D: Linking Better the European Economy to 'Foreign' Sources of Knowledge and Making EU a More Attractive Place for R&D Investment*, Brussels: European Commission.
Gertler, M.S. (2001), 'Best practice? Geography, learning and the institutional limits to strong governance', *Journal of Economic Geography*, **1**, 5–26.
Hillier, J. (2000), 'Going round the back? Complex networks and informal action in local planning processes', *Environment and Planning A*, **32**, 33–54.
Howells, J. (2005), 'Innovation and regional economic development: a matter of perspective?', *Research Policy*, **34**, 1220–34.
IRE (2006), *Mutual Learning Platform. Synthesis Report*, Luxembourg: Innovating Regions in Europe.
IRE (2008), *The IRE Network: Inspiring Innovation Innovating Regions in Europe (IRE)*, Luxembourg: Innovating Regions in Europe.
Jessop, B. (2004), *From Localities via the Spatial Turn to Spatio-temporal Fixes: A Strategic-relational Odyssey*, Bonn: University of Bonn.
Jessop, B. (2009), 'Cultural political economy and critical policy studies' *Critical Policy Studies*, **3**, 336–56.
Lagendijk, A. (2007), 'The accident of the region: a strategic relational perspective on the construction of the region's significance', *Regional Studies*, **41**, 1193–207.
Lagendijk, A. and Cornford, J. (2000), 'Regional institutions and knowledge – tracking new forms of regional development policy', *Geoforum*, **31**, 209–18.
Laranja, M., Uyarra, E. and Flanagan, K. (2008), 'Policies for science, technology and innovation: translating rationales into regional policies in a multi-level setting', *Research Policy*, **37**, 823–35.
Latour, B. (2005), *Reassembling the Social. An Introduction to Actor-Network-Theory*, Oxford: Oxford University Press.
Loasby, B.J. (1998), 'Industrial districts as knowledge communities', in T.M Bellet and C. L'Harmet (eds), *Industry, Space and Competition. The Contribution of the Economists of the Past*, Cheltenham, UK and Northampton, MA, USA: Edward Elgar, pp. 70–85.
MacLeod, G. (2001), 'Beyond soft institutionalism: accumulation, regulation, and their geographical fixes', *Environment and Planning A*, **33**, 1145–67.
Massey, D. (2005), *For Space*, London: Sage.
McFarlane, C. (2009), 'Translocal assemblages: space, power and social movements', *Geoforum*, **40**, 561–7.
Molle, W.T.M. (1983), 'Technological change and regional development in Europe', *Papers of the Regional Science Association*, **52**, 23–38.
Oughton, C., Landabaso, M. and Morgan, K. (2002), 'The regional innovation paradox: innovation policy and industrial policy', *Journal of Technology Transfer*, **27**, 97–110.
Porter, M.E. (2000), 'Locations, clusters and company strategy', in G.L. Clark, M.P. Feldman and M.S. Gertler (eds), *The Oxford Handbook of Economic Geography*, Oxford: Oxford University Press, pp. 253–74.
Prince, R. (2010), 'Policy transfer as policy assemblage: making policy for the creative industries in New Zealand', *Environment and Planning A*, **42**, 169–86.
PRO INNO (2009), *Annual Report 2008–2009. Working Towards More Effective*

Innovation Support in Europe, Brussels: Commission of the European Communities, European Regional Development Fund.
Reid, A. (2008), *Analysing ERDF Co-financed Innovative Projects. Final Report Prepared in the Framework of the European Commission Study on the ERDF Co-financed Innovative Projects and Comparative Analyses*, Brussels: Technopolis Group.
Sassen, S. (2006), *Territory, Authority, Rights. From Medieval to Global Assemblages*, Basingstoke: Palgrave Macmillan.
Shore, C. and Wright, S. (1997), 'Policy. A new field of anthropology', in C. Shore and S. Wright (eds), *Anthropology of Policy: Critical Perspectives on Governance and Power*, London: Routledge, pp. 3–40.
Soete, L. (2009), *The Role of Community Research Policy in the Knowledge-based Economy. Expert Group Report*, Brussels: European Commission, Directorate-General for Research.
Tewdwr-Jones, M. and Morais Mourato, J. (2005), 'Territorial cohesion, economic growth and the desire for European "balanced competitiveness"', *Town Planning Review*, **76**(1); 69–80.
Thrift, N. (1997), 'The rise of soft capitalism', *Cultural Values*, **1**, 29–57.
Thrift, N. and Olds, K. (1996), 'Refiguring the economic in economic-geography', *Progress in Human Geography*, **20**, 311–37.
Todtling, F. and Trippl, M. (2005), 'One size fits all? Towards a differentiated regional innovation policy approach', *Research Policy*, **34**, 1203–19.
Torfing, J. (2011), 'Policy, discourse models', in IPSA (ed.), *Encyclopedia of Political Science*, Thousand Oaks, CA: Sage.
Uitermark, J. (2003), *The Multi-scalar Origins of Urban Policy: Towards a Policygenetic Approach*, Research programme Governance and places, Nijmegen, the Netherlands: Nijmegen School of Mangement.
Van Heur, B. (2008), 'Networks of aesthetic production and the urban political economy', Department of Earth Sciences, Berlin, Freie Universität Berlin.
Varrò, K. (2010a), 'After resurgent regions, resurgent cities?: contesting state geographies in Hungary and England', Nijmegen, University of Nijmegen.
Varrò, K. (2010b), 'Re-politicising the analysis of "new state spaces" in Hungary and beyond: towards an effective engagement with "actually existing neoliberalism"', *Antipode*, **42**, 1253–78.
Ward, K. and Jonas, A.E.G. (2004), 'Competitive city-regionalism as a politics of space: a critical reinterpretation of the new regionalism', *Environment and Planning A*, **36**, 2119–39.

PART III

The Future of Innovation and Prospects for Socio-Economic Integration

6. Innovation diplomacy as driver of democracy, innovation and development: the case of Greece

Elias G. Carayannis

1. INTRODUCTION

Chapter 1 touched briefly on innovation diplomacy as a means of bridging distance and other divides. It can unleash and help 'realize the creative potential and aspirations of people around the world so that markets will serve society . . . to the fullest possible extent' (Carayannis et al., 2011). We now build on that background to examine the current situation of and prospects for Greece.

In general, entrepreneurship and innovation are human endeavors and socio-economic phenomena that are intrinsic to human nature as well as constituting both social and political engines of positive change and growth provided they are balanced and guided by effective and transparent regulatory and incentive systems in place.

Current local (Greek), regional (European) and global economic and financial conditions and trends make the need to trigger, catalyze and accelerate high-quantity and -quality entrepreneurial initiatives that are based on high-quality and -quantity innovations (low-tech, medium-tech and high-tech) even more clear and urgent as this is one of the major ways and means to target and achieve real, sustainable and eventually accelerating GNP growth. Such growth is much more likely to come from new and qualitative different and superior initiatives (from 'sunrise' industries) rather than restructuring existing (and perhaps 'sunset') industries. It may be strategically more prudent to invest scarce and precious resources in carefully calculated strategic 'bets' rather than keep throwing them after waning industrial sectors and declining firms and in that sense, it may be best to provide aggressive socio-economic re-training, re-insertion and/or early retirement programs to allow for real growth strategies to be implemented.

Moreover, we believe that the concepts of robust competitiveness and sustainable entrepreneurship (Carayannis et al., 2008) are pillars of a regime called 'democratic capitalism' (Carayannis and Kaloudis, 2009) (as opposed to 'popular or casino capitalism'), where real opportunities for education and economic prosperity are available to all and especially the younger people.

This would be the direct derivative of a collection of top–down policies as well as bottom–up initiatives (including strong R&D policies and funding but going beyond that to the development of innovation networks and knowledge clusters across regions and sectors: Carayannis and Campbell, 2006):

- We define sustainable entrepreneurship (Carayannis et al., 2008) as the creation of viable, profitable and scalable firms. Such firms engender the formation of self-replicating and mutually enhancing innovation networks and knowledge clusters (innovation ecosystems) leading towards robust competitiveness.
- We understand robust competitiveness (Carayannis et al., 2008) as a state of economic being and becoming that avails systematic and defensible 'unfair advantages' to the entities that are part of the economy. Such competitiveness is built on mutually complementary and reinforcing low-, medium- and high-technology, public and private sector entities (government agencies, private firms, universities and non-governmental organizations).

Existing and new small and medium enterprises (SMEs) that can provide better solutions for less will always be winners – even and perhaps especially in down markets and recessionary economic cycle stages – and this is the area where fiscal, monetary, institutional, intellectual property rights (IPR)-related and other public–private sector programs and initiatives are needed to help unlock, capture and leverage fully the value-adding potential of the Greek knowledge creation infrastructure (i.e. universities, research institutions and private sector R&D facilities) by providing incentives and establishing a large number, scale and scope of pilots connecting organically and effectively all stages of the value-adding knowledge chain (from the lab to the market via world-class SMEs that will be both locally as well as globally oriented by design and the new ones from their inception).

2. OPEN INNOVATION DIPLOMACY

Building on the constituent elements of technology transfer and commercialization, open innovation diplomacy encompasses the concept and practice of bridging distance and other divides (cultural, socio-economic, technological) with focused and properly targeted initiatives to connect ideas and solutions with markets and investors ready to appreciate them and nurture them to their full potential. With respect to Greece, we recommend the development of efforts and initiatives as follows (Carayannis, 2011).

2.1 The What

1. Re-engineer mindsets, attitudes and behaviors in Greece to help people – especially young people – realize the true nature and potential of innovation and entrepreneurship as a way of life and the most powerful lever for and pathway to sustainable growth and prosperity, with positive spillover effects staunching the brain-drain, reduced cynicism and increased optimism and trust in the future and each other, reduced criminality and social unrest, higher assimilation of migrant groups and similar effects.
2. Engage in sustained, succinct and effective dialog with stakeholders and, policy makers within Greece as well as the EU to pursue the reform and, as needed, the reinvention of institutions, policies and practices that can foster entrepreneurship and innovation in areas such as related laws, rules and regulations, higher education, public and private R&D, civil society movements and non-governmental organizations.
3. Identify, network and engage purposefully and effectively with the Greek diaspora of professional and social networks to trigger, catalyze and accelerate their involvement and intervention in a focused and structured manner to help with goals 1 and 2 above, as well as help establish, fund and manage entrepreneurship and innovation, promoting and supporting initiatives and institutions such as business plan competitions, angel and other risk capital financing of new Greek ventures, mentoring of and partnering with these ventures to ensure their survival, growth and success both within Hellas and in the global markets. Of particular interest and importance would be communities of practice and interest among the Greek diaspora that would include the shipowners, large trading concerns and technology entrepreneurs in countries such as the USA, Canada, Australia, as well as the EU and the rest of the world.

2.2 The How

Greek companies (especially small- and medium-sized firms) need to begin with the high-quality tools and expertise at their disposal (in terms of business planning, risk capital financing guidance and sources as well as strategic partners, complementors, suppliers and customers – in short a business ecosystem they can thrive locally, regionally and globally).

1. This should begin with a mindset shift from short-term, survival-mode thinking, which is normal for entrepreneurs especially in their early business stages, to more strategic, globally as well as locally attuned thinking and acting which nowadays could be greatly enabled and empowered via social networking tools and methodologies as well as blended (real/virtual) teaching/learning/consulting/mentoring environments.
2. Moreover, in the case of a country like Greece, a local, regional and global perspective is critical, given the small size of the local market. In this regard, Greece should pursue an effective and efficient strategic integration of its knowledge-generating assets in the universities as well as its industry and its government sectors and leverage them fully along with EU and Greek diaspora resources, expertise and experience to promote the creation of a new breed of start-ups (preferably – but not exclusively – as high-tech as is sustainable technologically and commercially).
3. These start-ups would aim to form a critical mass of an entrepreneurial innovation ecosystem in the form of locally and globally internetworked and competitive firms that would more organically and sustainably allow Greek innovators and entrepreneurs to tap and expand into the world's markets while remaining, researching and creating in Greece.
4. I have called this concept 'co-location' in the sense that it aims to retain the knowledge creators and potential entrepreneurs based in their mother country while enabling them to set up a bridgehead and become active in larger markets such as the USA. I have been doing this for the last five years with some success with Hellenic high-tech spin-offs from R&D centers and universities in Greece co-locating in the USA.
5. A balanced approach with a win–win–win mindset is key, combining short-term with long-term considerations. People, culture and technology need to be organically aligned so that resources used lead to results obtained in as short a period as possible to establish credibility and gain cooperation and support from civil society.
6. For that, top-level champions are needed as well as a strategic leveraging of social networking structures and infrastructures. In the past, regions around the world – whether Silicon Valley in California, or the Route 128 region in the Boston area or others – have been identified as

success benchmarks for innovation and entrepreneurship. However, simply emulating those has not always led to success, as people and culture are finicky and there are higher-order interdependencies and complexities involved.

3. POLICIES AND FRAMEWORKS

Here are some ideas as to how to set up policies and frameworks to provide conditions as conducive as possible to the creation of a sustainable and competitive entrepreneurship and innovation ecosystem in Greece:

- Advocate the need for a non-political, institutionally and meritocratically established entity that would function as part of the government in Greece and all other EU countries and could be called 'Ministry for Innovation and Entrepreneurship' but set up in a flexible manner to avoid becoming part of the problem.
- Advocate the need for an 'Ombudsman for Entrepreneurs and Innovators' with proper authority, visibility and resources to intervene and resolve barriers to innovation and entrepreneurship (E&I) in Greece and across the EU (this is the institutional civil society role in support of E&I as part of the quadruple innovation helix concept: Carayannis and Campbell, 2009), with government, university and industry working effectively with civil society to support and promote E&I).
- Advocate the need for high-caliber volunteers among the Greek diaspora as mentors as well as potential risk capital investors and strategic partners – in this context, I would propose forming a 'Global Greek Diaspora Angel Investor Network' and 'The Global Greek Diaspora Bond Issue for Entrepreneurs & Innovators' and to have the funds managed by a professional entity that is subject to the diaspora members in a transparent and efficient manner. The intent would be to allow for a pooling of resources, so, along with large-scale donations, many small-sized but cumulatively substantial contributions could start being made on a streamlined and sustainable basis and always focused on supporting and promoting E&I initiatives and efforts (a working case of that can already be seen in Denmark where a micro-finance and micro-enterprise fund – 'My C 4' – is already succeeding in pooling thousands of investors, with thousands of entrepreneurs leveraging social networking and clear vision and execution: www.myc4.com).

4. ENTREPRENEURS AND ACADEMICS

My descriptions of entrepreneurs and academics, based on 20 years of experience working with academics as well as entrepreneurs, are as follows:

- Entrepreneurs exhibit strongly the attributes of 'obsessed maniacs' focused on realizing their vision and 'clairvoyant oracles' seeing the opportunities and how to exploit them ahead of all others and being able to share that vision effectively with their key partners, investors and other early stakeholders (Carayannis, 2000–2010, Carayannis and Formica, 2006, 2007). A case in point is Daniel Williamson and the venture 'Connexions', which he is helping to develop further (www.cnx.org).
- Academics ideally should be 'entrepreneurs of the mind in the business of growing people intellectually and spiritually' (Carayannis, 2007) – facilitators of a lot of 'happy accidents', that is knowledge exchanges and partnerships.

Based on these descriptions, one should aim to inspire, empower and liberate the individual aspiring entrepreneurs (whether academic researchers and/or graduate students in science and engineering as well as other fields) to dare to dream big and dream in scientific/technological as well as commercial terms and to dare to take the next huge step of forming a company and asking people to invest in their dreams.

One of the ways to do so would be to establish across all Greece's universities interlinked, complementary and reinforcing, cross-disciplinary graduate degrees focused on E&I with emphasis on practice and aiming to produce working prototypes in the related science and engineering fields of the participants (from medical devices to agricultural techniques to software programs) and provide support and guidance for proper follow-through leading to the establishment of intellectual property rights (patents, trademarks, copyrights, trade secrets) as well as the formation of companies to commercialize those prototypes. These companies should be supported by advisory boards as well as potential investors from both internal/domestic networks as well as the Greek diaspora including the 'Global Greek Diaspora Angel Investor Network' mentioned above.

5. THE GREEK–US BRIDGE

In the mind of the average American, Greece is a country associated with its history and culture, the weather and the landscape and its famous

Mediterranean diet.[1] Other than that the Greek economy has little to offer, let alone compete with in the fields of innovation, state-of-the-art technologies, disruptive solutions, modern entrepreneurship and the like.

Every Greek economic actor, from the trade offices the Greek state maintains in the USA to the bilateral chambers (i.e. the Greek–American Chamber of Commerce and similar entities), to the trade and business development agencies in Greece, to Greek companies seeking to do business in the USA, all face this long-lived and largely misleading prejudice. But, to those who have first-hand knowledge or prefer to dig a little further beneath the surface, things look different.

Despite the economic downturn there is a dynamic economic and innovation potential in today's Greece, which remains to a large extent untapped. This potential can be ascribed to three main factors:

1. Native human capital: scientists and researchers, doctoral and post-doctoral candidates, graduates of world-class universities and polytechnics, fellows in major institutes and research facilities, who return home and staff local academic institutions or start their own companies right out of their labs.
2. The entrepreneurial spirit: Greeks have been archetypical for their adjustability and innovative thinking throughout history, having not only survived but flourished in unfriendly terrains and uncharted markets. A recent example illustrating this spirit is the unprecedented penetration Greek companies have accomplished in Southeast Europe in the early 1990s, in a very volatile political, business and investment environment right after the collapse of the former Soviet bloc. Today, in some countries in the Western Balkans, Greek FDI stock ranks first among foreign investors, outpacing economic giants like Germany, the UK and the USA.
3. Smart thinking: inventive academics and business pioneers had to virtually bypass a systemic defect in the Greek R&D framework: the decoupling of basic from applied research, leading to a correlated decoupling of innovation from industry and markets.[2] Applied research was practically transferred away from the universities, where mainly basic research is conducted, to research centers and tech parks, where commercializing technology and creating tech-driven start-ups are much less complicated.

How well Greece scores in winning competitive EU funding is an indicator of both the existence and the impact of the above-mentioned factors when combined and applied in a proper manner and in a highly antagonistic environment. Table 6.1 highlights the performance of Greek 'players'

Table 6.1 EU funding for ICT: calls for proposals 1–5 (Dec. 2006 through Oct. 2009) (percentage (%) of final funding allocated per member state)

Country	1st call 12/2006–5/2007	2nd call 6/2007–10/2007	3rd call 12/2007–4/2008	4th call 11/2008–4/2009	5th call 7/2009–10/2009	Total average/ rank
Greece	4.79	4.64	2.73	4.46	4.20	4.16 (3)
Austria	4.18	2.83	5.30	3.72	3.46	3.89 (4)
Belgium	4.88	5.36	3.21	6.11	4.65	4.84 (2)
Denmark	1.22	1.36	0.39	1.65	1.23	1.17 (8)
Finland	3.30	3.84	0.97	1.81	2.35	2.45 (6)
Ireland	1.38	1.24	0.75	1.19	4.37	1.78 (7)
Netherlands	6.37	5.04	6.39	6.82	4.53	5.83 (1)
Sweden	4.08	5.11	2.49	3.57	3.59	3.76 (5)

compared to other member states in winning competitive EU funding in information and communication technologies (ICT), one of the most innovative and competitive sectors.[3]

Greece ranks third and almost on par with Belgium, ahead of globally recognized R&D and innovation 'role models' Sweden and Finland, and also the equally advanced Nordic economy, Denmark, in front of the reputed international FDI 'magnet' Ireland and dynamic Austria. This is a very positive sign for the Greek innovative ICT sector.

As a further qualitative indicator, in the 1st call (12/2006–5/2007), for example, 35.8 percent of all the submitted proposal (total: 1836) had a participating Greek entity and 85 of the total 318 successful (= funded) proposals (or 26.7 percent) had a Greek participation. Furthermore, 20 out of a total of 135 of the submitted proposals under Greek coordination were approved, a remarkable 14.8 percent success rate.

6. THE GREEK RENAISSANCE INITIATIVE

The stability and sustainability of the Greek economy and society are of strategic importance for Europe as well as the USA, given the geopolitical, geo-economic, geo-strategic and geo-technological (geo-STEP) interdependencies across the region and beyond.

Unfortunately, short-sightedness and short-termism among politicians and policy makers in Europe and the USA have led to an exacerbation of the situation and a slow and increasingly risky series of balancing acts (as

I write this, Greece has been assessed at being in 'selective default' with serious risk of both sudden and catastrophic deterioration as well as broad contagion effects).

The conceptual foundation of the Greek renaissance initiative rests upon the following ideas:

- Current stratospheric unemployment levels, especially among the young, constitute a moral failure and a self-destructive crime against the society and economy of a country that it is absolutely critical to control, mitigate and reverse. One answer may be the effort as it is unfolding in the University of Ioannina Innovation Odysseys Initiative (http://ok2012.uoi.gr) as well as other universities around Greece and in cooperation with angel and mentor networks in Europe and the USA, where about 30 researcher and entrepreneur teams are entering the process of business plan development, evaluation, and presentation to potential investors including seed funding, foundation and co-location of start-ups at the University of Ioannina Technology Park and locations in the USA, for instance the George Washington University Science and Technology Ecosystem.
- If these efforts reach critical mass and result in the formation and growth of an E&I ecosystem that is present in Greece as well as in other countries and markets, via the co-location of university spin-offs, we may see a new middle class emerge that is empowered with the wisdom of global and local experience as well as the resources and capacity to act as part of the Global Greek Entrepreneurship and Innovation Ecosystem, bridging markets and pushing the endless frontier of science, technology and innovation further forward.
- This new and emerging middle class of global entrepreneurs and innovators would also act as the foundation, platform and protective buffer for a new era of open, transparent and democratic institutions, dynamics and processes in Greece and help in the emergence and evolution of political parties and mechanisms that would be more empowered as well as accountable and transparent.

These efforts, however, need time, perseverance, esthetic sensibility and structured and disciplined use of knowledge, know-how, experience and expertise. That is why it is critical for the Greek Renaissance Initiative to succeed to have a team from among experienced, successful and inspired members of the global Greek diaspora (researchers, academics, entrepreneurs, investors, policy makers and other professionals) and could set the pace and prove the concept for a way forward which could also constitute a working prototype for the entire EU.

This would indeed establish sufficient opportunities, bridging of markets and leveraging of net-centric knowledge serendipity and arbitrage effects that could well transform the current dire brain-drain from Greece and other European countries into a formidable brain-gain (via both the physical presence of repatriated innovators and entrepreneurs as well as the virtual presence, participation and contributions of all others engaged in support of start-ups in Greece).

7. CONCLUSION: LESSONS LEARNED AND RECOMMENDATIONS FOR THE ROAD AHEAD

I believe that academics are – or should continually strive to become – entrepreneurs of the mind in the business of growing people intellectually, spiritually and socially. Entrepreneurship is, in my experience, a liberator of creativity and an enabler of inventiveness that converts human dreams into socio-economic realities. I consider teaching, research and outreach as three key pillars of the academic enterprise that are mutually complementary and reinforcing. Successful entrepreneurs are typically people of a certain character, culture and charisma that leverage the financial means they have earned to do good in a multitude of ways. In the same context, through my research and pedagogy, I have come to qualify entrepreneurs of any type – including those of the mind who, by the way, represent the dominant mode in a knowledge economy and society – as obsessed maniacs and clairvoyant oracles. I have been involved for a number of years, and on a voluntary, *pro bono* basis, in designing and implementing initiatives to help reform and revitalize the Greek education ecosystem and, in particular, the higher education component as it relates to the national innovation and entrepreneurship ecosystem of Greece.

The challenge and opportunity is to engage on a large enough scale to both upgrade existing SMEs and catalyze the formation of new ones with an expectation to both survive and prosper as well as to grow (Greece should aim to be the cradle of the next Google or Amgen in the next 10–15 years as the nature and dynamics of the underlying technologies demand resources that are now well within the grasp of Greek researchers and potential or current entrepreneurs). The real challenge is to convert past failures of courage and imagination into future successes and to learn to convert counterproductive cynicism into empowering dreams grounded in reality. The aim should be to identify and outline clearly and in a convincing manner to all Greek citizens (including those of the diaspora, especially communities of interest and practice including diaspora members as well as other innovation ecosystem stakeholders as potential partners and mentors of domestic current and aspiring entrepreneurs – especially younger ones) a vision for the future and a strategy for change that is comprehensive, feasible and convincing so as to overcome the 'cynicism premium' that politics in Greece has to pay to atone for prior failures of ommission and commission. In short, we believe that the E&I area is one of the key pillars on which a strategy for change that people can believe in can be built.

Specific areas of focus should be clean/green technologies, environmental remediation/recovery solutions, eco-tourism and other higher-value (lower cost–benefit ratios) tourism solutions, transportation/connectivity solutions, nano-biomedical therapies, advanced materials for civilian and other uses, organic farming to feed the world, generic medicines to heal the world, e-learning solutions to educate the world (many of these should be set up as regionally centered, EU-supported initiatives).

Some more examples and thoughts of where and how E&I interventions might be targeted are listed below:

(a) Entrepreneurship as a solution for the way ahead – make a bigger pie, don't just redistribute it.
(b) Environment and energy as key sectors for entrepeneurial initiative – destroy the monopolies and bring on democratic capitalism (see Carayannis and Kaloudis, 2009).
(c) New technologies as platforms for flexible and high-value-added manufacturing – use intangibles to build valuable tangibles as they are the cause of viable, long-term prosperity (not services in a globalized, slave-labor-cost-driven economy).
(d) Eco-tourism building on environmental remediation and safeguarding and green energy schemes as drivers of entrepreneurial initiative – Greece is the Saudi Arabia of renewable energy and should be a major green energy exporter.
(e) Generic medicines and organic foodstuff not only for Greece but also parts of the world (like Africa) where they are dearly needed (and GMOs cause harm) – this could again leverage Greek know-how with UNIDO/WB/EBRD/EIB funding schemes and become a major and targeted (and also protected) export driver.
(f) Trans-disciplinary university pilot programs where students from engineering, medicine, business and social sciences are brought together into practice-focused apprentice groups to support existing firms and help create new ones in a network of internetworked incubators across universities, R&D centers, and other locations of private sector firms and feed the experiences and lessons learned back into curriculum renewal and design.

These are examples of building and implementing the quadruple innovation helix concept and the MODE 3 knowledge production system (see Carayannis and Campell, 2009; see also chapter 1). This is happening in many North and Western European countries today, and we need to engage in Greece as well.

In closing, we wish to note that people are interested in solutions that they can relate to and trust in to make things better for them individually and socially and in a viable manner. Greece remains the land of Alexander and Ulysses and, by extension, Greeks within Greece may choose to embrace defeat and decline or rediscover the voices, dreams, innovation, entrepreneurship and competence of Alexander, Ulysses and their comrades at arms and reinvent and re-build modern Greece and its socio-economic and socio-political ecosystems, locally, regionally and globally.

NOTES

1. In a recent market analysis on US consumers' attitudes towards Greece and Greek products (Kairos Consumers for the Greek Exporters Association, October 2010: www.pse.gr/en), the test groups associated Greece with nothing but historical/cultural and geographical landmarks (i.e. Acropolis, ancient history, Pythagoras, islands, Athens etc.) and food products (i.e. feta cheese, olives, yogurt etc.). To the question 'Which 3 products would you label as "made in Greece"?' the responses further solidified the findings: ouzo, feta cheese, olive oil, grape leaves, yogurt etc. As one quoted answer perfectly epitomizes: 'Olives, olive oil, feta cheese, yogurt; I can't think of any other products that are produced in Greece other than food.'
2. Article 16 of the Greek Constitution, which regulates Education, Art and Science, especially the correlation of provisions 'Art and science, research and teaching shall be free and their development and promotion shall be an obligation of the State' (§1): 'Education constitutes a basic mission for the State and shall aim at the moral, intellectual, professional and physical training of Greeks' (§2) and 'Education at university level shall be provided exclusively by institutions which are fully self-governed public law legal persons. These institutions shall operate under the supervision of the State (. . .)' (§5) of this article has been widely and consistently (mis)interpreted as practically forbidding any kind of commercial implications (let alone exploitation) of academic research.

   This idealization (one is tempted to say sanctification) of academic research limited the transformation of research to tangible novel goods and procedures, despite the fact that a number of targeted laws have been enacted to revert that distortion. Paragraph 3A of law 2741/1999 (further amended in 2000 by law 2843) clearly states that 'The outcomes of research and the knowledge created in research centers, educational institutions, companies or other entities in Greece and abroad can be economically exploited in various ways, including:

   a. Direct commercial use by producing and trading goods or services from the very knowledge-producing institution. In case the entity is an academic institution, those activities can be undertaken by the companies managing the institution's property.

   b. Out-licensing the commercialization from the knowledge-creating institution to a third-party entity or company, under a concession agreement defining the economic terms.

   c. Founding a targeted subsidiary corporation or participating in a third-party company to commercialize the knowledge produced.

   d. Technology companies where the economically-exploitable knowledge-creating individuals (scientists, technologists and researchers) engage in entrepreneurial activity; the institution where the knowledge was created can participate in these companies in any desirable form as can third parties (individuals or legal persons).

e. A combination of any of the above mentioned forms and other ways.'

3. The mix of countries is arbitrary, chiefly by virtue of comparable size with Greece, yet also reputation and significance in the R&D and innovation field. Data provided by Directorate of International S&T Cooperation, European Union Division of the Greek General Secretariat of Research&Technology (www.gsrt.gr) and the Greek national contact points for EU ICT programs.

REFERENCES

Carayannis, E.G. (2000–2010), GWU Lectures on Science, Technology, Innovation and Entrepreneurship.

Carayannis, E.G. (2007), 'Higher education manifesto', *Industry & Higher Education*.

Carayannis, E.G. (2011), 'The open innovation paradigm and strategic options for EU–US innovation partnerships: the FREIE concept in the context of open innovation diplomacy', Keynote Lecture, BILAT Conference, Vienna, Austria, March.

Carayannis, E.G. and D. Campbell (2006), *Knowledge Creation, Diffusion, and Use in Innovation Networks and Knowledge Clusters: A Comparative Systems Approach across the United States, Europe, and Asia*, Westport, CT: Praeger Publishers.

Carayannis, E.G. and D. Campbell (2009), '"Mode 3" and "Quadruple Innovation Helix": toward a 21st-century fractal innovation ecosystem', *International Journal of Technology Management*, **46**(3/4), 201–34.

Carayannis, Elias G. and D. Campbell (2011), 'Open innovation diplomacy and a 21st-century fractal research, education and innovation (FREIE) ecosystem: building on the quadruple and quintuple helix innovation concepts and the "Mode 3" knowledge production system', *Journal of the Knowledge Economy*, **2**(3), 327–72.

Carayannis, E.G. and P. Formica (2006), 'Intellectual venture capitalists: an emerging breed of knowledge entrepreneurs', *Industry & Higher Education*, **20**(3), 151–6.

Carayannis, E.G. and P. Formica (2007), 'The concentration of resources and academic performance: reinventing learning and research in the 21st century', Guest Editorial in *Industry & Higher Education*, **21**(2), 121–3.

Carayannis, E.G. and A. Kaloudis (2009), *Japan Economic Currents*, January, 6–10.

Carayannis, E.G., A. Kaloudis and Å. Mariussen (2008), *Diversity in the Knowledge Economy and Society: Heterogeneity, Innovation and Entrepreneurship*, Cheltenham, UK and Northampton, MA, USA: Edward Elgar.

Carayannis, E.G., M. Provance and N. Givens (2011), 'Knowledge arbitrage, serendipity, and acquisition formality: their effects on sustainable entrepreneurial activity in regions', *IEEE Transactions on Engineering Management*, **58**(3), 564–77.

Information Technology and Innovation Foundation (ITIF) (2010), 'Refueling the U.S. innovation economy', Washington, DC: ITIF.

APPENDIX

This appendix is adapted from an interview by *The Lithuanian Business Daily* provided by the author in October 2010.

1. What is the importance of technology innovation for economic growth?

Innovations (high-, medium- and low-tech) are the oxygen of the economy and the key driver of economic growth.

(a) They are *socio-technical solutions* with higher value added (or units of benefit per unit of cost) compared to existing solutions, thus resulting in the expansion and improvement of current markets and/or the creation of new markets.
(b) The more innovative an economy and a society is (the knowledge economy and society goal is pointing in that direction), the higher its productivity levels and thus the higher the rate of improvement of the standard of living (per capita GNP) and the more sustainable those higher productivity levels thanks to their higher levels of competitiveness.
(c) In particular, a combination of high-quality and -quantity technology innovations allows an economy to keep winning in the global competition race by being sufficiently and consistently better in terms of value-added solutions (products and services) – Germany is a case in point with its *Mittelstand* (small- and medium-sized) firms.

2. How can technology innovation help us exit from the economic crisis?

As in the above comments, the more innovation-driven an economy becomes, the more sustainably competitive it will become and thus the more market share it will be able to claim from competitors, NOT on the basis of being cheaper but on the basis of being better on a comparative value-added basis.

(a) In this context, the USA is currently mistakenly – in my opinion – trying to compete on being cheaper via 'competitive dollar devaluations'. This is only a temporary and limited solution with an increasing intrinsic risk for the US dollar to cease being the preeminent reserve currency and a potential spiralling of its already very high borrowing costs.
(b) In the EU context, this would require a combination of balanced and well-coordinated top–down government, university and industry

sector policies and mandates as well as bottom–up initiatives and practices from individuals and grass-roots movements (civil society) (the elements of the quadruple innovation helix discussed below).

(c) Otherwise, 'the entrepreneurship and innovation fad' risks becoming just another concept with limited or unrealized potential that could further exacerbate the cynicism and disengagement of the polity.

3. *What are the tools for firms to adopt innovations successfully and what are the accruing innovation benefits for the business?*

Companies (especially small and medium-sized firms) need to begin with as high quality tools and expertise at their disposal as possible (in terms of business planning, risk capital financing guidance and sources, as well as strategic partners, complementors, suppliers and customers – in short a business ecosystem they can thrive in locally, regionally and globally).

(a) This should begin with a mindset shift from only short-term, survival-mode thinking, which is normal for entrepreneurs especially in their early business stages, to more strategic, globally as well as locally attuned thinking and acting, which nowadays could be greatly enabled and empowered via social networking tools and methodologies as well as blended (real/virtual) teaching/learning/consulting/mentoring environments.

(b) Moreover, in the case of a country like Lithuania, a local, regional and global perspective would be critical given the small size of the local market. In this regard, Lithuania should pursue an effective and efficient strategic integration of its knowledge-generating assets in the universities (this is also further discussed later) as well as its industry and its government sectors and leverage them fully along with EU and Lithuanian diaspora resources, expertise and experience to promote the creation of a new breed of start-ups (preferably – but not excluisively – as high technology as is sustainable technologically and commercially).

(c) These start-ups would aim to form a critical mass of an entrepreneurial innovation ecosystem in the form of locally and globally internetworked and competitive firms that would more organically and sustainably allow Lithuanian innovators and entrerpeneurs to tap and expand into the world's markets while remaining researching and creating in Lithuania.

(d) I have called this concept 'co-location' in the sense that it aims to retain the knowledge creators and potential entrepreneurs based in their mother country while enabling them to set up a bridgehead and become active in larger markets such as the USA. I have been doing this for the last five years with some success with Hellenic high-tech spin-offs from R&D centers and universities in Greece co-locating in the USA.

4. *Can you explain the ideal cooperation plan between business and education organizations seeking commercial success for products or services? Please give some examples from practice.*

First of all, there is no 'perfect' cooperation plan – any such plan needs to be a living and evolving entity adapting to domestic and global socio-economic and technological trends and changes.

(a) As per my above comments, a balanced approach with a win–win–win mindset is key combining short-term with long-term considerations. People, culture and technology need to be organically aligned so that resources used lead into results obtained in as short-term a context as possible to establish credibility and gain cooperation and support from civil society.
(b) For that, top-level champions are needed as well as a strategic leveraging of social networking structures and infrastructures. In the past, regions around the world – whether the Silicon Valley in California, or the Route 128 region in the Boston area or others – have been identified as success benchmarks for innovation and entrepreneurship. However, simply emulating those has not always led to success, as people and culture are finicky and there are higher-order interdependencies and complexities involved.
(c) Here are some ideas as to how to set up policies and frameworks to provide as conducive as possible conditions for the creation of a sustainable and competitive entrepreneurship and innovation ecosystem:

    (c1) Advocate the need for a non-political, institutionally and meritocratically established entity that would function as part of the government in Lithuania and all other EU countries and could be called 'Ministry for Innovation and Entrepreneurship' but set up in a flexible manner to avoid becoming part of the problem.
    (c2) Advocate the need for an 'Ombudsman for Entrepreneurs and Innovators' with proper authority, visibility and resources to intervene and resolve barriers to innovation and entrerpeneurship (E&I) in Lithuania and across the EU (this is the

institutional civil society role in support of E&I as part of the quadruple innovation helix concept I have written about (Carayannis and Campbell, 2009, 2011) – government, university and industry working effectively with civil society to support and promote E&I).

(c3) Advocate the need for high-caliber volunteers among the Lithuanian diaspora as mentors as well as potential risk capital investors and strategic partners – in this context, I would propose forming a 'Global Lithuanian Diaspora Angel Investor Network' and 'The Global Lithuanian Diaspora Bond Issue for Entrepreneurs & Innovators' and to have the funds managed by a professional entity that is subject to the diaspora members in a transparent and efficient manner. The intent would be to allow for a pooling of resources, so along with large-scale donations, many small-size but cumulatively substantial contributions could start being made on a streamlined and sustainable basis and always focused on supporting and promoting E&I initiatives and efforts.

(d) Moreover, my descriptions of entrepreneurs and academics, based on 20 years of experience working with academics as well as entrepreneurs are as follows:

(d1) Entrepreneurs exhibit strongly the attributes of 'obsessed maniacs' focused on realizing their vision and 'clairvoyant oracles' seeing the opportunities and how to exploit them ahead of all others and being able to share that vision effectively with their key partners, investors and other early stakeholders.

(d2) Academics ideally should be 'entrepreneurs of the mind in the business of growing people intellectually and spiritually' (Carayannis, 2007).

(d3) Based on these descriptions, one should aim to inspire, empower and liberate the individual aspiring entrepreneurs (whether academic researchers and/or graduate students in science and engineering as well as other fields) to dare to dream big and dream in scientific/technological as well as commercial terms and to dare to take the next huge step of forming a company and asking people to invest in their dreams.

(d4) One of the ways to do so would be to establish across all of Lithuania's universities interlinked, complementary and reinforcing, cross-disciplinary graduate degrees focused on

E&I with emphasis on practice and aiming to produce at their conclusion working prototypes in the related science and engineering fields of the participants (from medical devices to agricultural techniques to software programs) and provide support and guidance for proper follow-through leading to the establishment of intellectual property rights (patents, trademarks, copyrights, trade secrets etc.) as well as the formation of companies to commercialize those prototypes. These companies should be supported by advisory boards as well as potential investors from both internal/domestic networks as well as the Lithuanian diaspora including the Global Lithuanian Diaspora Angel Investor Network and others.

5. *What is the key to obtaining financing: cooperation or acting alone?*

First of all innovation is a team effort, so some type of cooperation (including co-opetition or collaborating with your competitors under the right sets of conditions) is a sine qua non.

(a) The first key challenge typically is to bridge/overcome the so-called 'valley of death' hurdle – the lack of financing for early-stage ventures to get to the next level of growth and beyond a level of financing easily achieved with one's own resources.
(b) The comments above are part of the answer, and also patient and persistent policies and strategies that will nurture the development of an innovation ecosystem and the re-engineering of the mindsets of potential entrepreneurs and investors so that they will work better together and become better risk takers and risk evaluators over time.

6. *Could you compare US and European practices in the innovation-adopting area? Why is USA the leader in that? Do you have any suggestions for the scientists who are potential innovators?*

The USA retains an apparently eroding lead (see ITIF, 2010) thanks to earlier efforts starting with the Second World War, to promote E&I and also more E&I-friendly fiscal policies as well as the presence of a more accessible and large enough market.

(a) Fragmentation of markets, bureaucracy, lack of transparency, lack of the right mindsets, impeding fiscal and monetary policies – all these help to contribute to make things more difficult in Europe. However, there are many rays of hope in many regions across Europe, where clusters of innovative companies and innovation networks across regions and industries have been emerging. The Baltic region may well be the next one in this trend.

(b) Moreover, this trend can be further reinforced via a comprehensive and focused strategy to empower individual start-ups or spin-offs to be created in Lithuania with the intent and the underlying strategy to target and benchmark against competitors in the USA and to plan and enact entry in the USA from very early on. This strategy of 'co-location' is described above.

7. *Do incentive prizes help catalyze innovation? Why?*

Incentive prizes always help trigger invention and catalyze innovation (such as the X Prize in the USA, among others) but they can not suffice to ensure both high-quality as well as -quantity innovation beyond isolated events ('happy accidents' again). For sure, they help focus people's minds and provide them with an opportunity to compete with each other and also attain an apparent achievable goal.

8. *What is the importance of academic education as a pillar and driver of innovation?*

Academic education is key in order to provide the technical literacy and readiness to understand and leverage the messages nature is sending us and which we tend to realize through observing and learning from nature with an educated eye. In this regard, albeit there are cases of entrepreneurs who made it big with minimal education, education that is also tied organically with practice is a sine qua non for technology-driven innovation and entrepreneurship in particular.

9. *Do you think that fundamental or applied science is more useful for the economy? Why?*

This is a pseudo-dilemma in my opinion. Applied science stands on the shoulders of basic science but it takes longer for the fruits of basic science to manifest their value-adding potential, so we need to plan for and support both basic and applied science but with appropriately long horizons in each case as both provide the knowledge foundation or 'soil' in which the seeds of invention need to take roots so that the tree of innovation can grow and prosper.

(a) In this regard, the end of the cold war and the resulting shift in shorter-term priorities for the USA have to a considerable extent been very detrimental for the science enterprise in the USA and Vannevar Bush (President Roosevelt's Science Advisor who wrote a seminal report entitled *Science: The Endless Frontier* in 1946) would consider 1989 the beginning of the end of the 'Endless Frontier' as we have come to know it.
(b) Of course, the US society and economy have been shown capable of adapting and overcoming any and all challenges cast upon them to date – and the jury is still out as to whether, over the long run, more or less democratic regimes are more or less innovative.

10. What are your recommendations for the Lithuanian business and scientific community? We have a great lack of cooperation between science and business.

As I mentioned above, a major shift in mindset from 'tactical fragmentation' to 'strategic integration', both within Lithuania and across government, university, industry and civil society as well as across the Baltic states, the EU and the world – and surely the USA. More specifically, some initiatives that may need to engage both the Lithuanian society and government as well as the Lithuanian diaspora (LD) are:

(a) A strategicaly flexible, non-political and supra-governmental, civil-service-type 'Ministry for Innovation and Entrepreneurship', led and staffed by independent experts (domestic and foreign) as well as members of the LD primarily and on a non-career basis.
(b) The formation of an Office of the Ombudsman for Entrepreneurs and Innovators (OOEI) again independent and supported by LD members and other non-political entities, foundations etc.
(c) The Global Lithuanian Angel Investor Network and the Global Lithuanian Diaspora Bonds for Entrepreneurs and Innovators Initiative to provide, in a transparent and professionally managed manner, seed funding and risk capital for Lithuanian (primarily but not exclusively) high-technology inventor–entrepreneurs and surrogate entrepreneurs who are ready to develop the linchpins of the Lithuanian knowledge economy and society over the next ten years (let us call this initiative Lithuania 2020 to parallel the EU's Europe 2020 Plan and also to remind us of what was not accomplished with the Europe 2010 Lisbon Plan to help us learn and, we hope, avoid repeating the same mistakes twice at the country or continent levels.

(d) To establish across all of Lithuania's universities interlinked, complementary and reinforcing, cross-disciplinary graduate degrees focused on E&I with emphasis on practice and aiming to produce at their conclusion working prototypes in the related science and engineering fields of the participants (from medical devices to agricultural techniques to software programs) and provide support and guidance for proper follow-through, leading to the establishment of intellectual property rights (patents, trademarks, copyrights, trade secrets etc.) as well as the formation of companies to commercialize those prototypes. These companies should be supported by advisory boards as well as potential investors from both internal/domestic networks as well as the Lithuanian diaspora including the Global Lithuanian Diaspora Angel Investor Network and others.

7. Spatial knowledge spillovers within and between European regions: a meta-analysis[1]

Urban Gråsjö, Charlie Karlsson and Peter Warda

1. INTRODUCTION

During the last decade we have been able to observe a veritable explosion of interest in 'knowledge spillovers'. A search using Google Scholar on April 2011 limited to 'business, administration, finance and economics' gave 18 000 hits of which more than 70 per cent were from the period 2002–11. This explosive increase in interest in the concept among researchers mirrors both an increased scientific interest and an increased interest among policy makers in the topic. The increased interest among researchers is undoubtedly stimulated by the developments in endogenous growth theory during the two last decades. Among policy makers, we can trace a substantially increased interest in 'knowledge spillovers', not least among those within Europe. In fact, 75 per cent of the 18 000 hits contain the word 'Europe'. In Europe, it is in particular within the European Union (EU) that 'knowledge spillovers' have come into focus. The Lisbon Agenda confirmed by EU leaders in March 2000, which aims to create a climate in Europe that stimulates innovation, competitiveness and economic growth, has put 'knowledge spillovers' on the European policy agenda.

The earliest reference to 'knowledge spillovers' that we have been able to find is Griliches and Lichtenberg (1984, p. 466), who define 'pure knowledge spillovers' as 'the cross-fertilization of one industry's research program by developments occurring in other industries', that is, as inter-industry spillovers. However, it should be observed that research and development 'spillovers' were discussed in, for example, Griliches (1979). These early contributions to the study of knowledge spillovers all disregarded the effect of 'the tyranny of distance' on knowledge spillovers; that is, they were totally non-spatial. It was not until the 1990s that researchers started to study the geographical extent of knowledge spillovers (Jaffe et

Table 7.1 Number of hits using Google Scholar, 10 April 2011

Search term	Number of hits	Number of hits when Europe is added
Interregional knowledge spillovers	89	84
Inter-regional knowledge spillovers	47	44
Regional knowledge spillovers	345	289
Local knowledge spillovers	487	399
Geographic knowledge spillovers	122	93
Geographical knowledge spillovers	123	111
Spatial knowledge spillovers	293	193
Intraregional knowledge spillovers	8	8
Intra-regional knowledge spillovers	20	18

al., 1993; Audretsch and Feldman, 1996). We found the first use of the term 'inter-regional knowledge spillovers' in Premer and Walz (1994), the first use of 'regional knowledge spillovers' in Englmann and Walz (1995), the first use of 'local knowledge spillovers' in Head et al. (1995) and Englmann and Walz (1995), the first use of 'geographic knowledge spillovers' in Anselin et al. (1997), the first use of 'spatial knowledge spillovers' in Keilbach (1998), the first use of 'intra-regional knowledge spillovers' in Dohse (2000) and the first use of 'geographical knowledge spillovers' in Wallsten (2001). In Table 7.1, we illustrate the total number of hits for all these terms according to Google Scholar on 10 April 2011. We can observe that an overwhelming majority of the publications dealing with spatial aspects of knowledge spillovers also contains some kind of reference to Europe.

The interest in spatial knowledge spillovers has its background in that the existence of localized knowledge spillovers is one possible explanation for the industrial clustering that we can observe (Krugman, 1991, 1998) – a clustering that is greater than would be expected if the geographic distribution of firms and jobs were random (Ellison and Glaeser, 1997). Evidences of knowledge spillovers that are geographically bounded have been found in many studies (see, e.g., Jaffe, 1989; Jaffe et al., 1993). However, many existing studies have explored these issues only within large geographic units, such as nations, states or very large regions such as the NUTS-2 regions within the EU, which has made it impossible to determine in more detail the spatial reach of knowledge spillovers (Wallsten, 2001). Since firms in an industry normally cluster at a finer spatial scale even within cities, and since the hypothesis is that firms located in proximity to each other benefit from knowledge spillovers, most studies give little specific information about how distance as well as the local firm density matter for knowledge spillovers.

How should we understand this huge interest in spatial aspects of knowledge spillovers in general and in Europe in particular? One obvious reason is the long-standing observation that regions within integrated economic areas such as the EU tend to diverge rather than converge with regard to per capita incomes and labour productivity. This is of course puzzling, not least for many economists. The observed patterns of divergence are not in line with the predictions of the spatial version of the neoclassical growth model, where mobility of capital and labour over the long run would even out differences between regions (Borts and Stein, 1964). Neither are they in line with the more recent endogenous growth theory *à la* Romer (1986, 1990) and Lucas (1993), which builds upon the presumption that new knowledge is instantaneously and freely available to all economic agents because knowledge is assumed automatically and instantaneously to spill over from the economic agent generating the knowledge to all other economic agents.

In a similar manner, Griliches (1992) perceived that knowledge would spill over from the economic agent investing in new knowledge to be used by other economic agents at low or no cost. Knowledge can spill over and thus generate externalities since, being an intellectual asset, it differs from other factors of production by being non-exclusive and non-rivalrous (Arrow, 1962) and thus generating appropriability problems for those economic agents generating new knowledge. Even if knowledge can spill over, it does not imply that spillovers are automatic and instantaneous. New knowledge is highly uncertain and context specific, and is primarily diffused by means of face-to-face interaction, which implies that the diffusion of new knowledge is associated with high transaction costs. Hence early diffusion of new knowledge tends to be geographically limited to a spatial scale that allows frequent face-to-face interaction, which is normally equal to the daily interaction space of people. The spatial diffusion of knowledge is associated with frictions, which increase with distance, which gives a clear advantage to locations where knowledge-generating activities for one reason or another have started to cluster. However, economists have in the postwar period developed various explanations for divergent economic development in different regions, such as the theory of development poles (Perroux, 1955), theories of cumulative causation in economic growth (Myrdal, 1957; Dixon and Thirlwall, 1975) and theories of economic agglomeration, such as the 'new economic geography' (Krugman, 1991), which highlights the links between economic integration and agglomeration.

To understand the diverging development within the EU and within its member states we need a theoretical framework that is able to explain the interaction between economic integration, the location of peoples and economic activities, and long-run growth in a system of regions. That growth affects location and location affects growth has strong theoretical foundations. It is in principle a basic characteristic of all endogenous growth models that they depend upon technical externalities in the form of knowledge spillovers or production externalities. That such externalities are connected with the spatial distribution of R&D activities and/or production has been documented empirically (see Eaton and Kortum, 1996). Against this background it is natural to assume that agglomeration of production and/or R&D activities will stimulate growth and that growth will stimulate agglomeration of production and/or R&D due to the existence of the actual externalities.

Thus there exists a theoretical framework capable of explaining the dynamic interaction between location and growth in a system of regions, when externalities are present. However, to understand the importance and spatial scale at which the actual externalities operate, we need detailed empirical studies. Thus there is a need to establish the pervasiveness of externalities based upon geographical proximity as well as the distances over which they operate (cf. Head et al., 1995). In the sequel, we will focus on one type of such externalities, namely knowledge spillovers. The empirical studies of the effects of knowledge spillovers in Europe have normally focused on the localized effects on either total factor productivity or knowledge production measured in terms of patent output.

The purpose of this chapter is to quantitatively review the empirical literature on spatial knowledge spillovers in Europe by means of meta-analysis to determine the extent to which such spillovers have been empirically documented, as well as their spatial reach. In addition, we will apply meta-regression analysis to analyse the determinants of observed heterogeneity across and between studies. Thoroughly assessed empirical information on these issues is particularly important for the design of policies at the EU, the national and the regional level aimed at increasing knowledge production.

Meta-analysis can be described as a set of statistical and econometric methods that can be used to summarize, analyse and evaluate the empirical results from a set of primary studies focusing on a specific research question (Stanley and Jarrell, 1989; Stanley, 2001). It offers a more systematic and objective way to evaluate the results from a number of empirical studies compared to conventional literature reviews, which have difficulties in comparing different empirical studies due to differences in theoretical frameworks, empirical models, econometric methods and data definitions. Meta-analysis makes it possible to statistically analyse the variation over studies by means of basic economic variables and variations in research design. By applying meta-analysis to empirical studies of knowledge spillovers in Europe, we will be able to estimate the effect of knowledge spillovers on total factor productivity and knowledge production in Europe as well as the spatial reach of these effects, which is of great interest to policy makers interested in promoting economic growth in Europe.

The outline of this chapter is as follows: Section 2 discusses spatial knowledge spillovers by definition, methodological approaches and some stylized facts. Section 3 presents the meta-analysis and the results from gathering the data for the meta-regression analysis. The chapter offers an overview of the meta-sample and descriptive statistics from the publications that have been analysed in order to obtain a sample. Section 4 comprises the meta-regression analysis. Here we present our methodology, empirical model and analysis. Two models are estimated, one for local knowledge effects and the other for spillover knowledge effects. The final section concludes.

2. SPATIAL KNOWLEDGE SPILLOVERS

2.1 Definitions

Griliches (1979, p. 104) describes 'knowledge spillovers' as 'working on similar things and hence benefiting much from each other's research'. However, there is of course no guarantee that both parties gain or even gain equally when knowledge diffuses between economic agents. The principal idea behind the use of the concept 'knowledge spillovers' is that they are associated with externalities; that is, that knowledge generated by one economic agent can be used by other economic agents without any compensation paid to the generating economic agent who has carried the costs for the knowledge generation. However, it is important that knowledge may flow as a result of knowledge transactions or as a by-product of other transactions and that 'pure knowledge spillovers' only make up a (possibly minor) part of all knowledge flows. The implication is that not all knowledge flows are associated with externalities (Breschi and Lissoni, 2009).

Karlsson and Johansson (2006) argue that from the perspective of a firm one can separate three groups of knowledge flows that may generate knowledge spillovers:

- transaction-based knowledge flows,
- transaction-related knowledge flows, and
- pure knowledge spillovers.[2]

Table 7.2 Classification of knowledge flows to a firm

Knowledge flow category	Knowledge flow type
Transaction-based flows:	• Flows from knowledge providers that sell knowledge that is used as an input to a firm's R&D activities • Flows in the form of inventions (innovations) that are sold to a firm (e.g. by licensing a patent) • Knowledge flows between firms that cooperate in an R&D project, where costs and benefits are regulated by an explicit or an implicit contract, which may or may not be associated with unintentional knowledge spillovers • A firm obtains access to knowledge via a merger or an acquisition
Transaction-related flows:	• A flow of knowledge that is embodied in the delivery of inputs from an input supplier to a firm • In the course of supplying inputs to a firm, knowledge from the input supplier spills over unintentionally to the input-buying firm • In the course of supplying inputs to a firm, knowledge from the input-buying firm spills over unintentionally to the input-selling firm
Pure spillover flows	• Unintentionally, knowledge spills over from one firm to a competing firm in the same industry • Unintentionally, knowledge spills over between firms belonging to different industries

Source: Karlsson and Johansson (2006).

The three categories are presented in Table 7.2 together with nine types of knowledge flows.

From a firm's point of view, one can make a distinction between upstream, downstream and horizontal knowledge and technology flows. Upstream knowledge flows are helpful in generating access to suppliers' knowledge and technology often embedded in inputs bought by a firm. Downstream knowledge flows include the sale of knowledge and technology to customers either as licences or embedded in products. Horizontal knowledge and technology flows include intended and unintended knowledge and technology flows between firms in the same industry. Upstream and downstream knowledge and technology flows are inter-sectoral, while horizontal knowledge and technology flows are intra-sectoral.

From Table 7.2 it is obvious that the extent to which knowledge flows are associated with 'externalities' obviously varies a great deal between the different types of knowledge flows. It is also clear from the table that 'knowledge spillovers' and thus 'externalities' may exist also in cases where market mechanisms are operating. To the extent that knowledge flows are connected with externalities, we may make a distinction between three types of externalities, which also are the three main agglomeration forces according to the 'new economic geography' approach:

- pecuniary externalities, i.e. externalities due to market interactions;
- technological externalities, i.e. externalities due to non-market interactions;
- human capital externalities, i.e. externalities due to the mobility between firms of employees with embodied knowledge.

Breschi and Lissoni (2001) argue that it is important to improve the understanding of the transmission mechanisms of knowledge in addition to measuring knowledge spillovers by a rather limited set of indicators. There are several mechanisms that support and facilitate the transfer and diffusion of tacit as well as codified knowledge (cf. Arrow, 1994) and technology:

- education
- communication channels that are interactive and have a high bandwidth (e.g. e-mail, the Internet etc.)
- deliberate policy (e.g. organizations setting up scouting and knowledge intelligence units)
- R&D collaboration
- special activities of people in order to obtain and disseminate knowledge (e.g. gatekeepers, cf. Allen, 1977),
- mobility of people with the relevant knowledge and skills
- trade in goods and services
- trade in knowledge and technologies
- direct investments
- intra-firm knowledge management
- imitation and reverse engineering (cf. Verspagen, 1994).

It is important to observe that even if each of these channels or mechanisms can be seen as partly independent, they are often linked to each other in different ways. It is in this connection important to observe that international collaborations are also a significant and increasingly important channel for transfer of knowledge and technology in both the private and the public sector (Archibugi and Coco, 2004). An increasing number of partnerships among firms, universities and public research centres as well as between individual researchers and inventors is a clear indication of the growing importance of collaboration (NSF, 2002). Collaboration permits the partners to share and acquire each other's expertise, thus enriching the overall know-how. It can function as a positive sum game, where the advantages outweigh the disadvantages even if the advantages are not always equally shared among partners (Archibugi and Lundvall, 2001). The total number and type of collaborations can be taken as a measure on the one hand of the vitality of the regional, national and international knowledge systems, and on the other hand as an indicator of the extent and types of knowledge and technology transfers. The attractiveness of the knowledge base of economic agents will determine the extent to which they are invited to participate in collaborative ventures.

However, due to spatial frictions, we can expect that different mechanisms for the transfer of knowledge and technology differ in their effectiveness in transferring knowledge and technology at different distances. As much knowledge and technology tends to have a degree of tacitness, to be highly complex and/or highly contextual, it is often assumed that knowledge spillovers are bounded in geographical space. This implies that it is important to understand why location matters for knowledge flows of different kinds (Autant-Bernard et al., 2007). We need not only understand the spatial reach of knowledge flows but also their time profile. There is also a need to understand the mechanisms by which different types of knowledge and technologies are transferred, why transfer is unequal over space and the implications in terms of innovative performance in different locations. To achieve a better understanding of knowledge flows and the mechanisms that stimulate innovation performance, there is a need to evaluate by means of meta-analyses the results of the numerous empirical studies of knowledge spillovers performed in recent years. Certainly, such a meta-analysis is not enough to understand why and how location matters. There is also a need for complementary analyses of phenomena such as mobility of researchers, foreign direct investments, R&D collaborations, imports of knowledge-intensive products and entrepreneurial activities using micro-data (Audretsch and Feldman, 2004). Furthermore, to evaluate fully the impact of the spatial dimension it is important also to consider the influence of other proximities than the geographical, such as technological, institutional, organizational and social. However, at least the three last of these proximities are a function, among other things, of geographical proximity.

2.2 Methodologies Employed in the Literature

2.2.1 Different methodological approaches

Studies of spatial knowledge spillovers fall within study field 'geography of innovation' (Karlsson and Manduchi, 2001; Audretsch and Feldman, 2004). One common approach here has been to estimate how the knowledge output of firms in different locations is influenced by the research and innovation activities of other firms in the same as well as other locations to determine the influence of proximity on knowledge output. The extent of knowledge flows and knowledge spillovers is generally measured by the patterns of patent and publication citations, technology licensing or the degree of co-patenting and co-publication activities of researchers at universities and research institutes and in industry (Jaffe et al., 1993; Audretsch and Feldman, 1996; Crespi et al., 2006; Ponds et al., 2007).[3]

Many researchers think that patent citations can be used as a measure of technological impact and knowledge spillovers, in the sense that one specific technological innovation explicitly detects several others as being the technological state-of-the-art on which it is based. Patent citations have been used to analyse questions concerning spatial knowledge spillovers (see, e.g., Jaffe et al., 1993) and spillovers from public research (see, e.g., Jaffe and Trajtenberg, 1996; Jaffe and Lerner, 1999). However, patent citations are by no means a perfect measure of knowledge spillovers or flows since citations to patents not known to the inventor(s) may be added in the patenting process. Thus patent citations are a noisy measure but they have a substantial information content (Jaffe et al., 2000).

Many studies have focused only on disentangling the effects of 'pure' non-market 'knowledge spillovers', that is, technological spillovers, but attempts have also been made to estimate the effects of market-based knowledge flows (Autant-Bernard and Massard, 2007; Miguélez and Moreno, 2010).

2.2.2 The knowledge production function approach

According to Feldman (1999), it is possible to categorize studies of knowledge effects in regions into four types: (i) geographic knowledge production functions; (ii) paper trails left in patent citations; (iii) ideas in people; or (iv) ideas in goods. Studying the literature reveals a clear dominance of the use of geographic knowledge production functions and this approach is also the focus of our meta-analysis. The framework for analysing the importance of knowledge and knowledge spillovers for innovative activity is usually based on the knowledge production function (KPF) of Griliches

(1979). The framework was later developed with a geographical dimension by Jaffe (1989).

Spatial spillovers and spatial dependence can be accounted for in various ways. Following Anselin (2003), the spatial effects can be either (i) unmodelled, (ii) modelled or (iii) both unmodelled and modelled. If the spatial spillovers are global, that is, every location is correlated with every other location, but the correlations decreases with distance, the inclusion of a spatial multiplier effect of the form $(I - \lambda W)^{-1}$ models the spatial effects. Equations (7.1) to (7.3) show the three structural forms.

Unmodelled effects: $$y = x\beta + (I - \lambda W)^{-1}u \tag{7.1}$$

Modelled effects: $$y = (I - \lambda W)^{-1}x\beta + u \tag{7.2}$$

Both effects: $$y = (I - \lambda W)^{-1}x\beta + (I - \lambda W)^{-1}u \tag{7.3}$$

with $(I - \lambda W)^{-1} = I + \lambda W) + \lambda^2 W^2 + \ldots$ and $|\lambda| < 1$

where y is the dependent variable, W is a spatial weight matrix, λ is a spatial autoregressive parameter, x is a matrix of independent variables, β is a vector of regression parameters and u is a vector of independent disturbance terms, $u \sim N(0, \sigma^2)$.[4]

The question is then which model to choose. The answer depends very much on the case under study. Let us assume that the objective is to find to what extent R&D can account for the variations in regions' patent production.

- If the interest is limited to the local effects of R&D; that is, how R&D conducted in region i affects patent production in region i, then the answer is unmodelled effects.
- If the interest is to find both the local effects and the spatial spillovers of R&D; that is, how patent production in region i is affected by R&D efforts in municipality i, j, k, . . ., then the answer is modelled effects.
- If the interest is to estimate local effects of R&D and spatial dependencies of patent production; that is, how patent production in region i is affected by patent production in region j, k, . . ., then the answer is both effects.

Our focus is to find and investigate studies that estimate the importance of spatial spillovers of explanatory variables (studies with 'modelled effects').

2.3 Stylized Facts

Botazzi and Peri (2000) estimate a production function of innovation for European regions using patent and R&D data for the period 1977 to 1995. The main aim of the paper is to analyse the geographical relation between market size and innovative activity. R&D employment and R&D expenditure are used as inputs for both local and spillover knowledge effects.[5] The authors find that knowledge externalities exist within a geographical area of 200 kilometres; however, it decreases fast with increased distance. Thus knowledge spillovers are not strong enough to generate sustained growth in the region. One effect that might cause knowledge spillovers in Europe is that regions close to each other use similar technologies.

Another paper by Botazzi and Peri (2003) uses similar methodology, variables and time period, but different weighting techniques in terms of distance. The results show that knowledge spillovers exist within a 300-kilometre distance. Similar to the former study, the spillover effects to neighbouring regions are rather small, though large in the local region. Doubling the R&D expenditure in a region increases innovation by 2 to 3 per cent within a 300-kilometre distance, whereas the region itself benefits from an increase in innovation between 80 to 90 per cent.

Crescenzi et al. (2007) analyse the dynamics of innovation in a Europe–USA perspective using a knowledge production function framework. The focus is on a set of territorial processes that influence innovative activity. Local knowledge effects are estimated in terms of R&D expenditure as a share of regional GDP, whereas the spillover effects are weighted through a spatial average of neighbouring regions' R&D expenditure.[6] They find that Europe is far behind the USA in innovation and technology. An imperfect market integration along with institutional and cultural barriers work against Europe in catching up with the USA. However, increased European integration through geographical processes such as advances in road systems, ICT and firm cooperation might help Europe to close the innovation gap.

Crescenzi and Rodrigues-Pose (2008) use multiple regression analysis to estimate effects from R&D, knowledge spillovers and proxies for regional innovation systems. A total of 25 EU members are analysed with the possibility to discriminate between local and non-local knowledge spillovers. Local knowledge effects are measured in terms of R&D expenditure as a share of gross regional product. The knowledge spillover inputs comprise weighted accessibility to extra-regional innovation. The empirical results show that the complex interaction between local and non-local research shapes the innovation capacity in all regions. Proximity is highly important for knowledge creation, since spillovers are strongly affected when the distance increases.

The central focus in Hauser et al. (2008) is to analyse how innovation is spatially distributed between regions in Europe. The authors suggest that the spatial pattern of input variables (such as R&D expenditure and human capital) in innovation processes drives patenting autocorrelation, that is, knowledge spillovers. To prove this relationship they use a knowledge production function that measures innovative activity in form of patent applications. The local knowledge effect takes the form of R&D expenditure per worker. The empirical results show that there is a high degree of spatial autocorrelation in patent applications. The spatial location of the input variables has a significant effect on patent applications, and hence drives knowledge spillovers.

Krammer (2009) analyses the innovation impact in transition countries, before and after the fall of communism in Eastern European countries. Innovative output, as explained by the number of patents, is estimated by a knowledge production function. Various factors that measure innovative output are considered, such as: skill of labour, productivity, R&D investment, existing stock of knowledge and other factors that influence knowledge creation in transition countries. Local knowledge effects are estimated in terms of R&D expenditure (total, private and public). The results confirm that universities and the existing knowledge base (in the form of private and public R&D) have a crucial impact in augmenting the number of patents as countries go into transition.

In Maggioni et al. (2007) the focus is on geographical and relational spillovers to study the effects of patenting activity in regions within five European countries. They use a gravity model of co-patenting that explains how knowledge flows between inventors in one region and inventors in another region. The model incorporates private and public R&D expenditure in local and non-regions, technological similarities, geographical distance, common borders and so on. Another gravity model is suggested to study the effect of co-patenting in the local region. OLS (ordinary least squares) estimations show that private R&D expenditure induces larger spillover effects from one region to another than public R&D expenditure. Moreover, technological similarities are proven to have a positive effect on co-patenting between two regions.

Moreno et al. (2003, 2005) analyse the spatial distribution of innovative activity and technological spillovers across 138 and 175 regions, respectively, in 17 European countries. Both papers estimate, for different time periods, a knowledge production function of innovative activity. Local effects are explained by R&D expenditure as a share of GDP, whereas the spillover effects are estimated via contiguity matrices of R&D and weight matrices with neighbours portion of local R&D up to 750 and 500 kilometres, respectively. In Moreno et al. (2003) the results show that spillovers are significant up to a distance of 500 km (i.e. up to a second-order neighbourhood). However, in Moreno et al. (2005) this relationship is only significant up to a distance of 250 km (i.e. up to a first-order neighbourhood). The results from both papers indicate that technological similarities between regions are important for knowledge to spill over.

In a working paper by Pinto (2010), the knowledge production function framework is adapted to analyse how regions within the EU transform specific inputs to local knowledge outputs (i.e. patents per capita). Panel data analysis is applied to 25 countries and 125 regions for the period 1999 to 2003. Local effects enter the knowledge production function in terms of private and public R&D expenditure as a share of GDP. The results show that private R&D expenditure tends to be more important for knowledge production in the local region.

Pinto and Rodrigues (2010) estimate a knowledge production function to draw conclusions on how regional innovation strategies have affected knowledge creation. A total of 175 European regions are analysed over the period 1994 to 2001. A model is fitted to explain how local knowledge, measured in terms of patents and high-technology patents, is related to local R&D activities. The knowledge production function uses private and public R&D expenditure as a share of regional GDP as input variables for local knowledge effects. The paper concludes that private R&D expenditure is of high relevance to increasing the number of patents within a region.

The purpose in Varga et al. (2010) is to analyse the effects of intraregional agglomeration as due to R&D productivity across 189 regions within the EU. The study utilizes a knowledge production function that explains how innovation (in terms of patents) is related to a local knowledge variable in form of lagged gross regional R&D expenditure. The study observes that innovation flows are more than proportionate to R&D inputs. Moreover, agglomeration of innovation systems has a positive effect on R&D productivity. Thus knowledge interactions within European regions are of high importance for innovative activity to flow.

The central focus in Greunz (2003) is to study the effects of interregional knowledge spillovers across 153 European sub-national regions. A regional knowledge production function is fitted to answer the question whether geographical and technological proximities matter for knowledge creation in Europe. Knowledge spillovers are measured in terms of patents and are explained by a set of local and spillover knowledge inputs. R&D expenditure per capita (total, private and public) enters the function as a local knowledge input. The spillover knowledge variable is represented by

R&D expenditure weighted by distance to geographical neighbours. Interregional knowledge spillovers seem to exist between regions close to one another and between regions with technological similarities. Moreover, the empirical results show that knowledge spillovers in Europe are mainly driven by private R&D expenditure. However, given that knowledge spillovers exist within a nation, its national borders tend to dampen the spread of interregional knowledge flows further in Europe.

From the above 13 publications we have managed to extract local knowledge effects in all publications (110 observations). The local knowledge effect is frequently reported in terms of R&D expenditure. On the other hand, the spillover effect has been far more difficult to interpret due to various methodologies adapted in the empirical regression analysis of these publications. Thus we have been able to isolate only 75 observations from 7 of the above publications. Most commonly the spillover knowledge effect takes the form of R&D-weighted contiguity matrices.[7]

3. A SIMPLE META-ANALYSIS

3.1 The Meta-Sample

The data for the meta-analysis on knowledge spillovers in Europe were collected via an extensive search for studies that correspond to a set of lowest common denominators. The time period for the studies analysed ranges from 2000 to 2010. Key phrases used to find publications of interest comprise: 'knowledge production function and Europe' and/or 'knowledge spillovers and Europe'. Additional requirements for a specific publication to be included in the analysis are: Europe must be the focus area; it applies quantitative methods; it includes a minimum of five European countries; and the publication must contain a specific knowledge coefficient measuring local and/or spillover effects from one region to another. Thus we are interested in publications that estimate spatial spillover effects using a knowledge production function framework for at least five European countries. Equation (7.4) presents a typical knowledge production function that has been encountered in the literature review:

$$Y_i = \alpha_0 + \beta_1 x_i + \beta_2 (Wx)_j + \sum_{k=1}^{n} \gamma_k z_{ki} \tag{7.4}$$

Y_i is the dependent variable indicating knowledge production (or output) in region i, for example through number of patents, patents per capita, total factor productivity or wages. x_i and x_j are the knowledge inputs in

Table 7.3 Meta-explanatory variables

1. Time period	2. Estimation method (e.g. OLS, GLS, ML)
3. Time lag between input and output (1, 2,. . ., years)	4. Testing for spatial dependence (spatial autocorrelation tests)
5. Number of countries	6. Type of spatial model (spatial lag, spatial error, accessibility, distance band, nearest neighbour)
7. Coverage of economy (services, manufacturing or total etc.)	8. Type of main explanatory variable (R&D and human-capital-related variables)
9. Type of data (panel, cross-section)	10. Type of dependent variable (in form of patents, wages, total factor productivity)
11. Type of geographic unit (NUTS)	12. Other variables that characterize the publication

region i and j ($i \neq j$), respectively, and comprise indicators such as R&D employment, R&D expenditures and human capital in form of educated labour. W is a spatial weight matrix. z_{ki} is a vector that measures other covariates in region i. α_0 is the intercept coefficient and β_1, β_2 and γ_k are coefficients. The variables Y, x and z can enter the function in log form depending on whether the structural form is additive by nature or multiplicative, for example taking the form of a Cobb–Douglas production function.

To perform the meta-regression analysis, the coefficient for β_2 (or β_1) needs to be specified in our empirical model as the dependent variable. Table 7.3 presents other meta-explanatory variables that have been considered when gathering information from the empirical literature on knowledge spillovers in Europe.

Most data for the Y_i variable in the relevant publications has been generated from the European Patent Office and Eurostat in the form of annual patent data. However, the main focus of the meta-analysis is aimed at the coefficients β_1 and β_2, along with their standard errors. Estimators like these are often characterized by either marginal effects (i.e. additive) or in form of elasticities (i.e. multiplicative).

If the interest is to conduct a meta-analysis on spatial spillover effects, then β_2 is the relevant coefficient; that is, what influence knowledge input in region j has on knowledge output in region i. Many publications in our review have not isolated the spillover effect, which thus encourages a further gathering of information about β_1 (i.e. the local effect of knowledge input). The majority of publications that fit our requirements have empirically analysed the effect of β_1 and used various weighting techniques to control for spatial dependence. In order to satisfy the aim of the meta-analysis, β_1 and β_2 are defined in equations 7.5 and 7.6:

$$\beta_1 = \beta_{Lip^c}, \tag{7.5}$$

$$\beta_2 = \beta_{Sjp^c}, \tag{7.6}$$

$$p = (1, 2, \ldots, n) \text{ and } c = (1, 2, \ldots, m)$$

where β_{Lip^c} is the local knowledge variable in region i and β_{Sjp^c} is the spillover knowledge variable in region j. The subscript term p refers to a specific empirical publication and c is the cth β coefficient in publication p. From now on we use the terms β_1 and β_2 in our discussion.

3.2 Results of the Meta-Analysis

Table 7.4 presents an overview of the publications that have been analysed in the meta-analysis. Each publication displays a certain amount of information that has been gathered in order to generate a data sample. The variables reported include the number of β coefficients (i.e. how many of each β_1 and β_2 there are per publication), what type of local and spillover knowledge variable is utilized, number of countries, time period, geographical unit (i.e. NUTS), dependent variable and the number of observations used in the empirical application.

The local knowledge variable in region i is usually reported as R&D employment or R&D expenditure. An important point of discussion regards the large variation between the coefficients for β_1 and β_2. Each publication has a unique approach to measuring knowledge production from one region to another (i.e. the knowledge inputs x_i and x_j differ a great deal between publications). While some use the total effect of R&D expenditure to measure spillovers, others apply the variable in per capita or per worker, as private or public expenditure, with natural logarithms or as a share of gross domestic product or gross regional product. Thus we need to evaluate carefully the implications of each specific measure of knowledge production spillovers in order to avoid any misinterpretation of the effect it has on the dependent variable (i.e. in Y_i).

The second column in Table 7.4 reports the total number of β coefficients per publication.[8] Our total sample of publications that use a quantitative approach is equal to 13.[9] Out of these, we have generated 110 β coefficients for the local knowledge variable in region i and 75 β

*Table 7.4 Meta-analysis sample overview**

Publication (p)	β_1 coefficients per study	β_1	β_1 coefficients per study	β_2	European countries	Time period	NUTS	Dependent variable = Y_i	N
Botazzi and Peri (2000): WP	16	$\ln RD_{EMP}$ $\ln RD_{EMP/W}$ $\ln RD_{EXP}$	16	$\ln RD_{EMP}$ $\ln RD_{EMP/W}$ $\ln RD_{EXP}$ weighted by distance	12	1977–95	1/2	$\ln YP_{APP}$; $\ln YP_{APP/W}$	86
Botazzi and Peri (2003): WP	8	$\ln RD_{EMP}$ $\ln RD_{EXP}$	8	$\ln RD_{EMP}$ $\ln RD_{SPE}$ weighted by distance	12	1977–95	0/1/2	$\ln YP_{APP}$	86
Crescenzi et al. (2007): WP	6	$RD_{EXP\%GRP}$	6	SWANR	8	1990–2002	1/2	$\ln YP_{APP}$	97
Crescenzi and Rodriguez-Pose (2008): J	11	$RD_{EXP\%GRP}$	11	AERI TAIPS AIPEA $AERI_{WEI}$	15	1995–2003	1/2	$\ln GDP_{CAP}$	166
Hauser et al. (2008): J	1	$\ln RD_{EXP/W}$	0	N/A	6	Average 97/99/01	1	$\ln YP_{APP/C}$	51
Krammer (2009): J	16	$\ln RD_{EXP}$ $\ln RD_{EXPG}$ $\ln RD_{EXPB}$	0	N/A	16	1990–2007	1	PGY	126–221

Maggioni et al. (2007): J	4	$RD_{EXPG\%GDP}$ $RD_{EXPB\%GDP}$	0	N/A	5	1995–2001	1/2	P	51
Moreno et al. (2003): WP	13	$lnRD_{EXP\%GDP}$	12	lnRD weighted by distance	17	1978–97	1/2	lnP_{CAP}	123
Moreno et al. (2005): J	11	$lnRD_{EXP\%GDP}$	9	lnRD weighted by distance	15	1978–2001	0/1/2	lnP_{CAP}	175
Pinto (2010): WP	4	$RD_{G\%GDP}$ $RD_{B\%GDP}$	0	N/A	25	1999–2003	1/2	P_{CAP}	125
Pinto and Rodrigues (2010): J	4	$lnRD_{EXPG\%GRP}$ $lnRD_{EXPB\%GRP}$	0	N/A	15	1994–2001	2	lnP lnHTP	175
Varga et al. (2010): WP	6	$lnRD_{EXP}$	0	N/A	23	2000–2002	1/2	lnP	567
Greunz (2003): J	10	$lnRD_{EXP/C}$ $lnRD_{EXPG/C}$ $lnRD_{EXPB/C}$	13	$lnRD_{EXP}$ $lnRD_{EXPG}$ $lnRD_{EXPB}$ weighted by distance	14	1989–96	0/1/2	lnP_{CAP}	1184–224
$\Sigma p = 13$ Total:	110		75						

Notes:
WP = working paper; J = article in journal.
* In order to fit Table 3.2 conveniently on to two pages, some meta-explanatory variables have been excluded in the presentation of the table. See Appendix for further details on the abbreviations in columns three (for β_1) and five (for β_2).

Table 7.5 Descriptive statistics for $\beta_1 = \beta_{Lip}$

Publication (p)	β_1 coeffi-cients	β_1				
		Mean	Std dev.	Median	Min.	Max.
Botazzi and Peri (2000): WP	16	0.966	0.100	0.965	0.830	1.280
Botazzi and Peri (2003): WP	8	0.855	0.065	0.835	0.790	0.960
Crescenzi et al. (2007): WP	6	0.369	0.449	0.395	−0.145	0.960
Crescenzi and Rodriguez-Pose (2008): J	11	0.171	0.037	0.166	0.137	0.268
Hauser et al. (2008): J	1	0.600	0.000	0.600	0.600	0.600
Krammer (2009): J	16	0.150	0.077	0.141	−0.050	0.274
Maggioni et al. (2007): J	4	0.230	0.323	0.235	−0.060	0.510
Moreno et al. (2003): WP	13	0.493	0.037	0.485	0.429	0.551
Moreno et al. (2005): J	11	0.260	0.022	0.257	0.225	0.294
Pinto (2010): WP	4	0.686	0.443	0.688	0.290	1.080
Pinto and Rodrigues (2010): J	4	0.237	0.346	0.256	−0.153	0.588
Varga et al. (2010): WP	6	0.833	0.160	0.780	0.688	1.082
Greunz (2003): J	10	0.320	0.194	0.400	0.030	0.570
$\Sigma p = 13$ Overall:	110	0.468	0.346	0.445	−0.153	1.280

Notes:
WP = working paper.
J = article in journal.
β_1 = local knowledge variable in region i derived from the cth β coefficient in publication p.

coefficients that measure the spillover of knowledge from region j. The number of countries that are analysed varies from 5 to 25, where most focus is on countries in the EU-15. The time period studied also differs between publications. Some begin as early as the 1970s, while other knowledge production functions are estimated from the mid-1990s and onwards.

A number of publications also mixes different geographical units. The most common unit varies between NUTS-1 (economic country-level data) and NUTS-2 (economic region-level data). Yearly patent applications and number of patents, in log form, take the form of the dependent variable in the majority of publications (i.e. the Y_i). The number of observations per empirical study (i.e. N) varies a great deal from one publication to another. The lowest number of observations is 51 and the highest is 1224.

Table 7.5 presents the descriptive statistics for the β_1 coefficients obtained from the 13 publications. The table includes the mean value, median, standard deviation from the mean value, as well as the lowest and highest value.

The publications we have analysed are issued in the period 2000 to 2010.

Table 7.6 Descriptive statistics for $\beta_2 = \beta_{Sip}$

Publication (p)	β_1 coefficients	β_2				
		Mean	Std dev.	Median	Min.	Max.
Botazzi and Peri (2000): WP	16	0.071	0.027	0.080	0.032	0.110
Botazzi and Peri (2003): WP	8	0.022	0.009	0.027	0.004	0.030
Crescenzi et al. (2007): WP	6	7.982	0.466	8.118	7.066	8.311
Crescenzi and Rodriguez-Pose (2008): J	11	0.008	0.008	0.013	−0.008	0.014
Hauser et al. (2008): J	0	N/A	N/A	N/A	N/A	N/A
Krammer (2009): J	0	N/A	N/A	N/A	N/A	N/A
Maggioni et al. (2007): J	0	N/A	N/A	N/A	N/A	N/A
Moreno et al. (2003): WP	12	0.280	0.149	0.268	0.045	0.548
Moreno et al. (2005): J	9	0.035	0.023	0.049	−0.011	0.056
Pinto (2010): WP	0	N/A	N/A	N/A	N/A	N/A
Pinto and Rodrigues (2010): J	0	N/A	N/A	N/A	N/A	N/A
Varga et al. (2010): WP	0	N/A	N/A	N/A	N/A	N/A
Greunz (2003): J	13	0.169	0.055	0.170	0.040	0.240
$\Sigma p = 7$ Overall:	75	0.736	2.157	0.080	−0.011	8.311
$\Sigma p = 6$ Overall adjusted:	69	0.106	0.117	0.052	−0.011	0.548

Notes:
WP = working paper.
J = article in journal.
β_2 = spillover knowledge variable in region j derived from the cth β coefficient in publication p.

They have been published either as working papers (WP) or as articles in journals (J). The number of β_1 coefficients varies per publication, from 1 to 16 coefficients, depending on how many regression models the publication has estimated. The mean value for the local knowledge coefficient is reported as between 0.150 and 0.966. The overall mean value of β_1 (i.e. for all 13 publications) is about 0.468, whereas the median is 0.445. The deviation from the mean of β_1 is high for some publications (e.g. Crescenzi et al., 2007; Maggioni et al., 2007; Pinto and Rodrigues, 2010), while it is low for others. The minimum and maximum values for the overall sample of β_1 coefficients are −0.153 and 1.280, respectively.

Table 7.6 reports the descriptive statistics for the knowledge spillovers from region j to region i (β_2). Out of 13 publications, 7 report coefficient values for β_2. The mean value for β_2 falls within the range 0.008 to 7.982. The high mean value corresponding to 7.982 is observed in Crescenzi et al. (2007). The study uses a spatially weighted average composed of several factors that measure flows of knowledge spilling over from the neighbouring region to the local region. It comprises various proxies that make it possible to measure accumulation of local skills. The spatially weighted average increases the estimated values of the spillover coefficients, however, excluding it from our sample would imply that we lose valuable information in identifying knowledge spillovers from one region to another.[10] However, to avoid a misleading interpretation of the overall descriptive statistics of β_2 we also include descriptive statistics that are adjusted for the high values observed in Crescenzi et al. (2007) in Table 7.6.

The overall adjusted mean value for the spillover coefficient is 0.106 and the standard deviation is 0.117. The median is close to the mean for all publications, which indicates that each publication has a rather normal distribution in the spillover coefficient. The overall adjusted median is equal to 0.052 and a standard deviation of 0.117. The lowest and highest values for β_2 are −0.011 and 0.548, respectively.

4. META-REGRESSION ANALYSIS

4.1 Methodology

A common econometric problem in meta-regression analysis is that observations from the same study can be correlated. Since we have used multiple estimates per study, the within-study dependence is accounted for by a static panel data framework called the cluster-specific random effects model (GLS-RE). Previous meta-analyses using this regression technique include Jeppesen et al. (2002), Disidier and Head (2008), and Melo et al. (2009). For comparison reasons we have also reported results from a standard OLS.

4.1.1 Meta-regression model

The general model utilized to analyse the local knowledge effects and the spillover of knowledge (i.e. β_z) in the meta-regressions is as follows:[11]

$$\beta_z = a_z + \sum_{d=1}^{24} b_d D_d + \varepsilon \qquad (7.7)$$

$$z = 1, 2$$

The dummy variables D_d are defined in Table 7.7. The constant a_z is equal to the local (β_1) and the spillover effect (β_2), respectively, if b_d and/or D_d is equal to zero for all $d = 1, \ldots, 24$. The parameter estimate b_d is zero when the chosen model cannot pick up any variations among observations

Table 7.7 Meta-dummy variables

Empirical dimension	Variable	Definition	Reference case, $D = 0$
Working paper or published in a journal	D_1	1 if working paper	Study published in journal
Type of R&D variables	D_2	1 if R&D per capita	Study uses log of total
	D_3	1 if R&D is not in log terms	R&D expenditure
	D_4	1 if R&D as a percentage of gross regional product (GRP)	
	D_5	1 if public (government) R&D	
	D_6	1 if business R&D	
Spatial model	D_7	1 if inter-regional spillovers are accounted for	Study does not account for spatial spillovers
Spatial weighting regime	D_8	1 if R&D is weighted by physical distance between regions	R&D is weighted by a binary contiguity matrix
	D_9	1 if R&D in neighbouring regions	R&D in non-neighbouring regions
Statistical significance	D_{10}	1 if p-value of local R&D > 0.05	Local R&D is significant at the 5% level
	D_{11}	1 if p-value of spillover R&D > 0.05	Spillover R&D is significant at the 5% level
Time structure	D_{12}	1 if average year of study period is after 1990	Average year of study period is before 1990
	D_{13}	1 if time lag between dependent and independent variables	No time lag between variables is used
Part of Europe	D_{14}	1 if regions from north, west and south only	Study includes countries from all parts of Europe (north, west, south and east)
	D_{15}	1 if regions from west and south only	
	D_{16}	1 if regions from east only	

Table 7.7 (continued)

Empirical dimension	Variable	Definition	Reference case, $D = 0$
Type of data	D_{17}	1 if panel data	Study uses cross-sectional data
Level of geographical unit	D_{18}	1 if NUTS-1 regions only	Study includes NUTS-2 regions
Dependent variable	D_{19}	1 if patents are not in log terms	Study uses log of patent applications as dependent
	D_{20}	1 if log patents per capita	
	D_{21}	1 if annual patent growth	
	D_{22}	1 if annual GRP growth	
Education level	D_{23}	1 if there are controls for higher education	Study does not control for differences in education level
Initial stock (patents or GRP value)	D_{24}	1 if initial stock is controlled for	Study does not control for initial stock of dependent variable

and studies. The dummy $D_d = 0$ demonstrates the case chosen as the reference case. The two models for explaining β_z differ in one respect. The model explaining variations in local effects does not include the variables about spatial weights (D_8 and D_9); instead the simple dummy for a spatial model (D_7) is used. Obviously, D_7 is excluded in the spillover model because when a spillover effect is estimated, this is done in a spatial model.

Due to a large amount of collinearities among the 24 dummies in equation 7.7, it is impossible to use all the variables simultaneously. In order to find the final models used in this chapter the following strategy was followed:

1. When two variables are collinear, omit the one with the lowest correlation to the β variable and save the other.
2. Continue with step 1 until the multicollinearity problem is sufficiently small.
3. Omit variables with statistical significance > 0.1.

After fulfilling this strategy, the following two final models were estimated:

Table 7.8 Meta-regression results: dependent variable = local effect (β_1)

Dummy variable		OLS	GLS-RE
D_1	1 if working paper	0.291***	0.297***
		(0.053)	(0.058)
D_5	1 if public (government) R&D	−0.235**	−0.248**
		(0.083)	(0.099)
D_7	1 if interregional spillovers are accounted for	−0.165***	−0.062***
		(0.040)	(0.023)
D_{10}	1 if p-value of local R&D > 0.05	−0.301***	−0.239***
		(0.056)	(0.027)
D_{15}	1 if regions from west and south only	0.310***	0.233***
		(0.063)	(0.072)
D_{22}	1 if annual GRP growth as dependent	0.257***	0.168***
		(0.062)	(0.051)
D_{24}	1 if initial stock is controlled for	−0.170***	−0.200***
		(0.028)	(0.034)
	Constant	0.523***	0.482***
		(0.052)	(0.061)
	Number of observations	110	110
	Number of studies	13	13
	R^2 (total)	0.795	0.775
	R^2 (within)		0.367
	R^2 (between)		0.870

Note: ***, **, * indicate significance at 1%, 5% and 10% respectively. The standard errors in parentheses are robust to heteroscedasticity and adjusted for intra-study dependence.

$$\beta_1 = a_1 + b_1D_1 + b_5D_5 + b_7D_7 + b_{10}D_{10} + b_{15}D_{15} + b_{22}D_{22} + b_{24}D_{24} \tag{7.8}$$

$$\beta_2 = a_2 + b_1D_1 + b_3D_3 + b_8D_8 + b_{11}D_{11} + b_{15}D_{15} + b_{22}D_{22} + b_{24}D_{24} \tag{7.9}$$

4.2 Results from the Meta-Regressions

The results of the meta-regressions are presented in Tables 7.8 and 7.9. Let us focus on the results from the random-effects GLS regression reported in Table 7.8. The reference case is as follows: if total local R&D expenditure in a region increases by 1 per cent, then the number of patents in the region, on average, increases by 0.482 per cent. If a study uses a spatial model of some kind, that is, a model that takes into account R&D spillovers from

Table 7.9 Meta-regression results: dependent variable = spillover effect (β_2)

Dummy variable		GLS-RE	GLS-RE
D_1	1 if working paper	0.066***	0.057***
		(0.011)	(0.004)
D_3	1 if R&D is not in log terms	7.769***	–
		(0.026)	
D_8	1 if R&D is weighted by physical distance between regions	0.093***	0.090***
		(0.024)	(0.024)
D_{11}	1 if p-value of spillover R&D > 0.05	−0.142*	−0.074**
		(0.087)	(0.046)
D_{15}	1 if regions from west and south only	−0.114***	−0.115***
		(0.032)	(0.033)
D_{22}	1 if annual GRP growth as dependent	−7.916***	−0.204***
		(0.082)	(0.036)
D_{24}	1 if initial stock is controlled for	0.112***	0.114***
		(0.032)	(0.030)
	Constant	0.079**	0.066**
		(0.034)	(0.030)
	Number of observations	75	69
	Number of studies	7	6
	R^2 (total)	0.997	0.708
	R^2 (within)	0.175	0.196
	R^2 (between)	0.999	0.951

Note: As for Table 7.8.

other regions, then the local effect on patent production will be smaller. This is according to expectations since if interregional R&D effects exist they probably will have a positive impact on local patent production and hence the local effects are exaggerated. Smaller local effects on patent production are also the case for the studies that control for initial patent stock or gross regional product (GRP) value in the region.

Moreover, on average, government R&D expenditure has a lower impact on patent production compared to the reference case, which is in line with the stylized facts in Section 3.2. Also, studies conducted on regions in the western or southern part of Europe demonstrate larger local effects from R&D efforts.

To control for possible publication bias we have introduced a dummy variable for whether a study is published or not. The hypothesis is that there is a preference for publishing statistically significant estimates of a positive relationship between R&D expenditure and patent production. If this is true, a published study should on average have a higher β-value. However, the result in Table 7.8 shows the opposite; that is, a working paper reports, on average, larger local R&D effects.

The meta-regression results with the spillover effect as the dependent variable are presented in Table 7.9.[12] In order to check the robustness of the results two regressions are conducted – one with the full sample (i.e. with 7 studies) and one where the outlying observations from Crescenzi et al. (2007) were omitted. According to the table, the spatial weighting regime seems to matter. If R&D expenditures in other regions are weighted by distance in kilometers or minutes (instead of a binary contiguity matrix), then the spillover effect will on average be larger. Studies conducted on regions in the western or southern part of Europe demonstrate smaller spillover effects from R&D efforts (contrary to the local effects; see Table 7.8). If the initial patent stock or GRP value is controlled for, then the region demonstrates higher spillover effects, which is also contrary to the local effects seen in Table 7.8. The other estimates reported in Table 7.7 are similar to the ones found for the local effects.

5. CONCLUSIONS

In this chapter we focus on one type of externality, namely knowledge spillovers. The empirical studies of the effects of knowledge spillovers in Europe have normally focused on the localized effects on either total factor productivity or knowledge production measured in terms of patent output. The purpose of this chapter is to quantitatively review the empirical literature on spatial knowledge spillovers in Europe by means of meta-analysis to determine the extent to which such spillovers have been empirically documented, as well as their spatial reach. In addition, we apply meta-regression analysis to analyse the determinants of observed heterogeneity across and between publications. Our results show that if total local R&D expenditure in a European region increases by 1 per cent, then the number of patents in that region, on average, increases by 0.482 per cent. Government R&D expenditure is found to have a lower impact on patent production compared to private R&D expenditure. Also, studies conducted in regions in the western or southern part of Europe demonstrate larger local effects from R&D efforts. The spatial weighting regime seems to matter. If R&D expenditures in other regions are weighted by distance in kilometres or minutes (instead of a binary contiguity matrix), then the spillover effect will on average be larger.

NOTES

1. Acknowledgement(s): ESPON TIGER work package 2.3.3.
2. Griliches (1979) makes a distinction between pure knowledge spillovers and rent spillovers, where the latter arise because new goods and services are purchased at less than their fully quality-adjusted prices. Transaction-related knowledge flows here represent rent spillovers.
3. It is interesting to note that research on other types of linkages between universities and industry other than those related to patents and publications are rare, despite the fact that other channels for knowledge flows and knowledge spillovers, such as consulting, contract research and training programmes, are probably more frequently used in practice (D'Este and Patel, 2007; Link et al., 2007).
4. The model with the unmodelled effects is usually called the spatial error model. The model with both unmodelled and modelled effects is the so-called spatial lag model.
5. Inputs for spillover knowledge effects are weighted by distance.
6. See Section 3.2 for further details.
7. Further discussion on the procedure of extracting the data is covered in Section 3.
8. Since most publications run several regression models, the number of β coefficients per publication can exceed 1.
9. We have reviewed more than 100 publications in total and selected about 40 publications for further analysis. However, the majority of this selection has used irrelevant methods of interpreting the knowledge variable or a quantitative approach not suitable for our purpose, thus narrowing down our sample to 13 publications.
10. In the meta-regression model we will control for these β coefficients by using a dummy variable.
11. Also included in the cluster-specific random-effects model is a study random effect that controls for study-specific effects that are common to all individual estimates from the same study.
12. Only the GLS-RE results are presented since the results from the OLS estimation were almost identical.

REFERENCES

Allen, T.J. (1977), *Managing the Flow of Technology*, Cambridge, MA: MIT Press.

Anselin, L. (2003), 'Spatial externalities, spatial multipliers and spatial econometrics', *International Regional Science Review*, **26**(2), 153–66.

Anselin, L., A. Varga and Z.J. Acs (1997), 'Entrepreneurship, geographic spillovers and university research: a spatial econometric approach', ERSC Centre for Business Research, University of Cambridge, Working Paper No. 59.

Archibugi, D. and A. Coco (2004), 'International partnerships for knowledge in business and academia. A comparison between Europe and the USA', *Technovation*, **24**, 517–28.

Archibugi, D. and B.-Å. Lundvall (eds) (2001), *The Globalizing Knowledge Economy*, Oxford: Oxford University Press.

Arrow, K.J. (1962), 'Economic welfare and the allocation of resources for invention', in R.R. Nelson (ed.), *The Rate and Direction of Inventive Activity*, Princeton, NJ: Princeton University Press, pp. 609–26.

Arrow, K.J. (1994), 'The production and distribution of knowledge', in G. Silverberg, and L. Soete (eds), *The Economics of Growth and Technical*

Change: Technologies, Nations, Agents, Aldershot, UK and Brookfield, VT, USA: Edward Elgar, pp. 9–19.

Audretsch, D.B. and M. Feldman (1996), 'Knowledge spillovers and the geography of innovation and production', *American Economic Review*, **83**, 630–40.

Audretsch, D.B. and M. Feldman (2004), 'Knowledge spillovers and the geography of innovation', in V. Henderson and J. Thisse (eds), *Handbook of Urban and Regional Economics*, Amsterdam: Elsevier, pp. 2713–39.

Autant-Bernard, C., J. Mairesse and N. Massard (2007), 'Spatial knowledge diffusion through collaborative networks', *Papers in Regional Science*, **86**, 341–50.

Autant-Bernard, C. and N. Massard (2007), 'Pecuniary and knowledge externalities as agglomeration forces: empirical evidence from individual French data', in J. Suriñach, R. Moreno and E. Vayá (eds), *Knowledge Externalities, Innovation Clusters and Regional Development*, Cheltenham, UK and Northampton, MA, USA: Edward Elgar, pp. 111–35.

Borts, G.H. and J.L. Stein (1964), *Economic Growth in a Free Market*, New York: Columbia University Press.

Botazzi, L. and G. Peri. (2000), 'Innovation and spillovers: evidence from European regions', CESifo Working Papers, No. 340, CESifo, Munich, Germany.

Botazzi, L. and G. Peri. (2003), 'Innovation and spillovers in regions: evidence from European patent data', *European Economic Review*, **47**, 687–710.

Breschi, S. and F. Lissoni (2001), 'Localized knowledge spillovers vs. innovative milieux: knowledge "tacitness" reconsidered', *Papers in Regional Science*, **80**, 255–73.

Breschi, S. and F. Lissoni (2009), 'Mobility of skilled workers and co-invention networks: an anatomy of localized knowledge flows', *Journal of Economic Geography*, **9**, 439–68.

Crescenzi, R. and A. Rodriguez-Pose (2008), 'Research and development, spillovers, innovation systems, and the genesis of regional growth in Europe', *Regional Studies*, **42**(1), 51–67.

Crescenzi, R., A. Rodriguez-Pose and M. Storper (2007), 'The territorial dynamics of innovation: a Europe–United States comparative analysis', Working Paper, London School of Economics, London.

Crespi, G., A. Geuna and L. Nesta (2006), 'Labour mobility of academic inventors: career decisions and knowledge transfer', EUI Working Papers RSCAS No. 2006/06, European University Institute, Florence.

D'Este, P. and P. Patel (2007), 'University–industry linkages in the UK: what are the factors underlying the variety of interactions with industry?', *Research Policy*, **36**, 1295–313.

Disdier, A.-C. and K. Head, (2008), 'The puzzling persistence of the distance effect on bilateral trade', *Review of Economics and Statistics*, **90**(1), 37–48.

Dixon, R. and A.P. Thirlwall (1975), 'A model of regional growth-rate differences on Kaldorian lines', *Oxford Economic Papers*, **27**, 201–14.

Dohse, D. (2000), 'Technology policy and the regions – the case of the bioregion contest', *Research Policy*, **29**, 1111–133.

Eaton, J. and S. Kortum (1996), 'Trade in ideas: productivity and patenting in the OECD', *Journal of International Economics*, **40**, 251–78.

Ellison, G. and E. Glaeser (1997), 'Geographic concentration in US manufacturing industries: a dartboard approach', *Journal of Political Economy*, **105**, 889–927.

Englmann, F.C. and U. Walz (1995), 'Industrial centers and regional growth in the presence of local inputs', *Journal of Regional Science*, **35**, 3–27.
Feldman, M.P. (1999), 'The new economics of innovation, spillovers and agglomeration: a review of empirical studies', *The Economics of Innovation and New Technology*, **8**, 5–25.
Greunz, L. (2003), 'Geographically and technologically mediated knowledge spillovers between European regions', *The Annals of Regional Science*, **37**(4), 657–80.
Griliches, Z. (1979), 'Issues in assessing the contribution of research and development to productivity growth', *The Bell Journal of Economics*, **10**, 92–116.
Griliches, Z. (1992), 'The search for R&D spillovers', *Scandinavian Journal of Economics*, **94**, 29–47.
Griliches, Z. and F.R. Lichtenberg (1984), 'R&D and productivity growth at the industry level: is there still a relationship?', in Z. Griliches (ed.), *R&D, Patents and Productivity*, Chicago IL: University of Chicago Press, pp. 465–502.
Hauser, C., G. Tappeiner and J. Walde (2008), 'Regional knowledge spillovers: fact or artefact?', *Research Policy*, **37**, 861–74.
Head, K., J. Ries and D. Swenson (1995), 'Agglomeration benefits and location choice: evidence from Japanese manufacturing investment in the United States', *Journal of International Economics*, **38**, 223–47.
Jaffe, A. (1989), 'Real effects of academic research', *The American Economic Review*, **79**, 957–70.
Jaffe, A. and J. Lerner (1999), 'Privatizing R&D: patent policy and the commercialization of national laboratory technologies', NBER Working Paper No. 7064, National Bureau of Economic Research, Cambridge, MA.
Jaffe, A. and M. Trajtenberg (1996), 'Flows of knowledge from universities and federal labs: modeling the flow of patent citations over time and across institutional and geographical boundaries', *Proceedings of the National Academy of Sciences*, **93**, 12671–677.
Jaffe, A., M. Trajtenberg and M. Fogarty (2000), 'The meaning of patent citations: report of the NBER/Case Western Reserve survey of patentees', NBER Working Paper No. 7631, National Bureau of Economic Research, Cambridge, MA.
Jaffe, A., M. Trajtenberg and R. Henderson (1993), 'Geographical localization of knowledge spillovers as evidenced by patent citations', *Quarterly Journal of Economics*, **108**, 577–98.
Jeppesen, T., J.A. List and H. Folmer (2002), 'Environmental regulations and new plant location decisions: evidence from a meta-analysis', *Journal of Regional Science*, **42**, 19–49.
Karlsson, C. and B. Johansson (2006), 'Dynamics and entrepreneurship in a knowledge-based economy', in C. Karlsson, B. Johansson and R.R. Stough (eds), *Entrepreneurship and Dynamics in the Knowledge Economy*, New York: Routledge, pp. 12–46.
Karlsson, C. and A. Manduchi (2001), 'Knowledge spillovers in a spatial context – a critical review and assessment', in M.M. Fischer, and J. Fröhlich (eds), *Knowledge, Complexity and Innovation Systems*, Berlin: Springer, pp. 101–23.
Keilbach, M. (1998), 'Marshallian externalities and the dynamics of agglomeration and regional growth', Working Paper No. 1998/19, Technical University, Berlin.
Krammer, Sorin M.S. (2009), 'Drivers of national innovation in transition:

evidence from a panel of Eastern European countries', *Research Policy*, **38**, 845–60.
Krugman, P. (1991), *Geography and Trade*, Cambridge, MA: MIT Press.
Krugman, P. (1998), 'Space; the final frontier', *Journal of Economic Perspectives*, **12**, 161–74.
Link, A., D. Siegel and B. Bozeman (2007), 'An empirical analysis of the propensity of academics to engage in informal university technology transfer', *Industrial & Corporate Change*, **16**, 641–55.
Lucas, R. (1993), 'Making a miracle', *Econometrica*, **61**, 251–72.
Maggioni, M.A., M. Nosvelli and E. Uberti (2007), 'Space vs. networks in the geography of innovation: a European analysis', *Papers in Regional Science*, **86**(3), 471–93.
Melo, P.C., J.D. Graham and R.N. Noland (2009), 'A meta-analysis of estimates of urban agglomeration economies', *Regional Science and Urban Economics*, **39**, 332–42.
Miguélez, E. and R. Moreno (2010), 'Research networks and innovators mobility as drivers of innovation: evidence from Europe', Working Paper 2010/01, Research Institute of Applied Economics, University of Barcelona.
Moreno, R., R. Paci and S. Usai (2003), 'Spatial spillovers and innovation activity in European regions', Crenos Working Papers, No. 2010:10, Cagliari, Italy.
Moreno, R., R. Paci and S. Usai. (2005), 'Spatial spillovers and innovation activity in European regions', *Environment and Planning*, **37**, 1793–812.
Myrdal, G. (1957), *Economic Theory and Underdeveloped Regions*, London: Duckworth.
NSF (2002), *Science and Engineering Indicators*, National Science Foundation, US GPO, Washington, DC.
Perroux, F. (1955), 'Note sur la notion de pôle de croissance', *Économie Appliquée*, **7**, 307–20.
Pinto, H. (2010), 'Knowledge production in European Union: evidence from a national level panel data', MPRA Working Paper No. 27283, Algarve, Portugal.
Pinto, H. and P.M.M. Rodrigues (2010), 'Knowledge production in European regions: the impact of regional strategies and regionalization on innovation', *European Planning Studies*, **18**(10), 1731–48.
Ponds, R., F. van Oort and K. Frenken (2007), 'The geographical and institutional proximity of research collaboration', *Papers in Regional Science*, **86**, 423–43.
Premer, M. and U. Walz (1994), 'Divergent regional development, factor mobility, and non-traded goods', *Regional Science and Urban Economics*, **24**, 707–22.
Romer, P.M. (1986), 'Increasing returns and long-term growth', *Journal of Political Economy*, **94**, 1002–37.
Romer, P.M. (1990), 'Endogenous technological change', *Journal of Political Economy*, **98**, S71–S102.
Stanley, T.D. (2001), 'Wheat from chaff: meta-analysis as quantitative literature review', *Journal of Economic Perspectives*, **15**, 131–50.
Stanley, T.D. and S.B. Jarrell (1989), 'Meta-regression analysis: a quantitative method of literature reviews', *Journal of Economic Surveys*, **3**, 161–70.
Varga, A., D. Pontikakis and G. Chorafakis (2010), 'Agglomeration and interregional network effects on European R&D productivity', IAREG Working Paper, No. 5/22, University of Pecs, Hungary.
Verspagen, B. (1994), 'Technology and growth: the complex dynamics of convergence and divergence', in G. Silverberg and L. Soete (eds), *The Economics of*

Growth and Technical Change: Technologies, Nations, Agents, Aldershot, UK and Brookfield, VT, USA: Edward Elgar.

Wallsten, S.J. (2001), 'An empirical test of geographical knowledge spillovers using GIS and firm-level data', *Regional Science and Urban Economics*, **31**, 571–99.

APPENDIX

Abbreviation of variables in Table 7.4:

AERI	accessibility to extra-regional innovation
$AERI_{WEI}$	weighted accessibility to extra-regional innovation
AIPEA	accessibility to innovation-prone extra-regional areas
GDP_{CAP}	gross domestic product per capita
HTP	high-technology patents
P	patents
P_{CAP}	patents per capita
PGY	patents granted per year
RD_{EMP}	R&D employment
$RD_{EMP/W}$	R&D employment per worker
RD_{EXP}	R&D expenditure
$RD_{EXP/W}$	R&D expenditure per worker
$RD_{EXP/C}$	R&D expenditure per capita
$RD_{EXP\%GRP}$	R&D expenditure as percentage of gross regional product
$RD_{EXP\%GDP}$	R&D expenditure as percentage of gross domestic product
$RD_{EXPG\%GDP}$	R&D expenditure as percentage of gross domestic product, public
$RD_{EXPB\%GDP}$	R&D expenditure as percentage of gross domestic product, private
RD_{EXPG}	R&D expenditure public
RD_{EXPB}	R&D expenditure business
RD_{SPE}	R&D spending
SWANR	spatially weighed average of neighbouring regions' R&D
TAIPS	total accessibility to innovation-prone space
YP_{APP}	yearly patent applications
$YP_{APP/W}$	yearly patent applications per worker
$YP_{APP/C}$	yearly patent applications per capita

8. Innovation, efficiency and economic integration

Aikaterini Kokkinou

1. AN INTRODUCTION TO PRODUCTIVE EFFICIENCY

Nowadays, the economic role of innovation and efficiency enhancement in economic integration and convergence is even more important, taking into consideration the slowdown and the effects created by the current financial crisis. Within this framework, the key factors influencing the integration and convergence process are creation and diffusion of innovation, along with productive efficiency enhancement, mainly around three key areas: innovation and research, strengthening networks and clusters; and efficient use of production factors.

Within this framework, when one considers productivity comparisons, an additional source of productivity change, called technical change, is possible. This involves advances in technology that may be represented by an upward shift in the production frontier. This is represented in Figure 8.1 by the movement of the production frontier from $0F_0$ to $0F_1$ in period 1.

In period 1, all firms can technically produce more output for each level of input, relative to what was possible in period 0. When we observe that a producer has increased productivity from one period to the next, the improvement need not have been from efficiency improvements alone, but may have been due to technical change or the exploitation of scale economies, or from some combination of these three factors (Coelli et al., 2005).

The optimum level of production is defined in terms of the production possibilities frontier (PPF). Technological change is assumed to push the frontier of potential production upward, while efficiency change will change the capability of productive units to improve production with available inputs and technology. Figure 8.2 illustrates this idea.

As illustrated in Figure 8.2, F_1 and F_2 are production frontiers in periods 1 and 2, respectively. Technical efficiency, which is represented by a movement towards the frontier from A to B, refers to the efficient

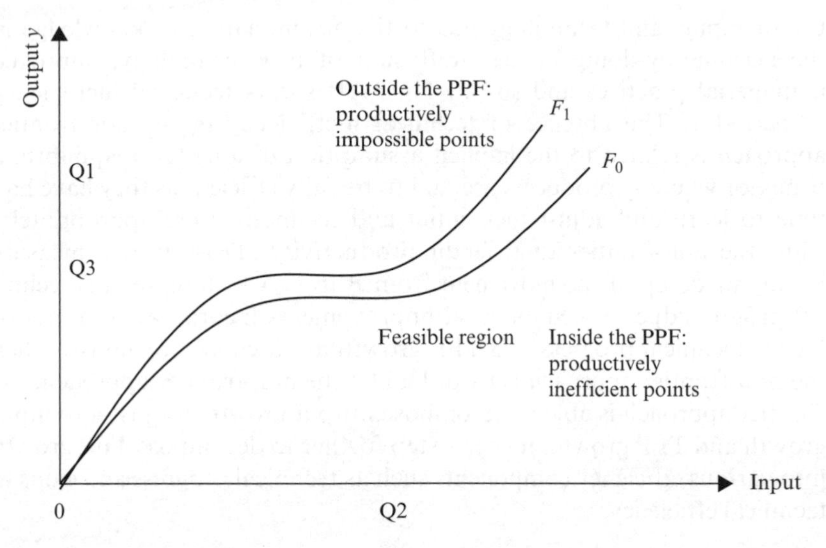

Source: Based on Coelli et al. (2005), p. 6.

Figure 8.1 Production frontiers and technical efficiency

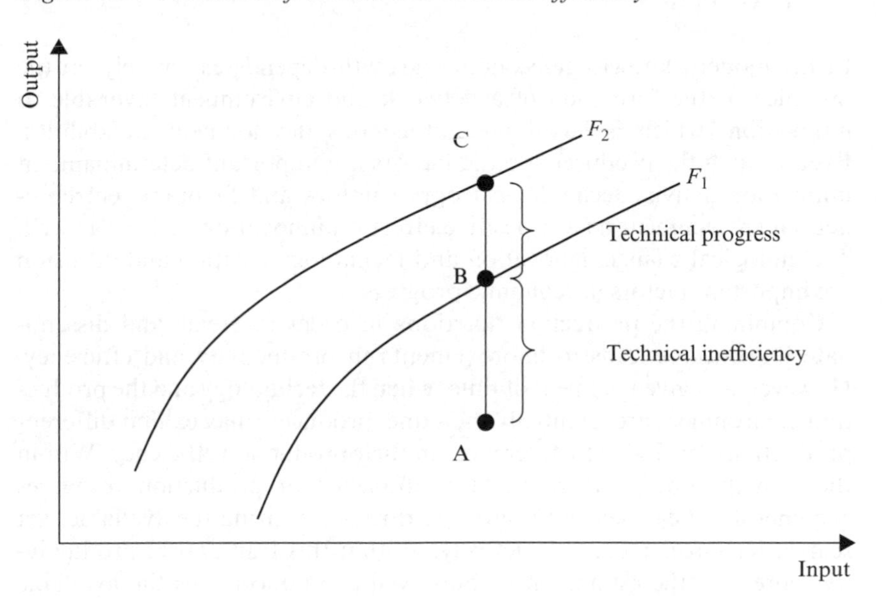

Source: Mahadevan (2002), p. 7.

Figure 8.2 The frontier and non-frontier total factor productivity growth measure

use of inputs and technology due to the accumulation of knowledge in the learning-by-doing process, diffusion of new technology, improved managerial practices and so on. Thus AB shows technical inefficiency in period 1. The absence of technical inefficiency in the non-frontier approach is related to the implicit assumption of long-term equilibrium behavior whereby producers are said to be fully efficient as they have had time to learn and adjust their input and technology use appropriately. Thus the non-frontier total factor productivity (TFP) growth measure is only made up of the movement from B to C, which represents technical progress due to technological improvements incorporated in inputs. Hence technical progress and TFP growth are used synonymously when the non-frontier approach is used. Unlike the non-frontier approach, the frontier approach is able to decompose output growth not just into input growth and TFP growth; it goes a step further to decompose TFP growth into various efficiency components such as technical progress and gains in technical efficiency.

2. PRODUCTIVE EFFICIENCY DETERMINING FACTORS

In the modern knowledge economy, growth depends extensively on the presence or the formation of a network and environment favorable to innovation, which is based on endogenous development capabilities. Even though the producer-specific factors are important determinants of innovation activity technological opportunities and favorable entrepreneurial environment have a positive effect on innovation activity as well. Technological change, innovation and technology creation and diffusion are important factors in economic progress.

Combining the production functions in order to create and disseminate innovations leads to improvements in productivity and efficiency. However, at a given moment of time, when the technology and the production environment are essentially the same, producers may exhibit different productivity levels due to differences in their production efficiency. Within the growth process, therefore, the efficiency of production resources becomes a critical element in growth, through utilizing the available, yet scarce, resources more productively. Within this framework, productivity represents the estimation of how well a producer uses the available resources to produce outputs from inputs. However, the productivity theory literature has emphasized factors such as productive efficiency, mainly through technological spillovers, increasing returns, learning by doing, and unobserved inputs (e.g. human capital quality), whereas the empirical industrial organization literature has emphasized the degree of openness of countries to imports and industry structure (Koop, 2001).

Consequently, one of the main tasks is to investigate the relationship between inefficiency and a number of factors which are likely to be determinants, and measure the extent to which they contribute to the presence of inefficiency. These factors are neither inputs to the production process nor outputs of it, but nonetheless exert an influence on producer performance. Such factors are widely referred to as efficiency explanatory variables.

Within this framework, based on Wang (2007), since R&D is one of the most crucial elements in promoting growth, it is argued that any production unit that uses R&D resources inefficiently may be subjected to a growth penalty in the form of a much smaller benefit from R&D investment. If R&D resources are not used effectively, additional investment may be of little help in stimulating economic growth. Literature has already been devoted to investigating the economic aspects and effects of R&D investment. It has been considered that R&D could result in better production technology and also raise the productivity as well as the rates of return on investment at both the producer and industry levels.

Technology and innovation play an important role in productive efficiency with a multiple role: as motive force they direct the producers to ambitious and long-term objectives, lead to the renewal of methods of production, supply and distribution, and management and marketing, as well as industrial structures and the appearance of new industries of economic activity, achieving a wider spectrum of products and services, as well as relative markets. Inputs affect the intermediate inputs, which consequently affect and define the productivity and competitiveness level. As mentioned earlier, technological change, innovation and technology creation and diffusion are an important factor in economic progress.

On the other hand, as broadly described in Gallié and Roux (2010), in the last two decades R&D cooperation has attracted a considerable amount of attention. Many empirical studies, in economics or in management, have investigated the motives for and potential benefits of cooperation as compared to internal R&D. Cooperation enables firms to internalize knowledge spillovers, facilitates knowledge transfers between them (in particular between firms and universities), helps them gain access to complementary knowledge and technologies, generates scale economies of research, enables firms to speed the commercialization of new products or technologies, to avoid duplicative R&D efforts, to share costs and risk and to gain access to foreign or new markets. After R&D collaboration, cooperation was most often captured as a homogeneous object (i.e. R&D cooperation versus internal R&D).

Following the main findings from the literature survey, there are two complementary sets of conditions that need to be satisfied for industries to sustain productivity and efficiency in a competitive environment. The first is that they must have suitable levels of both physical infrastructure and human capital. The second is that, in the new knowledge-based economy, they must have the capacity to innovate and to use both existing and new technologies effectively. Industrial and innovation policy is aimed at strengthening the competitiveness of producers by promoting competition, ensuring access to markets and establishing an environment which is conducive to R&D. As recognized, lack of innovative capacity stems not only from deficiencies in the research base and low levels of R&D expenditure, but also from weaknesses in the links between research centers and businesses, and slow take-up of information and communication technologies. Knowledge and access to it have become the driving force of productivity, much more than natural resources or the ability to exploit abundant low-cost labor have become the major determinants of economic competitiveness, since it is through these that industries can increase their productive efficiency. Innovation, therefore, holds the key to maintaining and strengthening efficiency, which in turn is essential for achieving sustained economic development.

These environmental factors are spatially confined externalities with different scales of influence. Some factors, such as the legal and cultural framework or large research institutes, operate mainly at national level, generating national systems of innovation (Lundvall, 1992). Other factors, such as skilled labor supply and networks linking firms and support institutions, have a more limited territorial span, and are the basis of regional systems of innovation (Braczyk et al., 1998).

3. PRODUCTIVE EFFICIENCY AND ECONOMIC INTEGRATION: THE CASE OF THE EUROPEAN UNION

As technical efficiency enhancement becomes an increasingly important issue, production must draw on a wide range of production ideas, component technologies and complementary capabilities. Within this framework, it is rather difficult for any single industry to incorporate and take advantage of the relevant technological advances, as well as the underlying industrial and innovation policies. This means that the actions of industries involve the targeted development of specialized knowledge assets, which are integrated from a wider range of knowledge areas (Kessler et al., 2000).

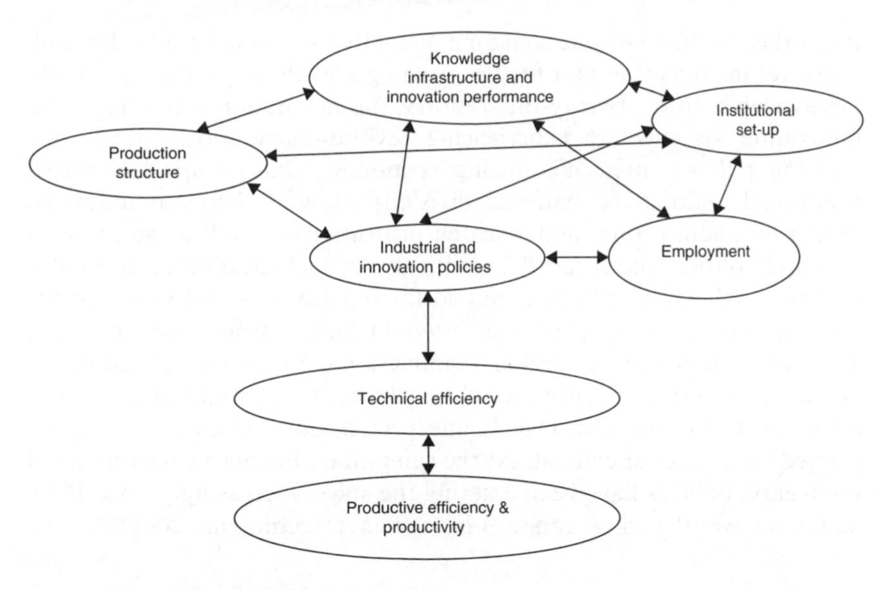

Source: Own elaboration.

Figure 8.3 Productive efficiency and institutional framework

European technology and innovation policies are no longer exclusively in the hands of national authorities: increasingly, national initiatives are supplemented by or even competing with regional innovation policies or transnational programs, in particular the activities of the EU.

At the same time, industrial innovation increasingly occurs within international networks. Research, technology and innovation policies of European countries clearly reflect the profiles of their national (and regional) 'innovation systems', understood as the various institutions, corporate actors and processes contributing to industrial and societal innovation. Figure 8.3 highlights the interactions among the main policy elements regarding the enhancement of technical and productive efficiency.

The spectrum of the implemented instruments of research, technology and innovation policy is widely differentiated in the meantime, reflecting the scope of institutions and interests involved: it stretches from public funding of research institutions over various forms of financial incentives to the conducting of research and experimental development in public or industrial research labs, up to the design of an innovation-oriented infrastructure, including the institutions and mechanisms of technology transfer. In many European countries, these instruments have dominated the practice or research and technology policy for the last three decades.

As further instruments one could mention efforts to guide public demand, measures in education and further training and the regulatory possibilities available. In the twenty-first century, though, national and (regional) innovation systems are experiencing revolutionary shock waves: the growing pull of internationalizing economic relationships has mixed traditional regional or national divisions of work between industrial enterprises, educational and research institutions as well as administration and politics, and it has debased many of their traditional strengths. Internationalization, however, has so far not led to a uniformity of the national innovation systems, which would finally mean their abolition. The various national and regional innovation cultures and related policy arenas react very differently, which partly leads them into crises, partly stabilizes, but partly also reveals unexpected, novel chances in a transformed international context. At the same time, European transnational innovation policies have been entering the stage, increasingly since 1985, and now cover the whole range of instruments (Kuhlmann, 2001).

4. PRODUCTIVE EFFICIENCY AND INNOVATION POLICY: THE CASE OF THE EUROPEAN UNION

Innovation policy seeks to help firms or industries to improve their capacity to innovate. This includes the provision of scientific infrastructure in research and education, and direct and indirect support for research and technological development. It also includes a wide range of policies which aim to build networks, to make markets more conducive to innovation, to facilitate the transfer of technology, to help firms to acquire relevant capabilities, and to provide a supporting infrastructure in areas such as standards and intellectual property. Public innovation policy aims to strengthen the competitiveness of an economy or of selected industries, in order to increase societal welfare through economic success (Kuhlmann, 2001). Hence the EU has made innovation a top priority through several strategies, funding opportunities and assessments. The pressures of globalization have brought innovation to the fore as a key element in increasing productivity along with technical efficiency and underpinning industrial competitiveness, taking into consideration the underinvestment in business R&D and other innovative activities, strongly linked to the fragmented condition of European markets.

Innovation policy is essential for EU productive efficiency and an important driver in enabling the EU to enhance competitiveness, increase efficiency and growth and consequently to compete on a global scale. However, policy makers have also underlined the need for interaction between innovation policy and other policy areas to improve the environment for innovative enterprises (Chesbrough, 2002; Nilsson, 2004; Georghiou, 2006).

On the other hand, Europe's national innovation systems differ substantially, as do their innovation performances. Therefore member states have undertaken great efforts to improve their innovation support measures by investing in research and implementing new or better instruments in support of innovation. This level of financial engagement is at risk in the current global economic crisis and, as a direct impact, the innovation gap in the EU is widening again. The implication of this is that innovation policy must consider the needs of a wide set of industries – policy initiatives need not be confined to a small group of highly innovative sectors. The EU is challenged in the global arena by emerging economies when it comes to capturing and capitalizing on knowledge and technology in the context of innovation. In the past few years, the budget for R&D has been increased and several initiatives have been launched to strengthen Europe's competitiveness. So far, however, these efforts have not made the EU more competitive.

The majority of public initiatives are still mainly developed in national policies offered by national institutions. While in recent years member states increasingly tended to compete with each other in the field of innovation policy, strong industrial or financial capital actors have been appearing more frequently on the scene – multinational enterprises, international strategic alliances of national enterprises – who act globally and across the national innovation systems. In the member states of the EU this policy initially took the form of initiatives for stimulating research, improving innovation financing and promoting technology absorption and innovation management.

Additional priorities such as intensifying the cooperation between research, industry and universities, promoting 'clustering' and other forms of cooperation among enterprises and other organizations involved in the innovation process, and encouraging the start-up of technology-based companies were added to the national innovation policy (Nilsson, 2004).

As part of the Europe 2020 strategy, in 2010 the Commission launched an ambitious new industrial policy that highlighted the actions needed to strengthen the attractiveness of Europe as a place for investment and production, including the commitment to monitor member states' competitiveness policies. The changing nature and scope of global innovation activities creates very significant consequences for EU innovation policy, requiring a substantial review of the pillars of EU innovation policy, involving both the scope and the governance of innovation at the EU and national level (Anvret et al. 2010).

The EU has identified the following key areas where the competitiveness of the EU economy could be further strengthened in order to make significant progress towards the Europe 2020 goals (European Commission, 2011):

- facilitating structural changes in the economy, in order to move towards more innovative and knowledge-based sectors that have a higher productivity growth and have suffered less from global competition;
- enabling innovation in industries, in particular by pooling scarce resources, by reducing the fragmentation of innovation support systems and by increasing the market focus of research projects;
- promoting sustainability and resource efficiency, in particular by promoting innovation and the use of cleaner technologies, by ensuring fair and undistorted pricing of energy and by upgrading and interconnecting energy distribution networks;
- improving the business environment, in particular by reducing the administrative burden on businesses and by promoting competition among service providers that use broadband, energy and transport infrastructure;
- benefiting from the single market, by supporting innovative services and by fully implementing the Single Market Regulation, in particular the Services Directive;
- supporting small and medium-sized enterprises (SMEs), in particular by favouring access to finance, by facilitating internationalization and access to markets.

EU industry must accelerate its efforts to adopt these technologies to keep its competitive edge in the world, with research and innovation driving productivity growth and industrial competitiveness. A transition towards a sustainable, resource-efficient economy is paramount for maintaining the long-term competitiveness of European industries. Overall, European member states have made significant progress in defining and implementing consistent national legislative frameworks for stimulating efficiency. However, some lack the experience and the administrative capacity to do this and for these countries the framework legislation at the EU level can provide guidance and support.

The quality and availability of infrastructure (energy, transport and broadband) make an important contribution to an efficiency-promoting environment. Industrial sectors need a modern public administration, able to deliver efficient and high-quality public services (European Commission, 2011). Coordinating clusters and networks improve industrial competitiveness and innovation by bringing together resources and expertise, and promoting cooperation among businesses, public authorities and universities. EU industrial and innovation policies should aim to overcome existing market failures and funding gaps, especially to supply the bridge between technical efficiency and productivity enhancement.

5. POLICY IMPLICATIONS AND CONCLUDING REMARKS

Nowadays, the role of manufacturing industries in the economy is even more important, taking into consideration the slowdown in the world economy and the effects on the business environment created by the financial crisis. Thus manufacturing industries have a very important role in creating opportunities, making an important contribution to economic growth and development. However, due to their nature, manufacturing industries are characterized by great heterogeneity since they differ in their endowments of resources as well as on the risks involved in their productive activities. For this reason, it is of great importance, on the one hand, to analyze their efficiency level and potential, and, in addition, to analyze the factors that determine their efficiency potential.

The key factors influencing the competitiveness of the EU manufacturing industry are access to innovation, R&D and international trade. The main recommendations revolve around three key areas: innovation and research, and strengthening networks and clusters; responsible use of natural resources; and the need for open world markets with fair competition. Clustering, collaboration and the formation of strategic alliances are becoming increasingly important. Continuous R&D and innovation efforts are essential elements in guaranteeing the long-term competitiveness of Europe's manufacturing industries. European research, technical development and innovation policies should focus on developing the framework conditions that stimulate innovation, entrepreneurship and, thus, growth and employment. Innovation for sustainable manufacturing requires paying attention to the interfaces of R&D policies with other critical policy fields. Strong emphasis needs to be placed upon the management of the interfaces of R&D policy and other policy realms – competition policy, intellectual property rights, standardization, education and training, environmental policy, the labor market, employment and social policy – to facilitate the creation of a sustainable European manufacturing industry environment, along with fiscal instruments and incentives. Understanding future challenges and issues is important in future developments in manufacturing. Industrial change driven by new technological opportunities will impact on the manufacturing structures in the EU contributing to sustainable growth and improving technical efficiency.

The potential for technical efficiency enhancement is considered to a large extent to depend on the EU's capability to transform the economy into one that makes more productive use of its resources. Much will depend on the capacity of markets to facilitate the reallocation of resources to industries that show rapid productivity growth. However, it is difficult to predict which industries will be the most productive in the future, as technology and innovation trends are inherently difficult to forecast. For now, a productive use of a larger input from skilled employment and the exploitation of information and communication (ICT) investments in manufacturing industries appear the most successful policy avenues for a European productivity revival.

Promoting technical and productive efficiency in the EU has resulted in a growing challenge for policy makers. Productive and regional disparities and inequalities are an increasing issue for the EU to resolve; as a result, policy makers have to adapt the policy agenda considering industrial and innovation policy in order to enhance technical and productive efficiency capabilities.

Moreover, efficiency and policy planning is a major matter which, due to its wide interpretations and implications, should have a clear mix of principles and priorities, mainly focusing on the effectiveness of the related EU policies. EU industrial and innovation policy should aim to bridge the technical efficiency gaps, both at industrial and country level, benefiting economic cohesion, allowing member states with a backwards economy or backwards industries to modernize and thus compete in European and international markets, promoting convergence, competitiveness and cooperation. Infrastructure, innovation and investments should be among the main goals.

European governments are in need of a more coherent, more coordinated approach towards industrial technical efficiency support. However, the pressure on public budgets adds to the urgency of this matter in different policy areas of industrial and innovation policy. The range of explicit innovation policies being applied is very much concerned with the supply side and even more with R&D support of various types, ranging from funding of science in public institutions through to fiscal incentives for firms to increase R&D spend. A comprehensive approach to industrial and innovation policy can be achieved by supporting markets for innovative goods and services, and excellence in research in new technologies, including ICT, introducing a more focused strategy to facilitate the creation of areas for action, and in particular introducing a more focused strategy to facilitate the creation and marketing of new innovative products and services. Within the domain of industrial and innovation policy, regulatory reform is seen to affect innovation indirectly by affecting the funds available for investment and market size and structure, and directly through its impact on the promotion of technical efficiency and productivity (Lengrand, 2003).

An open, efficient and competitive business environment is a crucial catalyst for growth in a global context. Improving the business environment covers policies in areas ranging from improving infrastructure to shortening the time needed to obtain a building license. In many cases, better institutional mechanisms need to be functioning as a single research area, business environment and innovation system. There need to be strategic approaches that promote closer interaction not only among sectors but also among policy makers (from different policy fields and different levels of government). European innovation and industrial policy is therefore recommended to develop strategic approaches that integrate R&D, innovation and industrial policy along with a more coherent EU strategy for innovative competitiveness, giving special attention to ICT in innovation and industrial policy (ETEPS, 2011).

At the national level, governments could set up agencies funded by public bonds with the mission to provide venture capital, investment credits and R&D support to new activities in the above fields. Productive efficiency and competitiveness would be strengthened by:

- pooling scarce resources to help to achieve critical mass in bringing innovation to the market; and by increasing cooperation in innovation to create large-scale demonstration projects and pilot test facilities;
- reducing the fragmentation of innovation support systems, facilitating bringing innovative solutions to the market, and increasing the market focus of research projects;
- developing support for innovative services based on measurable outcomes;
- facilitating the growth of manufacturing industries by ensuring that regulations do not pose obstacles to expansion; by favoring access to appropriate finance; and by providing support services for accessing new markets, and publicizing these.

A new generation of policies must overcome the limitations and failures of past experiences, such as collusive practices between political and economic power, heavy bureaucracy, lack of accountability and entrepreneurship. They have to be creative and selective, with decision-making mechanisms that are more democratic and inclusive of different social interests. These new approaches to industrial and innovation policies could play a key role in pulling Europe out of the current crisis. The politics behind such a new departure must be based on a wide social consensus over the distribution of the productivity and efficiency gains deriving from new technologies and economic activities (Pianta, 2010).

Industrial and innovation policy programs and projects claim to contribute to technical efficiency. This implies that policies should concentrate on areas in which there is expansion and therefore good prospects for growth. Community businesses should become more competitive, and scientific and technological progress is expected to offer a medium- or long-term potential for dissemination and exploitation (Kuhlmann, 2001). An open, efficient and competitive business environment is a crucial catalyst for growth in a global context. Rising to these challenges can improve the competitiveness of European manufacturing industries, and the Commission aims to help the member states to use their limited resources efficiently in order to increase the global competitiveness of their industries. Addressing these challenges will improve the growth prospects of industries. A competitive industry can lower costs and prices, create new products and improve quality, thus contributing decisively to wealth creation and productivity growth throughout the economy.

The difficult fiscal environment sets limits to policy action, but robust growth will reduce the burden of public deficit and debt, in line with the goals of the Stability and Growth Pact. For this an environment that favors new ideas and new businesses is required. Innovation is the primary driver of a successful and sustainable industrial policy. A strong lead in R&D and innovation is Europe's key competitive advantage and of central importance in finding solutions to economic challenges (European Commission, 2011). With increased globalization, one can only hope that industry will be an engine for the spreading of social progress, environmentally friendly technologies and innovations worldwide (Soete, 2007). To achieve a truly sustainable, positive effect for manufacturing industry and the workforce it employs, the EU and its member states should aim to avoid the relocation of manufacturing activities and related services (e.g. R&D, ICT) and support the permanent upgrading of European manufacturing industries.

REFERENCES

Anvret, M., Granieri, M. and Renda, A. (2010), 'A new approach to innovation policy in the European Union. Innovation Policy: Boosting EU Competitiveness in a Global Economy, CEPS Task Force Report, 8 July.

Braczyk, H.J., Cooke, P. and Heidenreich, M. (1998), *Regional Innovation Systems*, London: UCL Press.

Chesbrough, H. (2002), *Open Innovation: The New Imperative for Creating and Profiting from Technology*, Boston, MA: Harvard Business School Press.

Coelli, T.J., Rao, D.S.P., O'Donnell, C.J. and Battese, G.E. (2005), *An Introduction to Efficiency and Productivity Analysis*, 2nd edn, New York: Springer.

ETEPS (2011), Innovation and Industrial Policy, IP/A/ITRE/ST/2010-06, Brussels: European Parliament.

European Commission (2011), *Industrial Policy: Reinforcing Competitiveness*, COM(2011) 642 final, Brussels.

Gallié, E.-P. and Roux, P. (2010), 'Forms and determinants of R&D collaborations: evidence based on French data', *Industry & Innovation*, **17**(6), 551–76.

Georghiou, L. (2006), 'Effective innovation policies for Europe – the missing demand side', PREST, Manchester Business School, University of Manchester.

Kessler, E., Bierly, P. and Gopalakrishnan, S. (2000), 'Internal vs. external learning in new product development: effects on speed, costs, and competitive advantage', *R&D Management*, **30**(3), 213–23.

Koop, G. (2001), 'Cross-industrial patterns of efficiency and technical change in manufacturing', *International Economic Review*, **42**(1), 73–103.

Kuhlmann, S. (2001), 'Future governance of innovation policy in Europe – three scenarios', *Research Policy*, **30**, 953–76.

Lengrand, L. (2003), 'Innovation tomorrow – innovation policy and the regulatory framework: making innovation an integral part of the broader structural agenda', Directorate General for Enterprise Innovation Papers No. 28, EUR 17052.

Lundvall, B.-Å. (ed.) (1992), *National Systems of Innovation: Towards a Theory of Innovation and Interactive Learning*, London: Pinter.

Mahadevan, R. (2002), 'New currents in productivity analysis: where to now?', Productivity Series 31, Asian Productivity Organization, APO, Tokyo.

Nilsson, J.E. (2004), *Innovation Policy as an Alternative to Institutional Changes*, Bollschweil: Hagbarth Publications.

Pianta, M. (2010), 'After the crisis: towards a sustainable growth model', available at http://works.bepress.com/mario_pianta/69.

Soete, L. (2007), 'From industrial to innovation policy', *Journal of Industry, Competition and Trade*, **7**, 273–84.

Wang, E.C. (2007), 'R&D efficiency and economic performance: a cross-country analysis using the stochastic frontier approach', *Journal of Policy Modeling*, **29**(2), 345–60.

Index

Comecon and the Politics of Integration

Henry Wilcox Schaefer

Comecon and the Politics of Integration

PRAEGER SPECIAL STUDIES IN INTERNATIONAL POLITICS AND PUBLIC AFFAIRS

Praeger Publishers New York Washington London

PRAEGER PUBLISHERS
111 Fourth Avenue, New York, N.Y. 10003, U.S.A.
5, Cromwell Place, London S.W.7, England

Published in the United States of America in 1972
by Praeger Publishers, Inc.

Library of Congress Catalog Card Number: 79-151957

Printed in the United States of America

" 'The first thing I've got to do,' said Alice . . . as she wandered about in the wood, 'is to grow to my right size . . . and the second thing is to find my way into that lovely garden. I think that will be the best plan.'

"It sounded an excellent plan, no doubt, and very neatly and simply arranged; the only difficulty was, that she had not the smallest idea how to set about it. . . ."

Lewis Carroll,

Alice's Adventures in Wonderland

PREFACE

Since the mid-1950s the pursuit of the Marxist-Leninist dream of one "socialist" world economy has centered on the more prosaic task of improving the forms and methods of economic cooperation within Comecon (Council for Mutual Economic Assistance). This organization has had four phases since its creation in 1949: a dormant phase until 1955; an activization phase from then until 1962; a consolidation phase between 1963 and 1968; and a reactivization phase after 1968. During this last, a "complex integration program" was formulated which is supposed to guide the first fifteen-to-twenty-year period of "socialist" economic integration. After a short introductory chapter, this book picks up the story of Comecon after the invasion of Czechoslovakia in August, 1968, and carries it through the initial reactions to the approval of the integration program in July, 1971.

The approach taken is chronological rather than topical, and is more political than economic, in that it tries to determine the positions adopted by the members during their discussions of Comecon, as well as the results of these discussions, in order to provide a partial record of intrabloc relations during this period and to gain some insight into the still differing concepts of integration that have evolved. Accordingly, no attempt is made to define integration a priori or to fit its socialist version into Western economic or political theory. By and large the differences over topical issues within individual member countries are ignored, and the focus is on the more official media and spokesmen, instead of on academic thinking. The familiar barriers to integration within Comecon—the weakness of its executive, the lack of rational prices or effective incentives to specialization and cooperation, the tendencies toward autarky and bilateralism, etc.—are not elaborated on but are introduced only when necessary to a discussion of the positions and programs of Comecon members. Likewise, there is no attempt made to weigh Comecon's achievements against its failures or to marshal evidence in regard to such aspects of integration as trade growth, specialization, cooperation, or flows of the factors of production.

Any attempt to decipher such a political-economic dialogue among communist countries of necessity involves the selective use of a large amount of information which is itself very incomplete, particularly when it comes to the proceedings of closed-door meetings. To a large extent, therefore, what follows must be taken as a first approximation. The definitive history of Comecon developments can only be written from the inside, and to date there has been no indication that anyone in the East has the temerity to try it.

Munich, December, 1971

ACKNOWLEDGMENTS

In writing this book I have contracted a greater debt to others than is normally the case. My source material has been culled from the press and airwaves of Comecon members (see Appendix B for a listing of primary sources). For the most part this has not been done by me but by the monitors, translators, researchers, and editors at Radio Free Europe, the Foreign Broadcast Information Service, the Joint Publications Research Service, and elsewhere. For economy of space the monitoring/translation services have not been noted in the footnote references. To them I extend my thanks. I would also like to express my appreciation to J. F. Brown and Charles Andras for their wise counsel as this book took shape, and to Susan Hoover, Rose Marie Manger, and Unity Evans for typing and editorial assistance. Especial thanks go to Nancy for putting up with me while this effort was under way.

CONTENTS

LIST OF NEWS AGENCIES CITED

Agency		Country
ADN	Allgemeiner Deutschar Nachrichtendienst	East Germany
AFP	Agence France Presse	France
Agerpres	Agentia Romana de Presa	Rumania
BTA	Bulgarska Telegrafna Agentsia	Bulgaria
Ceteka	Ceskoslovenska Tiskova Kancelar	CSSR
dpa	Deutsche Presse Agentur	West Germany
MTI	Magyar Tavirati Iroda	Hungary
PAP	Polska Agencja	Poland
Tanjug	Telegrafska agencija Nova Jugoslavija	Yugoslavia
TASS	Telegrafnoe Agentstvo Sovetskogo Soiuza	USSR

Comecon and the Politics of Integration

CHAPTER

1

INTRODUCTION

Comecon* was founded in 1949, but it did not become active until the latter half of the 1950s. Between 1956 and 1962 many steps were taken to strengthen the organization: in 1956, twelve standing commissions were established; in 1960, it finally got a formal charter; and, in 1962, the "Basic Principles of the International Socialist Division of Labor" were ratified and the Executive Committee, composed of deputy premiers, was set up.[1] However, fears of the hegemonic aspirations that some had for Comecon and of the development and specialization schemes which were being considered led to growing misgivings in Eastern Europe. In 1962 Nikita Khrushchev's proposal for a "united planning organ" produced a sharp reaction, and, largely owing to Rumania's objections, the proposal was dropped.[2]

This rejection of the supranational approach to the development of economic relations within Comecon has been of major significance for its subsequent history. The modest possibilities for effective institutional innovations were reflected in the very limited impact of the agreement in 1963 to establish a new multilateral clearing scheme and a Comecon bank (International Bank for Economic Cooperation); the second multilateral scheme, like the first in 1957, proved abortive, and the bank has remained essentially a bookkeeping

---

*The Council for Mutal Economic Assistance, also known as CEMA or CMEA. Its members are Bulgaria, Czechoslovakia, East Germany, Hungary, Poland, Rumania, the USSR—and Mongolia. Because of its marginal role, Mongolia will be largely ignored in this study.

organization.* Moreover, two of Comecon's basic principles, which were now embodied in its charter, proved a continuing barrier to the development of closer economic ties.

These were the principles of interestedness and unanimity, the combination of which turned out to be a two-edged sword.** While primarily intended to preserve the principles of "full equality of rights, respect for one another's sovereignty and national interests, [and] mutual advantage" which were also embodied in the charter, the right to declare a lack of interest in a particular issue also carried with it the possibility that a member might declare interest with the intention, through the unanimity requirement, of preventing action by others who might be much more vitally concerned with the matter. Thus the principles of interestedness and unanimity could be turned into a right of veto.

After Khrushchev's efforts to strengthen it in the early 1960s had failed, Comecon found itself with the interested-party and unanimity principles still intact. Yet now Rumania, which continued to lead the struggle against change, was if anything even more wary and assertive of its interests and evidently was not adverse to using its statutory rights to weaken, delay, or veto not only projects which it felt posed an immediate economic threat but also steps toward "integration" which threatened to weaken its longer-run economic and political independence. (It should be noted that even if pressured into accepting a decision a member had two further lines of resistance open: its government could refuse to adopt the Comecon recommendations or simply not implement them effectively[4]—and Comecon had no executive authority to prevent the latter.) The problem of how to proceed with cooperation among those who wished to do so while preserving Comecon's principles became a much debated one, and

---

*The failure of Comecon's second multilateral scheme has been acknowledged with increasing candor in recent years, particularly in the more reform-minded East European members.

**Article four of the charter states:

> All recommendations and decisions by the Council shall be adopted only with the consent of the interested member countries of the Council, and each country shall be entitled to declare its interest in any matter considered by the Council. The effects of recommendations and decisions shall not extend to countries which have declared their lack of interest in the question concerned.[3]

the indications were that not only the Soviet Union but also some others in Eastern Europe were annoyed by the Rumanian tactics.[5]

One way around the problem was to establish separate branch associations which would operate outside of the Comecon framework, and two such groups (Intermetall and the Organization for Cooperation in the Ballbearing Industry) were formed in 1964, without Rumanian participation. However, no more were formed during the next five years even though others were discussed. It has been conjectured that Rumania was "probably responsible for blocking what in its view may have been an undesirable proliferation of international agencies with some degree of executive authority, which could play a significant integrating role within their respective economic sectors."[6]

Comecon thus came through its first activization phase with a broadened and more complex organization, but without having progressed institutionally to the point of being really capable of effectively promoting closer economic ties. Comecon was a more active meeting place, a larger depository of information and a busier bookkeeper, but it still had an essentially passive role, having little or nothing to do operationally once a meeting was over and the national representatives had gone home. A major problem was, of course, what they went home to, the economies of the members of Comecon being still run essentially on the highly centralized model, with its well-known adverse impact on international trade, investment, specialization, and cooperation.

Nevertheless, by the mid-1960s there were new grounds for the hope that progress might soon be possible along more flexible, decentralized lines. The economic reform movement was much more widespread (at that time the only abstaining country was Rumania) than its abortive predecessor of the late 1950s, and, most significantly, the USSR was joining in. Even when the reform programs adopted did not incorporate the most progressive proposals, they were generally vague enough or experimental enough that one could hope for liberal interpretations and ultimately for more progressive revisions. One could foresee that, if the economic reforms made meaningful progress toward the decentralization of some domestic decision-making, it would be logical to permit such decisions to extend across national borders, particularly among the fraternal socialist countries, and that this could lead to some real institutional changes for Comecon. Especially among the more reform-minded members in Eastern Europe, it was increasingly felt that a greater use of economic criteria, a wider role for "commodity-money" relations, and decentralization of decision-making should be encouraged by Comecon, which, therefore, ought to be reformed in parallel with the changes in the individual member countries.

REFORM MOMENTUM BUILDS: 1967

Comecon entered 1967 amid growing concern over its ineffectiveness. The growth rate of intra-Comecon trade had been declining markedly, and this trade had grown more slowly in 1961-66 than trade with outside markets. Among other things this reflected the very limited success of specialization and cooperation and the failure to coordinate investments or to achieve multilateralism, as well as the great economic attraction of the West. Particularly when it was compared to the European Economic Community (EEC)—which East Europeans increasingly did—Comecon was an obvious failure.

During 1967 the pace of discussion of Comecon reform quickened in Eastern Europe. A particular need for reform was felt by the Hungarians, who in January, 1968, were planning to embark on their bold, carefully planned economic reform. They rightly saw that without changes in Comecon they would soon begin to meet the same institutional problems in Comecon trade which Yugoslavia (a Comecon observer since 1964) had increasingly met since the introduction of her far-reaching reforms in 1965 and 1966. Accordingly, the Hungarians saw the need to adapt Comecon institutions to the principles which their reform embraced. They advocated a devolution of decision-making from central planners and ministries to enterprises and associations (Hungary itself did not anticipate establishing the latter, but most of the other Comecon members were doing so) and emphasized the need to attack the closely related problems of multilateralism, exchange rates, credit, interest, convertibility, and the introduction of commercial principles, on which the development of any real market within Comecon depended. Jozsef Bognar, a leading architect of the Hungarian reform and a former Foreign Trade Minister argued that "Hungary's task . . . is to promote, through appropriate suggestions and proposals, the creation of a new mechanism for the economic relations among the Comecon countries. . . ."[7]

Discussion was also lively elsewhere in Eastern Europe, particularly in Czechoslovakia and Poland. At a time when their domestic reforms were not making notable progress, some Polish authors were boldly calling for operational exchange rates among Comecon currencies as the basic condition for an effective price system and for the multilateralization of settlements and were urging that "various experimental solutions" be introduced into Comecon foreign trade in order to broaden and stimulate the flow of goods.[8]

As part of the campaign for reform, some commentators were extremely critical of the results achieved by Comecon to date. For example, in reviewing the organization's recent efforts, a leading Czechoslovak journal complained that:

> In coordinating the plans for 1966-70, a number of projects set forth at the 19th meeting of Comecon were not carried through. A number of important problems remained to be solved at the bilateral meetings, having not been solved on a multilateral basis. In the field of coordination, the main directions of specialization in machinery production were not clarified. Investment plans were not coordinated, and no over-all analysis was made of key problems in relation to the proportions and rate of development of basic production branches.[9]

Although it was recognized that there were basic differences in the various economic reform models, because of these reforms and the widespread recognition of Comecon's failings, by the end of 1967 to many observers the prospects for some real changes in Comecon appeared quite good. Hungary was introducing its comprehensive reform on schedule; the prospects for Czechoslovak reform were much improved, as Antonin Novotny appeared to be on the way out; Rumania had just announced a new (if limited) reform program; and, for all its inaction, Bulgaria was still officially committed to its progressive-sounding reform model. Moreover, the reform movement was having a significant impact on Comecon discussions. At the twenty-first Council session in December, 1967, it was reported to be "in the spotlight during the general debate."[10] As a result Piotr Jaroszewicz, the Polish representative to Comecon and the leading Polish spokesman on Comecon matters, saw the difficulties of 1966 and 1967 as being of a "transitory character" because new approaches, including the establishment of direct links between producing and foreign trade enterprises, would "gradually overcome" Comecon's problems.[11] A leading Hungarian economist had the temerity to state at the end of 1967 that he was "absolutely certain that by the end of this decade many further steps will have been taken for greater multilateralization of finance," although in a more circumspect passage he added that, while the new period of diversified economic reforms required new solutions to Comecon's problems, in this process the role of the USSR would be decisive.[12]

The USSR's view in 1967 was somewhat enigmatic, in part reflecting the fact that, since Khrushchev had forced the supranational issue in 1962 and had been defeated, the USSR knew much better what it didn't want for Comecon than what it did want. It apparently didn't want economic relations among East European members to become significantly closer unless the Soviet Union was also included. It didn't want Comecon members to become too economically involved with Western countries or to develop relations with the EEC. Perhaps most significantly, it did not want Comecon reform to lead the domestic reform movement or to help to provide its members with the means to slip out from under the Comecon yoke.

At the same time, despite its growing complaints about the economic burden of Eastern Europe, the USSR had no clear idea of the sort of new institutional forms really needed to solve Comecon's problems and thereby to bolster the East European economies and to reduce the economic burden on itself. A primary reason for this was the uncertain outcome of its own economic reform, which—in 1967—was just being introduced. Although the Soviet concept was conservative by East European standards, at that time one could still imagine that either the reform itself might take on a more progressive aspect after its initial phase or that, given the marginal role of foreign economic relations in the Soviet economy, it might be made to adjust to more progressive reforms in Eastern Europe and in Comecon institutions.

But the Soviets were generally wary of Comecon reform. An article in the spring of 1967 by Nikolai Fadeyev, Comecon Secretary since 1958, reflected the cautious Soviet approach to change.[13] Unlike many observers in Eastern Europe, Fadeyev did not view Comecon's difficulties over specialization, cooperation, and trade as deriving from a basic institutional failing which require a major overhaul of the organization itself, but rather approached these problems piecemeal and sought more prosaic causes for them. He felt that the situation did not require major changes in the approach to plan coordination but that a shift in emphasis in the "levers" used to carry out these plans was needed. His approach to specialization and cooperation was similar. After claiming that the major objective difficulty with specialization was the difference in economic levels among Comecon members, he said that the basic reasons Comecon specialization recommendations are not always carried out are:

> First, changes in the national economic plans of the Comecon countries, notably in capital investment (which leads to a change in the country's requirements for specialized products); and secondly, failure of the producing countries to develop in time the production facilities to ensure the manufacture of the products earmarked for delivery under the recommendations, or delay in developing production of these items. Departures from the adopted recommendations are also due to the fact that equipment made in some Comecon countries fails to meet the required technical standard or is of low quality.

Clearly there was no sense of the basic institutional failing of Comecon here, and, in fact, there was a quite determined attempt to find the causes of Comecon's problems elsewhere.

A similar approach to the significance and methods of plan coordination and specialization was adopted a few months later by the Soviet permanent representative to Comecon, Mikhail Lesechko, in his report on an Executive Committee decision on organizating plan coordination for 1971-75.[14]

PRE-AUGUST, 1968

In 1968 Comecon's problems promised to be exacerbated by the further introduction of economic reforms, notably in Hungary and Czechoslovakia. This was recognized early in 1968 in Pravda when a leading Soviet commentator on Comecon affairs, Oleg Bogomolov, in discussing closer integration, acknowledged that new methods of cooperation would have to be evolved because the economic reforms were enhancing the role of economic considerations and of decentralized decision making.[15] Already economic reforms were being blamed for part of the trade slowdown because they "considerably reduced the effectiveness of the forms of promoting trade hitherto in use."[16] The problem was seen to be that the binding force of intergovernmental agreements was being weakened, while new means of promoting trade, specialization, and cooperation had not yet been developed.

Differences over how Comecon should react to the reform question were still being debated at the highest Comecon levels. A Yugoslav correspondent reported that

> Some members think that the economic reforms must adjust themselves to the necessity of coordinating national plans. This is an opinion which was defended by individual participants in the discussion at the last meeting of the Comecon Executive Committee in Budapest, who blamed the economic reforms for all the difficulties. Others, however, think that the form of cooperation in Comecon and its work methods should not reduce the room for economic reforms in individual countries.[17]

However, during the spring of 1968, the issue of Comecon, as with the question of economic reform in Czechoslovakia, became progressively more political.

This was in large part due to the increasingly outspoken views of the Czechoslovaks. In January, at a meeting of the Czechoslovak delegations to permanent Comecon organs, the representative to Comecon, Otakar Simunek, criticized it for not advancing as rapidly as the economic reforms in its member states and stated that during 1968 the attention of the Czechoslovak representatives would be primarily directed at reforming Comecon operations.[18] Criticism of Comecon intensified, particularly in Czechoslovak news media. In reporting on the Thirty-third session of Comecon's Executive Committee at the end of February, Radio Prague complained that the chronically insufficient information about Executive Committee discussions "bespoke a certain stagnation in the activity of this organ."[19] A few days later the "one-sided half-truths" about Comecon successes which led to "distrust" were criticized in a panel discussion.[20] Official spokesmen were not much more charitable. In an interview, the Deputy Minister of Planning, Vitezslav Vinklarek, noted that Comecon's economic role was "altogether insufficient" and that as an institution Comecon had "undoubtedly become outdated," but, since no new concept had been found, stagnation had taken place.[21]

The problem of the divergence of economic reforms was clearly recognized. Because Czechoslovak enterprises were to have greater power than those in most other countries, new arrangements were seen to be necessary, yet it was also argued that the necessity for equal partnership required that the partner of an enterprise in one country should not be the government agency of another.[22] The implication appeared to be that either others had also to reform or Czechoslovak enterprises might have to look elsewhere for equal partners.

This seeming threat gained support from the shifting emphasis on questions of convertibility and credit. Czechoslovakia's impatience was evident, for example, when, in a discussion of Comecon problems, one commentator stated;

> I have visited all the socialist countries and in each I asked leading representatives to what extent they were interested in convertibility of currency. The Poles say they are interested; so do the Hungarians, just as we are, but not at the moment. They want to achieve it only gradually. In Rumania, in Bulgaria, and in the Soviet Union, this problem is not even considered.[23]

Independent Czechoslovak action on the convertibility question was suggested and was linked to the questions of participation in international monetary institutions and foreign credit. In his speech to the Central Committee Plenum on April 1, Bohumil Sucharda, the Czechoslovak Finance Minister, discussed the prospects for eventual convertibility of the crown.[24] He argued that convertibility would require structural changes and, perhaps, foreign credits, as the essential condition for crown convertibility was the "convertibility" of Czechoslovak products (i.e., the availability and acceptability of

Czechoslovak goods on world markets). Shortly thereafter the employees of the Czechoslovak Finance Ministry passed a resolution which found the "weakness of the Czechoslovak crown on an international scale [to be] a situation unworthy of the Czechoslovak economy and one which causes much political and economic damage."[25] They called for convertibility to be achieved within the next five years and for the restoration of Czechoslovak participation in international monetary institutions. Recurring reports that the Czechoslovaks were negotiating for Western credit—even with the Vatican—while simultaneously trying to arrange a loan from the USSR, strengthened the impression that closer Western economic cooperation was considered a very real alternative to Comecon. Some remarks by Premier Oldrich Cernik on August 17 were interpreted to mean that Czechoslovakia was considering massive loans from the World Bank, but, on August 19, in one of history's more futile footnotes, this was denied in both Prague and Washington.[26]

The public reaction to the increasingly independent Czechoslovak position vis-a-vis Comecon in the rest of Eastern Europe was largely one of watchful silence. It was generally understood that both the unilateral pursuit of convertibility and massive Western credits were anathema to the USSR; some countries, including Hungary, were careful to urge that the Comecon members move toward convertibility as a group, with Soviet support. In April, Hungarian Premier Jeno Fock managed to praise the "positive development" and "progressive ideas" in Czechoslovakia and to criticize "outdated forms" in Comecon in the same interview,[27] but this was exceptional.

Meanwhile, it had become increasingly clear that Comecon affairs were getting too serious to be handled through normal channels. The Dresden meeting of top political and economic leaders in March agreed to hold an economic summit in the near future. Although more prosaic long-range economic questions naturally were submerged as attention shifted increasingly to the political and social developments of the Prague Spring, at the height of the crisis in early August the issue was felt to be significant enough for the Bratislava declaration to assert the "urgent need to call a top-level economic conference in the immediate future." It was never very clear, however, just what the purpose of the summit conference as then conceived would be, or even who would attend.

Rumania was absent from the Dresden and Bratislava meetings, which led to speculations that the Soviets had decided to revamp Comecon (and the Warsaw Pact) without full Rumanian acquiescence or participation. Although Rumania later objected to decisions being taken in its absence, there was considerable evidence that a certain detachment from Comecon, among other things, was just what the

Rumanians wanted. They had been absenting themselves more frequently from routine Comecon meetings, and their success in shifting trade to the West and the relatively good harvests in 1966 and 1967 had strengthened their confidence. While reasserting its willingness to cooperate within Comecon, Rumania was still quick to reject any idea smacking of supranationalism. Although the Rumanians sometimes appeared hypersensitive on this latter question, it seemed clear that some of those behind the Dresden and Bratislava calls for an economic summit were not thinking in terms of accommodating Comecon either to economic reforms or to semi-independent members, but quite the opposite. At a minimum the Rumanians were very uncertain, not only about the outcome in Czechoslovakia but even about what the Soviets would have wanted for Comecon without the Czechoslovak complication.

This Rumanian uncertainty reflected the continued lack of any clear Soviet idea of what Comecon ought to be, even among the specialists. On the increased need for economic integration of Comecon and such general goals as improvement of the principles and methods of coordinating plans, there was general agreement. On the means of achieving these goals there was none, as was acknowledged in a Soviet review of a major Soviet work on Comecon, which observed that nowhere in the Soviet literature on Comecon was there yet an "integrated system of views."[28]

NOTES

1. For details see Michael Kaser, Comecon: Integration Problems of the Planned Economies (Second edition; London: Oxford University Press, 1967), chs. 5, 6.

2. N. S. Khrushchev, Kommunist, 12 (August 1962), and in his report to the Central Committee plenum in November, 1962.

3. As translated in Michael Kaser, op. cit., p. 238.

4. According to the charter, only decisions on organizational and procedural matters are exempt from ratification by "governments or competent authorities in accordance with their national legislation," while on all matters of cooperation only recommendations can be made, and these then require such approval. Ibid., pp. 237-38.

5. See, for example, the citations in Hertha Heiss, "The Council for Mutual Economic Assistance—Developments Since the Mid-1960s," in Economic Developments in Countries of Eastern Europe: A Compendium of Papers (Washington D.C.: Joint Economic Committee, U.S. Congress, 1970), p. 530.

6. *Ibid.*, p. 537.

7. Jozsef Bognar, *The New Hungarian Quarterly*, Summer, 1967.

8. Stanislaw Polaczek, *Gospodarka Planova*, August-September, 1967; and Artur Bodnar, *Zycie Gospodareze*, July 9, 1967.

9. *Planovane Hospodarstvi*, May, 1967.

10. Statement by the Yugoslav representative, Aleksandar Grlickov, as reported by Tanjug, December 20, 1967.

11. Piotr Jaroszewicz, *Trybuna Ludu*, December 30, 1967-January 1, 1968.

12. Lecture by Michael Simai, Columbia University, December 5, 1967.

13. *International Affairs*, April, 1967.

14. *Ekonomicheskaia Gazeta*, August 4, 1967.

15. Oleg Bogomolov, *Pravda*, January 13, 1968.

16. Jaroszewicz, *op. cit.*

17. Slobodan Vujica, *Borba*, April 19, 1968.

18. Report on Otakar Simunek's address, Radio Prague, January 26, 1968.

19. Radio Prague, March 1, 1968.

20. Radio Prague, March 4, 1968.

21. Interview with Vitezsav Vinklarek in *Prace*, May 18, 1968.

22. Interview with Radoslav Selucky in *Svobodne Slovo*, reported by Radio Prague, April 20, 1968.

23. Tomas Randak, speaking at a panel discussion over Radio Prague, March 4, 1968.

24. *Rude Pravo*, April 2, 1968.

25. Resolution passed at a meeting of Ministry of Finance employees on April 8, 1968 (Ceteka, April 8, 1968).

26. Cernik's reply to an Austrian television reporter in an interview was the source of the problem; Czechoslovak media claimed he was misinterpreted (Ceteka, August 19, 1968).

27. Jeno Fock, in an interview with Hungarian television and Radio Budapest, April 23, 1968.

28. Petr Alampieyev, Voprosy Ekonomiki, 10 (1968), reviewing Oleg Bogomolov, Teoriia i Metodologiia Mezhdunarodnogo Sotsialsticheskogo razdeleniia truda [The theory and methodology of the international socialist division of labor] (Moscow: Mysl' Publishing House, 1967).

CHAPTER

2

THE AFTERMATH OF INVASION

The invasion of Czechoslovakia had important consequences for Comecon. For one thing, it arrested the incipient disintegration. Both Czechoslovakia and Rumania, along with Yugoslavia, came under sharp attack for their independent economic policies, and there was now no question of Czechoslovakia's going it alone in terms of convertibility or economic relations with the West. Although Rumania was shortly to reassert its position on the issues of supranationalism and "integration," it became much more a part of the group, regularly in attendance at Comecon meetings, and not flaunting its relations with the West.

More significant was the invasion's impact on prospects for a market-type solution to Comecon's problems. Czechoslovakia—as well as Yugoslavia—was strongly attacked for its economic reform ideas, and the hopes for a second (besides Hungary's) market-oriented reform within Comecon were dashed, the obituary to the abortive liberal Bulgarian reform having already been written in July, 1968, at the Party Central Committee Plenum. The impression quickly got around that there might be "some scheme forthcoming which would make the economic systems of the Comecon member countries more uniform."[1] This notion received a significant boost at the Ninth Plenum of the East German Party Central Committee in October, when Party Chairman Walter Ulbricht stated:

> Since our countries have identical social-economic foundations and since, therefore, the objective economic laws of socialism work in the same way, we would like to advocate the idea that the basic principles of the economic system of socialism should be implemented in all our countries.[2]

However, the threat of supranationalism was a much more widespread fear in the aftermath of the invasion than was that of directly imposed uniformity in the domestic economic sphere. It was widely anticipated that the USSR, supported by East European hard-liners, would push through plans for a much strengthened and more inward-looking Comecon with some supranational powers. Such a development was seen as the logical economic counterpart to the anticipated political and military tightening up and also as a direct implication of the attacks on relations with the West and on too-progressive economic reforms which supported such relations. According to the Soviet Army daily, Comecon's correct course was to develop with the "least possible dependence on capitalist countries."[3] A subsequent editorial in Pravda lent support to fears of supranationalism by ignoring the oft-repeated reference to "respect for sovereignty and national interests" (from Comecon's charter) when it spoke of

> further strengthening of economic and scientific-technological ties on the basis of respect and equality among the partners, of territorial integrity, independence and socialist solidarity.[4]

Because this statement coincided with enunciation of the new "Brezhnev doctrine" on limited sovereignty, the omission could easily be interpreted as an indication of that doctrine's extension into the economic sphere.

Ulbricht at the Ninth Plenum also gave support to the idea that plans were afoot to turn Comecon inward, when he said,

> In the bitter dispute between socialism and imperialism on a world-wide scale, there is one law of the class struggle between the socialist and imperialist states that is now taking shape; this is the law that the community of socialist states must solve each and every important scientific-technological, military, economic, or other problem through its own strength and with its own resources. . . .[5]

The expectations of a hard line on Comecon were further intensified when, at the Fifth Congress of the Polish Party in November, Partyleader Wladyslaw Gomulka argued that:

> economic integration demands the strengthening of the complex economic links among the Comecon countries [and is] not only an economic necessity . . . [but is also of] immense political importance in the present phase of the struggle and competition between the [capitalist and communist] systems.[6]

An article in the Bulgarian party daily shortly after the Fifth Polish Congress forcefully presented the arguments for a much strengthened Comecon, along centralist lines, and supported Ulbricht's position on relations with the West. The author urged that economic cooperation "must be basically carried out among the socialist countries which have identical economic, political and ideological foundations." He maintained that dependence on capitalist states must be avoided, for the "independence of socialist countries, and especially of the relatively small ones among them, is guaranteed by their membership in the socialist community," and he polemicized with those who were in favor of "direct interenterprise relations without general coordination," asserting that "socialist countries are facing a clearly mapped out future."[7]

Thus, a certain consensus appeared to have been reached among the hardliners as to the general economic implications of the Czechoslovak experience.

Many who were expecting the blow to fall thought that it would come at the oft-delayed summit which was widely expected to coincide with Comecon's twentieth-anniversary meeting in January. When in December a prominent Soviet economist, Gennady Sorokin, spoke of the present stage of coordination of plans as "only the introduction to a single economic plan for all socialist countries" and argued that the "question is not so much the intensification as a new organization of general planning," this was taken by some to be the harbinger of a Soviet-dictated "solution" to the Comecon problem.[8] However, although this position undoubtedly reflected some high-level views, particularly in the Soviet Party, these ideas were offered as a personal opinion, and it was acknowledged that there were two views on the future of Comecon.

This acknowledgment was well warranted for, despite the growing hard line on Comecon, which was discernible, there was no evidence that the confusion and division over what to do about Comecon in terms of a concrete program had been overcome. At the Fifth Polish Congress neither Gomulka, Leonid Brezhnev, nor Ulbricht—all of whom discussed Comecon—actually suggested supranationalist solutions, or any particular solutions. In sharp contrast to his usual political bombast, Ulbricht hardly sounded like Ulbricht when, in discussing Comecon, he remarked:

> We have formulated our concepts . . . and made them available to the interested fraternal parties. The other Parties have also prepared and sent us their concepts. I hope we will soon see good results in this field and make progress.[9]

There were some very good reasons for hesitating over a more supranationalist, self-centered solution to Comecon's problems. The most obvious was that it wouldn't work. Few familiar with the mounting problems of the still over centralized Soviet economy or with economic centralism's failings in Czechoslovakia could see much hope for a viable solution along such lines. It was also widely recognized that both Eastern Europe and the USSR badly needed economic and technological help from the West.

Moreover, even those in Eastern Europe who might have felt forced to accept tighter political and military control were not necessarily ready to relinquish a significant measure of economic control, any more than they had been in the past. Rumania continued to come out strongly against any renunciation of the principles embodied in Comecon's statute, asserting that any form of economic supranationalism was unacceptable and that, while perfecting and intensifying collaboration within Comecon was proper, "integration" was not.[10]

Hungary had also decided, as in the case of its internal economic reform, that the best defense was a good offense. As early as September, Hungary's representative to Comecon, Antal Apro, was warning against isolation from the world economy and arguing that closer Comecon integration necessitated a common currency, for which Hungarian experts were preparing proposals.[11] Magyar Hirlap, the official organ of the Hungarian Government, was arguing that nothing essential had changed in East-West relations and was urging the continued development of détente.[12] In November, Apro was speaking forcefully for Comecon reform in line with Hungary's progressive internal economic reforms.[13] A few days later Radio Budapest boldly suggested that it might be worth adopting some of the proven methods of the EEC within Comecon—foreign trade, for example, where the "quota system should be abolished and foreign trade liberalized," noting that this had taken place long ago in Western Europe and asserting that the "socialist countries have reached the appropriate stage of development for adopting liberalization now."[14]

Moreover, though naturally muted, there were still voices in Czechoslovakia critical of Comecon and arguing that basic reform in the financial sphere, rather than coordination of planning, was the crucial issue.[15] Any attempt to give Comecon some sort of a supranationalist role or to cut off its members from the West was clearly still going to cause a fight.

Even in December there were indications that a tightly centralized solution was not necessarily to be the basis of the Soviet position. One Soviet writer took a quite moderate line, arguing that

> [during the] present stage, socialist integration consists of independent national economic complexes.

> . . . The only basis on which decisions are implemented is the voluntary consent of the countries and their economic interest in joint activities. That is why [plan] coordination at the present stage is the best and only possible method for Comecon's work. . . .[16]

The idea was of course not simply to stick with the old unsatisfactory plan coordination but to improve it greatly. But it was asserted that the "real meaning" of plan coordination does not lie in a coordination of general plan indicators, but rather in closer coordination by branch. To achieve this it was felt necessary to have, in conjunction with the introduction of new management systems, an increased role for individual industrial enterprises and foreign trade organizations, an increase in direct ties at various levels, greater material interest in enterprises, a more active use of "commodity-money instruments," and greater emphasis on production cooperation than on (mere) specialization.

As an important corollary, there appeared a determination to overcome the veto problem by modifying the principle of interestedness in order to exclude those not really interested in a "positive solution" to a particular problem:

> In the coming period, the principle of interestedness will be applied within the framework of Comecon to a considerably greater extent than formerly.
>
> This will mean that important questions of economic cooperation will be discussed and resolved by a definite number of countries—namely, those interested in their solution. Moreover, the countries will not insist on discussion of each question by all Comecon countries, that is, by those which are not directly interested in them. As a result, many problems which were formerly shelved owing to some Comecon countries taking different positions may find a positive solution in the coming five-year period. . . .[17]

There was thus a comprehensive, activist Soviet model, which, while advocating significant innovations, promised voluntary participation in plan coordination and held no threat of supranationalism for the foreseeable future. While the duration of the "present stage" was left open, it was not presented, as Sorokin had done, as "only the introduction" to a single economic plan, and there was no call for a "new organization" of over-all planning.

Pravda, moreover, was now arguing soothingly that

> The cardinal difference between the development of economic ties among our socialist countries and the so-called economic integration under capitalism is that [our system] does not infringe in any way on the sovereignty of any partner.[18]

A few days later Radio Moscow presented an interview with the Bulgarian delegate to Comecon, Tono Tsolov, in which he sounded remarkably like a Rumanian when he stated,

> The basic principles on which the activity of Comecon is built are known. They are set out in the organization's documents which are widely published and they have been used successfully for 20 years in the work of Comecon. I should like to stress just two points: there is no precedent in past practice for the council's adopting a decision or recommendation by which the interests of any country would be infringed in any degree whatsoever. It could not be otherwise, because decisions and recommendations can only be implemented with the agreement of all interested parties. Moreover, the countries carry out the recommendations which have been adopted only after they have been approved by their governments, or by another competent organ in accordance with the laws of the states concerned.[19]

Thus, by the end of 1968, the fears of an imminent Soviet-led push to grant Comecon supranational powers over member economies or to close the area more tightly to outside economic influence appeared to have been exaggerated, for the moderates were coming on strongly, even within the USSR.

In January, 1969, Comecon faced its twentieth birthday. Although its members were not ready for the long-promised summit and there was little to celebrate, protocol called for a meeting at which at least a modicum of unity and enthusiasm would be expressed. Twenty-second Comecon Council session of January 21-23 was intended to provide a suitable occasion.

In the early weeks of January, the moderate Soviet line continued in what appeared to be a determined effort to reduce the fears of those who felt the anniversary meeting might be used to push through plans for a more centralized Comecon. The Soviet press seldom even mentioned "integration," much less suggested supranational planning, and on the eve of the meeting Fadeyev took a very moderate line in <u>Pravda</u>, as did the Soviet deputy permanent representative to Comecon in Izvestiia. Fadeyev noted that "Comecon's work excludes any form of compulsion being applied to any state. All recommendations and decisions are adopted only by agreement with the countries concerned and apply only to them."[20]

A similar effort was apparently made at a symposium of Comecon specialists in Warsaw in mid-January. In reporting on the meeting Jozef Pajestka, newly appointed deputy chairman of the Polish State Planning Commission, was at pains to show understanding for those who had qualms about the evolution of Comecon.[21] He noted that

> We can accept as correct the principle that the more developed a country is, the more strongly it feels the need for integration. . . .
>
> The symposium agreed that it is still necessary for Comecon to preserve the principle of promoting individual undertakings by the states concerned without exerting any pressure.

Although Pajestka noted that the "very idea of integration met with full approval," he went on to say:

> The symposium assessed as unjustified concepts involving the introduction of planning on the scale of the entire socialist community—that is, supranational planning. International planning should be the basis of action—that is, planning which develops through the agreements among individual countries, while these countries retain their sovereign right to decide whether they want to participate in certain planning schemes or not. In addition, a country, if participating, is free to select solutions it wants to accept.[22]

At the symposium Sorokin was said to have supported Pajestka's view that in the foreseeable future a combination of plan coordination and financial instruments had to be employed, and reportedly acknowledged that the conditions for supranational planning did not exist and might only be created "in the very long run."[23]

DIFFERING VIEWS ON THE FUTURE

Rumania

Although the Rumanians were not present at this symposium, they undoubtedly had a good idea of what transpired and had followed the Soviet press closely. Despite the conciliatory efforts, the Rumanians could not be mollified—or silenced. While more cooperative on questions of participation and discussion, their campaign against a strengthened Comecon continued to reject not only supranationalism but also proposals for "integration," which, it was argued, clearly implied a limitation of sovereignty. All forms of economic integration, including the EEC, were attacked for inhibiting the necessary trend toward collaboration with all states. Lenin was invoked when it was argued that the danger of capitalist-style international monopoly, i.e., external economic control, was inherent in joint enterprises.[24] The basic Rumanian position was that there were still many possibilities for closer cooperation within the existing Comecon framework and that, while forms and methods might be improved, nothing should be done to change the principles of cooperation in any way.

A number of reasons for such an outspoken resistance to change, despite the assurances given, can be suggested. The Rumanians were naturally hypersensitive since the old battle over supranationalism with Khrushchev and, as then, undoubtedly feared for their ambitious comprehensive industrialization plans, should new industries become the focus of integration, as some people had been suggesting. They were also uncertain and suspicious of the ultimate aims of the Soviets and of East European advocates of integration, perhaps feeling that any concessions would be just the thin end of the wedge, and probably saw a minimalist position on change within Comecon as the best tactical approach to warding off more substantial future threats to their economic sovereignty.

The Rumanian position also derived in large part from its unique economic situation in Eastern Europe. Since it possesses more natural resources, notably oil, than the rest of Comecon's East European members and had shifted a major share of its trade to the West in recent years, Rumania saw Comecon much more as a vehicle for reasserting Soviet economic hegemony than did the rest of Eastern Europe, where bilateral dependence on Soviet supplies and markets was still very great. Rumania was also one of the least developed and, largely as a result of this, one of the least reform-minded of the Comecon countries in the economic sphere. Therefore, it had been under much less pressure to pursue intensive development and to participate in the socialist division of labor or to try to make Comecon institutions reform in line with a changing domestic economic system.

Rumanian resistance to strengthening Comecon and its stress on sovereignty, however, appear to have been perhaps even more a matter of principle that had its basic motivation and major implications in the political and military fields. The Brezhnev doctrine and the strengthening of the Warsaw Pact would serve the same Soviet general interests as would a strengthened Comecon and, particularly at that time, in the aftermath of the invasion, posed a much more immediate and direct threat to Rumania's national independence. Then, as always, Rumanian polemics over supranationalism and sovereignty within Comecon had implications far beyond the economic field.

Although generally not sharing the economic motivations of the other East European Comecon members, Rumania did find herself in agreement with some of them on a number of basic politically significant issues. This was particularly true in the case of Hungary, despite the fact that its was the most far-reaching internal economic reform and that as a result it was calling for a radical overhaul of Comecon.

Hungary

Hungary's basic position was spelled out publicly in two stages. The first was in an article in December by Antal Apro.[25] He criticized Comecon and argued the case for a major overhaul of its operations, using the EEC as both an example and a threat. He noted that there were basic differences in economic approach in member countries and that "the practical coordination of these strongly differing ideas is hardly imaginable." His answer was to create a new, more flexible framework that would preserve national sovereignty over economic policy and reforms. Essentially, Comecon would become more integrated from the bottom up; general policy only would be coordinated at the top.

> The continuous coordination of economic policy ideas of basic importance from the point of view of development would provide stability and security for the countries to work out their independent economic plans, and for the manifold coordination of the plans.

Operational powers would even have to shift increasingly away from Comecon to organizations within member countries.

> Some of the tasks of specialization and cooperation have been transferred from the permanent committee and ministerial level of Comecon to the agencies and enterprises directly interested. In all probability we shall have to proceed in this direction.[26]

Apro then outlined some of the steps Hungary advocated for providing the framework for integration through decentralized decision-making.

These included the introduction of multilateral settlement, the establishment of a customs system and a "socialist duty-free zone," and the use of commercial credits. Thus, the Comecon system envisioned would closely parallel Hungary's internal market-type economic reform under which broad policy is made at the top but operational decisions are made by enterprises and new institutions are introduced for guiding these decisions and directing the economy toward the desired centrally determined goals.

The Hungarian proposals were outlined in more detail in the midst of Comecon's anniversary session, during a lecture by Rezso Nyers (Hungarian Politburo member, secretary of the Central Committee, and a leading architect of the Hungarian economic reform).[27] Nyers began by arguing the universality of the necessity for integration and asserting that capitalist and socialist integration

> will be similar, in that economic efficiency, the measure of profitability, will come under the control of the international market in both cases, and technological development will take place in an international climate.

He then argued that the "difference will be decisive" because competition among monopoly capitalists is bad, while competition among "socialist" enterprises is good. This cursory dialectical bow to ideology served to justify the subsequent argument for a reform program which would introduce market integration at the Comecon level and leave the preservation of "socialism" to its individual members.

After emphasizing the political importance of the Comecon reform question, Nyers set out certain questions of principle which he felt must be settled before a definitive program for Comecon could be determined. On the issue of the maintenance of national independence he rejected "joint planning at the Comecon summit" in favor of the "fundamental" necessity for national independence, but acknowledged that

> Economic development brings about an intensification of the jointly dependent status of the national economies. Assumption of mutual interdependence is possible on a sensible basis, while preserving the essence of national independence.[28]

This greater mutual interdependence would be built on the basis of direct voluntary relations between enterprises and trusts and a new system for promoting and guiding the economic interest of these organizations. Nyers elaborated on Apro's proposals, suggesting, among other things, a flexible foreign trade price system and partial convertibility of the common currency.

The Hungarians thus envisioned Comecon reform as a unified process under which internal economic reforms and foreign trade liberalization would be paralleled by a progressive adaptation of the financial and trading practices among member countries and under which the isolation of enterprises due to central planning would be overcome across state lines just as it was being overcome within Hungary. Trade liberalization, multilateralism, increased price flexibility, and the advance toward convertibility would proceed together in a coordinated step-by-step process.

All of this was seen as a rather long-term process. Nyers stated:

> Once such a program is accepted, implementation can be gradual. The first years of the 1970s may be regarded as a period of transition, the second half as the period when integration is brought into play.[29]

Although such a lack of urgency appeared difficult to reconcile with the rapidly evolving Hungarian economic reform which was the motivation for the Hungarian Comecon model, it reflected the basic premise on which the Hungarian proposals were built. This premise was that, for all the present incompatibility of other members much more conservative economic reforms and for all the setbacks to even these limited efforts, during the next few years these countries would move toward the sort of market reforms that Hungary was pioneering. Given the precariousness of its internal economic reform, particularly following the invasion, and the urgency of moving ahead with it, the Hungarian position could hardly be otherwise, for, if such an evolution did not eventually take place, the long-range prospects for the new Hungarian system would be jeopardized, no matter what its current success or acceptability to the USSR.

Hungarian proposals for such a radical overhaul of Comecon also appear to have served an important purpose in the shorter run. By strongly advocating an eventual full market solution to Comecon economic relations, Hungary must have hoped to forestall the centralists with their threats of supranational powers for Comecon. The climate for both internal economic reform and a liberal overhaul of Comecon could hardly have gotten much worse than it was at that time, and Hungary's immediate hope must have been simply to prevent the hardliners from taking the opportunity to push through centralist solutions that would reinforce conservative domestic reforms and prove difficult to undo in the future.

Thus, while Rumania and Hungary advocated very different programs for Comecon, their basic goal was the same: hold off the centralists. They also had similar aims in a number of other areas.

In order to prevent restrictions on their economic relations they both argued against a closer grouping and urged that Comecon be outward-looking with respect both to other communist countries and to the West, and felt that a basic aim in improving Comecon should be to help to make its members' economies competitive on the world market. They both stressed sovereignty and claimed the right to opt out of any particular scheme, seeing state or enterprise (in the Hungarian case) interests, not some higher bloc interest, as the motive force for decision-making in the economic relations among Comecon members. Whatever their differences on economic grounds, on the gut political issues Rumania and Hungary had much in common.

Czechoslovakia

Although at the official level much subdued and concerned with being absolved of its past criticism of Comecon, Czechoslovakia generally supported the flexible, market approach advocated by Hungary.[30] Czechoslovak economists recognized that the problem was not so much the oft-debated one of establishing a price base but rather one of price formation under market relations and the application of commercial principles. They clearly saw the limitations of ad hoc efforts at cooperation in the absence of a new system embodying real exchange rates, effective interest and credit policies, etc. It was noted that "Czechoslovak economists, like the Rumanians, are against infringement of sovereignty, but they are strong advocates of integration," although Comecon should remain "open to the world economy."[31] Thus, except for a not unexpected greater emphasis on integration with Comecon, the Czechoslovak position still reflected the preinvasion reform model. Hopes of retaining as much as possible of that model were probably a major factor in the Czechoslovak economists' arguments at this time, but Czechoslovakia could hardly expect to have much influence in Comecon debates so soon after the invasion.

Poland

As was reflected in Gomulka's remarks at the Fifth Party Congress and elsewhere, integration was as much a political as an economic necessity for the Poles. Both the need to hold off the West and the need to consolidate the camp were seen to require closer economic integration. Poland also had strong economic reasons for seeking closer Comecon relations. As one of the moderately developed members of Comecon it still had much to gain from cooperation with the group's most developed states, East Germany and Czechoslovakia. Poland was going through—or trying to go through—a transition period from extensive to intensive development and saw that the necessary rationalization and specialization could only be served through an effective division of labor.

Poland's conservative foreign policy, which was still highly critical of Czechoslovakia's preinvasion economic moves toward the West, led it to look more to Comecon than did Rumania or Hungary, while the focus of internal reform on economic policy, rather than on the economic system, led Poland to advocate a more complex and centralist set of measures for tightening integration than Hungary or Czechoslovakia desired. Comecon integration and the policies it would allow Poland to implement internally could even be seen as a sort of substitute for a real reform of the Polish economy.[32] There was also a feeling that Poland was losing out to other members of Comecon in the competition to sell industrial products, particularly machinery and equipment, within the area, and it was apparently hoped that tightened discipline over specialization would help both to preserve and to open these markets to Polish industry. In addition, Poland evidently hoped to become a net importer of capital if Comecon took a role in the allocation of investment within the area.

Although the Poles hardly can be said to have spoken with one voice, their approach to the reform of Comecon was essentially twofold.* On the one hand, it clearly recognized the "solid economic

---

*The Poles have probably written more on Comecon reform than any other member country, yet their official position has not always been very clear. This has stemmed in part from the fact that since 1956 they have launched and then partly or totally aborted three economic reform efforts, and, at any given time, including 1968-69, there has been a great deal of uncertainty over just how the Polish economic system was going to work, and hence over what sort of Comecon reforms Poland really should strive for. An interesting survey of some of the Polish discussion on Comecon reform during 1968 appeared in an article by M. Misiak in *Polish Perspectives*, February, 1969. The arguments for a differentiated approach to Comecon's problems were laid out succinctly by J. Soldaczuk and J. Gierzgala in *Gospodarka Planowa*, November, 1968. The closest thing to an official Polish position before the twentieth anniversary meeting appears to have been Piotr Jaroszewicz's article in *Trybuna Ludu* on December 30, 1968. What follows is an attempt to characterize what appeared to be the general Polish position at that time based on a variety of sources, including the subsequent reports (cited below) of the Polish position at the twentieth anniversary meeting and at the twenty-third Council session.

barriers"[33] separating the economies of the Comecon states and, like Hungary and Czechoslovakia, the limited scope, under existing conditions, for ad hoc approaches and such specialized associations as Intermetall. Therefore, Poland was a strong advocate of multilateralism, more realistic and more operational exchange rates, a form of convertibility, the greater use of credit and interest rates, some decentralization, etc. The release of market forces, however, was in the beginning to be only a small part of the Polish program. Liberalized exchange of goods was to be introduced gradually (and implicitly only as domestic economic reforms permitted), beginning with the consumer goods sphere. The main purpose of the Polish financial reform proposals was to support Comecon integration with the same sort of financial levers that were being introduced as an aid to central planning in most member countries. Partial convertibility of debt obligations into convertible currency obligations and higher interest rates were viewed as essentially disciplinary tools to be applied to chronic debtors. Multilateralism and restructured exchange rates were looked upon primarily as prerequisites of planned integration, not as preconditions for the release of market forces. As Jaroszewicz emphasized:

> The point is to equip our countries' planned coordination of economic development with appropriate economic instruments. . . .
>
> It should be strongly emphasized that the economic instruments and development of trade and financial relations will not replace conscious and planned coordination of economic development or long-term planning of international economic relations and division of labor.[34]

New financial instruments were seen as the necessary, but not the sufficient, condition for the integration that was sought.

The Poles did not believe that a new set of institutions designed to encourage economic relations through new levers and incentives would be sufficient by itself. They had discussed more than anybody else how difficult it would be to make external incentives interact effectively with the diverse economic systems of Comecon members and saw most clearly that, unless everyone unexpectedly turned suddenly to market socialism, the Hungarian proposals were essentially incomplete. Many felt that it was necessary to coordinate economic reforms more closely and argued that if centrally dictated prices (or price-determining policies) still prevailed in most member countries, some agreed approach to pricing (e.g., a uniform method of calculating domestic production costs) was necessary in order to rationalize internal and external decision-making criteria and the resulting division of labor. But it was felt that, even if such complex, technical problems could be solved through a certain amount of coordination of the economic reforms, the essentially directive-promulgated central planning prevailing in most countries would have to have its planning counterpart within the Comecon framework for integration to be effectively implemented.

The Poles therefore went beyond the Hungarian and Czechoslovak positions and urged a second set of reforms. These involved the planning of the things which it was thought that market relations—actual or simulated—could or would not do effectively for the Comecon countries. Their answer, however, was not dogmatic, but pragmatic: Approach each trade, specialization, or cooperative problem in the way that would best expand economic ties. Thus, if consumer goods could best be exchanged multilaterally on market principles, that approach should be adopted in that sphere. If, owing to scarcities, essential raw materials had to be bartered for each other under long-term agreements, that was acceptable—at least while Comecon worked toward more flexible, multilateral agreements through price and production rationalization. Because their determination was essential to integration, basic investments were to be included in the coordination of development plans; but because specialization, particularly for new industries, could not always be determined on the basis of current costs and comparative advantage or by any other available economic criteria and because even if it could, it was often too important strategically (e.g., in the fields of electronics, computers, or atomic energy) to be determined by such criteria alone, other considerations had to be taken into account.

Agreement had to be reached somehow: If effective specialization and investment allocation required political decisions and then a greater level of economic pressure to achieve effective fulfillment, the appropriate steps had to be taken. Once basic agreement had been reached, it was in everyone's interest to submit to the operational demands of Comecon in implementing it. Thus, it appeared that the Poles had a genuine interest in developing closer economic ties and had formulated a comprehensive program for reaching their goal.

The Poles, however, made a sharp distinction between integration and "full integration" or supranationalism.[35] It was necessary to muster the political will and to devise the economic instruments required finally to break through the barriers to a successful multilateral division of labor—one which would be more favorable to Poland and would further its intensive development—but this was not to be at the expense of national sovereignty or independence. The rationale for their position appeared to be that either the economic or the political benefits of greater multilateral interdependence should appeal to most of the rest of Comecon (Rumania being the exception), with both types of benefits appealing to the USSR—particularly after the Czechoslovak experience.

Their attitude contrasted most sharply with that of the Rumanians, who wanted neither integration nor any real changes in Comecon; but it was also more at odds with the Hungarian view (and with the Czechoslovak position, such as it was by then) than many observers recognized. For the Poles, convertibility and so on were basically the economic means to an end—integration. The goal was not so much a Comecon market which would facilitate and encourage internal market socialist reforms among members, but rather the use of actual or simulated market solutions to foster integration. Moreover, this integration was for political reasons essentially inward-looking and not deliberately designed to facilitate economic relations with the West.[36]

Bulgaria

Prior to the invasion of Czechoslovakia, at the July Bulgarian Central Committee Plenum, Party leader Todor Zhivkov rather unexpectedly had outlined a fairly comprehensive program for Comecon.[37] He called for closer integration within Comecon, but emphasized that for Bulgaria this "should be based on even greater rapprochement and interlinking between our economy and the economy of the USSR." He saw much in the integration process for Bulgaria, arguing that:

> The process of socialist integration and of increased socialist mutual aid should contribute to the rapid economic advance of the less-developed socialist countries, to equalizing the economic level of such countries with that of the economically advanced socialist countries.

He went on to call for

> the coordination of long-range forecasts and long-range plans in combination with the better use of the socialist market and of commodity-financial relations . . . a gradual development of international socialist trusts . . . mass production, in large series, of commodities for the entire camp; . . . [for] joint investment [and a] common investment policy with long-range prospects for the creation of enterprises, with Bulgarian stock participation in the development of major sources of raw materials; . . . [for the] creation of international

> production-trade organizations; . . . the organization of joint purchases and sales, including those on the capitalist market; . . . [and] developing international socialist medium and long-term investment credits on the basis of joint bank capital.

He called for a real international bank, as opposed to the existing clearing center, direct cooperation among associations, the gradual elimination of quotas, and for "developing, together with the other socialist countries, a system of measures leading to convertibility of the currencies of the socialist countries."

Zhivkov concluded by noting that these problems had been outlined only in their most general aspect and would be "reviewed and developed by the corresponding authorities so that our country may contribute to the creation of a more effective mechanism of cooperation among the socialist countries." They appear, however, never to have been very much "reviewed and developed" in Bulgaria, at least not publicly; and following the invasion the Bulgarian position appeared to stiffen, the emphasis shifting from the economic to the political, while those aspects of Zhivkov's remarks which had a more liberal cast were played down. As mentioned at the beginning of this chapter, an article in the party daily in November called for a strengthened and relatively self-sufficient Comecon along centralist lines and criticized those who favored interenterprise relations without proper control. In another article the director of the Bulgarian Foreign Trade Bank talked of the "fusion of the economies of the separate countries into a single organism" and, in discussing the prospects for convertibility, was considerably more circumspect than Zhivkov.[38] Although Zhivkov's July remarks on Comecon were nominally reaffirmed in principle in January—just prior to the twentieth-anniversary meeting—they do not appear to have been elaborated further, and these endorsements appeared largely ritualistic.[39]

This rather curious performance can perhaps best be explained by Bulgaria's economic position, the invasion, and the uncertainty which followed it. Although well known for a tendency to hyperbole, given their great economic and political dependence on the USSR, the Bulgarians would not normally be expected to urge such a seemingly far-reaching program unless they had seen clear signs that Comecon was moving in such a direction with Soviet approval. Assuming Zhivkov's July remarks were an attempt to appear in the vanguard while reminding everyone of Bulgaria's interests, they evidently reflected a conviction that the time was ripe for changes in Comecon. However, in view of what was happening in Czechoslovakia and the fact that the quite progressive original Bulgarian reform model was suffering a major setback at that same Plenum, it is questionable how seriously Zhivkov intended to promote the more liberal-sounding aspects of this Comecon program. In any case, Bulgaria's comparative reticence and shifting emphasis on Comecon reform after the invasion would seem to indicate that Zhivkov may have felt overexposed on the issue and was awaiting a new set of signals from Moscow.

East Germany

There evidently was considerable optimism in East Germany that the concepts of systemic uniformity and quasi-isolationism voiced by Ulbricht at the Ninth Plenum in October would get a favorable hearing in the immediate aftermath of the invasion of Czechoslovakia.[40] It was apparently felt that, along with strengthened bilateral economic ties to the USSR (and the Brezhnev doctrine), these approaches would prove sufficient to permit the development of a cohesive, viable bloc and the furtherance of East German interests. The political rationale for an inward-looking economic group which would solve "each and every" important problem on its own was directly linked by Ulbricht to the threat of imperialist subversion through creeping dependence if economic "concessions" were made to the West, and this quasi-isolationist theme became an oft-repeated one, with Comecon representative Gerhard Weiss reiterating it in his speech to the Twenty-second Council session and Premier Willi Stoph doing the same at a postmeeting reception.[41]

How economic problems were to be solved and top-level world standards still achieved, however, was not very clear, for the East Germans appeared to have little real enthusiasm for Comecon reform or for integration. They did not share others' interest in rationalizing the system of Comecon relations through multilateralism and some form of convertibility. It was argued rather that the "fundamental tasks" facing Comecon in the production sphere had to be tackled, and that financial problems were secondary. Liberalization of trade agreements was rejected because concrete agreements are essential for the planning of national economies.[42] But this left little room for institutional change and appeared to put the East Germans in the rather awkward position of being strong advocates of bloc cohesion but without any very tangible program, in the economic sphere, for achieving it.

They attempted to compensate for this by arguing strongly, albeit pretty vaguely, for a complex, systematic approach to co-operation problems and to the expansion of economic ties. A "tightened closing of ranks among the socialist countries" and "deliberately harmonized exploitation" of the Comecon countries' potential were called for, which required the "constant adjustment of the planned nature of foreign economic relations" and "planned long-term co-ordination" of scientific-technological relations.[43] Yet it was felt to be basically a question of using the full existing potential of socialist economic principles and of Comecon. There were "enormous reserves . . . still hidden" in the scientific-technological field,[44] and to develop them required a concerted attack on the barriers to cooperation. Planning must be extended, particularly into research, and the basic needs were for complex coordination, binding agreements, and better material incentives, while it was also necessary to expand such things as technical and servicing organizations which promote trade. Expansion of cooperation along these lines would eventually provide the prerequisites for the further development of Comecon's trade-and-payments system and for multilateral relations, but the time was not yet ripe for any institutional innovations in these spheres.[45]

The emphasis was on bilateral agreements, with Comecon itself playing a coordinating role. Comecon should help in the "clarification of fundamental, structure-determining questions of the economic development of the member nations," for this makes "it possible to synchronize the working rhythm of the bilateral agreement negotiations during the preparatory phase, and the conclusions of agreements in the required co-ordination phases." The fulfillment of these bilateral agreements could then be the subject of conferences of Comecon agencies.[46]

Despite the evidence of a political interest in strengthened economic ties, a singular lack of enthusiasm for Comecon was still evident in the East German media as the twentieth-anniversary meeting approached. Much attention was devoted to socialist laws, to the principles of economic reform, to the socialist foreign trade system, to the implications of the scientific and technological revolution and, of course, to convergence and revisionism, but comparatively little to integration or to Comecon per se. In fact Comecon was ignored even when it appeared rather undiplomatic not to say something, for example in the remarks on economic matters by Premier Stoph and by the secretary of the Central Committee in charge of economic affairs, Gunter Mittag, in the issues of *Einheit* immediately preceding the anniversary meeting.[47] Their continuing reluctance to urge much change in Comecon was reflected in Weiss's generally bland speech on the opening day of the anniversary session, in which he said:

> International coordination is of great importance for drawing up national plans, for *parallel planning* in our countries, and for working out long-term aims and problems of economic development. [Emphasis added.][48]

One got the impression that whatever interest the East Germans may have had in reinforcing socialist unity and preventing too much contact with the West, they did not view Comecon as a primary vehicle for achieving these aims.

If East Germany was hesitant about strengthening Comecon or reforming it along multilateral lines, there were sound economic reasons for this. As the most highly developed East European member of Comecon, East Germany had less to gain from cooperation than any other East European country and undoubtedly felt that any specialization planned from an over-all Comecon perspective could easily work to the benefit of less developed members, giving them opportunities in advanced industries that they could not have won competitively. East German articles reflected a great preoccupation with the attainment of the highest world levels of science and technology—something they could not get from other countries of Eastern Europe and would not normally find embodied in their products. The East Germans may also have felt that their economic reform (the earliest to be introduced) was essentially complete and required little help from a reformed Comecon. They evidently felt others had not yet gone far enough in rationalizing prices for multilateralism or convertibility moves to make much economic sense and did not want to decentralize foreign trade to the extent that some were projecting. Both economically and politically they seemed to fear the openings to the West that such reform moves might eventually provide for other Comecon members.[49] They may also have feared that eventually they would be forced toward market socialism should those favoring a greater use of market relations push through some significant changes.

Perhaps most to the point, East Germany had developed highly important, and in many ways unique, special relationships with the two countries which were able to supply it with advanced technology and the markets that it required—the USSR and West Germany. Although the debt to the latter has never been acknowledged, much of what was written at that time stressed the overwhelming importance attached to relations with the USSR. It is difficult to see how the East Germans could have convinced themselves that closer economic integration with the rest of Eastern Europe would offer many major economic advantages.

Ironically, if the East Germans did not attach any great urgency to integration, seemed wary of institutional changes, and adopted an essentially bilateral approach to relations with other Comecon countries, then, although at opposite poles in terms of their political interests, the East German and Rumanian positions regarding Comecon may not have been so far apart at that time.

USSR

The Soviet Union, however, was still the prime centralist suspect, despite the continuing variety and imprecision of its views. Many members felt that the USSR must want to tighten up Comecon along centralist lines simply because this seemed a logical extension of its over-all policy and, hence, that the soft line prior to the January meeting was a smoke screen to lull suspicion. By this reasoning, Sorokin's article was a maximalist position but reflected a real intent, and actual Soviet hopes could be seen in paler reflections of his line, which called for "strengthening of the mechanism of planned regulation of the process of economic cooperation."[50]

However, whatever its supposed rationale, Soviet commitment to the sort of integrated regional grouping that would include some sacrifice of Soviet sovereignty and increasing dependence of the East European countries on each other—particularly in new industrial fields and for advanced technology—had to be ambiguous at most. What was frequently interpreted as an almost self-evident Soviet interest in a strengthened, centralist Comecon was often simply the much more self-evident Soviet interest in bilaterally binding these states to itself. Moreover, the supranational threat to Western Europe posed by the EEC was a very popular theme at this time, as was the plan for an international Communist conference, and a drive for a supranational Comecon would hardly have served Soviet interests either in developing an alternative design for Europe or within the Communist movement. Although Eastern Europe might be an increasingly costly burden to the USSR and although it was clear that, for the long-run economic viability of the Comecon area, a more sophisticated approach had to be found than in the past, the way out had not yet been determined. It was not to be sought through a simplistic linear extrapolation of the political thinking of the Soviet and East European hardliners into the economic field.

NOTES

1. V. Popovic from Warsaw, Tanjug, September 4, 1968.

2. Walter Ulbricht's speech to the Ninth Central Committee Plenum, Neues Deutschland, October 25, 1968.

3. Krasnaia Zvezda, September 12, 1968.

4. Pravda, September 30, 1969.

5. Ulbricht, op. cit.

6. Wladislaw Gomulka's closing speech to the Fifth Congress of the Polish Party, November 16, 1968, Trybuna Ludu, November 17, 1968.

7. Zhak Aroyo, in Rabotnichesko Delo, November 21, 1968.

8. Gennady Sorokin in Voprosy Ekonomiki, December, 1968.

9. Ulbricht's speech to the Fifth Congress of the Polish Party, as reported in Neues Deutschland, November 13, 1968.

10. Gh. Constantinescu, in Viata Economica, November 29, 1968; and in N. Ceausescu's speech to the Rumanian parliament, November 29, 1968, broadcast live by Radio Bucharest.

11. Antal Apro's speech in Mako on September 20, 1968, Radio Budapest, same day.

12. Magyar Hirlap, September 22, 1968.

13. Antal Apro's speech to the opening meeting of Comecon's Standing Committee on Light Industry, November 20, 1968, Radio Budapest, same day.

14. Radio Budapest (for Hungarians abroad), November 29, 1968.

15. Prague Television, December 2, 1968.

16. Yu. Belayev in International Affairs, December, 1968.

17. Ibid.

18. Pravda, December 12, 1968.

19. Interview with Tano Tsolov; Radio Moscow, December 15, 1968.

20. Nikolai Fadeyev, in Pravda, January 21, 1969; Alexander Zademidko, in Izvestiia, January 21, 1969.

21. Jozef Pajestka in an interview with Zycie Warszawy, January 12-13, 1969.

22. Ibid.

23. P. Bozyk in Handel Zagraniczny (Warsaw), 4, 1969.

24. N. S. Stanesca in Scanteia, January 24, 1969.

25. Antal Apro in Tarsadalmi Szemle, December, 1968.

26. Ibid.

27. Delivered to the Political Academy of the Central Committee on January 22, 1969; an abridged version appeared in Nepszabadsag, January 23, 1969.

28. Ibid.

29. Ibid.

30. V. Kyprova in Hospodarstvi a Pravo, October, 1968; J. Pleva in Zahranicni Obchod, December, 1968; Marcel Brozik in Rude Pravo, January 23, 29, 1969.

31. Marcel Brozik in Rude Pravo, January 29, 1969.

32. Neal Ascherson in The Observer (London), January 26, 1969.

33. A. Wasilkowski in Trybuna Robotnicza (Katowice), December 19, 1969.

34. Piotr Jaroszewicz in Trybuna Ludu, December 30, 1968.

35. D. Fikus in Polityka, December 7, 1968.

36. For a discussion of the differences between the Hungarian and Polish concepts as reflected at the January, 1969, symposium in Warsaw, see Bela Csikos-Nagy in Kozgazdasagi Szemle, February, 1969; also Gospodarka Planova August, 1969.

37. Rabotnichesko Delo, July 25, 1968.

38. Nesho Tsarevsky in Trud, November 13, 1968.

39. Naruchnik Na Agitatora, January, 1969; Stefan Sharenkov in Rabotnichesko Delo, January 11, 1969.

40. Neues Deutschland, October 25, 1968.

41. Gerhard Weiss's speech to the Twenty-second Council meeting, January 21, 1969, as reported in Neues Deutschland, January 22, 1969; Willi Stoph's "toast" at the reception on January 28, 1969, Neues Deutschland, same day.

42. See, for example, Gerhard Wyschka and Helmust Koenig in German Foreign Policy, 2, 1969 (to press January 1969).

43. Gerhard Wyschka in Deutsche Aussenpolitik, October, 1968.

44. Wyschka and Koenig, op. cit.

45. See, for example, K. Enkelmann in Sozialistische Aussenwirtschaft, 1, 1969.

46. H. Koenig, Sozialistische Aussenwirtschaft, 2, 1969 (to press on 10 January 1969).

47. Interview with Willi Stoph, Einheit, January, 1969; Gunter Mittag in Einheit, December, 1968.

48. Weiss's speech to the Twenty-second Council meeting.

49. A similar rationale was suggested on the eve of the Twentieth-anniversary meeting by V. Milenkovic in Ekonomska Politika (Belgrade), January 13, 1969.

50. P. Almpiev and Yu. Shiryaev in Voprosy Ekonomiki, January, 1969.

CHAPTER

3

AN ANNIVERSARY AND A SUMMIT

The Twenty-second Council session celebrating the twentieth anniversary of Comecon began on a "festive" note with the opening address of Comecon Secretary Nikolai Fadeyev.[1] After hailing the organization's success, Fadeyev went on rather blandly, noting:

> Further improvement in coordinating the plans of the Comecon countries is a topical task, particularly in view of the work presently being done in member countries to improve the planning and directing of the economy.

He appeared unhurried in referring to the changes being considered and suggested that a summit, "to be held soon," rather than the present Council meeting, would deal with the basic issues before Comecon.

Although public revelations of the Council proceedings by Comecon members suggested few problems, a number of news reports indicated that the differences were in fact sharp. In general the picture which emerged was one of the USSR and Poland pushing for tighter central control, and Yugoslavia (which apparently took a more active role than usual), Rumania, and Hungary, with some support from a subdued Czechoslovakia, providing the opposition.[2] According to one report, the attempt at centralized control extended to trade with the West.[3] From the news reports the East German position remained obscure: some included it with the USSR and Poland as a supporter of tighter controls; others did not. The East Germans were said to have strongly resisted the idea of convertibility, fearing that they would end up subsidizing poorer Comecon members and apparently insisting that, until others followed their example by introducing more rational price reforms, convertibility made no sense.[4]

The reports agreed that little had been achieved, and some suggested that the opposition to strengthening Comecon was so strong that its proponents had simply abandoned their original proposals.[5] According to one source, however, the Rumanian delegation made "certain minor concessions concerning the specialization problem."[6]

It was also reported that the Soviet, Polish, and East German delegations were initially pushing for an early summit meeting, preferably immediately following the Council session.[7] However, they apparently backed down, having decided to postpone a confrontation on the key issues, partly because of strong resistance and partly because they did not want to add to the problems of convening the international conference of communist parties scheduled for the spring.[8]

Although generally vague, the final communiqué of the council session appeared to confirm that tightened control had been effectively resisted. It reaffirmed the principles of full equality of rights and respect for sovereignty and national interests, and it saw the "coordination of plans" as the "principal instrument for the development of the socialist international division of labor." The communiqué stated further that member countries and Yugoslavia (Comecon organs were not mentioned) would "submit proposals on selected problems affecting their economic and scientific-technological cooperation," and reported that the meeting had "recommended" to these countries, but "instructed" the council organs, to "speed up the formulation of recommendations for the specialization and coordination of production of products <u>selected by the interested countries</u>" (emphasis added). A similar "recommended . . . instructed" formula was used in referring to completion of coordination of the next five-year plans, thus again clearly distinguishing between the Council's authority over its own organs and its authority over member countries. This distinction was reaffirmed by Fadeyev shortly after the meeting when, in an interview, he contrasted the "suprastate" nature of the EEC with Comecon, which was "not such an organization [but] is based on the most just principles, [for] no decision or recommendation can be adopted if one of the interested countries does not agree."[9]

In another interview Fadeyev indicated that agreement on the need for some form of convertibility had been reached.[10] He noted that "obviously, the time has matured for our national currencies to have better, more real mutual relations . . . more real coefficients [ratios]. This we have to solve as soon as possible. . . . A certain program already exists in this respect." He then stated that the "solution of the question which the Council has not solved so far, that is, the convertibility of currencies, is facing us in the future" and called for a step-by-step approach. In more concrete terms Hungarian Finance Minister Peter Valyi reported that the "question of the gradual establishment of the so-called clearing ruble convertibility . . . is now under discussion and in the near future a joint program will be formulated on the basis of mutual consent among the socialist countries to the benefits of its realization."[11] This still didn't sound like much, but it evidently reflected a better consensus on the general direction in which progress should be sought.

Nevertheless, both on convertibility and on broader reform, the Council meeting merely reached an agreement on the need to try to agree in the future on a concrete program. This, however led Jaroszewicz to remark in his closing speech—while acknowledging the continuing "quite considerable" differences of view—that "without exaggerating, we can say that for the first time our discussions proved that we are willing to make further efforts clearly to improve Comecon's performance."[12]

TOWARD A LONG AWAITED SUMMIT

Following the twentieth-anniversary meeting, the Soviet position on Comecon began to develop clearer direction. In February, articles by the chairmen of the Comecon Commissions on Economic Questions and on Coordinating Scientific and Technological Research set the tone by adopting a quite matter-of-fact, pragmatic approach to the problems that they faced.[13] It was acknowledged that economic reforms were raising the significence of financial autonomy and economic incentives and necessitated more progressive forms and methods of cooperation; no grand designs or provocative arguments were produced.

In March, a major article by Mikhail Lesechko suggested that the USSR had decided on a new approach to the bloc's economic relations with the West and to the role of Comecon in them.[14] Lesechko began with a familiar theme: He strongly emphasized the importance of scientific and technological progress and its close relationship to production and the division of labor, particularly in the most rapidly growing new industries. He made the important admission that, in the present state of rapidly expanding human knowledge, which necessitates huge investments, "no single country, not even a large one, is in a position to embrace by itself all the trends of scientific and technological progress in such a way as to maintain material production branches at the permanent level of world achievements." He went on to stress that the Comecon countries take an active part in the development of international technological progress and that the "world is the richer" for their contributions. Then followed a key passage:

> Naturally, the Comecon countries are endeavoring to utilize foreign scientific achievements and technical innovations even more effectively, insofar as this is permitted by the potentials of the world market. . . .
>
> With this in view they are seeking to coordinate their world market activities in order to avoid unjustified parallel expenditure and to obtain all that is best from other countries. But of course the socialist states have to take into consideration that the utilization of the capitalist market for the acquisition of machinery and equipment, although important, is not the main means of accelerating technical progress in the socialist countries. Everyone knows that at the very moment when even the latest machine appears on the world market it is already to a certain extent obsolete, in the sense that the designers will have begun work on a new, improved version. And it is no secret that not all doors are open to the socialist countries when they wish to benefit from more effective acquisitions in capitalist countries. This circumstance makes it all the more necessary to improve the coordination of the fraternal countries' activities on the world market where machines, patents, and licenses are involved. Much remains to be done in this respect. [Emphasis added.]

Thus, the problems of relations with the West were not seen to be the dangers of economic dependence and political penetration, but those of imported obsolescence and the restrictions imposed by Western trade barriers. The need within Comecon was to get together to ensure exploitation of the latest, worldwide scientific and technological developments, to avoid duplication, and to speed up the acquisition of new developments and continuously incorporate them into current plans. Comecon should not be an essentially autarkic grouping, as the East Germans had been arguing, but should be outward-looking, utilizing "all that is best" in the West—and this required closer coordination of foreign economic relations.

Lesechko's March article coincided with another major signal of a change in attitude toward the West. The "Appeal of the Warsaw Pact," issued after a meeting in Budapest which reiterated the call for a European security conference, adopted a noticeably mild approach to West Germany.[15] However, although the beginnings of a new policy toward the West appear to have been made at the Budapest meeting, an economic approach along the lines of Lesechko's article does not seem to have been adopted, for the appeal was notably restrained in its economic proposals to the West. While reiterating the call for "all-round cooperation on an all-European basis" of the July, 1966, Bucharest Declaration, when proposing specific areas of economic cooperation it omitted the 1966 declaration's references to scientific-technological cooperation and focused on more grandiose projects which would involve the Comecon area—and Europe—as a whole. It was to be several more eventful months before a Warsaw Pact appeal elevated East-West economic relations to the new position of prominence that Lesechko's article foreshadowed.

In a subsequent article, published just prior to the summit and probably indicating the Soviet position, Lesechko took up the question of planning economic ties within Comecon.[16] He said;

> In our opinion, there is an urgent need to put the work of planning foreign economic ties for the most important interlinking branches of production on the level of independent sectors of planning activity, using all the practical tools which the socialist countries have accumulated in solving domestic problems of long-term development and production siting.

Lest anyone get the wrong idea and think that supranationalism was again being suggested, he immediately continued;

> We have in mind working out, according to plan and in good time, technical and economic reports and forecasts, long-term plans for drafting and survey work for construction in future years, and other measures which come well within the field of domestic practice, as appropriate to interstate relations, of course. . . .
>
> The implementation of such measures wholly depends on the wishes of interested Comecon countries and must be founded on their voluntary participation, observing the principles of full equal rights and respect for sovereignty, mutual benefit, and comradely mutual aid.

In Poland a more centralist approach to joint planning seemed to be advocated in the party ideological monthly, which argued;

> Sovereignty means the right to a free undertaking of duties arising from common projects, the right to relegate certain tasks, previously accomplished single-handedly and in scattered fashion, to a central body, [but] this does not include international bodies entrusted with over-all economic planning. . . .

> Each country has the sovereign right to show or decline interest in this or that common undertaking. No decision made by one country can be binding upon another country which refuses to agree with it.[17]

While both the Soviet and Polish statements were vague on the role of central bloc organs in planning per se, the Polish statement appeared the more forceful of the two, for it made it quite clear that "certain tasks" should be turned over to these organs.

In general, however, the Poles did not appear very optimistic after the anniversary meeting. They noted that this meeting had not passed any resolutions which "might change the existing state of affairs to any marked degree," and, while they found this understandable, as such decisions were reserved for the summit, they also noted that there were "frequently serious differences of opinion" and that, while the need for multilateralism and new currency and price relations was generally agreed, "it would appear that it is in these areas that the differences of opinion may persist the longest."[18] At the Thirty-ninth Executive Committee meeting in early April, the usually rather ebullient Jaroszewicz, while pressing for reform, evidently took a critical and not very hopeful line.[19] Although apparently still determined to push its ideas at the upcoming summit meeting, Poland's broader policy began to reflect this discouragement as well as the opening up of opportunities elsewhere. After the Budapest meeting in March, Poland's position on the EEC began to moderate, and the historic shift in the Polish stand on West Germany began.

Significantly, in East Germany, a considerably less ambitious approach to improving plan coordination was adopted. Improvements in the contractual system and an expansion of the existing forms of cooperation through negotiations at the production level were seen as the primary means of increasing specialization and cooperation.[20] In an interview during this period, Weiss made a notably low-key approach to plan coordination, referring first to the growing role of the central plan in determining the development of individual Comecon countries and deducing from this that "Necessarily, coordination of economic plans will also gain in importance in international cooperation. The prospects for raising the quality of this effort are steadily improving since the scientific character, standards, and methods of planning are continuously being upgraded in the countries involved."[21] He went on to urge the domestic organs of the Comecon countries—but not Comecon itself—to concern themselves with export policies, emphasizing rationalization through the proper use of norms and efficiency criteria. East Germany still did not appear very enthusiastic about the Soviet and Polish suggestions for joint planning or for any other schemes for really changing or tightening up Comecon.

Czechoslovak spokesmen were now becoming notably more loquacious. In an interview, Frantisek Hamouz, the representative to Comecon (since April, 1968), supported decentralization, less detailed trade agreements, and convertibility, stating that "Czechoslovak concepts are based on the principles of our economic reforms and therefore they respect the principle of the relative independence of the enterprise."[22] Commentators in Rude Pravo rejected charges that Czechoslovak economists had worked against "socialist integration," and they condemned supranationalism, coming out strongly for independence in economic policy-making for those within integrated groupings and boldly maintaining that if someone were to push for supranational powers for Comecon it would lead to the breakup of the organization.[23] At a government meeting in late March, the principles that the Czechoslovak delegation would follow at the summit were discussed.[24] Financial reforms, "especially those required for the achievement of realistic exchange rates and, in the long term, convertibility of national currencies," were to be urged by Czechoslovakia.[25] On the eve of the summit, Hamouz saw integration not as an immediate aim, because the conditions for it still had to be created, and argued against supranationalism and isolation.[26] Czechoslovak economists were reportedly again actively discussing the future of Comecon with their Hungarian counterparts and reaching a certain consensus.[27]

In Hungary it was stressed that "socialist integration and sovereignty are not concepts which exclude each other." It was even suggested that "perhaps relations between the socialist countries had developed in a historically more intricate way than Lenin had foreseen" and hence that their economic cooperation—the need for which he rightly foresaw—might also be carried out differently (i.e., not through central direction or a common plan).[28] Although the Hungarian position appeared somewhat subdued after a Nyers-led visit to Moscow in early March,[29] the Hungarian media seemed to bounce back quickly: Radio Budapest was soon plugging for convertibility with the West.[30] A former deputy finance minister explicitly rejected Sorokin's views and gave priority to monetary relations over plan coordination, arguing for a loose form of strictly voluntary integration which would prevent differences in internal economic mechanisms from creating problems.[31] Another Hungarian official advocated a much freer flow of labor among the Comecon countries, based on economic criteria,[32] thus supporting the Hungarian reform principles and a practice that Hungary had pioneered. A week before the summit, the chairman of the National Planning Office reiterated in the party daily the Hungarian principles for Comecon reform and argued strongly that differences in internal mechanisms would not impede integration, asserting that the mechanisms were essentially the same and that "differences stem mainly from a certain discrepancy in phase sequence in efforts to perfect the mechanism." He concluded that therefore a gradual diminishing of essential differences could be expected.[33]

The focus of Rumania's concern now appeared to shift. Although evidently relieved that, for the time being at least, tightened control of economic relations by Comecon had been resisted, Rumania's defensiveness grew, evidently because a new determination to move ahead within Comecon was being manifested and because there was continued uncertainty over what the summit meeting—which it now seemed Rumania was destined to attend—held in store. While national economic sovereignty continued to be stressed, Rumanian concern seemed to turn to more specific problems. Conformity in domestic management and planning practices was strongly rejected: it was argued that there are no single, universally valid prescriptions for organizing economic life under socialism, that solutions should not be taken over automatically from others, and that only the national parties and governments were capable of introducing improved measures. It was also argued that plan coordination must be completely dependent upon national economic plans, and not the other way around, for national plans are essential attributes of national sovereignty. The need to base cooperation on contractual agreements was also stressed. Thus, the primary fear did not appear to be of a rapid push for comprehensive supranationalism, but rather of a complex of pressures and compromises under which Rumania would end up having to adapt both its economic plans and its economic system to the demands of closer economic ties within Comecon.

Rumania now found itself, however, in a growing dilemma. In February, 1969, Ceausescu noted;

> We start from the incontestable reality that, in view of today's enormous technical and scientific progress, the progress of every country is dependent on its active participation in the international division of labor. Isolation results only in stagnation, in lagging behind, with serious consequences for the whole economic and social development of the country in question.[34]

Although he stressed that Rumania would cooperate with all countries, irrespective of social system, it was obvious that the pressing issue was cooperation within Comecon. There evidently was a developing fear that Rumania might opt out or be left out of cooperative efforts in which it found it had an important economic stake, for it was now also argued that an initial decision not to participate should not prevent a country from joining a cooperative scheme later on. Rumania was evidently feeling more acutely the growing conflict between its desire to preserve both uncompromised economic sovereignty and Comecon's principles, on the one hand, and the demands of the scientific-technological revolution and of the renewed push for closer ties by the rest of Comecon's members, on the other.

Because of the very real economic need to increase cooperation, as well as the evident desire to improve the atmosphere before the summit, in early 1969, Rumania developed a growing enthusiasm for expanding economic ties with Comecon members. In an article in Lupta de Clasa, the Rumanian Central Committee's theoretical monthly, it was stated (with some exaggeration) that "Rumania has actively participated in all Comecon operations, making its contribution to the development of fruitful collaboration among the member nations."[35] The author went on to note that economic cooperation was becoming increasingly more important and could profitably include foreign investment and that scientific and technological cooperation was shifting the emphasis of economic relations between countries from trade to production, asserting that "Rumania is making every effort to initiate and to organize programs of cooperation and production specialization."

A more definitive sign of rapprochement came in mid-April when an article by Gheorghe Radulescu, Rumania's Comecon representative, appeared in a prominent Soviet journal.[36] Radulescu also stressed Rumania's cooperativeness and involvement in Comecon activities, listing the various approaches which "can substantially promote the extension and deepening" of cooperation. He was careful to note that plan coordination involved only "consultation, reciprocal information, and the useful exchange of experience" and that the well-tried principles of relations embodied in the Comecon charter should be the basis of any improvements, but stated that Rumania "supports the search for new and efficient forms of cooperation" and emphasized the close Soviet-Rumanian economic bonds. While making no real concessions—this had all been said before in different contexts—Radulescu managed to emphasize the positive side and, given the vehicle for these remarks, contrived to further improve the atmosphere for the approaching summit meeting.

As the summit approached, moreover, Rumania's often vague—but sweeping—definition of integration appeared to become more qualified, thus making rejection of integration less offensive. Forms of integration which had a supranational character, which would lead to a closed grouping, or which would abolish Comecon's principles, were rejected, as was "full-scale" integration, by Ceausescu,[37] but it appeared less certain that all forms of "integration" were viewed as objectionable. This undoubtedly reflected a desire not to be forced into a volte-face at the summit a few days later if other members proved uncompromising and, for example, insisted on using the term in the communiqué. Nevertheless, Rumania sought as much outside exposure of and support for its position as possible. To make sure that the West was fully apprised of it, on the eve of the summit, in a speech to the U. N. Economic Commission for Europe, the Rumanian delegate aired his country's views on integration, supranationalism, and closed economic groupings.[38]

In the meantime there were signs within Comecon of a new will to take pragmatic steps to improve economic relations in non-controversial areas of cooperation. With Rumanian participation, a new scientific-technological information center was agreed upon.[39] The first conference of internal trade ministers of the Comecon countries took place, in an effort to increase trade in consumer goods, including frontier trade, and to promote new forms of more direct contact,[40] which presumably would by-pass the rigid centralized trade agreements as much as possible. At the Executive Committee meeting in early April the question of settling accounts and the role of the Comecon Bank, as well as scientific-technological cooperation, were the major topics of discussion, and some progress was apparently achieved.[41] Later that month the first organizational meeting of the Comecon members' labor ministers was held to discuss cooperation and the exchange of information, and working groups were set up to explore certain common problems in anticipation of regular future meetings.[42] Although fundamental differences as well as objective barriers remained, the atmosphere had improved markedly since January, and a new willingness to move ahead appeared to be developing. The time for a Comecon summit was at last ripe.

THE SUMMIT AT LAST

From April 23-26, the long-awaited summit meeting, the Twenty-third "special" Council session, took place in Moscow, with top state and party leaders in attendance. On the eve of the summit, Pravda was urging East Europeans to put aside "nationalistic prejudices" and criticized those who failed to coordinate state interests with common socialist interests.[43] Moscow Radio was reassuring the Rumanians by arguing that the "socialist division of labor" helped to equalize development levels and noting that all Comecon members had a developed industry in which all the principal branches were rapidly expanding.[44] Polish sources indicated that Poland would continue to push its complex program for integration, but noted that voluntary participation was a basic principle of Comecon.[45] Czechoslovak media affirmed that the Czechoslovak delegation would urge greater enterprise involvement and a restructuring of exchange rates, and Rude Pravo reflected Czechoslovakia's more assertive approach when it recommended the creation of international branch associations on a "contractual basis and working on purely commercial" principles.[46] Rumania reiterated its objections to supranationalism and majority rule and called for Comecon to be an organization open to cooperation with all states, but it was at pains to show that the forms of expanded cooperation within Comecon which were acceptable were virtually unlimited as long as Comecon's principles were not violated and no coercion was involved.[47] It was reported that East Germany was thought to be still "wary of moves which might cramp her style" in Western markets.[48]

The reports emerging during the summit negotiations confirmed that, while basic differences remained, a willingness to move ahead had developed. Poland, the Soviet Union, and Bulgaria were reported to have been the most forceful advocates of closer economic coordination, Gomulka devoting a considerable portion of his speech to the need for an investment bank.[49] However, these countries were said to have voiced opposition to anything which would tend to harden their present roles as suppliers of raw materials and purchasers of industrial goods from East Germany and Czechoslovakia,[50] and, according to Yugoslav sources, while strongly urging the improvement of plan coordination, specialization, and cooperation, the USSR remained essentially neutral when it came to backing any particular scheme.[51] Kosygin reportedly emphasized the questions of scientific-technological cooperation and joint industrial projects,[52] and Brezhnev was said to have favored the "maximum development of bilateral and multilateral economic relations, without, however, the creation of common organs which would have the power to make decisions binding on the governments and parliaments of the various countries."[53] It was also reported that the Soviets appeared primarily interested in the political aspects of cooperation and in the manifestation of unity among Comecon members.[54]

Although Rumania again led the resistance to the more far-reaching proposals, it evidently had considerable support, particularly from the East Germans, and also from the Hungarians. Ceausescu predictably resisted any limitation on national sovereignty, but he was also reported to have agreed to a larger convertible currency contribution to the Comecon bank, some form of cooperation in joint production schemes, and specialization in certain fields.[55] This time there appears to have been no question about the East German position. According to some dispatches, Ulbricht supported Rumania in resisting anything which would encroach on its industrial development plans and was hostile to any scheme which would encourage the establishment of industries in other Comecon countries in competition with existing East German industries.[56] It was reported that East Germany "this time took a stand according to which no essential changes should be introduced into Comecon's manner of functioning."[57] Hungary too offered resistance to the strengthening of Comecon organs and strongly insisted on voluntary participation, undoubtedly still arguing that the principles of its economic reform should be the basis of any institutional changes in Comecon.[58] Nevertheless, despite their evident differences on other issues, Hungary and Poland reportedly still were in basic agreement on the need for financial reforms as a prerequisite to effective cooperation.[59]

The summit communiqué was unrevealing, containing a little something for everybody but reflecting the lowest common denominator on significant issues.[60] It reaffirmed respect for sovereignty and national interests, among other things, as not just Comecon but Marxist-Leninist principles. It reiterated the goal of gradually equalizing development levels and supported relations among economic organizations at all levels, including trusts, enterprises, and research institutes. It advocated the development of ties with all countries "regardless of social system." It called for the creation of new organizations by "interested countries according to necessity" and agreed to the establishment of an investment bank and to improvement of the activity of the existing Comecon bank. However, references to plan coordination, specialization, cooperation, and the financial system were extremely vague, and the provocative (to some) term "integration" was not mentioned. The communiqué said that it was agreed that proposals would be worked out for improving the work of the Comecon organs and increasing their role in the organization of cooperation, but, at the same time, it noted that "the session raised many problems of deepening relations between the national economies which must jointly be further studied in order to work out mutually acceptable solutions."

Postsummit reports from member countries helped to clarify what had been agreed upon at the summit. It turned out that an unpublished twenty-five-point protocol had been (unanimously) adopted—a protocol which evidently spelled out in considerably more detail things only vaguely alluded to in the communiqué. In discussing the protocol's points at a press conference shortly after the summit, Hamouz stated that it respected national sovereignty and "absolute voluntaryism" throughout, foresaw no supranational organs, and would not "touch on questions of internal planning, financing, or the economic activity of organizations."[61] He revealed that the twenty-five points had time limits, "some of them extremely short," and that the first efforts to work out concrete steps were to be evaluated as early as the first part of 1970; but he predicted that the first results of the program would not be evident for about three years, as the new measures would be introduced in stages. One short (and evidently largely unmet) time limit, he noted, involved decisions by individual states as to which types of production they would agree to share in planning jointly. These were seen as important decisions, for, "while decision is voluntary, the implementation of tasks undertaken is binding."

Also according to Hamouz, joint planning was to be subordinated to the traditional plan coordination which was to remain the "fundamental method" of cooperation and "would go as far as coordinating the economic policies" of the member countries. In addition, "in some spheres, the need arises to change from annual and five-year plans to a concept of an unbroken [planning] sequence." Where possible, trade agreements were to become more flexible, substituting over-all value commitments by general type of goods for binding quotas, but the "proportion between the firmly fixed quotas and freely exchanged goods could, needless to say, vary in different countries as to quantity and type." Trade prices would (once again) be re-examined with world prices still being used as the basis, and exchange rates would be adjusted "so that gradually we will go over to evolving a program of mutual convertibility of national currencies." Some documentation was to continue to be exchanged free of charge (one of Comecon's earlier and much criticized "principles"), but more important documentation, e.g., licenses and patents, could be sold (something which had actually been agreed upon previously).[62] Subsequently it was confirmed that the summit had "considered it advisable" to begin introducing joint planning in the course of coordinating the plans for 1971-75, although, as Hamouz and others had done, it was still carefully noted that this planning was to be only "between interested nations in certain mutually agreed-upon industrial branches."[63] Although the deadline was seldom alluded to, this protocol evidently also anticipated completion of the comprehensive program by the end of 1970.[64]

A number of other significant points also emerged from later reports on the summit decisions. It was said that it had been decided to extend planning to "cover longer periods of 10, 15, or even 20 years, and this will be accompanied by joint forecasting of the development of the economy, science, and technology. . . ."[65] It was also reported that

> For the elaboration of individual scientific and technological problems which are of mutual interest, the session recommended that coordinating centers, international scientific-research institutes, design organizations, temporary international scientific collectives, and other such bodies be set up.[66]

Just what was foreseen in the awkward field of financial reform was not so clear and evidently had been largely left to future negotiation. A number of reports stressed that moves in this field would be difficult, complex, and long-range. One step expected was exchange rate realignment, which, Hamouz noted, was to include the rates among the national currencies and the rate and gold content of the transferable ruble-accounting unit. Another step expected was a change in the Comecon bank's regulations on trade credit, with an increase in interest rates and perhaps longer-term credits anticipated.[67] On the much-debated question of whether convertibility should (first) involve Western currencies or only Comecon currencies—including the transferable ruble—the decision evidently went against any form of convertibility into Western currencies for the near future.[68]

The April summit apparently also saw the beginning of a breakthrough on one of the two major barriers to effective cooperation within Comecon—the principle of interestedness, which along with that of unanimity had long tended to stall Comecon's development. As noted, the communiqué called for the creation of new international organizations by "interested countries according to necessity." Shortly after the summit, the long-anticipated branch association Interchim was set up with the participation of all members except Rumania and Mongolia. At the time of Interchim's establishment it was reported that the agreement "envisages that a council resolution will be adopted only upon agreement of the contracting parties after they have stated their interest in solving a given problem."[69] While this formulation was unclear, it appeared that, although the unanimity principle was preserved, obstructionist tactics by those not really interested in "solving" a problem were not going to be tolerated. With the establishment of Interchim the summit could be regarded as having paved the way to the formation of more quasi-independent associations,[70] and it appeared that the interested-party principle, which had carried with it the right to veto, was giving way to the "voluntaryism" to which Hamouz referred, which prevented a member from being coerced, but also prevented it from inhibiting action by others who were <u>really</u> interested.

In apparent confirmation of this, a rather subtle shift appears to have taken place in Rumanian statements after the summit. Rumania now stressed that the basic principles of Comecon for which it had fought had been preserved. But in an article by the vice-chairman of the Government Commission on Economic and Technological Cooperation, it was argued that Comecon cooperation did not involve supranational agencies or affect internal planning or financial and administrative activities, and that, on the contrary, each country could "freely demonstrate its interest and participate in any kind of collaboration at any time."[71] While this formulation did not specifically exclude the right to declare interest before a matter was taken up and then to exercise a veto over the whole idea, its thrust appeared to be defensive, and the sense appeared to be that only previously established collaboration was under discussion. The omission of any reference to the setting up of cooperative arrangements here, along with the subsequent references to voluntaryism in Rumanian media, suggest that Rumania was now concerned with preserving its right to opt in or out of cooperative arrangements without being coerced, but that it was resigned to the fact that others were determined to move ahead with new and more effective forms of cooperation whether Rumania concurred in their operating procedures or not.

The main result of the summit appeared to be the impetus given to the search for new approaches to the development of economic ties within Comecon, rather than any concrete agreement on these approaches themselves. The scope and methods of plan coordination and joint planning were still largely to be worked out, as were the more complex institutional reform questions such as multilateralism and convertibility. What evidently had been achieved at and just prior to the summit was a better consensus on the general directions in which reform should be pursued, as well as a certain legitimatization of the reform discussion and the criticism of Comecon, which in the past had been too easily construed as attacks on the international socialist system itself.

INITIAL REACTIONS

Despite the apparent erosion of their veto power, the Rumanians seemed particularly pleased with the outcome. Rumanian Premier Ion Gheorghe Maurer told Rude Pravo,

> We did good work in Moscow. We have not for a long time achieved such useful and successful results in our mutual negotiations as on this occasion. . . . We cudgeled our brains a lot, [and this brought] really good results, or more precisely, good foundations were laid down. . . . I consider the outcome of the talks very, very positive.[72]

Scanteia, too, was quite happy with the results, naturally taking the opportunity to stress the fact that the principles for which Rumania had fought had been reaffirmed.[73] An article in Probleme Economice demonstrated just how loose Rumania intended to stay. While avoiding any mention of joint planning, it managed to treat everything positively. Closer plan coordination, for example, is a good thing when seen in the following Rumanian terms:

> Future plan coordination will proceed mainly by means of mutual exchanges of experience and information, as well as by means of the bilateral and multilateral discussion of certain problems regarding the main directions of the economic policies of each country. It is, therefore, considered both useful and possible to intensify exchanges of opinions and information on problems of mutual interest during the preparation period of the economic development plans of each country so that later, by successive analyses, those aspects which might form the object of collaboration could be better brought out. The countries involved would thus be able to take into consideration the results of the exchanges and discussions when preparing their national plans.[74]

Rumania evidently felt that, whatever others might do, her freedom of action had been largely preserved—probably to a greater degree than she had anticipated the previous fall.

Hungary and Czechoslovakia also seemed quite happy. In Hungary it was found that the resolutions approved completely suited the socialist community and that Comecon had taken the "road to renewal."[75] In Czechoslovakia the meeting was seen as having been "very successful in drawing up and approving projects which form the basis of a new phase in the development of collaboration between the Comecon countries," and it was argued that the differences over Comecon were not nearly so great as foreign observers had suggested, for the "results of this session show clearly that a joint resolution has been found which is satisfactory for and corresponds in principle to the interests of all concerned."[76] In both of these countries the primary reason for satisfaction was undoubtedly the absence of forced solutions, especially to such questions as specialization and joint planning, and the continued tolerance of some diversity in internal economic policy and reform.

The East Germans and Bulgarians also seemed reasonably satisfied. Ulbricht was "gladdened" by the summit session which, in formulating its program, took the "interests of all the Comecon member countries into consideration," while Weiss stated that his government evaluated highly the session's results.[77] It appeared that East Germany's reported objections to any interference in industrialization plans had been sustained. Any reservations on its part probably involved the questions of cohesion of the bloc and the degree of relations with the West which was to be tolerated.

In Bulgaria a favorable attitude in part reflected that country's constant enthusiasm for all things "socialist," but it also reflected more concrete satisfactions. While it had been less concerned than others over Comecon's principles and over a flexible Comecon organization to further economic reforms, Bulgaria was certainly happy about the maintenance of the goal of equalizing development levels (which in practical terms served as a lever for more Soviet aid) and about the reaffirmation of everyone's right to industrialize in all spheres as they saw fit.

Poland, in part through its comparative silence, as was reported at the time, appeared to be the least happy over the summit's outcome.[78] This reflected the lack of firm commitments to closer ties—to "integration," and was the logical counterpart of the relative contentment recorded by others, most notably the Rumanians. Although a brave front was put up, in Poland the summit outcome was evidently taken as an economic and political setback. Here one should note that it was three weeks later that Gomulka made his bid to West Germany on the Oder-Neisse question, de-emphasizing the issue of recognition of East Germany.[79] It would appear that these developments within Comecon, in particular the apparent further hardening of the East German position, were an important factor in the timing of Gomulka's bid, just as earlier the results of the Budapest meeting of the Warsaw Pact and perhaps the twentieth-anniversary meeting had been factors in the development of the new Polish line on West Germany and the EEC.

The USSR appeared to have gotten largely what it wanted at the summit. _Pravda_ was enthusiastic and stressed the meeting's importance for political unity.[80] With the international conference of communist parties imminent and the Czechoslovak invasion providing more than enough problems, the USSR clearly was more concerned at that time with short-term political considerations than with long-term economic ones and undoubtedly much preferred that as far as possible the East Europeans' resentment over Comecon be focused on each other rather than on the USSR. This helps to explain why in the face of opposition the Soviet Union had not pushed the issue of an immediate summit in January and had consented to its postponement to April, an obviously more propitious time for those resisting a strengthened Comecon, and also why the Soviet position became progressively more moderate and conciliatory and why the USSR was reported to have been comparatively neutral at the April summit. This was possible because, contrary to widespread impressions—which lingered even after the summit—the Soviets were not committed to a more supranationalist, self-contained Comecon. The reaction in the USSR, however, was not necessarily uniform. It was reportedly felt in Eastern Europe that the summit outcome represented a "small victory" for the more progressive Soviet forces and a defeat for those who still wanted a tightened Comecon but that both factions agreed that unity before the international conference was the primary consideration.[81]

NOTES

1. N. Fadeyev's opening address was "festive," according to the East German news service ADN, which reported it on January 21, 1969.

2. Reuters report from East Berlin, January 24, 1969; Radio Zagreb, January 24, 1969; RFE Special/Schleich (Berlin), January 23, 1969; Frankfurter Allgemeine Zeitung, January 25, 1969; The Economist (London), January 31, 1969; David Binder in The New York Times, January 31, 1969.

3. Binder, op. cit.

4. Binder, op. cit.

5. This was reported in the Frankfurter Allgemeine Zeitung, January 25, 1969; RFE Special/Schleich (Berlin), January 23, 1969; and The Economist, January 31, 1969.

6. An East Berlin source, reported in RFE Special/Schleich (Berlin), January 31, 1969.

7. Ibid.

8. Binder, op. cit.

9. N. Fadeyev interview broadcast over East Berlin Radio, January 29, 1969.

10. N. Fadeyev interview broadcast over Czechoslovak Television, January 23, 1969.

11. Interview with MTI, February 1, 1969.

12. P. Jaroszewicz's closing speech at the Twenty-second Council session on January 23, 1969, as reported in Trybuna Ludu, January 24, 1969.

13. A. Bachurin and D. Gvishiani in Ekonomicheskaia Gazeta (Moscow), 7, February, 1969.

14. M. Lesechko in Ekonomicheskaia Gazeta, 10, March, 1969.

15. Warsaw Pact Appeal, MTI, March 18, 1969.

16. Ekonomicheskaia Gazeta, 17, April 1969.

17. S. Kuzinski in Nowe Drogi, March, 1969.

18. J. Wysocinski in Zycie Gospodarcze, February 2, 1969.

19. Jaroszewicz's speech on April 9, 1969, as reported by PAP, April 10, 1969.

20. M. Heinze in Sozialistische Aussenwirtschaft, 3, 1969.

21. Interview with G. Weiss in Sozialistische Aussenwirtschaft, 3, 1969.

22. Interview with F. Hamouz in Hospodarske Noviny, March 7, 1969.

23. M. Brozik in Rude Pravo, February 27, 1969; D. Machova in Rude Pravo, March 13, 1969.

24. Ceteka, March 27, 1969.

25. Interview with F. Hamouz, Radio Prague, March 27, 1969.

26. Interview with F. Hamouz, Radio Prague (in English to Africa and Asia), April 21, 1969.

27. Radio Bratislava, April 15, 1969.

28. J. Redei in Nepszabadsag, February 15, 1969.

29. For example, in the official communiqué on the Central Committee and Council of Ministers meeting of March 5-6, in Nepszabadsag, March 8, 1969.

30. Radio Budapest, March 18, 1969.

31. B. Sulyok in Kozgazdasagi Szemle, April, 1969.

32. S. Kopatsy in Valosag, March, 1969.

33. I. Pardi in Nepszabadsag, April 15, 1969.

34. Electoral speech in Bucharest, carried live by Radio Bucharest, February 28, 1969.

35. N. Belli in Lupta de Clasa, March, 1969.

36. G. Radulescu in Ekonomicheskaia Gazeta, 16, April, 1969.

37. In a speech to Rumanian student leaders in Bucharest, reported from Vienna by UPI, April 18, 1969.

38. Speech by Rumanian delegate N. Ecobescu, April 21, 1969.

39. At a meeting of science and technology ministers in Moscow, February 26-27, reported in PAP, February 27, 1969.

40. Meeting of the internal trade ministers, February 18-21, 1969, reported in PAP, February 21, 1969.

41. TASS, April 10, 1969.

42. E. Banyai, in Mankaugyi Szemle (Budapest), May, 1969.

43. Pravda, April 22, 1969.

44. Radio Moscow (in Rumanian), April 22, 1969.

45. Zycie Warszawy, April 23, 1969; Radio Warsaw, April 22, 1969; J. Hlebowicz in Slowo Powszechne, April 23, 1969.

46. Radio Prague, April 22, 1969; M. Brozik in Rude Pravo, April 22, 1969.

47. R. Caplescu, Scanteia, April 23, 1969.

48. Ronald Farquhar dispatch from Warsaw, Reuters, April 22, 1969.

49. UPI dispatch from Moscow, April 25, 1969; Zycie Warszawy, July 15, 1970.

50. Lars-Erik Nelson dispatch from Moscow, Reuters, April 25, 1969.

51. Tanjug dispatch from Moscow, April 25, 1969.

52. Moscow correspondent J. Merunka on Radio Prague, April 23, 1969; East European sources reported in a UPI dispatch from Moscow, April 23, 1969.

53. A. Guerra, l'Unita, official organ of the Italian Communist Party, April 26, 1969.

54. Tanjug dispatch from Moscow, April 25, 1969.

55. UPI dispatch from Moscow, April 23, 1969.

56. Adam Kellett-Long dispatch from Moscow, Reuters, April 25, 1969; Lars-Erik Nelson dispatch from Moscow, Reuters, April 25, 1969; J. Raffaelli dispatch from Moscow, AFP, May 3, 1969.

57. Tanjug dispatch from Moscow, April 25, 1969.

58. UPI dispatch from Moscow, April 27, 1969; Tanjug, quoted by Radio Zagreb, May 3, 1969; lecture by Professor T. Nagy at Columbia University, New York, May 7, 1969.

59. *Kurier Polski*, April 23, 1969.

60. Communiqué on the Twenty-third Special Comecon session, April 26, 1969.

61. Press conference by F. Hamouz, May 5, 1969, in Ceteka and Radio Prague, May 5, 1969.

62. *Ibid.*

63. Editorial, *Novo Vreme* (Sofia), June, 1969.

64. P. Jaroszewicz in *Trybuna Ludu*, December 31, 1969, and January 1, 1970; PAP, May 11, 1970.

65. T. Tsolov in *Rabotnichesko Delo*, August 10, 1969.

66. Editorial, in *Novo Vreme*, June, 1969.

67. V. Karpich in *International Affairs*, June, 1969.

68. Editorial in *Novo Vreme*, June, 1969.

69. V. Karpich in *Ekonomicheskaia Gazeta*, 31, July, 1969.

70. Hertha Heiss, "The Council for Mutual Economic Assistance—Developments Since the Mid-1960s," in *Economic Developments in Countries of Eastern Europe: A Compendium of Papers* (Washington, D. C.: Joint Economic Committee, U.S. Congress, 1970), p. 537.

71. R. Constantinescu in *Probleme Economice*, May, 1969.

72. Interview with Ion Maurer, Rude Pravo, April 28, 1969.

73. Scanteia, April 29, 1969.

74. R. Constantinescu, op. cit.

75. Nepszabadsag and Nepszava, April 29, 1969.

76. J. Lapsansky in Smena, April 29, 1969.

77. Walter Ulbricht at the Tenth Central Committee Plenum, as reported in Neues Deutschland, April 29, 1969; G. Weiss in Pravda, July 2, 1969.

78. Poland was reported to be the most disappointed of all Comecon members, by Eric Bourne in Christian Science Monitor, May 19, 1969.

79. In his speech to an electoral meeting in Warsaw, May 17, 1969, as reported in Trybuna Ludu, May 18, 1969.

80. Pravda, April 28, 1969.

81. D. Binder in New York Times, May 1, 1969.

CHAPTER

4

REGROUPING

After the first reactions to the summit, much of the discussion of Comecon began to revert to familiar problems and in some cases to a reiteration of former positions. This reflected the long-term nature and vagueness of what the summit had decided. However, major reassessments and realignments also began to emerge.

RUMANIA

Rumania's approach to Comecon now began to change. The earlier polemics led by Scanteia, Agerpres, and Ceausescu were replaced by a more subtle and less conspicuous presentation of the Rumanian position. The thrust of the Rumanian argument was now twofold: Don't be hasty, and preserve Comecon principles as much as possible. At the more esoteric level elaborate Marxist-Leninist arguments were developed or reiterated to back up Rumania's continuing fight for sovereignty.

In discussing Comecon at the Rumanian Tenth Party Congress in August, 1969, Ceausescu praised the April summit for creating new opportunities to perfect and develop forms of economic cooperation but quickly turned once again to defending sovereignty and independence, rejecting not only supranational bodies but anything which affected national economic plans or the independence of economic units within each country.[1] However, Ceausescu was more defensive when he stated that

> our country's Party and government believe that the relations of economic, technological and scientific collaboration must not be affected in any way by differences of opinion which may appear in ideological matters concerning

the building of socialism, the Communist movement, or international life.

This probably reflected fears of being cut off from desired cooperation and the squabbles at the Moscow international conference in June.

An attempt was made to contribute more directly to the discussion of what was actually to be done within Comecon. Shortly after the Tenth Congress, it was admitted that the establishment of new international institutions would be useful.[2] It was argued that these should be set up on a contractual basis with provision for other countries to join later, and that they should preserve the principle of equal rights (though contributions should be based on members' level of development). It was also maintained that decisions on organizational problems should be unanimous and that recommendations should apply only to those countries interested in the particular problem under consideration.

Besides reflecting Rumania's heightened interest in such organizations, this was perhaps the first indication that Rumania was anticipating a further erosion of its ability to prevent actions within the organizations set up by Comecon. The emphasis appeared to have shifted from the principles of decision-making within Comecon itself—that is, the rules for the setting up of new organizations—to the principles on which such Comecon offspring would operate—with or without Rumania's presence. While the concern again was to prevent coercion (to preserve voluntaryism), it appeared to be implicit in these remarks that on nonorganizational questions an "interested" party might object but could be overridden by others, who would then be free to proceed without it.

Other Rumanian arguments appeared to be similarly defensive, if not resigned. The plea that Comecon should be an open organization in whose activities nonsocialist as well as socialist countries would participate was reiterated, the idea presumably being that, whether ever utilized by nonsocialist countries or not, emphasis on such an existing provision would help to prevent coercion in institutions set up by Comecon. Supranationalism or anything affecting internal economic control continued to be rejected and sovereignty to be defended, but intensification of the socialist international division of labor and multilateral cooperation were accepted with evident sincerity and even enthusiasm. Arguments to the effect that nonparticipation in one activity of Comecon should not affect participation in others and that the new forms of cooperation envisaged should be introduced with great caution and patience again suggested that Rumania was trying to accommodate to a situation within Comecon over which it now had relatively little control.[3]

From such arguments, however, a more concrete Rumanian alternative "model" for Comecon was evolving. Whereas the earlier signs of cooperativeness on the part of Rumania had tended to focus on the specific forms of bilateral arrangements it would entertain, there now appeared to be an effort to address the broader issues of the new program which had been under discussion since the summit. Predictably, the Rumanian view of such questions as plan and policy coordination tended to emphasize forecasting and consultation, and making the "broadest possible use of existing possibilities."[4]

Rumania also became more cooperative in her bilateral economic relations with the Comecon states. As on the eve of the April summit, Rumanian writers tended to refer positively to the extensive Rumanian economic cooperation with the Comecon countries, and they harked back to earlier proposals for expanded production cooperation (at the March, 1967, Central Committee Plenum) to demonstrate Rumania's long-standing willingness to cooperate within Comecon. They even cited favorably the increase in Comecon's share of Rumanian trade in 1968, which followed many years of decline as Rumania shifted her trade to the West. Reports of bilateral economic relations indicated that cooperation was moving ahead and that such innovations as cooperation in the purchase and application of foreign licenses with Poland and investment in Soviet iron ore and other raw material deposits were being considered.[5] Relations with the USSR appeared to be receiving particular attention, and one concrete result of this new economic rapport was an agreement in March, 1970, that the USSR would help Rumania in the construction of a large nuclear power station.

Of particular interest in view of subsequent developments was a discussion of investment just two months before the Twenty-fourth Comecon Council session (at which, as discussed below, Rumania abstained from joining the new investment bank).[6] After speaking approvingly of collaboration in the construction of investment projects and of consultations on investment policy, the author stated that investment collaboration is an important and integral part of plan coordination and should be oriented toward the utilization of raw materials which are in excess of the needs of one country and can be used to satisfy the needs of other countries. He then argued that, after preliminary information has been exchanged on prospective investments, the countries

> should examine and determine the concrete areas of reciprocal interest relative to the projects and products which will be obtained, then examine the possibilities of realizing the constructions and projects, and, finally, include the agreed-upon projects within the framework of agreements.

Rumania thus appeared to be preparing to enter into joint investments with Comecon members but preferred to do this through the familiar processes of plan coordination and contractual relations rather than through any new institutional departures within Comecon.

This more positive approach to ties with the East in part reflected the faltering in Rumania's economic turning toward the West. While apparent for several years, this became more acute in 1969, and, in the face of a second bad harvest, the drying up of Western credit, and a huge convertible currency debt, Rumania was forced to begin to retrench. As was reflected in the policies announced at the Tenth Party Congress, Rumania was then looking inward both materially and organizationally for the main sources of her future economic development, but the counterpart of her growing economic problems in the West was a certain forced economic rapprochement with the East.

HUNGARY

Although evidently relatively satisfied with the summit's outcome, Hungary soon returned to a strong advocacy of Comecon reform along market lines. Picking up certain themes agreed to at the summit—financial reforms, direct contacts among economic units, and coordinated economic policies—Hungary still argued for eventual convertibility with the West and the use of market relations in order to integrate Comecon economies at the operational as well as interstate level.[7] It was reaffirmed that integration of "individual economic units not only with the planning authority, but also with each other [is] the official view of the Hungarian government," while at the interstate level, it was argued, coordinated economic policy should mean "coordinated developmental, market, credit, and monetary policies."[8] While this latter concept was something well suited to Hungary's own economic reform (and readily understandable in the West), it was clearly not exactly what some of the other members of Comecon had in mind when they agreed at the summit to the coordination of economic policies.

In the party daily the idea of policy coordination was given an even bolder twist when it was argued:

> An identical system of internal economic direction in individual countries is not a prerequisite for integration. It is inconceivable, however, that participants in the integration would not have to coordinate fundamental means of economic policy from the viewpoint of international exchange and cooperation. . . .[9]

The idea was to introduce tariffs, subsidies, and taxes in the place of quotas, and then to reduce these new, more sopisticated trade barriers preferentially (just as, it was noted, the EEC had been doing), for

> a cardinal question in any integration is the removal of such import restrictions and the opening of the internal market to imports from member countries, which is supplemented later, as a result of gradual development, by a liberalization of investments—the traffic of capital—and the flow of credits and the labor force. . . .

In fact, the

> ultimate long-term goal is to abolish the tariff and tax system within the integrated area by joint decision and to accomplish a joint external tariff boundary.

This appears to have been the most explicit statement of the implications for other members of Hungary's long-range concept of Comecon. To achieve integration, the other members must follow Hungary's lead in introducing market-type reforms, or at least simulate them so well in the international sphere that Comecon economic relations could become true market relations and a customs union could be formed.

The forceful reassertion of Hungarian views so soon after the April summit suggested that, while happy enough that certain negative things had not happened there, Hungary did not anticipate that the review of Comecon institutions then getting under way would be very favorable to her proposals, and was anxious again to present a maximalist position in the hope of securing as favorable conditions as possible for her economic reform. The impression that Hungary's avowed position was still essentially tactical, at least in the short run, gained support from an interview with a leading Hungarian economist in which he acknowledged that the full-scale transformations necessary to introduce true monetary relations in other Comecon countries were not yet in sight, and that until such internal changes could force these others toward adopting an area-wide "monetary system," the impact of the Hungarian reforms would be mainly domestic.[10]

Still, the economic reform was having a significant impact on Hungary's relations with Comecon, as was reflected in Hungary's approach to such immediate questions as joint planning. Although, in discussing the instruments of integration, joint planning of cooperation at the branch level was mentioned abroad at least twice (once in Pravda) by Nyers, during this period prior to the Twenty-fourth Council session, it does not appear to have been referred to in the Hungarian media.[11] The basic problem appears to have been that the things that others would expect joint planning to achieve administratively—elimination of duplication, creation of optimal capacities, coordination of investment, industrial cooperation and specialization—are the things which under the Hungarian reform should be left much more to the enterprise and the market.

While maintaining its ultimate aims, the Hungarian position on short-range questions nevertheless began to be modified in an apparent effort to find common ground on Comecon reform, particularly with the Poles. In a joint interview in late 1969, following a session of the Hungarian-Polish standing committee on economic cooperation, the delegation heads, Antal Apro and Polish deputy premier Stanislaw Majewski, stressed their identity of views about the future of economic cooperation, and, despite some sidestepping of controversial issues (joint planning was avoided, and a point made by Majewski on the fundamental importance of investment coordination under long-term agreements was ignored by Apro), there was a determined attempt to indicate agreement on basic reform questions such as prices, multilateralism, and trade liberalization.[12]

In December the Hungarian Minister of Finance, Peter Valyi, appeared to make an important concession to the Polish position.[13] Whereas the Hungarians had tended to see the achievement of trade liberalization, multilateralism, and convertibility as a unified process which would require simultaneous steps on all three fronts, the Poles foresaw a separation of the questions of trade liberalization and multilateral clearing, at least during the initial phases of Comecon reform. For the Poles, liberalized trade exchange would proceed slowly from the bottom up with only a limited number of goods, primarily consumer goods, being exchanged on a quotaless basis to begin with. This liberalized trade would expand as the availability of goods and progress in economic reforms permitted. Multilateralism, however, should start soon and be an integral part of planned integration with the partial convertibility of clearing balances into Western currencies used as one of the disciplinary levers. Without assenting to the Polish goal of a more planned integration, Valyi now subscribed to this partial convertibility idea, seeing it as increasing the creditors' interest in accumulating claims and by implication the pressure on debtors to pay off in acceptable goods or the means (Western currency) of acquiring such goods. Such partial convertibility was also seen as a spur to exports and competition, to the harmonization of Comecon prices with world market prices, and, hence, to integration.

The Hungarian accommodation to the Polish view continued further in early 1970. At a conference in Moscow the Hungarian case for a customs union was reiterated with the proviso that initially a limited list of restriction-free goods would be drawn up and that this list would then be expanded in the future.[14] An interesting aspect of this presentation was that, besides criticizing those countries where foreign trade enjoyed an excessive socialist monopoly (i. e., overly centralized control), it was argued that the USSR was unique due to its size and small dependence on foreign trade and also due to its world power role, which brought political interests to the fore in economic policy determination. This could be taken as a suggestion that if the USSR did not want to adjust economically to the more urgent needs of the rest of Comecon it should at least not hold them back from reform as long as socialist political interests were not jeopardized.

Hungarian media subsequently reflected the rapprochement with Poland by talking separately about introducing price liberalization in certain spheres of goods traffic and the broader problem of a new Comecon currency mechanism, acknowledging that Hungary uses a special method in linking foreign and domestic prices. While in another effort to reflect mutual interests on Comecon as the Twenty-fourth Council session approached, Hungarian Premier Jeno Fock, in an interview with the Polish party daily, again stressed the importance of financial reform within Comecon.[15]

It made considerable sense for Hungary now to seek a closer alliance with Poland on Comecon reform. It was clear that only if others began to release market forces internally and to introduce them from outside, as Hungary was doing, could the link between trade liberalization at operational levels and some form of multilateral settlement at the central financial level become as close as Hungary would like it to be. However, the prospects of anyone else following Hungary's reform lead in the near future continued to diminish with the "normalization" of Czechoslovakia, and the more modest Polish reform concepts for Comecon evidently now appeared to be the maximum feasible goals to pursue in the first rounds of negotiation over the integration program.

Moreover, although a constant theme in Hungary was that the economic barriers to integration were crucial and could not be broken down without new approaches, there was considerable wariness of outside coercion or of any forced uniformity of approach along the lines of somebody else's model. Concern about encroachment on Hungary's national economic prerogatives was reflected in Apro's speech to parliament in March, 1970, in which he argued that integration should affect only "certain" functions and counseled "tremendous patience" in developing new approaches to integration.[16] Intensive economic development was said to bring with it the need to develop one's own domestic system, adapted to one's own distinct conditions, and there was considerable sensitivity over Hungary's reform principles. This was also reflected in an authoritative review in the party daily of a major East German treatise on socialist economies.[17]

In this review a basic "error" in the German thinking was found to be that enterprises must be given obligatory plan directives. It was asserted that Hungarian reform experience demonstrated the contrary. This difference was of course crucial to the differing Hungarian and East German concepts of integration, as well as of domestic economic reform. In direct contrast to the emerging East German position (discussed below), the Hungarians continued to push their long-range program for financial reform, including convertibility into Western currencies.[18]

CZECHOSLOVAKIA

In Czechoslovakia the renewed, more assertive discussion of the future of Comecon, which was seen prior to the April summit, continued temporarily despite Alexander Dubcek's removal as first secretary. As in the case of Hungary, the main problem from the economic point of view was still seen to be that of financial—particularly currency—reform. The stress, however, was increasingly political, with the need for and the defense of close Comecon relations as the main theme. Comecon—and of course Soviet—economic ties were praised as the backbone of Czechoslovakia's foreign economic relations, and an alleged attempt to break away from Comecon was frequently cited as one of the deviations of the Dubcek leadership. The "revisionists" were attacked for forcing upon Czechoslovakia a "departure or at least a deviation from Comecon," and for recommending that Czechoslovakia "leave Comecon and integrate with the imperialists."[19]

By late 1969 there were signs of a tougher stance on the program of integration itself developing in Czechoslovakia, as the inexorable process of "normalization" proceeded. It was even suggested that during negotiations it might be expedient to reassess the voluntary principle and the practice of issuing only recommendations, and it was claimed that, in suggesting that Czechoslovakia examine the successful reforms of other countries, the summit had settled the diversification problem by calling for coordination of reforms.[20] "Subjectivist voluntaryism" was criticized for having contributed to Czechoslovakia's and Comecon's problems, and any lack of binding commitments in trade relations was found to be untenable.[21] Isolated preparations for convertibility with the West without a coordinated course of action with the other Comecon countries were attacked as antisocialist.[22] Contradictory trends and lack of unity of views were criticized, and Comecon was seen as the hope for restoring a dynamic growth rate according to plan.[23] Comprehensive planning and joint planning by branch—rather than financial reform—were now seen to be of paramount significance for integration.[24] The Czechoslovak position on Comecon was beginning to reflect the general tightening and progressive rejection of the past seen in other fields, including that of economic reform. When expressed at all, progressive ideas appear to have had to be left to guest commentators from other countries.[25] Once a strong ally of the reformers on many Comecon issues, Czechoslovakia was now moving from ineffectualness to opposition.

POLAND

Poland contined to be an enthusiastic supporter of integration, especially "planned" integration. This was particularly reflected in her statements on joint planning. At one extreme, in discussing Polish-Czechoslovak economic relations the army daily argued that the "economic structures of the two countries must be readjusted on the basis of joint bilateral and multilateral planning."[26] More moderate voices, however, while still urging comprehensive efforts to integrate Comecon economies, attempted to allay the fears conjured up by the idea of such planning. An article in the Planning Commission's monthly called for "gradual introduction of elements of joint planning by Comecon member countries in the development of definite areas of production, research or technology," but it went on to note that "there is sometimes some misunderstanding on this question of joint planning."[27] It reassured its readers that there is no danger of the creation of a supranational administrative center but that in fact the term joint planning is so broad as really to encompass existing practices:

> So-called joint planning may mean a number of things, of varying degrees of "jointness." A certain element of joint planning would become apparent, as a matter of fact, as soon as mutual contacts and general cooperation among various planning bodies (planning commission, ministries, industrial associations, institutes, and sometimes even individual enterprises) were to become so close that the transmission of information about the intended development trends in certain countries would influence to a sufficiently strong degree the over-all plans in all other Comecon member countries.

This was certainly a much more acceptable concept of joint planning to countries like Rumania and Hungary than some prevous

Polish statements had suggested, and in fact this approach was probably connected with the effort at rapprochement between the Polish and Hungarian positions on Comecon.

There were additional indications, besides this statement and Majewski's joint interview with Apro, of resignation to a more moderate, evolutionary approach to Comecon reform in Poland. Pajestka, at a Moscow conference on "Lenin and Economic Integration," after quoting Lenin's thesis on the idea of one worldwide socialist plan and noting that it is "beyond the range of economic policy under present circumstances," stressed the comprehensive nature of the changes necessary for integration.[28] These were seen to include both the sphere of economic relations and that of the "sociopolitical superstructure." It is just as necessary, he argued, to adapt the "inner rules and forms of economic activity to the requirements of intensive development" as it is to develop reforms in the international area. In fact "the difficulty lies mainly in the fact that our countries must adapt themselves to the economic cooperation system. . . . This adaption requires changes in many spheres; in working methods, institutions, and so forth in each country," and these changes "appear to be a very difficult problem." But a forced uniformity was not the answer, and it was strongly reiterated that a dual approach was essential, that is, that plan coordination is no substitute for reforms in the financial field.[29]

Nevertheless, continued Polish frustration over the slow progress of integration and on Comecon reform was quite evident. In reporting on the outcome of Polish-Czechoslovak talks, for example, Radio Warsaw complained that "in spite of considerable efforts Poland and Czechoslovakia have failed to achieve essential progress in the division of labor, particularly in the field of cooperation."[30]

At the turn of the year, in his annual review of Comecon relations, Jaroszewicz still plugged hard for a "planned tightening and developing of mutual economic, scientific, and technological links.[31] This included a call for "joint planning both in selected industrial spheres, . . . in branches of production, [and for] selected groups of products," particularly in the machine building industry. There was no notion of delegating powers to central organs, however, and instead he called for an "increased role and responsibility" for member states' planning organs in the planning of cooperation. When it came to a discussion of concrete steps, things were still very much in the preparatory stage. Jaroszewicz noted:

> Polish experts, among others, have prepared the initial material concerning both the range and the working principles of a common currency to be used in the Comecon

> countries' financial transactions, and also the methodology of the national currencies' exchange-rate formation and the conditions and ways of introducing these exchange rates. On the basis of these proposals a project for the formation of an international investment bank is being prepared. . . .

But things were not necessarily going smoothly:

> The implementation of the recommendations of the special April Comecon session requires time, patience, and a huge amount of work. This is neither a simple nor an easy matter. It is a matter which leads to conflicts. In many spheres, opinions and estimates vary; a struggle with old habits continues. So does the struggle between autarkic trends and new currents which are only beginning to break fresh ground in human consciousness and activities.

Initial examination of some proposals at the Twenty-fourth Council session was now anticipated by Jaroszewicz at the "end of the first or the beginning of the second quarter" of 1970, and since a comprehensive program was still expected to be presented to another council session "toward the end of 1970," if these deadlines were to be met, there was seen to be little time left. Jaroszewicz appeared resigned, however, to a long, hard slog when he concluded that "despite difficulties, doubts and differences of opinion, we are progressing step by step along this difficult path."

Expressions of impatience continued in early 1970. Criticism of the slow progress in the socialist division of labor was a theme at a conference in the Central Party School, and shortly thereafter a particularly frustrated commentator was arguing:

> It is no secret that Comecon is not meeting the socialist countries' needs. . . . We are not engaged in socialist construction merely to continue forever to chase the production standards determined by the capitalist groups; we are trying to outstrip them. . . .
>
> Our countries will never accomplish this by themselves and unassisted. We have no alternative but finally to make common efforts within Comecon. There lies our only chance.[32]

The political significance of economic integration was still in the forefront, at least for Gomulka. In an article published both in <u>Pravda</u> and <u>Trybuna Ludu</u>,[33] Gomulka argued that economic integration is of tremendous political importance in the present competition with capitalism, because, although successful Western integration is preparing capitalism for its transformation into socialism, as Lenin predicted, "today [this integration] increases the strength of capitalism in the struggle against socialism." As Gomulka saw it, the socialist countries must integrate rapidly in order to exploit more fully the possibilities of their system of planned economy, to strengthen their political alliance, and to compete successfully with the West.

The need to integrate, in part to compete with the West, however, did not preclude expanded economic ties with the West. In early 1970, with the prospects for economic reform improving, hopes for economic openings in the West were rising. In addition, stress was still given to financial reforms in Comecon, and some continued to foresee eventual convertibility into Western currencies. Relatively free trade in consumer goods and even a "free" flow of labor within Comecon were also anticipated—this latter again reflecting a parallel with Hungarian concepts.[34] Just how such progressive economic ideas were reconcilable with the conservative political inclinations of Gomulka remained one of the continuing enigmas of his ill-starred regime.

BULGARIA

Following the summit, Bulgaria continued to register its enthusiasm for closer economic ties with Comecon countries, especially the USSR, and to exhibit few inhibitions about how these ties were formed. As noted above, in June a Bulgarian journal indicated with approval that joint planning was to begin during the process of plan coordination for 1971-75.[35] Enthusiasm was also expressed for increasing interdependence through the (further) joint creation of international economic complexes, particularly with the USSR, and in Pravda a Bulgarian professor got carried away to the point of offering the ever closer Bulgarian-Soviet economic integration as a "standard" for the other countries of Comecon.[36]

Shortly thereafter Zhivkov revealed, not surprisingly, that the Soviet Union would be Bulgaria's first joint planning partner, when he stated in Moscow that "we shall . . . gradually move on to joint planning in a number of branches."[37] However, despite mutual commitment in principle, when the Bulgarian-Polish commission on economic cooperation met in November to decide on new forms of cooperation "in accordance with the decisions and recommendations of the 23rd special Comecon session," agreement on joint planning was not mentioned.[38] Only in late February, following talks in Warsaw, was agreement on joint planning between Bulgaria and Poland rather cautiously announced. The head of the Bulgarian half of the joint commission, Ivan Mihailov, acknowledged that "integration . . . processes are very complicated, take a very long time, and require much effort and knowledge from both countries. What we still need is more study of each other, because our talks showed that there still is a great deal to do."[39] He then stated that "we agreed that our planning bodies would work out methods of joint planning and would stipulate sectors of production in which such planning can be carried out." Since the designation of sectors suitable for joint planning had been scheduled in April, 1969, for decision "in a few months,"[40] even this appeared to be a rather belated and hesitant step forward.

Probably reflecting their new reading of Soviet thinking, Bulgarian writers became more assertive and polemicized with what they took to be overly progressive concepts.[41] A regulated socialist market, the "premature introduction" of extensive quotaless trade, and freedom to establish direct contacts were rejected, as was partial convertibility into gold or convertible currency. Planned convertibility of the socialist currencies with a "convertible" ruble was advocated. The basic idea was that such convertibility and financial relations in general should be subordinated to planned production relationships and should develop only as these latter permitted. Convertibility would be part of a system of financial levers which supplemented and reinforced plan coordination, but was not to provide an independent driving force under which elements of spontaneity might develop. Interestingly, in rejecting convertibility into gold or convertible currency even as a disciplinary measure, one Bulgarian author argued that this approach wouldn't work because penalty clauses calling for gold or convertible currency payments which had long existed in bilateral trade agreements within Comecon had in fact never been used.[42]

EAST GERMANY

In the immediate aftermath of the summit the East Germans appeared to maintain their reserve, continuing to make much of bilateral economic relations, particularly of scientific-technological and investment ties with the USSR. East German media still took a low-key approach to such topical issues as plan coordination and joint planning, and showed no real interest in tightening up, or reforming, Comecon. There was still no particular interest shown in financial reforms. East Germany had not begun to develop a program of its own which might offer anything to the rest of Eastern Europe. In July, writing in Pravda, where maximum enthusiasm is expected, Weiss was bland and noncommittal.[43]

However, it was becoming increasingly evident that others, including the USSR, had not accepted Ulbricht's positions. There was to be continued tolerance of some diversity among economic systems (notably in Hungary), and economic ties with the West were to be encouraged. Moreover, with the summit, a renewed search for ways to improve Comecon—to achieve "integration"—was under way. Some adjustments in the essentially negative East German position appeared to be in order.

In the latter part of 1969 the East Germans began to develop a greater interest in Comecon and in the integration program being developed. While bilateral ties with the USSR were still foremost, such topical questions as joint planning, financial reform, and even the accelerated industrial development of the less advanced Comecon members were now at least acknowledged, and there began to develop a greater concern for the complex solutions to Comecon's problems which were more actively being sought.[44]

To mark the twentieth anniversary of the German Democratic Republic, a lengthy quasi-official treatise (with a foreword by Ulbricht) on socialist economics was published.[45] In this treatise a comprehensive discussion of Comecon and integration set out the basic framework within which, in the East German view, the reform of Comecon should be pursued. To start, it was argued that the economic and scientific-technological integration of the Comecon states was made necessary by the economic laws of socialism, the demands of the scientific-technological revolution, and the sharpening economic competition with capitalism.

In elaborating on the requirements of the socialist economic system, considerable attention was first devoted to polemics with "revisionists." It was found that the foreign trade monopoly must be further developed into an all-encompassing monopoly of foreign economic relations and that one should not leave the regulation of economic relations to a customs system or succumb to the thesis that nationalization and the existence of a state foreign economic policy were sufficient. Decentralization and enterprise autonomy were a threat to socialist control. Rather, the laws governing the socialist economy established the form of "integration" of a nation's foreign economic system into its over-all economic system and, hence, defined the direction of the expansion of the socialist monopoly in the foreign economic field.

The East German concept of the admissible foreign trade system allegedly was based on certain inherent principles of socialism which must be embodied in every domestic economic model. These principles require a combination of the use of goods-money relations with a development of the responsibility and initiative of the enterprise or association. Financial interest must be raised, and production must feel the consequences of trade activity. A complex system of economic levers must provide the instrument for active state guidance of foreign economic relations on the basis of the plan. Operations research and electronic data-processing help to make this possible. In short, central planning stimulates the market through economic, particularly financial, levers in so far as modern technology allows and efficiency demands. But there must be no risk of loss of control by the center, and spontaneity and "market socialism" are not to be tolerated.

In systematic fashion, the East German answer for Comecon integration followed quite logically from this foreign trade model, just as this model followed from the economic "laws" of socialism as reflected in the domestic economy. The integration concept was rather weak on specifics, however, although it closely followed the Soviet and summit ideas of a complex, multifaceted attack on the barriers to closer ties. But there was still no urgency about pushing ahead with multilateral integration or with the institutional, particularly the financial, reforms necessary to support it. Lenin's idea of a common plan was cited, but the new economic unity developing was not seen as leading to any loss of the states' role. On the contrary, the organizational role of the socialist state would be raised, for the "voluntary" integration process must be guided at the state level.

The approach to Comecon as spelled out here reflected the fact that East Germany was still more concerned with bloc unity and conformity than with economic integration per se. The great concern with socialist laws and revisionism and the stress on the derived nature of integration and the threat of imperialism focused attention on the internal economic model as the basic determinant of Comecon reform and of socialist orthodoxy. The main thrust of the antirevisionist polemics was aimed at Hungary, and the sharp Hungarian rejoinder, noted above, reflected the fact that the East Germans were the chief critics of the Hungarian reform model as well as of the Hungarian concepts for Comecon.

There were also still strong East German reservations about pushing through integration schemes which might impinge on national economic prerogatives or established positions. East Germany's preoccupation with its own interests and its economic focus on the USSR continued to be paralleled by an unwillingness to collaborate fully with the rest of Eastern Europe. This naturally helped to impel the rest of Eastern Europe to look to the West for technological help and cooperation. Yet the special East German economic relationship with West Germany and the privileged access to the EEC that this provided caused growing resentment, particularly as the East Germans opposed bilateral contacts with the West by others. East Germany reportedly tried to forestall the development of Hungarian ties with West Germany and to limit Czechoslovakia's receipt of Western credits and its competitive exports to the West. It was also accused of trying to use its leading and privileged position to expand the dependence of the rest of Eastern Europe on East German technology—even to the point of annoying the USSR.[46] (One result of the East German obstructionism was to induce others to gather evidence of East Germany's own close economic ties with West Germany. This reportedly was especially true just prior to the December, 1969, Warsaw Pact conference.)[47] The dilemma for East Germany was still how to formulate a program capable of reinforcing socialist internationalism and satisfying some of the economic demands of the rest of Eastern Europe, while at the same time not sacrificing the privileged East German position in Soviet and Western markets or accepting a bloc-wide rationalization of production and trade which would undermine East Germany's leading role in advanced industries.

In early 1970, considerable interest was shown by East German economists in overcoming this dilemma and in filling in the basic framework provided by the twentieth-anniversary treatise. Although much attention was still devoted to negative strictures, in a spate of articles on Comecon an East German integration concept began to emerge more clearly. A basic line of argument began with the familiar thesis that the struggle with imperialism is focused on the scientific-technological field and that top-level world standards must be met in research, investment, and production; this, it was maintained, can only be done to a limited and carefully controlled extent by borrowing from the West [under a common policy] and hence the emphasis must be on the most advanced countries within Comecon, the USSR and East Germany; given the existing lack of uniformity in internal economic systems (due in large part to revisionism), multilateralism, convertibility, and financial reform were still for the more distant future, and bilateral links, with the weak depending on the strong, would continue to dominate for the foreseeable future; the USSR is in fact the "integration center," and it and East Germany are setting an "example for adjustment and coordination of national planning and management systems as well as for development of completely new [types of cooperative arrangements] which increasingly become a model for shaping socialist economic integration as a whole, . . . for a higher level of cooperation is being introduced here bilaterally than was hitherto, or is yet, possible on the multilateral level."[48]

In order to justify this continuing focus on bilateralism when others were clamoring for multilateral solutions, the East Germans emphasized the prerequisites to effective multilateralism. Continuing to reject market solutions which would lessen plan control, they argued in effect that multilateralism could only be built up on the basis of uniformity in domestic economic systems of planning, forecasting, and management, with common methods of calculating costs and returns showing the mutual benefits of each step toward integration. Still foremost was the argument that, because integration is to take place among sovereign, independent states, the effectiveness of plan coordination and the rate of integration depend on the development of the internal economic systems, on the degree of similarity of the national planning and guidance systems. It was even suggested that a binding mechanism was needed, not to promote integration directly but to regulate tasks and responsibilities of state organs involved so as to guarantee their parallel development.[49]

The East German concept of integration thus involved the integration of foreign economic relations into the domestic system and uniformity of domestic systems, with operational integration essentially confined to the bilateral level for the foreseeable future. This led the East Germans not only to resist multilateralism and basic financial reforms but also to criticize those who went too far with Lenin's idea of a common plan.[50] Although plan coordination should begin before national structural concepts are worked out, voluntary cooperation was still necessary, under which each state draws up its own plan while attending bilateral and multilateral conferences to decide on the cooperation opportunities to be grasped in the spirit of socialist internationalism. The binding nature of plan coordination was to increase (only) as trade agreements and contracts were signed.[51] It was at this point that the uniformity of domestic economic systems became crucial, for to carry out these obligations successfully, central planning had to be directive and reinforced by the improved application of financial levers such as interest, credit, prices, and exchange rates.

Although this new-found concern for Comecon reflected the necessity to enter into the discussions begun after the summit, the increasingly embattled political position of East Germany within the bloc was quite probably also a major factor. There were growing indications that East German political interests might be compromised in the drive to improve relations with the West, particularly with West Germany, and, in late 1969, following the accession of Willy Brandt's government to power, the East German tactics on East-West relations had begun to change. Seeking to confine potential new bloc contacts with Bonn to a multilateral framework, East Germany began to give much greater support to the proposal for a European security conference,[52] while within the Comecon sphere this was reflected not only in the constant emphasis on the need for integration in the sharpening struggle with imperialism, but in the arguments for the unique form which socialist integration must take—its "completely new quality" in contrast to capitalist integration.[53] One's approach to socialist integration must be based on opposition to Western models, as well as on socialist laws, and it was necessary to rebut convergence theorists who were linked to Western plotting against Czechoslovakia and to the machinations of the new West German government.[54] A common approach to the West was necessary, and a strict foreign trade monopoly had to be preserved in order to protect the socialist states from the capitalist market and from inducements to decentralize in order to facilitate trade with capitalist firms.[55]

But the need for economic relations with the West was no longer so categorically rejected. One writer, while arguing that the threat of Western economic subversion was still strong, now gave Ulbricht's dictum a new twist when he asserted that, because the socialist countries were capable of solving every important problem with their own resources, they were able to "make use of relations with the capitalist countries without becoming dependent upon them."[56] This appeared to tie in with the emergence of the renewed East German drive for Western recognition. At the Leipzig Fair, the Minister for Foreign Economic Relations said that there would be far greater prospects for trade and cooperation if "normal interstate relations were established between the GDR and the capitalist industrial states."[57] In early 1970, there evidently was a growing feeling that a negative approach to Comecon and to expanded economic ties with the West was only isolating East Germany further in bloc councils and that more comprehensive and positive ideas were essential if East German interests were to be preserved during a period of changing bloc approaches toward external economic relations.

USSR

Soviet spokesmen, like those in Eastern Europe, continually emphasized the importance of the April summit. Great potential was seen in such "new" departures as joint planning, joint research organizations, joint forecasting, longer-term planning, continuous plan coordination, policy coordination, direct contacts at all levels, contractual relations, new foreign trade methods, and an enhanced role for financial incentives (including sanctions). At the same time the limits of change foreseen within Comecon were set out.

In an article in *Pravda* in June discussing the results of the summit, Mikhail Lesechko went out of his way to criticize the anti-Soviet hysteria of the bourgeois press in predicting a fruitless summit, and to attack bourgeois ideologists for foisting advice on the Communist countries and recommending that they abandon "socialist foundations" for the "anarchy of so-called free market relations."[58] He maintained that "it is obvious that the envisaged intensification of the role of commodity-money relations by no means implies a turn to the conditions of market relationships, which are incompatible with the planned economies of the fraternal countries." He also emphasized, however, that the new methods of cooperation, including joint planning, would be "based on intergovernmental agreements embodying established principles for cooperation," and that the new organizations established "cannot and will not perform supranational functions, [for] their prerogatives will be fully defined by the rights and spheres of competence of the national organs which take part in them; these are regulated by the domestic laws of the individual sovereign Comecon member countries."

Another commentator, moreover, took a notably cautious approach to the question of joint planning, at least to its role in the short term. He observed that the summit

> recognized that it was advisable for the interested countries to work out joint plans for individual types of production or branches as an experiment during the coordination of the national economic plans for 1971-75.[59]

He saw joint planning as a "further development in the coordination of national economic plans," although it would give rise

> to various new problems of a methodological and organizational nature. . . . Naturally, the methodology and organizational forms for working out joint plans will be based on the available experience of plan coordination and will proceed from the existing principles for economic cooperation among the Comecon countries.

Joint planning was to be supported by a "whole system of agreements reflecting the concrete pledges of each country." Eventually, however, he foresaw that

> As joint planning experience accumulates, it will probably be necessary to create international branch organizations of a financially autonomous nature whose participants will be the countries' economic organizations [enterprise associations, combines, main administrations, and individual major enterprises].

Great stress was placed on the importance of expanding direct contacts and strengthening contractual relations within a planned framework. Another commentator argued, for example, that, in future, direct collaboration from the ministerial level on down, rather than centralized collaboration organized at the interstate level, would be the primary method of cooperation. Contractual relations between these lower level organizations were seen as "a significant new element" in this cooperation.[60]

This interest in direct contacts and contractual relations was followed up within the Comecon Executive Committee where the Soviets introduced a proposal on the "organizational, economic, and legal preconditions" for the establishment of direct ties, including those between research institutes. According to the proposal, these ties would be based on contractual relations under which the material interestedness and responsibility of the member countries should be increased.[61] This was not to suggest, however, that "alien mechanisms," such as market socialism—which would bring in its wake such dreadful results as the dismantling of weak enterprises and open exposure to the world capitalist economy—were suddenly being contemplated.[62] Rather it reflected the fact that, whatever latent notions some might have about developing comprehensive criteria for assessing Comecon's over-all prospects and enforcing "optimal" development, present technical capability was still far from able to supply much support.[63]

Some insights into Soviet thinking on Comecon were also provided by a discussion among leading Soviet specialists broadcast by Radio Budapest.[64] Whereas "in the past the [Comecon] plan had no independent part to play [and] came into being only in the course of coordinating the [individual] economic plans," now all of the new approaches to be made and the reforms being worked out were to contribute to making the planning of economic ties among the Comecon members a more continuous process of mutual interaction, encompassing research and marketing as well as trade and production. The old separation of production from finance and foreign trade was to be eliminated by a new system of "interrelated interests"; specialization was to extend to research as well as production; and new organizations were to become involved. The USSR had in fact already taken action, and further involvement of production enterprises in foreign economic relations was to be encouraged. One participant noted:

> Decisions have already been taken at government level which grant specific authority to specific ministries, and several of them have already concluded agreements fully designed to further the objectives of close integration and coordination. In the Soviet Union and in other Comecon countries enterprises are springing up which in the sphere of production already take foreign relations into consideration, and I believe this should be further expanded in the future.

There were also indications that the Soviets would support exchange-rate adjustment and higher interest rates in Comecon trade,[65] two steps that it seemed likely could come out of the working group discussions, for while both are prerequisites to rationalization, neither is a determinant of the ultimate institutional approach to multilateralism and convertibility.

The great importance of science and technology was continually stressed. The accelerating development of scientific-technological relations among the Comecon states was linked to the need for developing direct contacts and contractual relations.[66] Interestingly, it was argued that although the scientific-technological revolution was a basic cause of the need for new approaches to integration, it was also a barrier to any simple solutions: While things were getting more and more complicated, the productive lifetimes of technology and its products were decreasing; hence it was necessary to develop much more sophisticated and effective methods of forecasting, planning, and coordinating activities; but there were many contradictions involved which complicated the search for new approaches and required "extensive scientific and practical elaboration."[67]

The great potential for Soviet-East European cooperation in this field was a constant theme, and Fadeyev predicted in Izvestiia that "socialist economic integration will facilitate the victory of socialism in the peaceful economic competition with capitalism, primarily in the decisive field of this competition—in the sphere of scientific and technological progress."[68]

In this period the Soviet position on Comecon was gaining in complexity and sophistication, and a clearer Soviet concept for Comecon had at last begun to develop. Although the grand designs, if there were any, were only for the long term, and, unlike some East European countries, the USSR did not feel that major institutional breakthroughs at the broadest level (for example, through the establishment of real multilateralism or some form of convertibility) were the basic answer to Comecon's problems, a consistent program emerged. The USSR had become an activist in changing Comecon at the operational level where expansion, improvement, and sometimes innovation were pushed on the basis of old and proven methods. Even joint planning was treated as just one of many approaches which were essentially extensions of past practice.

A great deal of work was seen as necessary in order to achieve effective closer economic relations among the Comecon countries. The main areas into which cooperation had to be extended were production, investment, and scientific-technological research, particularly in the newest, high-technology industries. The primary method of controlling and promoting this cooperation was to be through contracts and other agreements enforced by financial rewards and penalties. All available means were to be developed—legal, financial, organizational, and moral—and all the latest techniques were to be employed, for integration was a multileveled, multifacited operation which required a modern complex solution. The Soviet approach to Comecon thus well reflected its approach to domestic economic reform, which could be characterized as the "new form of bureaucratic spirit [which uses] the sciences in order to supply politics with a method of employing techniques in the solving of individual problems within the framework of the existing system."[69]

As the next council session approached, the general confidence and determination of the Soviets also appeared to increase. Reassurances on the preservation of national independence, voluntary participation, and equality were given, while supranational organs and closed groupings were rejected. Yet "subjective" problems presented by "departures from socialist internationalism" or concessions to "*petit-bourgeois* ideology and capitalist remnants" were clearly not to be tolerated, and the long-run concept of integration now increasingly had an aura of Leninist-inspired inevitability.[70] Nevertheless, although the stress was on the need for the planning of direct contacts and of contractual relations rather than decentralization of decision-making, these Soviet formulations, particularly in their acknowledgment of the complexity and interrelatedness of economic ties, appeared to reflect a better understanding of the problems of integration and, one could hope, of at least some of the arguments of the decentralization advocates and of their institutional reform programs.

NOTES

1. N. Ceausescu's report to the Rumanian Tenth Party Congress, August 6, 1969 (Radio Bucharest, same day).

2. R. Negru in *Viata Economica*, September 19, 1969.

3. I. Ionescu in *Viata Economica*, February 13, 1970; R. Moldovan in *Lupta de Clasa*, March, 1970.

4. Moldovan, *op. cit.*

5. *Zycie Warszawy*, February 21, 1970.

6. Moldovan, *op. cit.*

7. Hungarian Finance Minister Peter Valyi in a report to Parliament, July 2, 1969, as reported by Radio Budapest, same day; Rezso Nyers's interview in l'Unita, the Italian Communist Party paper, July 1, 1969; G. Becsky in the Hungarian Review, July, 1969; Bela Sulyok in Nepszabadsag, September 3, 1969.

8. Becsky, op. cit.

9. Sulyok, op. cit.

10. Bela Csikos-Nagy, in an interview reported by David Binder in the International Herald Tribune, June 27, 1969.

11. Rezso Nyers's interviews in l'Unita, July 1, 1969, and in Pravda, January 20, 1970.

12. Joint interview with S. Majewski and A. Apro, Nepszabadsag and Trybuna Ludu, November 11, 1969.

13. Press conference reported in Magyar Hirlap, December 21, 1969.

14. Lecture by T. Kiss at a joint conference of Comecon and the Soviet Academy of Science on January 28, -February 4, 1970, published in Kozgadsagi Szemle, May, 1970.

15. Jeno Fock's interviews in Magyar Hirlap, March 13, 1970, and Trybuna Ludu, April 2, 1970.

16. Radio Budapest, March 5, 1970.

17. Review by Istvan Friss, a leading architect of the Hungarian reform, a member of the Hungarian Central Committee, and the director of the Economic Institute of the Hungarian Academy of Sciences, in Nepszabadsag, March 14, 1970. The East German treatise in question was by G. Mittag et al., Politische Oekonomie des Sozialismus—und ihre Anvendung der DDR (Political economy of socialism and its application in the GDR) (East Berlin: Dietz-Verlag, October, 1969).

18. Peter Valyi, The New Hungarian Quarterly, Summer, 1970 (written before the Twenty-fourth Comecon session in May).

19. Radio Prague, November 30, 1969.

20. B. Horak, Mlada Fronta, November 11, 1969; F. Kolar over Radio Prague, November 30, 1969.

21. J. Blazek over Radio Prague, January 5, 1970.

22. Pravda (Bratislava), January 10, 1970.

23. J. Terek in Rude Pravo, February 27, 1970; Rude Pravo, January 23, 1970.

24. O. Marusiak in Pravda (Bratislava) March 2, 1970.

25. For example, the interview with J. Soldaczuk, director of the Warsaw Institute for International Trade, published in Hospodarske Noviny, January 23, 1970.

26. M. Misiak in Zolnierz Wolnosci, June 21, 1969.

27. Z. Kamecki in Gospodarka Planowa, October, 1969.

28. PAP report on J. Pajestka's speech at the Moscow conference, in Trybuna Ludu, January 29, 1970.

29. D. Fikus in Polityka, August 2, 1969; Z. Kamecki in Gospodarka Planowa, October, 1969.

30. Radio Warsaw, December 4, 1969.

31. Piotr Jaroszewicz in Trybuna Ludu, December 31, 1969, and January 1, 1970.

32. PAP report in Trybuna Ludu February 26, 1970; A. Mroczek in Slowo Powszechne, March 2, 1970.

33. Wladyslaw Gomulka in Pravda, March 31, 1970, and Trybuna Ludu, April 1, 1970.

34. Interview with J. Soldaczuk, director of the Warsaw Institute for International Trade, in Hospodarske Noviny (Czech), January 23, 1970; J. Jakubowski in Panstwoi Prawo, May, 1970.

35. Novo Vreme, June, 1969.

36. G. Popisakov in Pravda, August 4, 1969.

37. Todor Zhivkov's speech at the opening of the Bulgarian Jubilee Exhibition in Moscow, September 26, 1969, reported in Rabotnichesko Delo, September 27, 1969.

38. Radio Sofia report on the communiqué, November 13, 1969.

39. Interview with Ivan Mihailov in Trybuna Ludu, February 23, 1970.

40. Press conference by Frantisek Hamouz, May 5, 1969, as reported by Ceteka and Radio Prague, same day.

41. M. Stoimenov in Ikonomicheska Misul, November-December, 1969; I. Dimov in Finansi i Kredit, March, 1970; V. Ivanova in Ikonomicheska Misul, April, 1970.

42. I. Dimov, op. cit.

43. G. Weiss, Pravda, July 2, 1969.

44. G. Weiss, Einheit, 9-10 (special twentieth-anniversary issue), 1969.

45. G. Mittag et al., op. cit.

46. A. Herman in Financial Times, November 26, 1969; H. Ellis in Christian Science Monitor, November 4, 1969.

47. D. Binder in New York Times, December 3, 1969.

48. O. Hofmann in Sozialistische Aussenwirtschaft, 2, 1970.

49. O. Weitkus in Sozialistische Aussenwirtschaft, 5, 1970.

50. G. Proft in Sozialistische Aussenwirtschaft, 5, 1970.

51. K. Morgenstern in Wirtschaftwissenschaft, May, 1970.

52. See A. Ross Johnson, "The Warsaw Pacts' Campaign for 'European Security'" (Santa Maria, Calif.: The RAND Corporation, November, 1970), p. 61.

53. I. Hauke, Sozialistische Aussenwirtschaft, 4, 1970.

54. A collective team of authors, led by Professor Kupferschmidt, in Sozialistische Aussenwirtschaft, 3, 1970.

55. S. Wenger in Sozialistische Aussenwirtschaft, 3, 1970.

56. R. Bauer in Sozialistische Aussenwirtschaft, 4, 1970.

57. H. Soelle's press conference as reported by ADN, March 3, 1970.

58. M. Lesechko in Pravda, June 21, 1969.

59. S. Plakain in Ekonomicheskaia Gazeta, 29, July, 1969.

60. Interview with D. M. Gvishiani in Rude Pravo, June 25, 1969.

61. Radio Sofia, March 1, 1970, reporting on the forty-fifth session of the Comecon Executive Committee, February 24-27, 1970.

62. A. Eremin in Nauchnye doklady vysshei shkoly—ekonomicheskie nauki, 11, 1969.

63. G. Prokhorov, Voprosy Ekonomiki, 11, 1969.

64. Discussion recorded by Radio Moscow between O. Bogomolov, director of the Economic Institute of the World Socialist System, his deputy, Dudinsky, and the chief of the institute's department on Comecon cooperation, Shilayev (Radio Budapest, 16 December 1969).

65. K. Nazarkin in Vneshnyaya Torgovlya, January, 1970; Karpich, op. cit.; O. Bogomolov in Mirovaya ekonomika i mezhdunarodnye otnosheniya, April, 1970.

66. Interview with D. M. Gvishiani, op. cit.; see also V. Karpich, op. cit.

67. Iu. Medvedkov in Mirovaya ekonomika i mezhdunarodnye otnodshesiya, 12, 1969.

68. N. Fadeyev, Izvestiia, March 27, 1970.

69. Professor M. Zivotic, Covek i Brednosti (Man and Values) (Belgrade: Prosveta, 1969).

70. N. Fadeyev, Izvestiia, March 27, 1970; O. Bogomolov, in Mirovaya ekonomika i mezhdunarodnye otnosheniya, April, 1970.

CHAPTER

5

AN INTERIM ASSESSMENT

Following the summit one could see some evidence of rapprochement in thinking on the role of Comecon and a certain willingness to accommodate in intrabloc relations. The two most comprehensive reform positions brought to the anniversary sessions of January, 1969, the Polish and the Hungarian, showed considerable convergence in terms of immediate operational means, if not in ultimate ends. At the same time, however, the emergence of a more forceful and clear-cut East German position added a new dimension to the differences over Comecon's future, while the shifting of Czechoslovakia's stance removed from the side of the reformers what little weight that country carried in Comecon affairs since its invasion.

As the Twenty-fourth Council session approached, the debate over the basic principles on which cooperation within Comecon was to be expanded continued undiminished. It turned out (predictably) that the individual members which had been assigned the tasks of preparing proposals on direct contacts and new organizations took differing approaches and that "therefore the preparation of a joint proposal was accompanied by difficulties in trying to unify different views, particularly with regard to the role of central organs and economic organizations, structure and management, etc."[1] Major differences reportedly developed over whether direct relations should be determined "only on the impulse" of central state organs and through high level agreements or to some extent through the initiative of economic organizations themselves. There were also differences over the responsibility of economic organizations for the implementation of agreements, particularly when central organs "unilaterally" interfere.

By the spring of 1970 voluntaryism was apparently accepted as a principle of economic cooperation among socialist countries and codified in the proposals being worked up for submission as part of the over-all integration program. The debate was now to a large extent over unanimity. In the proposals drafted by the working group on questions of planning a distinction was made between _interstate_ and _international_ economic organizations. It was proposed that the former operate with "unanimous agreement of the interested countries as the basic principle of decision-making," but the principles of decision-making were left open in the case of the latter, which were subdivided into associations and joint enterprises. The associations were expected, among other things, to handle "coordination of investments in which the participating countries are interested." These associations had few a priori stipulations to face. They were to have management and executive organs, but the structure of these organs was to depend on the organizations' particular mission. Significantly, the management organ was to run things "on the basis of the principles indicated in the agreement establishing the organization." Moreover, it was envisioned that the agreement could stipulate that an association was _not_ subject to the national legislation of the country in which it operated. Thus the idea was to establish machinery under Comecon for the setting up of international associations which virtually gave _carte blanche_ to those drawing up a particular agreement to establish the principles and procedures on which the association would operate. In theory at least, the participants could agree that the majority could take action which violated the national laws of the minority.[2]

Joint enterprises, the second type of international organization proposed, also appeared to have similar implications. They were to "have their own property, operate independently on the basis of _khozraschot_ [cost accounting] and [be] fully responsible for their obligations, which are guaranteed by their property." They could be established in a variety of ways, on the basis of shares which could also be defined in a variety of ways. In short, they too appeared to open up the possibility that a majority of shareholders could make decisions which affected economic operations on the national territories of their members. Not surprisingly, it was reported that the "problem of the standard forms and nature of (joint) economic organizations remained unsolved" by the working group, and that Rumania "conceived of (joint) economic organizations in a uniform manner, based to a considerable extent on the principles on which interstate economic organizations are to be built in the future."[3]

Although progress was reportedly made, only some of the disputed questions were resolved by negotiations in the Executive Committee to which the working group's findings were submitted, and the key issue, the principle of unanimity, was evidently carried to the Twenty-fourth Council session.

As Jaroszewicz had noted at the end of 1969 and as had been the case in the past, the search for financial reforms was also proving difficult. Still under discussion at Executive Committee meetings and to be taken up at the forthcoming Council meeting were proposals for the Comecon investment bank, the establishment of which in principle was agreed upon at the summit. Decisions on this bank and on exchange rate reform were making slow progress, as was reflected both in the rather long delay in the actual founding of an investment bank and in the lack of comment on these questions in the communiqué which followed the Forty-sixth Executive Committee meeting in April, despite the fact that the meeting was supposed to have discussed them.[4]

The discussions indicated that, in the financial sphere, more realistic (i.e., generally higher) interest rates on trade balances might also be anticipated, but little else was resolved. In an indicative commentary, the Polish news service was extremely cautious in discussing this sphere of reform. After noting the complexities involved in relating exchange rates to national price setting principles, it stated that "initial materials" for financial reform had been prepared and that the transition from bilateralism to multilateralism "may be carried out" on the basis of a common currency. It went on to say that the debates of Comecon commissions and special working groups "were concentrated on numerous subjects whose analysis and preparation will form an outline of the draft program of socialist integration" and that "the implementation of this program . . . is a continuous process spread over a period of time."[5]

Some decisions were also anticipated on plan coordination, organization, and regulation of cooperation. Fadeyev claimed that "the conclusion of an international agreement as a form of legal consolidation of the results of joint planning is envisaged," but this was not imminent, and after the next Executive Committee meeting in April it was rather laconically noted that joint planning of certain types of production was being elaborated.[6]

The December Executive Committee meeting called for the establishment of an international institute for economic problems, and Hamouz indicated that it would handle management, organization, and cybernetic questions.[7] There was evidently considerable urgency felt on this area, for, without waiting for the next Council session to take the matter up, a preliminary agreement on the establishment of international working groups in various countries to study such problems was reached in late April.[8]

As indicated in Fadeyev's statement on joint planning, there was considerable stress on the "perfection of the legal foundations" of economic cooperation. New measures to enhance responsibility for implementing agreements and to improve arbitration were proposed.[9] They were felt to be particularly necessary because of the new stress on direct contacts among organizations at all levels. The possibility of expanding the legal council, which was set up in December, 1969, into a legal institute was also raised.[10]

In these reports and commentaries on changes in Comecon one could detect an important, if inevitable, shift in emphasis. On the broad reform questions, notably those involving the financial system, the members were still in the preliminary stages of even the initial, and seemingly easiest, steps, and there was now less optimism over any quick progress toward convertibility or multilateralism. In part, undoubtedly, in compensation for this, increased stress was put on organizational questions and on regulating the more complex economic interrelations to be developed, particularly in new fields of cooperation. Although it appeared to be as difficult as ever to introduce effective change in these latter areas without parallel adjustments in internal mechanisms and broader Comecon financial reforms, an effort was being made to move ahead on the least controversial issues, while the debates over more fundamental systemic economic questions continued.

RELATIONS WITH THE WEST

There were suggestions that the summit had concerned itself with the question of external economic relations, but apparently little of what went on there in this sphere was revealed. The summit communiqué gave no hint that a common external policy was being considered. A few days after the summit, however, Polish Foreign Minister Stefan Jedrychowski suggested that agreements between Comecon, EFTA (European Free Trade Association) and the EEC would contribute to closer collaboration in Europe, and TASS claimed that "worldwide peaceful international cooperation also finds expression in the decisions" of the summit.[11] Moreover, Soviet commentators now appeared to be encouraging East Europeans to think in broader terms economically, using their guest privilege in East European media to argue, for example, that the question of scientific-technological cooperation is worldwide, "certain problems simply are of a global nature", and "all signs indicate that the output of [the machine] industry will not be able in the near future to find a market within the Comecon community of countries alone."[12] Despite the lack of open discussion on the topic, at least some minimum agreement on coordinating economic relations with the West may have occurred either at or just prior to the summit.

This conclusion would seem to be supported by the fact that the need that Lesechko had seen for coordinating world market activities was partially met by incorporating the gathering and dissemination of Western scientific and technological information into the functions of the new Comecon Information Center. The center, which went into operation in March, 1970, was expected to receive material both from its members' scientific-technological information services and from all over the world. In conjunction with members' organizations, uniform codes and methods of handling information were to be set up, and the center was to "develop wide contacts with international organizations," for "we cannot think of autarky in scientific information."[13] In order to perfect the information system itself (and by extension the systems of member countries), the center was also expected to keep abreast of international progress in information retrieval, to conduct its own research, and to provide training for member-country specialists.[14]

However, little had evidently really been settled on the coordination of Western economic policy on a broader basis, and there was continual sparring after the summit over the question of economic relations with the West. Although Comecon was not normally explicitly involved, the implications for its role in coordinating such ties were always present. This sparring was particularly evident in Soviet and Rumanian statements.

At the Tenth Party Congress, Ceausescu took the opportunity to defend Rumania's economic and scientific-technological relations with the West, while the Soviet delegate, Konstantin Katushev, responded with an attack on the "perfidious bridge-building and economic penetration policies of the West.[15] While the Rumanians were using the European security issue as a peg for rejecting zones of interest and closed economic groupings, Radio Moscow was arguing that the "loosening of links with the Comecon market is particularly dangerous when it is related to the broadening of trade with the capitalist states [for]this would sooner or later lead to the inclusion of one socialist country or another in the sphere of influence of the capitalist market."[16]

Rumania was quick to exploit the rapidly evolving Western contacts of other Comecon countries to counter suggestions that she was out of step. In his concluding speech at the party's Central Committee Plenum in December, 1969, Ceausescu even managed to present Rumania as the farsighted pioneer in improving relations with West Germany: after approving the beginning of Soviet and Polish talks with that country, Ceausescu noted that Rumania had consistently called for the normalization of relations between the socialist states and West Germany and went on to suggest that Rumania's policy had all along been the best way to inhibit the revanchist forces still at work there and to support the development of progressive forces.[17] An article in the Rumanian Central Committee theoretical journal Lupta de Clasa took a similar line, explicitly rejecting the argument that increased ties with the West endangered socialism and asserting that it was anachronistic to think that the more realistic stand of certain leading Western circles should be regarded a priori as an attempt to build bridges to the socialist countries in order to "undermine their unity or their social systems."[18]

Having accepted the necessity of an economic opening to the West the Soviets were obviously afraid of the possibilities for moving away from Comecon that this move might offer to Eastern Europe and of the great attraction of Western institutions. One answer to the difficulties presented by such a selective opening was to try to reinforce the collective approach, but it was not feasible simply to try to strengthen Comecon and then to use it as bloc spokesman and as the monitor of East European economic initiatives towards the West.

To begin with, Comecon had no experience or authority in these fields. Unlike other regional economic groupings, Comecon had not played any significant role in relations either with individual nonmember countries, other regional groupings, or international organizations, and its executive body could not speak for its members. To strengthen Comecon's role in external economic relations without first developing a more cohesive and viable system internally would appear artificial, at best, in the West, and would certainly provoke strong resistance in parts of Eastern Europe, notably Rumania. Moreover, bloc-to-bloc negotiations on economic questions did not at all fit in with the evolving broader Soviet designs for Europe.

This was in large part due to the changing view of the EEC, and of its potential for shaping the future of Europe, and to the strategy that was being worked out to contain it. As the EEC approached the end of its transition period and showed renewed signs of expanding, Soviet concern increased. At the June, 1969, International Communist Conference in Moscow a new realism and a suggestion of a new policy could be seen in Brezhnev's speech when, in examining the "special features of imperialism in the past decade," he stated,

> We cannot afford not to take into consideration the fact that imperialism in our time still possesses a powerful and highly organized production mechanism. . . . The imperialists, striving to respond to the challenge of socialism and to strengthen their position, are uniting their efforts on an international scale and resorting to various forms of economic integration. . . . There is no doubt that

> imperialism will continue to seek out new opportunities to prolong its existence. We must not fail to take all this into account in our policy. . . .[19]

How this was to be done became somewhat clearer from another declaration on European security which was issued after a bloc gathering in Prague in October, closely following Brandt's election. This declaration elevated the expansion of commercial, economic, scientific, and technological relations between East and West to the position of one of the East's two basic proposals. Thereafter, the idea of East-West cooperation quickly began to take on more concrete form, large-scale all-European projects in such diverse fields as oil and gas pipelines, pollution control, medicine, and nuclear research being foreseen if "artificial" barriers, including the discriminatory policy of the EEC, were removed.[20] Although a very sharp distinction was drawn between obtaining as much economic help as possible from the West and anything resembling "integration" with the West on its own terms, one visionary even maintained that at the various Communist Party conferences, including the June meeting in Moscow, a plan of action had been elaborated which was "designed to utilize to the full the natural process of economic integration in the interests of all European states. . . ."[21] The EEC was now being condemned not only for all the old reasons, but as the major barrier to the East's program for Europe—to a European security conference, to an all-European settlement, and to the "natural process" of all-European economic integration. It would now seem to have made even less sense for the Communist states to be at all accommodating toward the EEC and thereby to facilitate its formulation of a common external policy.

Yet they were evidently still thinking that some such move might eventually become necessary, if their design for Europe failed and the EEC made rapid progress, for at the end of 1969 the Bulgarian Deputy Secretary of Comecon came back to the idea of EEC-Comecon relations. He stated in an interview with the Hungarian broadcasting service that "Comecon, as a united body, would not be adverse to a declaration of readiness for cooperation from the organs of the European Economic Community"[22] (emphasis added). Because there was once again, as with the Polish Foreign Minister's remark following the summit, no elaboration of immediate follow-up, it is difficult to say whether this was a reflection of resignation over EEC developments (notably the success of the December meeting at The Hague), a response to a West German overture of the previous month,[23] an attempt to keep the West off balance, or an indiscreet revelation of a possible long-range strategy which had perhaps been discussed at the bloc gathering in Moscow earlier in December.

In any case, in early 1970 the East's alternative design for Europe began to take on an institutional form which appeared to require that Comecon and the EEC continue to play minimum roles. It was now suggested that the security conference should lead to the establishment of a permanent regional organization for the promotion of cooperation in Europe.[24] The idea was that this would be a pan-European forum in which all European states would participate as individuals, and alleged Western efforts to substitute a conference of "blocs" for a "general" European conference were strongly criticized.

However, it was now suggested more clearly that if the EEC's development proceeded successfully but the security conference idea didn't, some sort of a confrontation between Comecon and the EEC might become necessary. The EEC countries had to give up their discriminatory practices and cooperate in "organized endeavors in defense of the economic unity of Europe [or face] justified steps in joint defense of their vital economic interests [by] the member countries of Comecon, [which would] bring about a still clearer distinction between the two basic European economic organizations."[25] In order to prevent any such Comecon-EEC "clearer distinction" and to develop a complement to—or a potential substitute for—a new permanent regional organization, it was also urged that the U.N. Economic Commission for Europe (ECE) play a more active role in East-West economic affairs. In an address to the ECE in April, the Polish Ambassador made a wide-ranging appeal for East-West economic cooperation, voicing the East's fears of an expanded EEC and unhappiness over the slowdown in the growth of East-West trade.[26] He urged that the ECE give priority to five key problems, among which was a definition of changes in the ECE's structure and methods of work. In addition, Poland, Rumania, and the USSR, along with some Western countries, supported a Yugoslav proposal which called for a permanent center for promoting European industrial cooperation to be established under ECE auspices.[27]

Despite certain suggestions of a possible change, Comecon's role was still being kept to a minimum while other avenues for East-West economic cooperation and the containment of the EEC were being explored.

THE TWENTY-FOURTH COUNCIL SESSION

As the premiers of the Comecon states gathered in Warsaw for the Twenty-fourth Council session in May, 1970, there was general agreement among observers that sharp differences would emerge in the course of the meeting. The Soviets indicated that they were very much aware both of the political and economic significance of integration and of the difficulties of achieving harmonious agreement in both spheres. In a commentary on the morning of the Council's opening session Radio Moscow noted that "the political and economic cohesion of the socialist countries is the most important condition for victories in the historic competition between socialism and capitalism."[28] This overriding Soviet interest in maintaining cohesion in both areas helps to explain why at this session the USSR again appears to have played a moderating role.

From the discussions since the summit it appeared that it would be very difficult to come up with a comprehensive program for Comecon by the end of 1970, as had been anticipated. Nevertheless, on the eve of the Twenty-fourth Council session those most anxious to see such a program completed, the Poles, emphasized the great significance of the review to be undertaken and expressed considerable optimism over the progress being achieved, reminding everyone that the anticipated deadline was fast approaching.[29] In what appeared to be a last-minute thrust against the East German position, they argued that integration did not necessitate the elimination of differences in methods of planning, organization, or pricing, for such differences were "quite natural and presented no obstacle," forming an "objective departure-point" for the development of cooperation; they also stressed their interest in economic relations with the West and the need for multilateralism and for financial reforms.[30]

An apparent preview of the Hungarian line on topical questions at the session was presented in the party daily on the opening day by the chairman of the national planning office.[31] Closer coordination, it was asserted, imposed several important tasks, "primarily the task of furnishing appropriate information about the concepts of individual countries with respect to economic development," and this plan coordination was to be supported by policy coordination, which should be "primarily through consultations." On the question of internal reform, it was found that in other Comecon countries "changing trends similar to ours are manifest in the system of economic direction." The joint planning issue was now addressed cautiously, it being felt that joint planning should be applied largely to "certain chosen products" for the present, and that financial reform must proceed simultaneously with new approaches to plan coordination. Preservation of a Comecon framework within which it could pursue its economic reform still evidently was the primary Hungarian concern.

In his welcoming speech, Polish Premier Jozef Cyrankiewicz appeared to anticipate a difficult session when he noted that integration could only develop gradually, for it was a hard task which required the "bold Leninist vision of distant goals."[32] During the meeting, the Polish news service acknowledged that a "lively exchange of views, not devoid of controversial elements," took place, but also asserted that there had been a "rapprochement between the stands of the various states on many essential matters."[33] The Yugoslav news service, however, suggested that, because of the many differences, there might be some delay in meeting the deadlines for agreement set at the summit.[34] At the close of the session, Radio Sofia saw integration as a very complicated and difficult problem.[35]

Despite these signs of differences and caution, the communique on the Twenty-fourth Council session indicated that a number of decisions had been taken and claimed that, on examining the report of the Executive Committee, it was found that a "considerable part of the work on the preparation of a complex program" had been carried out.[36] The communiqué said, among other things, that the session had accepted the proposals submitted concerning the improvement of plan coordination and the holding of consultations on economic policy, and that the Executive Committee had been instructed to formulate and put into practice measures to ensure that the role of planning agencies in multilateral cooperation would be effectively increased. The session also approved the principles and proceedings, and the organizational, economic, and legal premises, for direct contacts, the principles of increasing material interest, and the admissible forms and organizational functions of joint organizations created by interested Comecon members. Here the communiqué preserved the distinction between the Council's right to instruct Comecon organs but only to exhort its members, it being merely recommended that members create conditions conducive to the creation of direct contacts and joint organizations. It was also decided to create an international institute for economic problems of the world socialist system, and certain recommendations concerning the Comecon bank's multilateral accounts and short-term credit were adopted. Most important, all of Comecon's members but Rumania approved the draft agreement and the draft statutes of an investment bank, and promised to sign the agreement by early July. Just what these various decisions, approvals, and recommendations really amounted to, however, was not too clear, for the details of these steps were not given, and even in the case of the investment bank several crucial questions remained open.

Subsequent remarks revealed more about what had transpired at the Twenty-fourth Council session and what were considered its most significant accomplishments. The session evidently was more involved in operational decisions than often implied, since it had discussed specific joint investment proposals and set deadlines for the completion of five-year plan coordination.[37] The importance of the session's decision to promote regular contacts among central planning authorities was frequently noted, and meetings of the chairmen of state planning organs were soon held to develop ways to improve cooperation and to "link integration measures more closely to long-term plans."[38] The Twenty-fourth Council session thus appeared to mark considerably more progress toward integration than it did toward reform, and the shift in emphasis seen prior to the meeting from more substantive reform issues to more practical cooperation questions was also reflected at the session itself.

FIRST ASSESSMENTS

In contrast to the seemingly self-satisfied tone of the communiqué, many observers felt that little had been achieved, either at this Council session or in the year of preparation since the summit. Western observers in particular noted the imprecision of the bulk of the communiqué and concluded that, despite final agreement on the investment bank and some other modest improvements, there had been no real progress toward financial reform: nothing had been said about price and exchange rate reform or about convertibility, even as limited, distant goals.[39] Hungarian Premier Fock appeared to agree when he spoke of the need for "long and persistent work [and] further efforts and understanding by every country," and said that the greater part of the work was still to be done, historically new problems having been raised for which solutions were only now being sought.[40] He also observed that different views on financial issues persisted and important aspects still had to be worked out, and he promised that Hungary would continue to struggle to push through its point of view.[41] In a similar vein Radio Budapest observed that the meeting had not marked a turning point in Comecon relations.[42]

One's view of progress was, however, in considerable part a question of perspective, and those who did not see financial reform as the heart of the matter tended to be more sanguine. The Soviets felt that important recommendations had been adopted, seeing this as evidence of a determination to consolidate economic ties, and they found the session's decisions to be of great practical importance.[43] In similar fashion, reflecting Czechoslovakia's less reform-minded, more Soviet-oriented position, Hamouz felt that important practical measures had been taken and argued that the meeting had not been expected to adopt basic documents but only the procedures and structure of the integration program.[44] He called for an "uncompromising" discussion of problems and said that an effort would be made to include some already-resolved questions of cooperation and specialization in current plan coordination. Significantly, he revealed that the conclusion of the integration program was not now expected until the spring of 1971—a delay evidently sanctioned at the Twenty-fourth Council session.

The Poles' reaction was mixed, but despite their candid recognition of differences and of the difficult road ahead, they now appeared on balance fairly well satisfied. They emphasized that the session marked an important step forward and played up the significance of the decisions taken. As did Hamouz, they saw prospects for important integration steps to be made in coordinating the upcoming five-year plans, without waiting for completion of the entire integration program. Although the continuing difficulties with multilateral plan coordination were lamented, they thought that concrete provisions on multilateral cooperation could be incorporated in these five-year plans through joint planning.[45] They felt that both prior to and during the session a rapprochement of stands on basic integration questions had taken place, and welcomed the fact that unanimity was no longer sacrosanct, seeing the new investment bank as setting a precedent for future Comecon organizations.[46] While the institutional reform side of integration was lagging, the Poles evidently placed considerable hope in the prospects for a multilateral division of labor opened up by the investment bank.

Others in Eastern Europe, notably East Germany and Rumania, appeared more reticent, suggesting that they may have felt that they had lost a round, the former probably in connection with systemic uniformity and relations with the West and the latter in connection with the unanimity question.

THE INVESTMENT BANK AND UNANIMITY

The idea of getting Comecon involved in joint investments was an old one. The 1960 charter foresaw the promotion of joint investments by Comecon, and initially some enthusiasts had hopes that the Comecon bank established in 1964 would eventually grant long-term investment credits. However, there appeared to be little serious public discussion of how investment credits and a bank to grant them might operate either before or after the summit agreed that such an investment bank should be set up. With member currencies not even convertible on trade account, much less on capital account, the relationship between the bank's capital or credits and actual goods and services presented complex problems, as did the closely related question of the relationship between the bank's investment credits and plan coordination. Neither of these basic questions had been settled when, with Rumania still abstaining, the agreement on the investment bank was signed in July.

Rumania's abstention from the investment bank at this time was closely related to the unanimity issue and to the broader question of "integration." The communiqué on the previous (summit) Council session had not used the term integration at all, and the communiqué on the Twenty-fourth Council session used it only once. This was in saying that those attending had discussed a report of the Executive Committee on the implementation of the resolution of the summit "connected with the preparation of a complex long-term program to tighten and improve cooperation, as well as to develop the socialist economic integration of Comecon member countries."[47] Later on, in the communique's discussion of proposals approved and principles adopted, the term integration did not appear. This strained separation of integration from cooperation and the references only to the latter in the descriptions of more concrete steps meant that Rumania had now obliquely acknowledged the generally accepted fact that, with the summit, Comecon had embarked on something called "integration" but that Rumania had not really committed itself directly to anything that could be so termed.

This could in part at least be explained by the fact that by now the Rumanian definition of integration had been narrowed to the point where rejection of integration was simply a defense of economic sovereignty, while the Soviet definition had broadened to include everything which anyone, including Rumania, was doing to develop closer economic ties. Thus, for the USSR, things which few Westerners would ever consider "integration," such as simple trade protocols, now came to be called significant steps toward integration. But for Rumania not even the most elaborate sort of economic cooperation was integration unless there was an element of supranationalism involved. Rumania was thus fighting for principle and the USSR for economic involvement, and there was still considerable room for the latter—as Rumania kept insisting—without violating principle. This is not to suggest that "economic sovereignty" is a less elusive and more satisfactory concept than "integration," but it does help to explain what happened about the investment bank.

In the bank's procedures, for the first time in Comecon's history some questions (but not questions of principle) are decided by a three-fourths majority vote. Thus at the Twenty-fourth Council session Rumania lost its fight to preserve the unanimity principle throughout Comecon and its offspring organizations. Moreover, although it did not agree to join the new investment bank, Rumania evidently did in fact officially accede to the breaching of the unanimity principle at this Council session, for, as noted, the communiqué stated that the session approved the admissible forms and organizational functions for joint organizations set up under Comecon. With the simultaneous agreement on the investment bank, these admissible forms clearly included organizations in which majority decisions could be taken. By the end of the Twenty-fourth Comecon Council session, therefore, the two basic principles which had long given Rumania veto power in Comecon—

interestedness and unanimity—had been modified by the concept of voluntaryism and, under certain circumstances, by the introduction of majority decision-making. Just what these circumstances were and what the implications of majority decision-making would be for the minority appear to have been at the heart of Rumania's subsequent negotiations with Comecon over the possibility of joining the new investment bank.

The problem of making the bank into a new institutional, as well as an organizational, departure and of fitting it into the over-all integration scheme, however, was much broader. As was clearly recognized by at least some of the bank's proponents, the need to create an international credit institution of a "new type . . . fundamentally different" from those in the capitalist world was more than one of mere propaganda.[48] The point was that

> [the] institutional connection between the bank and the other organs of Comecon . . . is closely connected with the theory advanced at the Twenty-third Comecon session about the necessity of preparing a detailed program of work designed to tighten integrational bonds among our countries. In this detailed program, the investment bank will find its proper place, which, however, will be determined by the way in which the other aspects of this complex problem are solved, above all the matters of currency and financial connections among our countries.[49]

These "currency and financial connections" represented the key to what ruble capital and ruble credits might mean.

The bank's capital, initially set at 1,000,000,000 rubles, was expected to be paid 70 percent in rubles and 30 percent in gold or convertible currency, with 17.5 percent to be contributed during the first year of operations (1971) and an equal amount in the following year—the rest being paid "successively, depending on the development of the bank's operations, and in a manner and installments determined by the bank's council."[50] (Capital contributions are based on volume of exports to member countries, the shares at that time (before Rumania joined) ranging from less than 0.5 percent for Mongolia to nearly 40 percent for the USSR.) In the preparatory work on the bank in the Comecon Currency and Finance Commission, "full assurance" of contributions was reported to be the primary concern.[51] It was said that the ruble share was expected to be covered by appropriate lists of commodities so that credit recipients would be assured of receiving the necessary investment goods.[52] It was also claimed that national economic plans would contain special sections for Comecon investment, and it was suggested that capital commitments be backed up in part by reserve production capacity.[53]

But these provisions wouldn't really solve the problem. If capital obligations were rigorously defined as to type and quantity of raw material, capital equipment, technical expertise, reserve capacity, etc., then the bank would have little leeway in selecting investment projects. Yet, if these obligations were loosely defined too much uncertainty would appear to be introduced into the planning of the bank's members.

Moreover, the puzzle remained of just what the bank's approval of a proposed investment might mean, if in fact plan coordination must produce agreement on a multilateral investment project before it is proposed in the first place. If the bank did nothing but monitor fulfillment of contractual delivery obligations and tap Western money markets for additional convertible currency capital, its disapproval of a project would not necessarily prevent the project from being carried out, and the importance of the bank would be very limited. But if, in connection with a particular project, the bank could draw on participants disproportionately or on nonparticipants, these obligations would have to fit in with plan coordination. What the bank would do with its ruble capital that its members couldn't perhaps do more easily and wouldn't have to do anyway through plan coordination remained a mystery.

Another major area of uncertainty about the bank's operations involved the criteria to be used to choose investment projects. It was provided that the bank would operate on strictly economic principles with projects being selected on the basis of competition among proposals.[54] The criteria for judging the effectiveness of proposals were said to be "exactly defined" in the agreement and statutes, with top-level world technological and quality standards, minimum costs, and prices which would not surpass world levels being demanded,[55] but in fact no methodology for applying these general criteria had been established in these documents.[56] Here the authority of the bank's staff was also a significant question, for it was supposed to apply these economic criteria in checking and verifying the investment proposals made by members. Given the rather chaotic pricing and costing systems with Comecon, this provision appeared to open up numerous opportunities for differences of view and perhaps for changes that attempts were being made to impose supranational criteria, if not authority, on investment decisions.

While all of these issues remained pending, the primary question concerning the new investment bank was still the impact which a majority vote would have on the dissenting minority, for the break with the unanimity principle had implications for relations throughout Comecon. This was also still the key issue for Rumania in deciding if and when to join.

NOTES

1. J. Tesar, Planovane Hospodarstvi (Prague), April, 1970.

2. Ibid.

3. Ibid.

4. Reports on the Forty-fifth and Forty-sixth Executive Committee sessions on February 24-27, and April 7-10, 1970, TASS, February 28, 1970; Ceteka, April 6, 1970; Tanjug, April 11, 1970.

5. PAP, March 23, 1970.

6. N. Fadeyev in Izvestiia, March 27, 1970; TASS on the Forty-sixth Executive Committee meeting, April 10, 1970.

7. Protocol of the Forty-fourth Executive Committee meeting, TASS, December 16, 1969; F. Hamouz in Hospodarske Noviny, February 28, 1970.

8. Zycie Warszawy, May 14, 1970; the agreement was signed on April 29.

9. Protocol of the Forty-fourth Executive Committee meeting, Radio Prague, December 16, 1969.

10. Radio Prague, May 11, 1970.

11. Press conference by Stefan Jedrychowski in Algiers on April 29, 1969, Reuters, April 29, 1969; TASS, April 28, 1969.

12. Interview with D. Gvishiani, Rude Pravo, June 25, 1969; Yu. Kormnov in Gospodarka Planova, May, 1969.

13. I. Csato, reporting on a discussion with Arpad Kiss, Magyar Hirlap, September 8, 1969; V. Frolov, the center's director, as quoted by TASS, January 9, 1970.

14. Arpad Kiss, op. cit.

15. N. Ceausescu's speech to the Tenth Party Congress, Radio Bucharest, August 6, 1969; K. Katuschev's speech, Radio Moscow (in Rumanian), August 8, 1969.

16. Radio Moscow to Rumania, November 29, 1969.

17. Speech on December 13, 1969, in Scanteia, December 14, 1969.

18. N. Nedelea and D. Csiki in Lupta de Clasa, January, 1970.

19. Speech to the International Conference of Communist and Workers' Parties, June 7, 1969, as reported in Pravda and Izvestiia, June 8, 1969.

20. I. Troyanovsky in Pravda, November 13, 1969.

21. K. Petrov in International Affairs, November, 1969.

22. Angel Todorov interviewed over Radio Budapest, December 22, 1969.

23. The SPD (Sozialdemokratische Partei Deutschlands) had proposed that the EEC and Comecon work out an agreement for closer cooperation; SPD press statement, Bonn, November 18, 1969, as reported by UPI the same day.

24. Trybuna Ludu, March 17, 1970; V. Shatrov and N. Yuryev in International Affairs, April 1970, among others.

25. Zycie Warszawy, April 7, 1970.

26. Polish Ambassador J. Wintewicz's address to the ECE, Geneva, April 16, 1970, RFE Special/Mahoney, Geneva, April 16, 1970.

27. RFE Special/Mahoney, Geneva, April 20, 1970.

28. Radio Moscow, May 12, 1970.

29. PAP, April 20, and May 10 and 11, 1970; Trybuna Ludu, May 11, 1970.

30. Zycie Warszawy, May 12, 1970; Zycie Gospodarcze, May 10, 1970.

31. I. Pardi in Nepszabadsag, May 12, 1970.

32. Trybuna Ludu, May 13, 1970.

33. PAP, May 13, 1970.

34. Tanjug, May 13, 1970.

35. Radio Warsaw, May 14, 1970; Radio Sofia, May 14, 1970.

36. PAP, May 14, 1970.

37. Trybuna Ludu, May 19, 1970; I. Dudinsky in Life Abroad (Moscow) 28, July, 1970.

38. Nepszabadsag, February 14, 1971; Ceteka, February 21, 1971; and quotation from SED (Sozialistische Einheitspartei Deutschlands) Politburo report by A. Norden, Neues Deutschland, June 15, 1970.

39. For example, Die Welt, May 19, 1970; Neue Zuercher Zeitung, May 17, 1970; and R. Marsch, dpa, May 15, 1971.

40. J. Fock in Vilaggazdasag, May 16, 1970.

41. J. Fock over Radio Budapest, May 15, 1970.

42. Radio Budapest, May 16, 1970.

43. Radio Moscow, May 19, 1970; the Central Committee and government reaction to the Soviet delegation's report on the council session as reported by Radio Moscow, June 1, 1970. See also O. Bogomolov in Kommunist, 8, May, 1970.

44. At a press conference reported by Radio Prague, May 22, 1970.

45. PAP commentary, May 16, 1970; Radio Warsaw; May 18, 1970.

46. Ibid., and Trybuna Ludu, May 19, 1970.

47. PAP, May 14, 1970.

48. V. Garbuzov, Soviet Finance Minister, in Pravda, July 11, 1970.

49. A. Solska in Trybuna Ludu, June 2, 1970.

50. L. Rusmich interviewed in Hospodarske Noviny, June 19, 1970.

51. L. Siemiatkowski, chairman of the Polish National Bank and Deputy Minister of Finance, interviewed in Zycie Gospodarcze, July 26, 1970.

52. P. Jaroszewicz interviewed on Polish Television, as rebroadcast by Radio Warsaw, May 22, 1970.

53. L. Siemiatkowski, op. cit.

54. P. Jaroszewicz interviewed on Polish Television, May 22, 1970.

55. PAP report on the Comecon investment bank, July 7, 1970; L. Rusmich interviewed in Hospodarske Noviny, June 19, 1970.

56. The agreement and statute of the international investment bank, Gesetzblatt der DDR, Part 1, 1071, No. 2; reprinted in "Der Ostmarkt im Comecon" (The Eastern Market in Comecon), a collection of documents on Comecon with a foreword by Alexander Uschakow, published by Nomos Verlagsgesellschaft, Baden-Baden, Germany, 1972.

CHAPTER

6

REGROUPING AGAIN

During the final period of negotiations over the integration program between the Twenty-fourth and Twenty-fifth Comecon Council sessions, attention turned further to the narrower, immediate issues involved. A more organic, step-by-step concept of integration evolved as the prospects for agreement on substantive reforms faded.

RUMANIA

After the Twenty-fourth Council session there appeared to be few regrets elsewhere in Comecon that Rumania hadn't agreed to join the new investment bank, and considerable optimism that it eventually would. Hungarian Premier Fock, on his return from the meeting, stated that Rumania had not joined "for the time being" because it had "reservations about the bank's mode of operation, but no objection in principle"—i.e., indicating that, as reflected in the communiqué, the unanimity principle per se was no longer the issue.[1] Jaroszewicz said that "Rumania did not join the bank at this stage, but I am fully convinced that in the next stage—which may be soon—Rumania will join this bank, because it can gain considerable advantage [by so doing]."[2] In reporting the signing of the bank agreement in July TASS stated that the Rumanian deputy permanent representative to Comecon had made a statement to the effect that his country would study the possibility of Rumania's participation in "one or another form" in the work of the bank and would "make its stand known as quickly as possible."[3] Thereafter Rumania refrained from publicly criticizing the bank's role or principles of operation. The door was thus kept open by both sides.

Rumania in fact faced a serious dilemma. If it did not join the bank, it not only could not exercise its veto on (potentially precedent-setting) questions of principle or try to prevent a three-fourths majority on projects to which it objected, but it would be ill-informed on what was going on in areas affecting its vital interests and would find itself excluded from multilateral investment projects of potential interest, some of which were to include joint efforts to obtain economic help from the West. If it did join, however, it would be acceding to Comecon's breaking of the unanimity principle in actual practice as well as in principle and—depending on the implications of majority decisions—would risk exposing its cherished economic sovereignty to greater outside influence.

A major reason for Rumania's continuing hesitancy was that this question of the meaning of a majority decision had still not been completely settled. In particular, it had evidently not been decided just what obligations a minority would have to the majority once a project had been decided upon over the former's objections. It was reported that the bank's council would decide fundamental questions unanimously and that these would include such things as changes in statutory capital, bond issues, acceptance of new members, changes in the charter, appointment of the board, and profit distribution.[4] Other issues, "especially the granting of credit," were to be decided by three-fourths majority vote.[5] But just how the majority was to exercise its right to dispense the bank's capital—including minority contributions—was evidently not resolved at the Twenty-fourth Council session, before the agreement was signed in July, or even at the bank's first council meeting in November.[6]

In the months before Rumania made up its mind on the investment bank a number of significant developments in its relations with Comecon and the USSR took place. Shortly after the Twenty-fourth Council session, while Rumania was still having serious floods, Ceausescu made an unexpected visit to Moscow (on May 18-19). It was reported that the impact of the floods had been "projected" into these talks and that is had been decided to "initiate a new phase" of economic cooperation regardless of differences in other spheres.[7] Since the talks were described as having been held in a "frank and comradely" atmosphere, there had clearly been some disagreement, but Ceausescu evidently did agree to be more cooperative. Ten days later Premier Maurer went to Moscow for further talks on economic cooperation with Kosygin, and shortly thereafter Fadeyev, the Comecon secretary, arrived in Bucharest for talks with Comecon representative Gheorghe Radulescu on the future activity of certain Comecon bodies.[8] During this period Rumanian media and Ceausescu himself were once again stressing independence in economic (and other) affairs,[9] but this was accompanied by efforts to project an image of cooperativeness in bilateral economic relations with the USSR, and a number of new cooperative agreements with the Soviets were concluded.[10] In July, the new Soviet-Rumanian friendship treaty was signed, and Rumania very quickly appeared to become more accommodating in Comecon. On bilateral questions talks continued actively, and the treaty was seen as the foundation for the development of further ties by the Soviets, who reported that new, direct ministerial links and mixed working groups had recently been established, and that the USSR was proposing increased cooperation in shipbuilding, the manufacture of agricultural machinery, etc.[11] Radio Moscow now became very active in telling Rumanians of the merits of Comecon integration, the new investment bank, and bilateral cooperation but employed a soft-sell approach and appeared relatively sanguine about the developing prospects.

Because Rumania was still very touchy about rationalizing Comecon production by eliminating inefficient operations, the Soviets attempted to be reassuring. They recognized that each country had to develop leading industrial branches in order to attain all-round development and that the existence of such branches is more important for a country than the actual output that they achieve. They also maintained that, while smaller, less-developed countries were inevitably more dependent on the division of labor, this could be compensated for by allowing them to specialize in products vital to others (i.e., to increase the Soviet Union's dependence on them) and by giving them a wider variety of specialized products in return.[12]

In early September a protocol on coordination of the Soviet and Rumanian five-year plans was signed. At the same time it was reported that Rumania had agreed to invest in the production of enriched iron ore in the Soviet Union and that in accordance with Rumania's wishes its deliveries of machinery and equipment to the USSR would increase at a much faster rate than either over-all trade or reciprocal Soviet deliveries of these products.[13] At the end of the protocol talks Radio Moscow did not pull its punches when, in broadcasting to Rumania, it quoted Gosplan (State Planning Committee) Chairman Nikolai Baibakov as saying that he had been guided in the talks by the recommendations of the Twenty-third and Twenty-fourth Comecon Council sessions, which aimed at the "economic integration of our states" and that the protocol was not only of economic but also of great political significance.[14] The iron ore agreement, calling for Soviet deliveries from 1972 to 1990, was signed on September 30, and although many more cooperative arrangements were still under negotiation (a number of them involving Rumanian investment in Soviet raw materials) Rumania had taken a major and long-resisted step toward closer economic dependence on the USSR.[15]

After the signing of the Soviet investment agreement, Rumania's relations with Comecon once again moved to the fore. In October Rumania agreed to join a new Comecon coordination center to be set up in Moscow (to study the prevention of corrosion) and subsequently joined additional new specialized coordination centers.[16] In November Rumania sent an observer to the first meeting of the new investment bank's council and a representative to the twelfth meeting of the Intermetall Council, who reportedly entered into the debate on joint investments.[17] It was also revealed that Rumania's Metalimport had "recently" concluded an iron-and-steel cooperation agreement with Intermetall[18]—which was perhaps linked, in substance as well as timing, with the agreement to invest in Soviet iron ore.

Rumania's active participation in Comecon affairs soon produced more significant results. In mid-December, 1970, Rumania joined its first branch association, Interchim, which had been operating since the first of the year. This step, along with the agreement with Intermetall, indicated that Rumania now accepted Comecon's production-oriented branch associations, as well as its distribution organizations (such as the power grid and the railway-car pool to which it had long belonged), as legitimate outgrowths of Comecon and suitable partners for Rumania. On January 12, 1971, Rumania applied for and was admitted (unanimously—as required by statute) to membership in the Comecon investment bank, at the second session of the bank's council.[19]

Exactly what this meant for Rumania in terms of economic sovereignty and independence, however, was still not clear, for the bank began operations on the first of the year under rather uncertain circumstances. It was not until the second bank council session that the principles of its credit and interest policy were endorsed and the procedure for paying in capital was claimed to have been (in part at least) determined.[20] This determination of procedure for capital contribution must certainly provide an important clue as to why Rumania decided to join the bank at that time. Details were not revealed, but it is likely that a formula for pledging investment resources to the bank was adopted, which Rumania could consider to be a prior contractual commitment and, therefore, one which would not imply supranational control over the disposal of Rumanian economic resources.

An insight into Rumanian thinking was given by an article in Viata Economica published shortly after Rumania joined the bank, in which the emphasis was on the limitations on the bank's authority and activity.[21] The handling of majority decision-making was particularly interesting, for it was asserted that only in "certain cases which necessitate prompt handling" could a three-quarters majority prevail. This seemed incompatible with previous claims that operational decisions by majority vote would include decisions as to which investment proposals the bank would support. Although it is doubtful that any major concessions were made to Rumania in the realm of majority decision-making, here as elsewhere the real meaning of the majority vote was left obscure, and the closely related question of how the bank's investment decisions would be related to plan coordination was also still unclear. From the vagueness surrounding these questions and the remarks in Viata Economica, it appeared that the bank's role may not have been so clearly defined as was often implied, and that the majority had little power to affect the minority. Majority decision-making therefore evidently did not imply any form of majority rule and possibly was essentially only a formalization of "voluntaryism" under which a majority could decide to prevent a minority from exercising a veto via the old interestedness and unanimity principles.

During the first months of 1971 Rumania continued to collaborate in many aspects of Comecon's work, agreeing, for example, to join in the establishment of Intergormash, a new organization for developing mining equipment. It was not, however, cooperating in everything, not being involved in the intergovernmental commission for computer technology or joining in adopting the principles of a unified computer system.[22] Moreover, increased cooperation with Comecon members was paralleled by stepped-up efforts to expand ties with China, the U.S., and Yugoslavia, among others, and by a sudden turnabout in policy toward economic cooperation. A new law provided for foreign investment in Rumania and appeared aimed primarily at attracting Western capital.[23]

At the same time, considerable interest continued to be manifested in what Comecon had been doing since the summit, which was found to have taken important decisions with active Rumanian participation.[24] General acceptance was also accorded the idea that Comecon ties were growing ever closer and more complex, in large part because cooperation had expanded into scientific-technological collaboration. Financial relations and multilateralism were seen to be deepening, with the Comecon bank playing a growing role—particularly following the adoption of the recommendations of the Twenty-fourth Council session.[25] In short, Rumania appeared to be making a real effort to be more involved in Comecon affairs.

But being involved allowed a more detailed elaboration of the Rumanian position. This now included not only a strong reassertion of principles but also the spelling out of reservations on future changes and endorsement of the restrictions placed on the various new departures within Comecon. Thus the improvement of multilateral settlements—which, it was acknowledged, was a problem that could not be solved independently—was seen to require exchange-rate adjustments, but each country, it was asserted, had the right to do this independently and to determine the impact of any changes on the domestic economic system. In similar fashion, when acknowledging the importance of Interchim and the Comecon bank, although recognition was given to the expansion of the rights of their management organs, the principle of voluntaryism, the preservation of unanimity on major issues, and the continuing right to opt in or out on specific questions were emphasized.[26] Since economic cooperation was becoming increasingly significant, it was seen to be very important to improve the exchange of information and of forecasting experience—so that independent national plans could be better coordinated. The focus was on a principled approach to specific problems, and any suggestion of major innovations was avoided. It was finally acknowledged, however, that integration was taking place within Comecon—although this was done rather backhandedly at first by citing it as one of the difficulties besetting closer economic collaboration with the West.[27]

Rumania was still fighting to preserve its freedom of action at the broadest level. It categorically rejected suggestions that "changes should be made in the meaning of internationalism in the contemporary era" or that problems within a state's exclusive area of competence be "subjected to international examination."[28] Probably the most forceful statement of the Rumanian position appeared in April when it was argued:

> Disregard of one principle or another, economic pressures of any kind, or interference in internal affairs in the name of alleged demands of internationalism would only create asperity, mistrust, and contradiction between socialist states, which obviously would affect their relationship in general. . . .
>
> [It is necessary to reject] proposals of an integrationist nature bordering on transgression of the independence of the socialist states, their sovereignty, their right to decide independently about their entire economic activity.[29]

This renewed assertiveness was accompanied by greater efforts to diffuse pressure to toe the line more closely in international affairs, including Comecon. In addition to the continuing efforts to improve bilateral relations with non-Comecon countries, the policy of developing ties with all states was focused on Western Europe and on the Balkans, where closer multilateral economic ties were quite obviously seen as counters to any "closed" integration under Comecon.

The strains in Rumania's position appeared to be recognized by Ceausescu when, in a major speech shortly before the Twenty-fifth Council session, in which he accepted integration for the first time, he said:

> It is necessary for us to discuss more seriously the relations between the national and the international, particularly

> because there are all sorts of confusion and erroneous ideas afloat in this connection. Here too—on a theoretical, principled plane—we must establish clarity as regards the role of the nation, the national factor, the interdependence between national and international, the mutual conditioning of these two factors. . . . In the same manner it is necessary to tackle with extreme clarity the problem of economic cooperation and the problem of socialist integration. The term integration has been introduced in international economic language. Integration is being discussed—both socialist integration and integration in the Comecon Market. Let us see what this means theoretically and in essence, and let us express our point of view, let us work out our party's clear orientation on this problem.[30]

He then revealed:

> We have come to a certain conclusion, together with the Comecon member countries, concerning the meaning of integration, to the effect that this does not affect national independence and sovereignty, does not lead to common planning and superstate forms of organization.

Here and subsequently Ceausescu stressed that the "first obligation" of closer ties within Comecon is to contribute to the development of each socialist state. A few days before the Twenty-fifth Council session he elaborated on this theme, while implicitly giving a first, if limited, definition of what constituted acceptable integration, when he said:

> Of course, the forms of cooperation can be diverse. But no matter how diverse they may be, no matter how much interdependence in production between various sectors of activity develops, this must not in any way lead to the transgression of national sovereignty, must not in any way influence the right of the communist party of each country . . . to independently decide its development program according to its own wish.[31]

At the same time it was publicized that the diverse forms to which he referred already included a wide variety of concrete projects, either concluded or under negotiation.[32]

HUNGARY

The Twenty-fourth Council session was followed by a further shift in Hungary's tactical, if not its strategic, approach to Comecon.

The emphasis now came to be less on over-all, long-range concepts or models—which in any case had already been quite thoroughly elaborated—than on the methods of plan coordination and cooperation which would promote Comecon integration, yet allow Hungary to maintain the principles and momentum of its economic reform. An interview with Hungary's representative to Comecon, Antal Apro, in *Nepszabadsag* in *late July* set the pattern.[33] He made it clear that Hungary's attention was focused on the "practical aspects" of the strategy for plan coordination being formulated in the executive committee and on the "new tasks of particular importance [which] will fall to member's planning bureaus." He was now willing to discuss joint planning at relative length, maintaining that the Comecon countries had

> drawn up their plans independently thus far, and they will continue to do so; that is, joint planning for the most important branches does not mean that the internal planning activities of countries and their independent national characters will diminish. . . . The productive capacities [established through joint planning] will remain national properties.

He also argued that joint planning would be most effective if based on agreements between governments and enterprises (meaning within the same country, so that planning would not simply be determined by high-level plan coordination and then presented to enterprises as a *fait accompli*), and he maintained that successful joint planning presupposed further progress in the financial field. But he did not elaborate on the latter remark, and, in addition to joint planning, his primary concern was with such other more topical questions as scientific-technological cooperation and the setting up of joint institutions.

One reason for the greater Hungarian concern with the immediate and the practical was that the finalization of five-year plans was due. This was particularly evident in September, when major agreements with the USSR were signed which called for a significant expansion of cooperation, including Hungarian investment in Soviet raw materials. In discussing these agreements Hungarian media stressed the role enterprises had played in their conclusion, the expanding role of direct contacts among enterprises and branch ministries, and the importance of joint organizations.[34] Apparently to demonstrate Hungary's ability and willingness to be cooperative, it was also maintained that Hungarian economic reform had *not* been accompanied by a real foreign exchange reform, although some preparatory elements had been introduced, and it was emphasized that any currency's convertibility depended on international cooperation, the Hungarian currency and the prospects for its eventual convertibility being tied to the collective socialist currency.[35]

Accommodation with the Polish position continued. While reiterating his argument about the preservation of independent national planning despite the introduction of joint planning, Apro asserted that Hungary and Poland took the same stand on economic cooperation within Comecon and pointed with satisfaction to their agreement to introduce quota-free trade for some consumer goods.[36] Again the Polish idea of a partial convertibility of trade debts into gold or Western currency in order to make the present financial system more effective was supported, it being acknowledged that "complete convertibility" would be a lengthy process, dependent upon the greater competitiveness of Comecon countries' goods.[37]

Despite the greater concern for more immediate issues, an effort was made to show that Hungary's broader concepts had not been abandoned. The ineffectiveness of administrative methods and the difficulties of market surveys without real markets were noted,[38] and at a major Comecon-sponsored conference on integration questions the Hungarians appeared to show no signs of weakening in the defense of their positions.[39] In his opening remarks at this conference Apro said that it had "daringly" placed the most difficult questions on the agenda, questions which had hardly been worked out even theoretically, in part because of differing economic interests and views.[40] He then appeared to go on the offensive on the economic reform question, calling for all countries to study each other's new systems and stating that the "results attained and experience acquired in individual countries can affect the economic direction systems of other countries." He extolled Hungarian successes with the challenging statement that "We believe and we can prove with facts that the reform of the Hungarian mechanism has stood the test of the past three years" and went on to say that "We gladly reveal our experience to date, but of course we do not regard the reform of our mechanism as the only possible solution." The Hungarians thus appeared quite willing to take up the East German challenge in the contest for Soviet support for proven economic reforms and in the performance stakes—where the now faltering East German economy had so long been touted as the East European success story.

At the conference another leading Hungarian authority, Bela Csikos-Nagy, reiterated the broad Hungarian position, arguing that the need for financial, particularly price, reform was closely linked to the principle of mutual advantage endorsed at the summit, and that, despite the improvements in comprehension at central levels only enterprises could effectively handle the details in the rapidly developing, heterogeneous industries.[41] He also reasserted the need for relying heavily on world market prices and for a preferential tariff system for Comecon. In similar fashion other Hungarian participants defended the Hungarian reform and strongly urged an expansion of market relations and greater enterprise freedom. A "heated discussion" on the question of monetary functions reportedly took place, with the Hungarians and East Germans very likely being the prime antagonists.[42] Although some clarification and convergence of views on certain questions could be claimed, there had evidently been little progress on the gut issues of money and prices. It was reported that the Polish and Hungarian delegations stood alone in their "active" concern with these latter questions—in further confirmation of the new Czechoslovak position, as well as of their own rapport.[43]

Right after this conference the Hungarian Tenth Party Congress took place. After Janos Kadar had pledged Hungary's support for the "fullest possible implementation" of Comecon integration based on independent national economies and reiterated Hungary's total loyalty to the USSR, Nyers put an official stamp on the new Hungarian line on Comecon which had been emerging.[44] He stressed the success of Hungary's reform, its contribution to the cause of integration, the significance of the enterprise's role, and the importance of bilateral relations with the USSR. But in discussing the over-all integration program he said that because it was such a big issue Hungary had always regarded not haste but thoroughness as of primary importance and that multilateral contacts would evolve only gradually. He stressed that the correlation among the program's main features—consultation, plan coordination, and economic regulators—had not yet been clarified, for, while it had been agreed that plan formulation was the sole right of member states, the whole system of economic regulation, the price, credit, and currency systems, and the approach to convertibility had not been agreed upon. Thus, he felt, much had to be done, these open questions precluded any over-all assessment as yet, and Comecon's members must look forward to a long drawn-out process of integration.

At the same time, considerable caution was shown at the congress on the foreign-trade side of Hungary's domestic reform. While the congress gave full endorsement to the continuation of the economic reform, as a seeming counterpoint to the earlier argument that no real change in Hungary's foreign trade system had taken place, both Kadar and Nyers urged restraint in the further expansion of independent foreign trade rights to enterprises. Although a case could be made that the extent and success of the expansion of foreign trade rights made some consolidation reasonable and that simultaneously rights were actually being extended where expedient, these remarks may also have reflected the general caution now being shown on broad Comecon reform issues and indicated an effort to be accommodating on the question of adapting one's reforms to those of others in the interests of promoting integration.

Convincing arguments could of course still be found for the Hungarian model for Comecon in terms of the longer-term political benefits it promised through the creation of a viable bloc economic system. At a more esoteric level an impressive attempt was now made to put the Hungarian approach in the broader context of the drive for bloc unity and of the competition with capitalism.[45] This was done by Nyers through a judicious blend of the unassailable, if incongruous, triumvirate of Brezhnev, Lenin, and the demands of the scientific-technological revolution. First, like Brezhnev at the 1969 international Communist conference, Nyers argued that there is to be a long period of competition between the two economic systems. Therefore, he maintained, economic performance is of paramount significance—perhaps, by implication, even more important than the short run reinforcement of the bloc. Second, political and ideological victory can only be won through the proper use of and distinction between strategy and tactics, and Lenin's example of flexible tactics, "sometimes even in a way perplexing to some of his contemporaries," should be emulated, while keeping the strategic goal in view. And, third, it follows that (implicitly as with Lenin and the NEP [New Economic Policy]) one must be pragmatic and seek the most effective means to promote economic development: As demonstrated by the capitalists, he argued, international market relations can stimulate growth and greatly speed up the penetration and propagation of science and technology, although within Comecon this would of course be done in the framework of socialist principles, which would preserve society's control and distinguish the whole process from capitalist integration. The point was to convince the Soviets and other doubters that the Hungarian approach to Comecon was the best long-range alternative politically and even ideologically—as well as economically.

The motivations for these apparent shifts in tactics on Comecon were undoubtedly complex. The thrust of the integration drive apparent at the Twenty-fourth Council session and the evident strengthening of the Soviet commitment to integration following it (see below) would appear to have engendered strong Hungarian reservations about multilateral Comecon integration in the absence of much institutional reform. Apro's stress on contractual relations and bilateralism in an interview with a major Soviet economic journal[46] as well as Nyers's cautious approach to multilateralism at the Tenth Party Congress would seem to support this explanation. At the same time, Hungary's efforts to maintain Soviet support of its internal reform and tolerance of at least some of its Comecon ideas had evidently come under mounting attack from the East Germans. The tactical decision appears to have been to hold back from too overt a confrontation on the broader Comecon reform issues; to face up to such pressing issues as joint planning and direct contacts and to impress the Soviets with Hungary's interest and flexibility in developing these practical approaches to integration; and to take advantage of their main opponent's economic weakening (and; perhaps, of its growing isolation in bloc circles on other issues) by taking up the reform model challenge and focusing on the success of Hungary's new mechanism. Given the very limited current prospects for Hungary's Comecon reform concepts, the policy was successful, for Hungary received continued public Soviet support for its internal economic reform—the sine qua non for its longer-run Comecon concepts—most notably from Brezhnev himself at the Tenth Party Congress.[47]

Nevertheless, as the integration program took final form in early 1971, a tone of resignation or defensiveness could sometimes be seen in Hungarian remarks. Foreign Trade Minister J. Biro explicitly recognized that the decisions of the Twenty-fourth Council session would lead to progress primarily in the field of planning, and Premier Fock lamented the lack of any progress toward a monetary system for Comecon, convertibility still being seen as a very long-term proposition.[48] Both the need to move ahead with integration without waiting for the talks on a comprehensive program to be completed and a step-by-step approach were stressed.[49] Care was taken to acknowledge that major issues would be dealt with centrally, but it was still noted that the Twenty-fourth Council meeting had called for an expansion of the number and authority of the organizations entitled to maintain direct contacts, and each member's right to determine the scope of these contacts according to its own internal economic mechanism was defended.[50] The need to reform domestic management systems, as well as financial relations, in order to promote direct contacts and voluntary participation continued to be argued, but these remarks now seemed more perfunctory and there did not appear to be an expectation that much progress was imminent.[51]

Reflecting this new caution, in his speech to parliament in June, Premier Fock said that integration was still in its initial phase and much had to be done, noting that there were great natural and economic differences among members.[52] In a similar vein, just before the Twenty-fifth Council session one Radio Budapest commentator said that there was nothing unusual about Comecon's members having "essentially different views" on integration stemming from differences in levels of development, relative importance of foreign trade, and internal economic mechanisms, while another noted that the adaptation to changed demands had naturally resulted in arguments, although, he felt, the exchange of views had contributed to the working out of the long-range program.[53]

In an apparent effort to demonstrate Hungary's willingness to accommodate, as well as to emphasize the orthodox basis of its economic system, the chairman of the planning office, Imre Pardi, was chosen to write an appropriately enthusiastic article on integration for Pravda a few days before the Council met to adopt the integration program.[54]

CZECHOSLOVAKIA

During the second phase of Comecon's search for an integration program, Comecon reform became of considerably less interest to Czechoslovakia than integration itself. Integration was regarded as absolutely essential for both political and economic reasons, and Rude Pravo saw prejudice, conservatism, and indolence—rather than institutional failings—as the major barriers.[55] The level of cooperation with Comecon, particularly with the USSR, was now seen as the basic determinant of economic progress, and sensitivity to Soviet complaints about delays in deliveries led to a preoccupation with the lack of state discipline which allegedly was the primary cause. Concern with the ineffectualness of many cooperation arrangements brought greater emphasis on binding contractual relations which would increase the incentives to cooperation.[56]

These preoccupations reflected the acute need to concentrate industrial efforts. The link between restructuring Czechoslovak industry and integration within Comecon was a constant theme, particularly for Premier Lubomir Strougal, who felt that the fundamental problem of short, inefficient production runs for far too many products could only be overcome by cooperation within Comecon.[57] These pressing structural problems, along with the internal debates over economic management and the "reintegration" of Slovakia and the Czech lands, undoubtedly helped to shape the new Czechoslovak thinking on Comecon.

According to Hamouz it was necessary to push ahead and to tighten up on all fronts because the focus of integration was shifting from mere trade to production.[58] As he saw it, internal mechanisms, including long-term planning, had to be improved in line with integration requirements; consultations should be held on all basic policy questions; much higher levels of accuracy and commitment were necessary in plan coordination; branch-level joint plans ought to be made formal commitments and incorporated in national plans; and central planning bodies had to be guaranteed their necessary leading positions in cooperation. Strougal also took an activist approach to integration at the December, 1970, Central Committee Plenum, at which he called for a greater role for enterprises within a carefully planned framework, and maintained that increased efficiency required complex rationalization, every concrete aspect of which had to become an inseparable part of the plan.[59] Financial reforms, including exchange rate reform and convertibility, also received high-level support, though not as intense as before the invasion, but still as essential, if subordinate, aspects of any comprehensive integration program. More extensive planning required improved financial methods, and these were espoused in the context of "closing economic ranks" within Comecon.[60] Some commentators, apparently having in mind the "new type" of socialist sovereignty reflected in the Czechoslovak-Soviet treaty (of May, 1970), took a hard line on the principles of cooperation and the new investment bank, claiming that integration required rapid decisions "independent of the will of possibly one single member" and suggesting that some sort of supranationalism might emerge from the bank's operations.[61]

There was also great stress on the need to adapt domestic reforms to integration requirements and to learn from the reforms of others. Rude Pravo took a strong stand on the need for greater uniformity in the various approaches, arguing that economic reforms could not be solely the concern of individual countries but were the concern of all countries and had to be coordinated to prevent barriers to cooperation.[62] Some in fact accepted the contention that East Germany had a model which was both orthodox and successful and hence, to some extent at least, to be emulated.[63] East Germany was also found to have set a good example in its bilateral cooperation arrangements with the USSR.[64] But in general a less specific commitment to learning from others seemed to prevail, although the USSR naturally was found to have gained much useful experience, particularly from its "logical and well considered" approach to economic reform.[65]

This discussion was paralleled by continued criticism of past approaches: the Novotny regime had failed to make adjustments in good time and thereby created Czechoslovakia's serious structural problems which now made integration that much more essential; and the right wing of course had been planning to solve Czechoslovakia's economic problems by selling out to the capitalists. The belaboring of these issues in part reflected the persistent and pervasive skepticism among the Czechoslovak people over the advantages of trade and co-operation with Comecon, which was very upsetting to those responsible for the carrying through of "normalization." Moreover, although Czechoslovakia had by now completed its metamorphosis on Comecon, and its views were probably carrying somewhat greater weight, it still did not appear to have developed any concepts incompatible with those of the USSR. In fact, following Gustav Husak's fulsome endorsement of the invasion and of the Brezhnev doctrine at the Soviet Twenty-fourth Party Congress, at the Czechoslovak fourteenth Party Congress in May the sycophantic loyalty to the USSR was painfully evident in Strougal's speech, in which mention of Comecon was all but submerged in praise for economic ties to the USSR.[66] The few concrete ideas about integration which did surface as the Twenty-fourth Council session approached appeared to reflect—particularly in retrospect—the general behind-the-scenes consensus on the integration program rather than any self-generated Czechoslovak position. Thus cautious calls for the "very careful" increase in manpower mobility or for eventual exchange rate unification do not appear to have been remnants of the earlier Czechoslovak concepts for a thorough-going Comecon reform, but rather indications of the state of general agreement.[67] Czechoslovakia's new, strictly orthodox stance was particularly evident on the convertibility issue. The Czechoslovak contributor to the World Marxist Review foresaw "in a more distant period . . . the introduction of mutually convertible collective and national currencies," and, while acknowledging that views on this differ and intensive research was required, he rejected the view of "some economists" who argue that "integration should start with streamlining financial arrangements—exchange rates, say, or convertibility, or exchange of national currencies for the freely convertible currencies of the capitalist world. . . ."[68]

POLAND

In the latter half of 1970, Poland continued to show its great interest in economic cooperation with other Comecon members, and in Poland too there was less emphasis on the grand design envisioned for integration and more on narrower issues, particularly on those most closely related to the immediate question of five-year plan coordination. The new investment bank received considered attention, Poland having been one of its foremost boosters and hoping to be a major beneficiary both of credit and of the industrial rationalization that the bank was to foster.[69] The elimination of the veto continued to receive approval, and the limitations on the bank's role in the absence of broader reforms were again noted and served as the starting point for the urging of further improvements in the methods of Comecon cooperation.[70]

The need for joint planning was also stressed. It was seen as leading to much closer cooperation than plan coordination because it could specify tasks and obligations more precisely on a multilateral basis and would enable planning to cover a full development cycle.[71] Yet at least one commentator made a sharp distinction between the obligation to coordinate plans on a broad basis and the supplementary and optional nature of more detailed joint planning.[72] In addition, the beginnings of practical implementation were still confined to bilateral relations, with a two-year experiment in joint planning with the USSR of certain scientific and technological projects reportedly under way.[73] The need for continuous plan coordination was also a major theme, there reportedly having been set up interdepartmental permanent working groups between Poland and the USSR as well as various other forms of continuing direct contact, particularly in research and development.[74]

Impatience with the slow progress, both in bilateral cooperation and in reaching agreement on broad aspects of Comecon reform, continued to be registered. Commentaries in connection with five-year plan cooperation arrangements noted the lack of progress to date in the form and content of agreements, and there were complaints that besides the lack of economic instruments to encourage cooperation some countries were not sufficiently interested.[75] Also maintained was the long-standing Polish insistance on the seriousness of institutional barriers to closer integration, particularly the lack of sound financial and legal provisions relating to obligations incurred under cooperation agreements.[76]

In late December following the ouster of Gomulka and Premier Cyrankiewicz, Jaroszewicz—who had been Poland's representative to Comecon for twelve years—became the new Prime Minister. In his first policy statement to parliament, on the day of his election, he pledged a continued active role in Comecon and reaffirmed Poland's commitment to integration and to the development of all forms of economic contacts.[77] A few days later the long-term trade agreement with the USSR was signed, great stress being placed on the significance of Soviet economic ties (and on the immediate importance of the 2,000,000 additional tons of grain which Poland had been promised), and "far-reaching integration" within Comecon was being called for.[78]

The constancy of Poland's position was again emphasized when Jaroszewicz's annual review of Comecon developments, evidently written in early December while he was still the Comecon representative, was published, as usual, at the turn of the year.[79] Following the pattern seen in other recent Polish commentaries, he stressed scientific and technological contacts and lamented the unsatisfactory state of specialization and cooperation. He then strongly reaffirmed the Polish position on the need for financial reforms, arguing that, while everyone was aware of the present failings, the efforts being made to overcome them were still insufficiently effective. Referring back to the summit and also to reforms in the conduct of foreign trade, he asserted that it was not just a question of programing production cooperation, but of developing financial instruments which would encourage trade and cooperation. Jaroszewicz, however, was cautious on the timing of financial reforms in Comecon, maintaining that the "solving of these problems would take many years and all decisions should be made cautiously and gradually because their successful implementation is dependent on difficult and complicated adaptive processes and changes which are bound to occur in the economic systems of individual Comecon countries."

This strong reassertion of the Polish position on financial reform in principle, but reserve on the timing of its actual introduction probably, as in Hungary, reflected the fact that it was clear by now that the integration program being drafted was unlikely to provide for much change in this sphere. Moreover, caution here was also appropriate because Poland was in the process of aborting yet another economic reform attempt, and, even if Gomulka's departure was a prerequisite to more consistent and extensive economic reforms in the future, it would be some time before things were sorted out enough for Poland to embark on a new reform model.

Commentaries on Comecon during the next few months were muted, although Poland's commitment to integration and to closer ties with the USSR received continual attention. Her unchanging stand on the need for reform was also reiterated, and she was still highly critical of the progress in specialization and of trade in industrial products. However, now a number of remarks suggested reconciliation to a further limiting of the prospects for change. The lack of progress on financial reform was still lamented, but talk of concrete steps now tended to focus on limited moves, such as exchange rate reform and better credit discipline. The long-term significance of harmonious—some suggested convergent—internal economic reforms was generally recognized and, particularly in view of Poland's own confused reform situation, evidently contributed to her lengthening perspective.[80] One commentator saw the first half of the 1970s as essentially a time for elaborating new methods, and did not anticipate a real deepening of integration until the latter half of the decade.[81] Another felt that "years would pass" before new forms of cooperation could be established and popularized.[82]

Yet, under the new leadership, the policy reorientation toward the consumer, the greater interest in foreign credit and the need to break with past investment and labor practices increased the urge to cooperate with the other Comecon states, despite the sober assessment of Comecon's prospects. This was reflected in efforts to improve bilateral economic relations with Comecon states, including East Germany. In contrast to the strain in relations back in mid-1969 as the work on and integration program was getting started, the talks between Premiers Jaroszewicz and Stoph, just ten days before the Twenty-fifth Council session, were conducted in an "extremely cordial and friendly atmosphere" and showed a "full conformity of views on all questions discussed," while a few days later it was reported that Polish workers were to go to East German factories.[83] In Poland, as in the only other remaining exponent of reform, Hungary, the drive for reform had gradually given way to resignation to slow and limited progress and to an increasing focus on the need to solve pressing economic problems essentially within the existing framework.

BULGARIA

Bulgaria continued to voice full support for Comecon integration, the Twenty-fourth Council session simply being added to the summit as the second major milestone. Strong emphasis was still given to the planned, controlled nature of socialist integration, which at its extreme was to bring even closer "convergence, interdependence, and—in future—unification of the national economic complexes of the socialist countries."[84] Scientific criteria were essential in order to select the optimal integration plan and to "ensure a planned process rather than spontaneity and competition."[85]

Comecon, and particularly the USSR, were still seen as Bulgaria's key markets, with the already very large Soviet trade share scheduled to increase still further. Provisions for closer ties between central planning organs and for joint planning were included in the coordination of Bulgarian and Soviet five-year plans.[86] Bulgaria still vied with Czechoslovakia and East Germany in trying to demonstrate that integration with the USSR was really of greater significance than that with the rest of Eastern Europe.

In Bulgaria's contribution to the discussion in the _World Marxist Review_, emphasis was placed on the development of "international production complexes [and] the need for integration in the fields of finance, currency and credits."[87] The author found new complexes necessary because the "growth requirements of many industrial branches—computer technology, metal-cutting machine tools, automobiles, tractors, ships, iron and steel, synthetic chemistry, etc.—create a range of problems that cannot be solved simply by coordinating plans or with the help of trade agreements." Exhibiting no qualms about sovereignty, he argued further that "as we see it, these complexes are _alone_ capable of supervising the most desirable _geographic distribution_ of the productive forces" (emphasis added). It was also necessary to "enhance the role of the transfer ruble [and to] call for an expansion of international crediting," while the "economic growth of the socialist countries and increasing integration make it possible to introduce higher forms of convertibility of both the transfer ruble and national currencies." Endorsement of such ambitious, if vague, objectives reflected Bulgaria's continued strong commitment to a comprehensive approach to integration.

This commitment and the political significance of socialist integration in the struggle against capitalism were increasingly emphasized as the Twenty-fifth Council session approached. Zhivkov himself rejected as unworthy of comment any allegation that cooperation within Comecon could limit economic independence or national sovereignty and even maintained that, in fact, Bulgaria's "successes" through this cooperation indicated just the opposite.[88] A few days before the Council session the party paper took the line that the "identical social system, identical ideology, and identical goals" of the socialist countries were the basic prerequisites for their integration process, and that in addition to the pressures of their own development needs, socialist integration was "imperative because of the exacerbated ideological and political struggle being waged by imperialism against the socialist system."[89] It followed that "economic integration is inseparable from political integration," yet, despite this, integration under Comecon was allegedly far more "perfect and progressive" than in the EEC, because of the former's observance of the sovereignty and equality principles.[90]

EAST GERMANY

The new-found East German interest in integration continued unabated after the Twenty-fourth Council session, and the great importance of actively pursuing the mandates of this and the summit meetings was constantly reiterated. While integration was, in practice, developing primarily in a bilateral fashion, East Germany now appeared somewhat more willing to join in multilateral specialization and cooperation arrangements.[91] Nevertheless, although passing reference was made to the need to "perfect goods-money relations," any "overestimation" of the significance of the financial sphere was still strongly rejected.[92] Interest was primarily in "strengthening the planned approach in [Comecon] relations and in solving concrete problems," with the East German delegation to the Twenty-fourth Council meeting reportedly having submitted "concrete proposals [which], under the growing role of planning organs in multilateral cooperation, [are] specifically aimed at jointly resolving structure-determining tasks and projects. . . ."[93] The idea was to agree upon unified systems of the highest world standards, e.g., for data-processing, and then to sign long-term contracts assuring compliance. This greater interest in cooperation within Comecon was paralleled by the argument that the integration program is not to come into force on a fixed date, but rather that, whenever a specific problem is solved, it must be immediately incorporated into the practical work of plan coordination, the coordination of five-year plans in practice requiring a series of specific commitments on a step-by-step basis.[94]

If possible, even greater political significance was attached to economic integration in the latter part of 1970, and Soviet media were exploited to demonstrate East Germany's enthusiasm for integration and its leading role in trade and cooperation with the USSR.[95] This undoubtedly reflected East Germany's deteriorating position within the bloc (the Soviet and Polish treaties with West Germany having been signed in August and December, respectively) and the continuing search for a new framework of intrabloc relations within which East German interests could be preserved. Some concepts now voiced on the relationship between the emerging new framework of socialist relations and economic integration, in fact, put the latter directly into the service of East Germany's broader political interests. The increased economic intertwining of the Comecon states under integration, it was argued, did not mean their merger or their centralized planning and management, but rather had far-reaching political effects and necessitated political measures.[96] The political and ideological "integration" of the Comecon states was at once a prerequisite to economic integration and, in effect, a substitute for economic supranationalism. Socialist integration was found to be "connected with the working out and implementation of joint strategy and tactics in foreign and military policy," because "consolidation of economic and political ties among the socialist countries presupposes joint political resolutions by the Marxist-Leninist parties of Comecon members" and the continuation of socialist integration will depend on "consolidation of political and ideological cooperation." In particular, because the economic laws of socialism necessitate "far-reaching coordination of the economic systems and methods of planning and management," it is "especially important to achieve the appropriate political-ideological prerequisites."[97]

At the Fifteenth SED CC Plenum in January, East German priorities were again demonstrated when Ulbricht maintained that the socialist countries are "gaining strength to the degree that they [are] mastering ideological tasks," as well as scientific-technological ones.[98] Shortly thereafter, in _Einheit_, the need for socialist integration was described as stemming from essentially the same three basic factors mentioned in the treatise of 1969: the inner laws of socialism, the requirements of the scientific-technological revolution, and the struggle against the West—although, apparently indicating growing East German concern, the "economic competition with capitalism" of the treatise now became the "class conflict with imperialism."[99] In similar fashion, the uniqueness of socialist economic integration and its political and ideological link with socialist internationalism were strongly stressed, as was the great need to perfect plan coordination through the convergence of internal economic systems under the economic laws of socialism.[100] Unfortunately for the latter idea, the credibility of the East German economic system as a model for the other Comecon states was deteriorating as economic problems mounted. The need for retrenchment was acknowledged at the Fourteenth Plenum in December and the Fifteenth Plenum in January, and a certain defensiveness over the East German system could be detected in references to current economic problems.[101]

In its contribution to the discussion in the World Marxist Review in May, the basic East German themes were again reiterated, and it was even maintained that "essential political and economic preconditions for integration are now at hand in all Comecon countries."[102] The father of this optimistic thought—which appeared to be at odds with the Soviet contributor's earlier reservation in the same journal (see page 128, below)—evidently was again the wish for a united front against the West, for it was found that socialist integration is a "new sharp weapon in the class struggle against imperialism [and that] common socialist interests require a collective, coordinated strategy towards imperialist policies and, in particular, early solution of the Comecon countries' economic problems." Comecon integration and a united front against the West now went hand in hand.

As a result, with the integration program in the process of finalization, East German media took an increasingly positive view on certain issues which earlier had received scant support. Joint forecasting was now seen to require further coordination of national economic indexes in order to develop a "uniform over-all system" for the Comecon countries, and a Comecon "data bank" was proposed.[103] Comprehensive planning, from joint forecasting to deliveries of the finished products, and including joint planning, was seen as the "qualitatively new element" in Comecon relations, while a major role for commodity-money relations was even foreseen in support of plan coordination.[104] At the same time an "uncompromising battle against revisionist economic theories and nationalist deviations" was demanded, and now the Rumanian foot-dragging on Comecon came under sharp attack.[105]

In part these developments may have reflected the new leadership. On taking over as party leader in May, Erich Honecker had quickly affirmed East Germany's commitment to integration, and East Germany now appeared less insistent on elevating its own interests to bloc interests, as well as more interested in economic cooperation with the other East European members of Comecon. The latter stemmed in large part, of course, from a desire to prevent them from turning to West Germany, as well as to help relieve East Germany's own mounting economic problems. The idea of improving the consumer's lot, as reflected in the new five-year plan, undoubtedly heightened East German interest in closer economic ties, and the apparent more genuine commitment to integration was soon followed by signs of determination to expand bilateral economic ties in Eastern Europe, including those with Poland noted above.

USSR

Following the Twenty-fourth Council session, Soviet commentaries became increasingly outspoken on the need for integration.

In part this simply reflected the fact that after a year of active discussion among Comecon members the limited feasiblility of any fundamental reform had become even clearer, and, in conjunction with the finalization of five-year plans, the time was ripe to push for immediate, practical steps toward integration. In addition, developments in relations with the West, especially West Germany, were moving along very rapidly and made strengthened Comecon cohesion increasingly urgent. A third, less tangible factor was the state of post-Czechoslovak-invasion ideological discussion: Economic integration had become, in Soviet eyes, but one facet of a much broader integration framework and was increasingly seen as the natural result of political and ideological cohesion, something which right-thinking socialist states pursued because of their internationalist outlook and not something separate from integration in other spheres.

This broader framework was fundamental to Soviet thinking on integration under Comecon, the distinction between what had to be done and how it was to be done being crucial. Loyalty to the joint cause—the search for integration—was seen as mandatory, and, when difficulties developed, the "point is, what attitude is adopted toward these difficulties?"[106] But the means to such still ill-defined ends as integration or a common plan are not preordained, and participation by everybody in everything is not expected. As it was put in Kommunist:

> Integration is a multifaceted field of activity; therefore, the Comecon countries are not faced with the obligation to participate in all measures connected with the acceleration of this process. Proceeding from its own internal potential, each country independently solves questions concerning the advisability of utilizing material resources, at the same time determining those forms and areas of foreign economic cooperation which most fully correspond to its economic interests at the present stage.[107]

Economic differences, moreover, were not viewed here as necessarily bad and in fact could be beneficial, a sharp distinction being made between nationalist contradictions, which are dangerous, and contradictions based on the logic of the historical process, which, if "not artifically exaggerated," do not hinder socialist cohesion. These latter include differences in levels of economic development, in socioeconomic structure, and in economic methods, and can, "by reflecting the complexity of reality, to a certain degree promote an enrichment of [socialist] experience in solving various economic and political problems." Correct approaches are those verified in practice. There could be no plurality of "models" of socialism, some of which rejected such fundamental principles as centralized state planning, an increasing party role, or socialist internationalism, but, according to Kommunist, life had confirmed the Leninist tenet that "'integral socialism' is born of all the best experience accumulated and checked by the [socialist] countries."

In addition to the USSR's enormous experience, it was recognized that there is now a wealth of other socialist experience, including that acquired in "improving the economic mechanism and political organization of society in the course of building developed socialism."[108] The need was "to hammer out a universal system based on a deliberate utilization of the objective economic laws of socialism."[109] But, in pursuing the Leninist concept of "integral socialism," from which Lenin's vision would gradually evolve, as Bogomolov argued in the World Marxist Review, "no good can come from speeding up processes not yet ripe. This is why socialist integration is justified only if the necessary prerequisites are at hand."[110]

At the pragmatic level these prerequisites included the familiar arguments for progress on all fronts. There continued to be great emphasis on the specific cooperation arrangements being worked upon, including joint projects, and on the significance of cooperation among central planning organs. Any real loosening up of trade planning or efforts to justify the combining of planned development with market relations were rejected, the emphasis being on commodity-money levers and contractual sanctions.

Joint planning now loomed somewhat larger, but there appeared to be a certain ambivalence in the Soviet attitude. Fadeyev saw it not as an "ordinary continuation of past forms, but as a qualitatively new and higher stage of planning," yet others still stressed continuity and the experience already gained in this field.[111] At the more propagandistic level, joint planning was seen as of fundamental significance for the socialist community's historic fate because it was already a manifestation of the common plan foreseen by Lenin.[112] In Kommunist, however, there were reassurances that joint planning was "not aimed at formulating some kind of general plan for the Comecon countries to replace national planning of this or that branch or complex of interconnected production processes."[113] There thus still appeared to be considerable sensitivity to the wariness with which many in Eastern Europe viewed the concept of joint planning, and, as with the specter of integration, there was even an element of reassurance in Soviet claims that in fact much already had been done and was being done successfully.

Nevertheless, in connection with the enhanced role foreseen for central planning organs, soon after the Twenty-fourth Council session the idea was broached that a "qualitatively new step" be taken by placing the "indicators of economic relations with the Comecon countries in a separate section of the national plan."[114] Although this possibility was subsequently raised several times by both Lesechko and Fadeyev, it did not appear to become a fixed part of the Soviet liturgy on Comecon, evidently because it received little support in Eastern Europe.[115]

Just prior to the Twenty-fourth Party Congress in March, Lesechko reviewed current Soviet thinking on Comecon in Kommunist.[116] In this article, supranational organs were again rejected, and after recognizing that each country has its own problems which it approaches from its own perspective, the need for trading experience and utilizing the best results of the "further search for means to improve organization and planning" was reaffirmed. Here it was seen necessary to try to "prevent the economic reforms from raising barriers to economic cooperation while, conversely, [making them] contribute to the formation of prerequisites for its effective implementation." Thus, for example, a convergence of internal practices of price-setting was anticipated, in order better to "formulate criteria for the evaluation of profitability and production effectiveness in integration processes," while, in a similar fashion forecasting would lead to the "coordinated adoption of the most rational concepts" if pursued on a multilateral basis. The basic approach was still eclectic and long-range, for it was argued that:

> All the proposals submitted by Comecon countries in the course of formulating the complex program are being thoroughly studied with a view to securing the maximal utilization of anything which could contribute to the rapid development of socialist economic integration. . . . Naturally, time is required to clarify the nature of problems and bring the various viewpoints closer to each other. Time is also necessary in the search for acceptable decisions which would be consistent with the interests of each fraternal country and of the entire socialist community.

An apparent attempt to disarm the Rumanians also was made here. Lesechko viewed economic integration not as a novelty, but as something which had been going on for a long time, which was already quite successful, and which was accelerating. The "new and exceptionally important fact" about the summit was that it formulated a joint strategy in all fields and on a long-range basis, that "for the first time in history" a "qualitatively new" complex program, which took in management, planning, and legal, organizational, and methodological problems, had been undertaken. Commitment ot this all-encompassing long-term program loomed much larger than any commitment to the controversial (and partially implemented) concept of integration itself, while, by implication, the obligation to help formulate this program of course helped to formalize the demands of socialist internationalism. Not subscribing to integration, therefore, did not appear to be a way out, if one had subscribed to the development of the complex program—as Rumania had done at the summit.

The Soviets in fact appeared increasingly optimistic about achieving integration. In addition to their renewed faith in relations based on socialist international principles, this optimism could in large part be explained by the prospects opened up by the scientific-technological revolution. The publication of the draft directives on the Soviet five-year plan and the Twenty-fourth Party Congress in the early months of 1971 confirmed the widespread impression that scientific-technological progress had replaced economic reform as the party's primary hope for rejuvenating the economy.[117] Planning and management were expected to become much more effective as data-processing and control techniques rapidly improved, and the extension of these new approaches to joint forecasting and joint planning were greatly to aid plan coordination within Comecon. Other themes of the Congress also closely paralleled Soviet thinking on Comecon: Kosygin, for example, stressed the need for longer-range planning and for more extensive and harmonious joint planning of interrelated industries.[118]

Of considerable potential significance for Comecon was the support given to the creation of more associations by Brezhnev and Kosygin at the Congress. Although associations have not played a major role in the USSR, they have been a significant feature of most of the economic reforms in Eastern Europe. It has been widely thought that such groupings are better suited than are enterprises to take over foreign trade, specialization, and cooperation arrangements from the ministries—enterprises often being too small and lacking in skilled personnel to be able to get involved in foreign operations efficiently. The introduction of new associations in the USSR promised to facilitate cooperation within Comecon by making the Soviet system more closely parallel those of Eastern Europe, and would be a logical consequence of the Soviet support for the adaptation of internal economic systems to the requirements of integration. That the Soviet economic system also had to adapt and that associations had a major role to play in expanding cooperation was in fact explicitly recognized at the time.[119]

The Twenty-fourth Party Congress, however, did not give new impetus to the Soviet discussion of the economics of integration. On the contrary, following it, there appeared to be a certain hiatus, at least on the more specific aspects of the program. In subsequent commentaries provocative ideas were avoided: the idea of a separate section in plans for integration does not appear to have been repeated by official spokesman, and in one article joint planning was not treated as novel departure, but as something already being introduced in plan coordination.[120]

This did not mean that the political prerequisites for integration were being neglected, but quite the opposite. Foremost among them were proper concepts of sovereignty and of socialist internationalism. The situation was summed up bluntly:

> What determines the importance of the present political, ideological, and theoretical struggle over the question of the sovereignty of the socialist state is that it concerns not simply the theoretical comprehension of one or another concrete political action, but the development of the principle of socialist internationalism as a practical, real basis of socialist international relations applied to the new, higher stage of the world socialist system, the state of socialist integration.[121]

Integration and the principles on which it was to be based were much more than economic issues. Politics had come to the fore, because

> It is a distinctive feature of [economic] integration that it is based on the preservation by each socialist state of its unlimited right to dispose of its own international resources, to engage in economic planning, and so on. In other words, the economic integration of the socialist countries in no way restricts their national sovereignty. From this it follows that socialist economic integration demands still greater responsibility from communist parties in combining, ably and suitably, the international and the national, in vigorously combating any manifestation of nationalism and national selfishness.[122]

While these remarks were in large part probably aimed at Rumania, the apparent shift in focus had much broader implications, not only within Comecon and within the USSR (where integration of the nationalities had become an especially topical issue since the Twenty-fourth Party Congress), but beyond. The downplaying of institutional questions helped to clear the way for rapid adoption of the new program. This suggested that something may have changed in the Soviet outlook, that perhaps grander political designs had made it inexpedient to let differences over the integration program delay its completion further. This something and these designs very likely involved the new drive for détente with the West which was in the making.

NOTES

1. Radio Budapest, May 15, 1970.

2. Polish Television, May 27, 1970, as rebroadcast by Radio Warsaw, same day.

3. TASS, July 10, 1970.

4. V. Garbuzov in Pravda, July 11, 1970.

5. PAP report, Zycie Warszawy, July 15, 1970.

6. A. Solska in Trybuna Ludu, June 2, 1970; Zycie Warszawy, August 11, 1970; interview with the bank's board chairman, V. Vovobyev, Izvestiia, December 13, 1970.

7. Radio Warsaw, May 29, 1970; l'Unità, May 30, 1970.

8. Radio Bucharest, June 4, 1970.

9. N. Ceausescu's interview in Figaro (Paris), May 20, 1970; Scanteia (on the first anniversary of the International Conference of Communist and Workers' Parties in Moscow) June 10, 1970.

10. See, for example, I. Ionescu in Viata Economica, June 26, 1970.

11. Ye. Karpeshchenko and Ye. Zaytsev in Ekonomicheskaia Gazeta, 30, July, 1970.

12. V. Zhamin, V. Zhukov, and Yu. Olsevich in Voprosy Ekonomiki, September, 1970.

13. Radio Moscow (in Rumanian), September 9, 1970.

14. Radio Moscow (in Rumanian), September 10, 1970.

15. Agerpres, October 1, 1970.

16. TASS, October 29, 1970.

17. MTI, November 12, 1970.

18. G. Radulescu, World Marxist Review, November, 1970.

19. With Rumania's entrance, the banks's statutory capital was raised from 1,000,000,000 to 1,052,600,000 transferable rubles. See V. Karpich in Izvestiia, March 10, 1971.

20. TASS, January 13, 1971; Magyar Hirlap, January 14, 1971.

21. N. Eremia in Viata Economica, January 22, 1971.

22. S. Stibor in Rude Pravo, March 24, 1971.

23. The law was approved by the Grand National Assembly on March 17, 1971; Scanteia, March 18, 1971.

24. I. Ionescu in Viata Economica, 6, 7, February 5 and 12; 1971; A. Resiga in Viata Economica, 7, February 12, 1971.

25. N. Eremia in Viata Economica, 8, February 19, 1971.

26. Ibid.; G. Comanici in Viata Economica, 2, January 8, 1971.

27. A. Albu and A. Puiu in Viata Economica, 11, March 12, 1971.

28. C. Lazarescu in Lupta de Clasa, March, 1971; A. Cristescu in Lumea, January 7, 1971.

29. I. Radulescu, Probleme Economice, April, 1971.

30. N. Ceausescu's speech on July 9, 1971, Scanteia, July 13, 1971.

31. Speech in Constanta on July 23, 1971, Scanteia, July 24, 1971.

32. Viata Economica, July 16 and 23, 1971.

33. A. Apro in Nepszabadsay, July 30, 1970.

34. Nepszabadsag, September 17, 1970; Radio Budapest, September 16, 1970.

35. Bela Csikos-Nagy in Kozgazdasagi Szemle, September, 1970.

36. A. Apro in Nepszabadsag, October 17, 1970, and interview with PAP, as reported in Trybuna Ludu, October 18, 1970.

37. G. Gyomai in Penzugyi Szemle, October, 1970.

38. E. Laszlo over Radio Budapest, November 4, 1970; Figyelo, September 16, 1970.

39. In Budapest on November 17-19, 1970, under the auspices of Comecon's Permanent Economic Committee.

40. Antal Apro's remarks as reported in Nepszabadsag, November 18, 1970.

41. Bela Csikos-Nagy's report, published in Kozgazdasagi Szemle, December, 1970.

42. K. Apatini's report on the conference in Penzugyi Szemle, January, 1971.

43. B. Csikos-Nagy in Vilaggazdasag, November 20, 1970.

44. Kadar's speech to the Tenth Party Congress, Radio Budapest, November 23, 1970; Nyers's speech as reported by Nepszabadsag, November 26, 1970, and Radio Budapest, November 25, 1970.

45. R. Nyers in The New Hungarian Quarterly, Winter, 1970.

46. A. Apro in Ekonomicheskaia Gazeta, 47, November, 1970.

47. Brezhnev's speech as reported in Pravda, November 25, 1970.

48. J. Biro in Nepszabadsag, February 14, 1971; J. Fock in Nepszabadsag, January 1, 1971, and Tarsadami Szemle, January, 1971; J. Fekete in The New Hungarian Quarterly, Spring, 1971.

49. Magyar Hirlap, March 9, Radio Budapest, March 11, 1971.

50. J. Szita in Nepszabadsag, March 24, 1971.

51. Valosag, May, 1971; F. Varnai in Nepszabadsag, July 4, 1971.

52. J. Fock's speech on June 23, Nepszabadsag, June 24, 1971.

53. I. Lipovecz over Radio Budapest, July 26, 1971; G. Bereczki over Radio Budapest, July 26, 1971.

54. Imre Pardi in Pravda, July 23, 1971.

55. Rude Pravo, August 26, 1970.

56. Foreign Trade Minister A. Barcak, Rude Pravo, November 6, 1970; A. Mrazek over Radio Prague, November 26, 1970.

57. Strougal's speeches on Prague Television, August 27, and October 10, 1970, and over Radio Bratislava, October 23, 1970 and April 18, 1971.

58. F. Hamouz in Zivot Strany, 20, September 28, 1970.

59. Strougal's report to the Central Committee Plenum on December 10, 1970, Rude Pravo, December 16, 1970.

60. J. Liparsky in Rude Pravo, September 30, 1970; F. Vencovsky in Rude Pravo, October 27, 1970; L. Rusmich in Tvorba, 40, October 7, 1970; J. Kraus in Rude Pravo, December 10, 1970.

61. M. Svoboda in Tvorba, September 19, 1970; J. Fidrmuc over Radio Prague, July 14, 1970; L. Rusmich in Hospodarske Noviny, June 19, 1970, and Praca, September 7, 1970.

62. Rude Pravo, January 8, 1971.

63. These included Premier Strougal, at least according to his remarks at a rally attended by Ulbricht and Stoph as reported over Radio Bratislava, October 23, 1970; see also A. Lantay in Pravda (Bratislava), October 23, 1970.

64. For example, A. Bak in Prava (Bratislava), January 22, 1971.

65. Speech by J. Lenart, the Slovak first secretary, to the Slovak Central Committee plenum on April 27, 1971, Radio Bratislava, same day.

66. Husak's speech as reported by Radio Moscow, April 1, 1971; Strougal's speech as reported by Radio Prague, May 26, 1971.

67. J. Fidrmuc over Radio Bratislava, July 19, 1971; interview with R. Roylicek, the Federal Finance Minister, in Pravda (Bratislava), May 7, 1971; J. Kalfus in Svet Hospodarstvi, May 6, 1971.

68. Vaclav Kves in World Marxist Review, August, 1971.

69. See, for example, Zycie Warszawy, July 15, 1970.

70. L. Siemiakowski in an interview with Zycie Gospodarcze, July 26; 1970.

71. Zycie Warszawy, August 25, 1970; A. Wasilkowski, Zycie Warszawy, October 15, 1970.

72. J. Charnicki in Trybuna Mazowiecka, October 12, 1970.

73. Z. Komender in Slowo Powszechne, November 4, 1970.

74. S. Majewski's speech as reported by Trybuna Ludu, September 5, 1970, and interview with Trybuna Ludu, September 6, 1970; Z. Komender, op. cit.; Trybuna Ludu, October 25, 1970.

75. For example, Radio Warsaw, October 30, 1970; S. Majewski in Trybuna Ludu, October 18, 1970.

76. See especially, A. Wasilkowski in Zycie Warszawy, October 15, 1970.

77. P. Jaroszewicz's speech to the Sejm, December 23, 1970, Trybuna Ludu, December 24-27, 1970.

78. Trybuna Ludu, December 30, 1970; S. Bratkowski in Zycie Warszawy, December 31, 1970-January 1; 1971.

79. Trybuna Ludu, December 31, 1970.

80. A. Solzka in Trybuna Ludu, January 18, 1971; P. Bozyk in Perspectywy, April 30, 1971; M. Dmochowski, Vice-Minister of Foreign trade, in an interview with PAP, April 7, 1971 and in Rynki Zagraniczwe, April 17, 1971; Trybuna Ludu, July 25, 1971.

81. P. Bozyk in Nowe Drogi, February, 1971.

82. J. Redlich, Radio Warsaw, July 7 and 26, 1971.

83. Joint communiqué as reported by PAP, July 17, 1971; Trybuna Ludu, July 23, 1971.

84. St. Sharenkov in Ikonomicheska Misul, 3, 1971.

85. N. Vulev in Gulgarski Profsuyuzi, 1, 1971.

86. Speech by T. Zhivkov at the conclusion of plan coordination negotiations as reported in Rabotnichesko Delo, August 29, 1970.

87. K. Zarev in World Marxist Review, May, 1971.

88. T. Zhivkov, interview with S. Pardera in l'Unita, June 8, 1971.

89. G. Popisakov in Rabotnichesko Delo, July 23, 1971.

90. E. Kamenov, Bulgarian delegate to a symposium on legal aspects of economic integration at The Hague, as reported by BTA, July 26, 1971.

91. For example, K. Fichtner, Deputy Chairman of the Council of Ministers, in Neues Deutschland, June 9, 1970.

92. G. Weiss, Neues Deutschland, May 30, 1970; P. Florin, German Foreign Policy, June, 1970.

93. Report to the Thirteenth Central Committee Plenum by Politburo member A. Norden as reported in Neues Deutschland, June 15, 1970.

94. G. Weiss in Neues Deutschland, May 30, 1970, op. cit.

95. E. Schuerer, Chairman of the State Planning Commission, in Pravda, November 3, 1970; K. Hager, Central Committee Secretary, in Izvestiia, August 28, 1970.

96. W. Seiffert in Staat and Recht, October, 1970.

97. G. Heiland and E. Schumann in Deutsche Aussenpolitik, September-October, 1970. W. Ulbricht's speech to a conference celebrating the 150th anniversary of Engels's birth also reflected the drive for ideological "integration." See Neues Deutschland, November 15, 1970.

98. W. Ulbricht's speech, January 28, 1971, as reported by ADN January 29, 1971.

99. E. Goehler and O. Weitkus in Einheit, 2, 1971.

100. Ibid.; M. Engert and H. Baer in Sozialistische Aussenwirtschaft (special supplement), January, 1971; H. Meiser in Die Wirtschaft, 18, May 5, 1971; P. Sydow and J. Streber in Sozialistische Aussenwirtschaft, April, 1971; K. Herrman in Horizont, 16, April, 1971.

101. Reports to the Fourteenth Central Committee Plenum by P. Werner, Neues Deutschland, December 10, 1970, and by

W. Jarowinsky, East Berlin Radio, December 14, 1970; report by W. Ulbricht to the Fifteenth Central Committee Plenum on January 28, 1971, *Neues Deutschland*, January 30, 1971.

102. W. Kunz in *World Marxist Review*, May, 1971.

103. F. Heiduschat in *Sozialistische Aussenwirtschaft*, June, 1971.

104. G. Weiss in *International Affairs*, June, 1971; H. Busch and W. Seiffert in *Staat and Recht*, April, 1971.

105. H. Busch and W. Seiffert, *op. cit.*; B. Mahlow in *Horizont*, 27 and 28, July, 1971.

106. O. Selyaninov in *International Affairs*, August, 1970.

107. Yu. Belyayev and Yu. Shiryayev in *Kommunist*, 11, July, 1970.

108. O. Bogomolov in *Kommunist*, 8, May, 1970.

109. B. Sukharevsky in *World Marxist Review*, August, 1970.

110. O. Bogomolov in *World Marxist Review*, November, 1970.

111. N. Fadeyev in *Rabotnichesko Delo*, August 10, 1970.

112. I. Dudinsky in *Life Abroad*, 28, July, 1970, and *International Affairs*, November, 1970.

113. Yu. Belyayev and Yu. Shiryayev, *op. cit*.

114. M. Lesechko in *Pravda*, June 30, 1970.

115. N. Fadeyev in *Rabotnichesko Delo*, August 10, 1970, and *World Marxist Review*, August, 1970; M. Lesechko in *Pravda*, March 27, 1971.

116. M. Lesechko in *Kommunist*, 5, March, 1971.

117. According to the draft directives, it was necessary to introduce

> Automated planning and management systems in branches, territorial organizations, associations, and enterprises, with a view to forming in the future a nationwide automated system for the collection and processing of

> information essential for the control, planning, and management of the national economy on the basis of the state system of computer centers and of the unified, automatic communications system of the country as a whole.

Pravda, February 14, 1971.

118. A. Kosygin's report to the Party Congress, April 6, 1971, in Pravda and Izvestiia, April 7, 1971.

119. M. Lesechko in Pravda, March 27, 1971.

120. I. Popov and V. Sviridov in Ekonomicheskaia Gazeta, 26, June, 1971.

121. E. Novoseltsev in International Affairs, May, 1971.

122. O. Selyaninov in International Affairs, July, 1971.

CHAPTER

7

TOWARD "SOCIALIST" INTEGRATION

By the spring of 1971 it had become clear that progress on the integration program had not been as rapid as had been hoped. In a candid moment after the Twenty-fourth Council session, it was acknowledged that this meeting had "not provided for a complete, complex program of improvement in plan coordination [and that certain] problems which were not prepared in detail and preliminarily agreed upon could not be discussed at the session," the latter including aspects of joint planning and investments.[1] A year later many problems were still largely unresolved.

Even the question of the final form in which the integration program would be codified was a confused, and evidently controversial, issue. Reportedly, the summit had "expressly resolved to submit the program of economic integration for preparation in the form of a legal document,"[2] but following the Twenty-fourth Council session, the Polish news agency said that only a "decisive majority" of the member countries had come out in favor of "imparting to the program for the development of integration, besides the character of a resolution of the session, also the character of an interstate agreement."[3] This indicated that some (Rumania?) still had reservations about signing a formal document. Yet, a few days later, the Polish party daily claimed that the Twenty-fourth Council session had, in fact, decided that the program would be given the form of a multilateral interstate agreement.[4] Subsequently, there were references to the preparation of an integration treaty, which was reported to be under examination, along with aspects of the program itself, by a drafting commission set up by Comecon's Executive Committee.[5] It appeared that work on some sort of formal agreement was under way, even though not all were necessarily committed to signing it. Mention of such a formal agreement appeared to die out in late 1970, however, at the same time that talk of deadlines for the program's submission also disappeared.

In the summer of 1970, it was anticipated that the comprehensive program would be "fully elaborated in 1970," and following the Forty-eighth Executive Committee meeting in July, it was said that the integration program would be submitted to member governments by the end of the year.[6] Following this submission, the program was now scheduled, as Hamouz had noted, for final approval at the Twenty-fifth Council meeting during the first half of 1971.[7] However, at the Forty-ninth Executive Committee meeting in October, it was merely decided to continue work on the preliminary drafts of certain documents,[8] and after the Fiftieth session in December, nothing was said about having completed the program or submitting it to the member governments. At the end of December, Jaroszewicz claimed that the program was almost complete, but then went on to note that comprehensive agreements concerning detailed principles governing scientific and technological cooperation were still being prepared for signature and implementation some time during 1971.[9] Although this was apparently never acknowledged, the target date for submitting the program to the member governments had obviously been missed.

In early 1971, progress was evidently still labored, the difficulties undoubtedly being compounded by the December developments in Poland and the delays in drafting the Soviet five-year plan. The communiqué on the Fifty-first Executive Committee session in late February merely noted that the committee had continued to work on the program.[10] Although the deputy Soviet Comecon representative now claimed that preliminary approval had been given to the draft program, his boss, Mikhail Lesechko, said only that work had entered the final stage, while TASS claimed merely that the program had been discussed.[11] Any approval was evidently very preliminary, for at the Twenty-fourth Soviet Party Congress a month later it was apparent that the program was still being worked out. After the Fifty-second Executive Committee session at the end of April, it was again reported simply that questions related to the integration program were discussed,[12] and, although the main point on the agenda of this session had been completion of work on the program, there were no subsequent statements as to when this might be accomplished or when the Twenty-fifth Council session might be held. In early May, Hungarian Premier Fock indicated that it was not imminent when he said that "after two years of work, a document on Comecon integration will be concluded during the current year."[13] It now appeared that the final integration program would not be ready for submission to the Twenty-fifth Council session during the first half of 1971, as planned.

UNDERLYING COMPLICATIONS

Behind these difficulties in formulating the program was of course much more than the question of the form that the integration document should take. A major factor was the continuing state of disarray over reform, both in Comecon and domestically. This was clearly reflected at a conference sponsored by Comecon's Permanent Economic Committee held in Budapest in November, 1970. Despite claims of a certain amount of theoretical and definitional progress—the discussion having shifted, for example, from the criteria of price formation to the role of prices, the fundamental differences remained, "especially concerning the estimation of the relationship between, and importance of, plan and market."[14] The currency system was still at the center of debate, and it was said that no progress was made on such key issues as the function of money or the internal price mechanism.[15] The latter question was closely connected with the coordination of domestic reform, the need for which reportedly was generally agreed upon, although "no acceptable concept of how to effect coordination has yet been worked out."[16] It was also reported that

> debate was particularly trenchant on the question of convertibility. In the opinion of some it is a fundamental requisite for the currency mechanism to be developed on the Comecon market, and according to others it should not be attempted, for the perfecting of mutual economic relations requires more planlike coordination of supply and demand. In their view convertibility would develop spontaneous dependence upon the capitalist market, and would import the currency crisis in the capitalist world economy into socialist financial relations.[17]

In sum:

> All speakers considered the increase and development of the effectiveness of cooperation in production to be important, and they also agreed that a whole complex of measures would be needed to achieve this goal. However, they were not all agreed on the means to be applied.[18]

This lack of agreement was reflected in the lag in legal cooperation. A legal council had not been set up until December, 1969, and it evidently got off to a slow start during the next year, amounting to something considerably less than the legal institution some had suggested. The first conference of legal representatives was not held until July, 1970,[19] and as late as September—just three months before the final program had been due for delivery to the member governments—it was being lamented that

> the working out of legal questions and institutions has been forced to some extent into the background, and therefore integration is faced with heavy tasks in this field. The new economic content of integration requires, instead of the sporadic legislation we have had thus far, the working out and developing of an institutional system.
>
> . . . The integration document for establishing closer economic cooperation among the states will require significant legal work. This includes the drafting of the various contractual forms for the goals, means, and ways of economic cooperation, and the selection of the necessary institutions. With this document and others to be drafted, at the same time we will have to work out the system of institutions for integration, the working order for certain institutions, the forms of decision-making, the relations of the institutions to one another, and so forth.[20]

What was clearly implied, since legal codification would be the last step in introducing new approaches in all of these spheres, was that as yet the lawyers had little, if anything, to work with, because the politicians had not yet come to any firm decisions.

Even by the spring of 1971 it was evident that little progress had been made on contentious questions. On convertibility, for example, it was clear that many still had very strong reservations, particularly about the "spontaneity" which might be fostered if any sort of direct convertibility of national currencies into Western currencies were to be introduced. Although occasional approval continued to be voiced for some ill-defined sort of convertibility within Comecon or between the transferable ruble and Western currencies, it was obvious that the members were no closer to a generally acceptable definition of the concept than in early 1969, when the vague commitment to convertibility was made at the twentieth-anniversary meeting and reaffirmed at the summit.[21] Lack of progress was evident not only on such broad institutional questions as financial reform or the coordination of domestic reform but also in more limited spheres, such as the regulation of joint enterprises, for which, it was acknowledged, appropriate rules had not yet been elaborated and ad hoc decisions were still to be required in each case on exchange rates, taxes, and other financial issues, as well as on any deviation from the laws of the country in which the enterprise was to be located.[22]

INTEGRATION À LA CARTE

By contrast, this same period was, in the natural course of events, the busiest time for working out the practical aspects of trade and cooperation for the next five-year plans. Multilateral cooperation was being expanded or introduced in a wide variety of areas, involving not only such things as computers, automobiles, air traffic control, domestic appliances, and specialist training, but also domestic banks, internal trade ministries, and chambers of commerce. Under the auspices of the new scientific and technological information center, specialists were designing a "single automated information retrieval and distribution system," reflecting the high priority given to scientific and technological cooperation and to starting collaboration with basic research.[23] Multilateral joint forecasting work was reportedly under way in many areas from the food industry to atomic energy production, and there was talk of multilateral joint planning (for example, in agricultural machinery). Even the more routine coordination of trade plans was being complicated by new bilateral and multilateral investment projects—the latter, including a large metallurgical works in the USSR, having been agreed upon without waiting for the new investment bank to begin operations.

At the organizational level things were also active. Organization of the new International Institute for Economic Problems of the World Socialist System was begun, and it was expected to coordinate research among the economic institutes of its members.[24] A number of new specialized coordination centers were agreed upon, and preparations were begun to set up an organization (Interatominstrument) to handle cooperation in the field of nuclear equipment[25] (thereby complementing the Dubna Joint Institute for Nuclear Research).

A new effort was also being made to improve the operations of the Bank for International Cooperation, on the recommendation of the Twenty-fourth Council session. In the summer of 1970 it was decided by the bank's council to restrict the automatic granting of credit and to extend the duration of credit plans in order to give credit extension a more significant role and to increase its flexibility; recommendations on simplifying credit categories, extending the time limits for credit, changing the interest rate structure, raising the bank's capital in convertible currency, and expanding the bank's role in credit planning were under discussion.[26] Probably in connection with this last, it was reported that the rights of the bank's board would be extended, "while preserving the principle of unanimity in the Council," thus suggesting that, as with the new investment bank, it was anticipated that certain operational questions—but not questions of principle—would be decided by majority vote.[27] As of January 1, 1971 the new provisions were introduced, including higher interest rates and a reduction of the types of credit from six to two (short-term automatic credits within a fixed limit and longer-term negotiated credits of up to three years), while during 1971 the bank's gold and convertible currency capital began to be "gradually" expanded.[28]

The investment bank was slowly getting organized. At the first session of the bank's council in November a number of organizational questions were agreed upon, but such crucial questions as the principles of granting, using, and repaying credits and of interest policy and the procedure for paying in capital were only "considered."[29] Although the idea of cheap capital had been rejected—not without some evident ideological embarrassment[30]—there appeared to be some uncertainty as to what the range of interest charged would be. (Following the first council meeting it was reported that interest rates would range from 5 to 7 percent.[31] This was reaffirmed after the second council meeting in January, yet it was claimed elsewhere that both transferable ruble and convertible currency loan rates would correspond to current rates on international markets, while an agreed range of 4 to 6 percent was also reported.[32]) In an interview, the bank's new chairman, Vitali Vorobyov, said that it would provide credit guarantees as well as credits,[33] the facilitating of convertible currency credit from the West very likely being a major objective. At the end of June, 1971, the first projects to be financed by the bank were approved "in principle" at the bank council's third session (two Hungarian and three Polish projects were reportedly involved, with the credits ranging from five to ten years in duration).[34]

In the early months of 1971, piecemeal progress toward multilateral cooperation continued elsewhere, despite the apparent difficulties in agreeing upon a comprehensive integration program. In January, for example, plans were announced for a large automobile factory to be built jointly by Czechoslovakia, East Germany, and Hungary, and the first meeting of a Coordination Council on Problems of Organizational Control, Cybernetics, and Operations Research was held.[35] Among other things the Fifty-first Executive Committee meeting in February approved the basic principles for drawing up long-term forecasts, adopted a joint plan for work in the field of standardization, and approved proposals for extending the authority of foreign trade arbitration bodies.[36] Plans for new coordination and research centers were reported, including new centers to study "ten vital problems" connected with improving industrial management.[37] A new organization for developing mining machinery and expected to carry out "commercial functions" was founded (Intergormash), and plans for a joint factory producing large trucks and for joint construction of power plants and power lines were reported.[38] During the Fifty-second Executive Committee session at the end of April an agreement was signed on the establishment of seven new research or coordination centers.[39]

On various specific cooperation aspects of the integration program, progress was also being reported. At a meeting of Comecon's commission for the chemical industry in May, for example, the primary measures contained in the draft program for cooperation in the chemical, cellulose, and paper industries were approved, and in June the commission for the food industry adopted the provisions in the draft program for forecasting development in the branches of that industry up to 1985.[40] During this period the first conferences of representatives of managerial training centers and of the scientific council of the new economic research institute were held.[41]

While it remained difficult to gauge how multilateral Comecon was actually becoming through all of this—multilateral coordination still normally being finalized through bilateral agreements—integration, particularly since the Twenty-fourth Council session, appeared to be becoming in practice more of a process than a program.

LOOKING WEST

Following the Twenty-fourth Council session in May, 1970, Comecon began to take a more active role in external economic affairs. Efforts appeared to be directed toward having Comecon play a greater role in pan-European endeavors and simultaneously developing the U.N.'s role in East-West economic relations. In June, 1970, the first ministerial-level all-European conference on science and technology was held in Paris, under the auspices of the United Nations Educational, Scientific, and Cultural Organization (UNESCO). In addition to ministers or deputy ministers from all the Comecon members (except Mongolia), four representatives of Comecon were among the observers, and at the proposal of the Comecon countries it was decided that UNESCO would promote further such conferences.[42] Subsequently it was reported that Comecon representatives would continue to broaden their international contacts and had plans to take part in forthcoming European conferences on labor, statistics, and population forecasting.[43] At the end of the year a conference on long-term technological forecasting, organized by the U.N.'s Economic Commission for Europe (ECE) on a Polish initiative, was held in

Warsaw at which, among others, delegates from Comecon, the EEC, and UNESCO took part in the debates.[44] In May, 1971, at the request of the Soviet delegate, Comecon was granted consultative status by the Board of the U.N.'s Industrial Development Organization.[45] While Comecon had participated in U.N. activities since the mid-1950's, notably in the ECE and in the Conferences on Trade and Development (UNCTAD) in 1964 and 1968, its role had been limited and clearly subordinate to that of its individual members. The impression now was that somebody wanted to expand Comecon's role.

This activity was paralleled by the evolution of the concept of a permanent pan-European economic organization. In June, 1970, at a Warsaw Pact foreign ministers' meeting, it was formally, if somewhat vaguely, suggested that "it would be useful to hold a number of European conferences and to set up an appropriate organ [to promote] security and cooperation in Europe."[46] After the signing of the Soviet-West German treaty in August, however, the concept of a permanent organ took on a more interesting aspect. It was suggested that it would be made up of representatives of individual states and that it "could . . . in accordance with the practice of existing regional organizations and under the rules of international law . . . adopt decisions based on the agreement of all its participants."[47] Thus we seemed to be working toward the idea that a regional organization could take over some of the organizational forms and perhaps the functions of Comecon and/or the EEC, evidently so that it could act as a partial substitute for the latter—as well as, of course, for Atlanticism.

This ambitious goal was part of a complex Soviet strategy which involved trying to promote a security conference, East-West economic cooperation, and a permanent regional organization, while at the same time establishing clearer limits on East European economic relations with the West and pushing hard for Comecon integration and a common bloc policy vis-à-vis the West. The difficulties were many. The Soviet concepts of East-West cooperation offered little to excite the West, but closely paralleled Soviet ideas for Comecon and domestic planning and appeared to be inhibited by the standard criticisms of the EEC and the U.S., notably on the question of foreign investment and ownership rights.[48] The recognition that "integration is not only an economic but also a political process" was particularly difficult to reconcile with the idea that pan-European economic cooperation should be substituted for regional integration in the West but not in the East, and anticipation of the ultimate triumph of socialist integration through a "long-term program of democratic changes in the EEC countries," sponsored by the Western communist parties, hardly seemed calculated to reassure Western leaders.[49] Moreover, the constant references to the uniqueness of Comecon, particularly in contrast to the EEC, were closely related to the efforts to construct a more durable political and ideological framework for socialist integration and to argue the necessity for a common policy toward the West—all of which appeared difficult to reconcile with the "Europe-of-States" line on the security conference.

Despite these complications, the signing of the Soviet and Polish treaties with West Germany in the latter half of 1970 and international developments in the first part of 1971—notably the diplomatic re-emergence of China and the much improved prospects for EEC expansion and further integration—contributed to, -if they did not inspire, -the decision to reinvigorate the security conference drive and to move on Berlin. This new diplomatic offensive by the Eastern bloc, along with increased Western pressure for EEC recognition,[50] made it more urgent that the USSR reconsider its timing, if not its tactics, vis-à-vis the EEC and the potential role of Comecon in East-West relations, and consolitate its rear through a successful completion—i. e., unanimous adoption—of the integration program.

In early 1971, as the EEC showed renewed signs of progress, the attitude of the Comecon countries toward it appeared to begin to moderate further. There was a small sign of accommodation in February when, after initially objecting to the implied recognition of the EEC, the USSR signed a new international wheat agreement which—somewhat artificially—gave the EEC the status of one country for signing purposes.[51] This may have in part reflected a sober assessment of the EEC's decision in early February to try to move toward full economic and monetary union, which appeared to come as a particular shock.[52]

In the spring a certain resignation appeared in Soviet commentaries, not only to the EEC's institutional evolution but also to its expansion. Implicitly at first, the probability of British entry began to be accepted, the focus now being on the impact that this would have on "splitting the European continent."[53] At the end of June, after agreement had been reached on all the outstanding major issues involved in Britain's entry, the likelihood of expansion was explicitly acknowledged, and an effort appeared to be made to prepare the Soviet public for this eventuality.[54]

In Eastern Europe during this period, Hungary in particular began to be more conciliatory toward the EEC and, in the process, to foresee a greater role for Comecon. The Hungarians appeared very keen to develop new forms of East-West economic contact which would closely parallel some Comecon concepts and not violate Soviet strictures, yet would allow Comecon and the EEC to find viable roles amongst a variety of permanent all-European arrangements.[55] Hungarian formulations in early 1971 were cautious (the Soviet line on big pan-European infrastructure projects being strong), but it was now suggested that the economic groupings which have developed in isolation in Europe should no longer do so, and instead the countries in them should widen their contacts in the framework of all-European cooperation.[56] In March, Kadar appeared to go much further when, in an interview with a Western news agency, he said that both Comecon and the EEC are realities and "obviously will remain so. Therefore I find it reasonable that some sort of contact be established between the two organizations, and most probably this is going to happen."[57] Thereafter, a leading Hungarian professor addressing a Western forum returned to this idea when, after noting that the expansion of the EEC was under way and that Comecon was emerging into a new phase of integration, he remarked that in consequence the "relation between the two economic organizations in Europe will gain a very important role in coming years."[58] Although the latter views do not appear to have been elaborated in domestic media and can be taken as primarily for Western consumption, given Kadar's loyalty to the USSR there can be little doubt that the dropping of such hints had Soviet backing.

In Poland too there were suggestions of bloc-to-bloc relations. One article, in fact, linked the anticipated increase in pressure for recognition of the EEC, following the introduction of common trade policies at the beginning of 1973, directly to the need to speed up the convocation of a security conference in order to deal with the question of East-West economic relations.[59] These various East European remarks undoubtedly reflected growing concern over the EEC's apparent progress, but, like the efforts to enhance Comecon's presence in East-West economic endeavors, they served essentially to help prepare the groundwork for a shift in policy without making any prior commitment to such a shift.

In May, when signs of enhanced Soviet interest in détente were fast accumulating, Comecon's international ambitions turned to new spheres. A Comecon delegation headed by the organization's secretary, Fadeyev, went to Cairo to meet with the secretary-general of the Arab League to discuss economic cooperation between Comecon and the league, and the results were considered significant enough to warrant a report to the Fifty-third Executive Committee session (at which the draft integration program was receiving final Executive Committee approval).[60] A few days after the Cairo meeting representatives of the National Secretariat of the Northern Council (made up of Denmark, Finland, Iceland, Norway, and Sweden) met with representatives of the Comecon secretariat in Moscow to "exchange information" on the activity of the two organizations, and, after a meeting with Fadeyev, Chile's Foreign Minister, Clodomiro

Almeyda, said that his country intended to develop contacts and study the possibilities of cooperation with Comecon.[61]

In July a certain precedent, if not a model, was established for negotiating and signing agreements with West European economic groupings. After nearly a year of negotiations, the USSR signed a commercial treaty and trade agreements which officially recognized Benelux for the first time. Although the agreements were with individual Benelux members, each agreement noted that the members were "acting in common" under the terms of the Benelux treaty.[62] This also served to rationalize bloc policy and to help clear the way for subsequent action, since, except for East Germany, the East European members of Comecon had recognized Benelux a decade ago.

All these moves, however, amounted essentially to contingency planning. In mid-1971 the Soviets evidently still felt that, with the integration program being rapidly finalized and with constant pressure being applied for a bloc approach to foreign policy, they could continue their efforts gradually to enhance Comecon's external role, without making any move to recognize, and thus bolster, the EEC. Nevertheless, while Comecon still remained in the background in bloc discussions of pan-European projects and of a permanent regional organization, a steady broadening of its role in external affairs was improving the basis for including it in the East's evolving designs for Europe, if and when it might be needed.

THE TWENTY-FIFTH COUNCIL SESSION

The Twenty-fifth Council session took place at the end of July in Bucharest with member delegations led by premiers, the absence of party chiefs lending credence to reports that no major political decisions were to be expected. The Executive Committee had accepted the draft program at the end of June, and, as Ceausescu had indicated early in July, a certain agreement had been reached on what integration would not entail.[63] But there had been no clear indications that the Twenty-fifth Council session was imminent until a few days before it began, and few clues were offered as to what concrete decisions to expect.

However, what had happened to enable such rapid progress, from apparent impasse to the holding of the Twenty-fifth Council session, had become clearer. A few days before the Council meeting it was explained by Radio Moscow that integration was, in fact, now conceived of as a two-stage process.[64] The first stage, according to the radio, was to last for three to four five-year planning periods and would carry out tasks for which the conditions had already ripened.

During this stage, improvement of traditional forms and methods of economic cooperation would be combined with the elaboration and introduction of new forms and methods. It was evident that it was only this first stage upon which some agreement had been reached, for the broadcast also reported that the forthcoming session would adopt a program covering a fifteen-to-twenty-year period, i.e., stage one, and it was very cautious in discussing the second stage.

This splitting of integration into two stages and the confining of the integration program to the first stage evidently opened the way to a compromise on the question of integration versus sovereignty. Rumania, in particular, was able to accept "integration" during the first stage because it could, as Ceausescu had done, redefine the term to meet its own stipulations on sovereignty. The USSR, on the other hand, was able to get unanimous agreement to a complex integration program, which included a substantial commitment by East European members to closer economic ties. The struggle over sovereignty and socialist internationalism within Comecon, as elsewhere, would continue, but the formulations in the program for the first stage of integration need no longer be the focal point of debate.

As the session opened, commentaries tended to stress the importance of the program but to be cautious on its actual content. In Poland the party daily noted that, while that country had always recognized the great significance of Comecon cooperation, "we are [now] attaching all the greater weight to it under our new political conditions, seeing in it a new important factor for the success of our plans. . . ."[65] Premier Stoph reflected the new East German position when he wrote in Pravda that "we fully understand the political significance of [economic] cooperation for the strengthening of the socialist community . . . socialist integration is to an equal extent both an economic, scientific, and technological problem and an ideological one.[66]

During this session, little information emerged as to what particular issues were being discussed, what positions were being taken by various members, or what the expected outcome might be. However, the reports of continuing differences of view, of a two-hour delay in the session's scheduled opening, and of numerous meetings in the lobbies indicated that important issues relating to the draft program on integration, as presented to the session by the Executive Committee, were still being negotiated.[67] This did not necessarily mean, however, that the broad interpretation of economic sovereignty or the meaning of integration were being debated, for, as indicated by Ceausescu's earlier remarks, because of the two-phase approach to integration and the absence of party chiefs, the basic political compromise had evidently already essentially been reached. In fact, during the session Radio Moscow was once again reassuring its Rumanian listeners, stressing national interests on which "nobody can impose" participation and the rigorous observation of Comecon principles throughout the organization's entire activity.[68]

At the session Czechoslovak Premier Strougal reportedly voiced his country's total commitment to the integration concept, seeing it as "virtually the only effective possibility" for the successful development of the Czechoslovak economy.[69] Similarly, Polish Premier Jaroszewicz saw the program as of crucial significance for Poland and declared that his country was "ready to accept the integration program in the form submitted [by the Executive Committee] for discussion."[70] He noted, however, that it did not provide "ready solutions" for such "very complicated" questions as contracting and the fulfillment of obligations stemming from cooperation and that it provided only general directions for the establishment and operation of joint economic organizations. Interestingly, he did not mention convertibility, even though he found the exchange rate and price reform provisions in the program to be important.

The communiqué revealed little about what "integration" would mean.[71] In keeping with the "fundamental tasks and guidelines" set by the summit of April, 1969, the Twenty-fifth Council session unanimously endorsed the "complex program of the continued deepening and improvement of cooperation and of the development of socialist economic integration," but the detailed program was left for later publication. This program, the communiqué affirmed, would be carried out stage by stage over a period of fifteen to twenty-years, and it would "rely on the experience amassed" over the past twenty-odd years. The emphasis on continuity and an evolutionary approach to change were also reflected in the reiteration of Comecon's principles (including respect for "state sovereignty, independence, and national interests"), the pledge that socialist integration would not involve the foundation of supernational bodies, and the promise that these principles would guide the carrying out of the integration program in the future.

The most tangible provisions in the communiqué were organizational. The closer cooperation among central planning organs called for at the Twenty-fourth Council session was now to be facilitated by a new Comecon Committee on Cooperation in the Sphere of Planning. In addition, the Commission on Coordinating Scientific and Technological Research was transformed into a Committee on Scientific and Technological Cooperation, and a new Commission on Post and Telecommunications was set up.

NOTES

1. I. Charnicki in *Zycie Warszawy*, July 5-6, 1970.

2. W. Seiffert in *Staat und Recht*, October, 1970, citing the unpublished "Resolution of the Extraordinary 23rd Comecon Council session."

3. PAP, May 16, 1970.

4. *Trybuna Ludu*, May 19, 1970.

5. PAP, July 14, 1970; Radio Moscow, September 17, 1970.

6. V. Karpich in *International Affairs*, August, 1970; interview with Hamouz as reported by Radio Prague, July 27, 1970.

7. F. Hamouz at a press conference reported by Radio Prague, May 22, 1970.

8. TASS, October 22, 1970.

9. *Trybuna Ludu*, December 31, 1970.

10. Communiqué of the Fifty-first Executive Committee, PAP report from Moscow, published in *Trybuna Ludu*, February 27, 1970.

11. A. Zademidko interview in *Izvestiia*, March 4, 1971; M Lesechko in *Pravda*, March 27, 1971; TASS, February 26, 1971.

12. TASS, April 29, 1971; Radio Prague, April 30, 1971.

13. Jeno Fock's speech to the Twenty-second Hungarian Trade Union Congress On May 7, 1971, Radio Budapest, same day.

14. Report on the conference by K. Apatini in *Penzugyi Szemle*, January, 1971.

15. *Nepszabadsag*, November 20, 1970; *Vilaggazdasag*, November, 20, 1970.

16. Report on the conference by I. Wiesel in *Kultureskedelem*, January, 1971.

17. *Ibid*.

18. K. Apatini, op. cit.

19. Pravda, July 30, 1970.

20. I. Szasz, Magyar Jog, September, 1970.

21. See, for example, S. Potac, chairman of the Czechoslovak State Bank, Hospodarske Noviny, July 23, 1970.

22. Magyar Nemzet, March 2, 1971; K. Houska in Hospodarske Noviny, May 14, 1971.

23. TASS, December 8, 1970.

24. TASS, July 29, 1970; A. Apro in Nepszabadsag, July 29, 1970.

25. The Preparatory Committee met in Warsaw in October; Zycie Warszawy, October 30, 1970.

26. Report on the bank's council session in Prague on July 6-7, Ceteka, July 7, 1970; V. Karpich in International Affairs, August, 1970; K. Nazarkin in International Affairs, July, 1971.

27. V. Karpich, op. cit. It was claimed in Sztandar Mlodych, the Polish youth newspaper, that "limitations on the principle of unanimity" for this bank had been decided upon at the Twenty-fourth Council session (W. Koczanowicz, August 31, 1970).

28. N. Eremia in Viata Economica, February, 1971; J. Kalfus, Svet Hospodarstvi, May 6, 1971.

29. TASS, November 19, 1970.

30. G. Mazanov in International Affairs, December, 1970.

31. TASS, November 19, 1970.

32. TASS, January 12, 1971; H. Kisiel in Trybuna Ludu, January 5, 1971; Prague Television, January 19, 1971.

33. Interview with V. Voroboyov in Nepszava, January 17, 1971.

34. MTI, June 30, 1971; Radio Moscow, August 2, 1971. It was apparently not revealed what, if any, other applications were made. Czechoslovakia said that it had not made any but would in the fall (Radio Hvezda, August 9, 1971).

35. Radio Budapest, January 18, 1971; ADN January 27, 1971.

36. Communiqué of the Fifty-first Executive Committee meeting, Trybuna Ludu, February 27, 1971.

37. TASS, March 24, 1971.

38. TASS, March 27, 1971; Radio Moscow (in Rumanian), April 21, 1971; Pravda, April 23, 1971.

39. TASS, April 28, 1971.

40. Neues Deutschland, May 11, 1971; Agerpres, June 8, 1971.

41. PAP, June 14, 1971; TASS, July 7, 1971.

42. RFE (Radio Free Europe) Special/Ovadia, Paris, June 26, 1970.

43. TASS, November 19, 1970.

44. PAP, December 11, 1970.

45. RFE Special/Opper, May 27, 1971.

46. Memorandum of the Warsaw Pact Foreign Ministers meeting in Budapest on June 21-22, 1970, as reported by PAP, June 27, 1970.

47. "New Stage in Preparation for All-European Conference" (unsigned), International Affairs, September, 1970.

48. See, in particular, A. Vetrov in International Affairs, September, 1970; Yu. Rubinsky in Izvestiia, December 27, 1970.

49. M. Maximova in World Marxist Review, March, 1971.

50. In particular at the meeting of EEC foreign ministers in Munich on November 19, 1970, and at the Assembly of the Council of Europe in Strasbourg, January 27, 1971.

51. Reuters dispatches from Geneva, February 19 and 20, 1971.

52. Yuri Zhukov in Pravda, February 12, 1971; L. Volodin in Izvestiia, February 16, 1971.

53. V. Mayevsky in Pravda, April 14, 1971.

54. In a discussion over Radio Moscow on June 27, 1971.

55. See, in particular, J. Bognar in Kozgazdasagi Szemle, November, 1970.

56. Premier Fock, as quoted in Tarsadalmi Szemle, January, 1971.

57. Interview with United Press International, reported by R. Longworth, UPI from Budapest, March 17, 1971.

58. Mihaly Simai at the Danube-European Institute in Linz, Austria, June 5, 1971, RFE Special/Vienna, June 9, 1971.

59. Michal Lytko and Stanislaw Michalowski in Sprawy Miedzynarodowe, April, 1971.

60. Pravda, May 21 and June 27, 1971.

61. TASS, May 27, 1971; Clodomiro Almeyda's news conference reported by T. Shabad in New York Times, May 29, 1971.

62. RFE Special/Dybvik, Brussels, July 14, 1971.

63. N. Ceausescu's speech on July 9, 1971, Scanteia, July 13, 1971.

64. Radio Moscow, July 22, 1971.

65. Trybuna Ludu, July 27, 1971.

66. Willi Stoph in Pravda, July 27, 1971.

67. Radio Budapest, July 27, 1971; PAP, July 28, 1971.

68. Radio Moscow (in Rumanian), July 28, 1971.

69. Radio Prague, July 28, 1971.

70. Piotr Jaroszewicz's speech on July 28, 1971, Trybuna Ludu, August 1, 1971.

71. Communiqué, Agerpres, July 29, 1971, and Pravda, July 30, 1971.

CHAPTER

8

HIGHLIGHTS OF THE INTEGRATION PROGRAM

In early August the press of the Comecon member states published the lengthy integration program.[1] It is broken down into seventeen sections which fall, somewhat arbitrarily, into four chapters. With the exception of a reference to the coordination of foreign economic policy, which is discussed subsequently in dealing with relations with the West, the highlights of the program are treated in chronological order in the following section.

CHAPTER ONE (SECTIONS ONE AND TWO)

Section One: Introduction

The first section presents the "fundamental principles, aims, paths, and means" of the program. Its opening paragraph is notable for its stress on the role of the efforts and development of each member, a favorite Rumanian theme which here seems to overshadow the parallel assertion that the community of socialist states is based on a single type of economic foundation, state system, and ideology.

After outlining the familiar reasons why closer cooperation and integration are needed, including the demands of the scientific-technological revolution and of the class struggle against imperialism, the introduction goes on to give a somewhat cumbersome and imprecise definition of the "deepening and improvement" of cooperation and the development of "integration" among the Comecon countries. They

> constitute a process of the international socialist division of labor, of the rapprochement of their economies and the formation of a modern, highly efficient national economic

> structure, of the gradual rapprochement and equalization of their economic development levels, of the formation of profound and stable ties in the fundamental sectors of the economy, science, and technology, of the extension and consolidation of these countries' international markets, and of the improvement of money-exchange relationships, a process regulated in a deliberate and planned manner by the Comecon countries' communist and workers' parties and governments.

This is followed by the statement that such cooperation and integration will

> continue to be effected in accordance with the principles of socialist internationalism, on the basis of respect for state sovereignty, independence, and national interests, non-interference in other countries' internal affairs, full equality, mutual benefit, and comradely mutual aid. . . . Integration is taking place on the basis of complete voluntaryism; it is not accompanied by the creation of supranational organs, and does not affect the activity of organizations so far as internal planning, finances, and economic accountability are concerned.

After listing the primary ways and means envisioned for carrying out the program, discussed in more detail in subsequent sections (and below), the introduction reaffirms the fact that the program is to cover a fifteen-to-twenty-year period, and

> contains the necessary economic and organizational measures, which will be implemented gradually within the deadlines set by the comprehensive program, taking into consideration the interests of each country and of the community as a whole.

The opening section concludes with a number of vague formulations about the future role in all this of Comecon as an organization. While its role was expected to increase in general, the only specific considerations mentioned are that Comecon's organs are to organize multilateral cooperation and render assistance in implementing it, to analyze and generalize its results, and to formulate recommendations for its further improvement. While the rest of the program was interesting and/or revealing in varying degrees on a number of issues, little more is said about the role of Comecon and its organs. *

---

*On this question, see the discussion of Section Sixteen, Chapter Four, of the program below.

Section Two: Leveling

Section Two, which completes the first chapter, is devoted to the "gradual rapprochement and equalization of the levels of economic development of the Comecon countries." This is described as an "objective historical process in the development of the world socialist system." To facilitate it, the industrially less developed Comecon members are promised "preferential conditions for cooperation" in certain areas. These involve opportunities to participate in new sectors of production and to be allocated a stable and constantly expanding market (providing they guarantee a high technical standard and a high quality of output); assistance in the scientific-technological field (including the lending and training of specialists); and some (undefined) preference in the granting of credits by the new investment bank. Only Mongolia is singled out as holding a "special" place, for its development "demands considerable capital investment and assistance" on the part of other members. However, the elevation of the long-standing—but vague—principle of leveling to something approaching a concrete program appears also to be aimed at inducing other members, notably Rumania, to cooperate more closely with Comecon, the prerequisite for receipt of "preferential conditions" very probably being agreement to cooperate fully in the particular field involved.

CHAPTER TWO (SECTIONS THREE THROUGH NINE)

Chapter Two is the most interesting, for it discusses the spheres in which the possibilities of some institutional changes are foreseen. These sections cover policy consultation, planning, science and technology, foreign trade, currency and financial relations, direct ties and joint organizations, and standardization.

Section Three: Policy Consultation

Section Three first states that the Comecon countries will hold mutual consultations on the main questions of economic, scientific, and technological policy, in order to expand the division of labor and gradually work out and realize the directions of a "coordinated strategy" for improving cooperation and developing integration. The forms, level, and procedures of these consultations, as well as the problems and questions discussed, are to be decided upon by interested members. These consultations are then held "according to a procedure whereby information is given and opinions are exchanged." Then the (still) "interested countries will given concrete form to these consultations on agreed questions through the adoption of appropriate agreements, protocols, or other joint documents." This formulation sets a pattern which occurs throughout the remainder of the program, viz., a commitment in principle to do something, but preservation of the right in individual cases to determine what that something will amount to, and to opt out (sometimes at more than one stage).

Included among the anticipated areas of consultation are utilization of the labor force, the "material stimulation" of labor, internal finance and credit, price formation, improvements in the systems of planning and management, and the basic directions to be taken by foreign economic policy.

Section Four: Planning Cooperation

Section Four, on the "basic directions and tasks in developing cooperation in the sphere of planning", is potentially the most revealing of all the sections, for, as we are constantly reminded, in this document and elsewhere, integration is to be a process "regulated in a deliberate and planned manner." It is first stressed that the central planning organs will bear the responsibility for cooperation in planning, especially "all work on the coordination of plans," both bilateral and multilateral, with the "broad participation of the appropriate Comecon organs, ministries, departments, associations, and major enterprises." The chairmen of the central planning organs are charged with implementing planning cooperation. Thus it is made clear that the responsibility for carrying out this key facet of integration rests on the central planners of the individual members, not on Comecon per se—a practical corollary of the continued rejection of supranationalism.

Planning cooperation is to be developed in five directions: forecasting, long-term plan coordination, five-year-plan coordination, joint planning, and the exchange of experience in improving planning and management. These are taken up separately, but the discussion of them is quite general, and it is said that the actual "program for engaging in cooperation in the sphere of planning" was scheduled to be worked out during the remainder of 1971.

What is stressed throughout this section, in addition to the primary role of members' planning organs, is the voluntary nature of cooperation in planning. To begin with, the interested countries will determine the areas of cooperation to be included in forecasting. On the sensitive question of joint forecasting, the areas must first be agreed upon by Comecon members, and the actual joint forecasts will then be based on agreements reached under the "guidance of the appropriate competent organs" of the interested countries. Comecon's organs will participate only when these areas have been defined. In similar fashion, the coordination of long-term plans will be dependent upon the revelation of mutual interest and will be effected through bilateral and multilateral consultations between representatives of the interested countries' planning organs. The results of this coordination will then be examined by the planning chairmen, so that interested countries can conclude the appropriate contracts and agreements. Five-year-planning coordination will continue to take place "on those problems in whose joint solution the Comecon countries display interest . . . the sphere of problems to be coordinated and the depth of their elaboration [to be] determined by mutual agreement between the Comecon countries."

When it comes to joint planning, the stipulation that only interested countries will participate is elevated to the subtitle, as is the provision that only individual sectors of industry and types of production will be involved. Here virtually all that has been agreed upon are the limitations on this "new form" of planning cooperation. It is stipulated that the independent nature of domestic planning and national ownership of production capacity and resources are to be maintained during joint planning. The period, content, number of participants, domestic organs involved, and the form and level of agreement are all explicitly left open, while it is again made clear that Comecon does not get involved until the interested countries have agreed to joint planning. It is said, moreover, that, in view of its newness, special attention will be devoted to the formulation of an efficient mechanism for the effective implementation of joint planning and that, in the initial stage, only a small number of sectors and types of production will be involved, joint planning to be extended gradually as experience accumulates.

Only on the final issue, that of exchanging experience in improving national economic planning and management, is this section more noncommittal; the only thing of any moment said in this connection is that this exchange will be for the purpose of promoting the utilization of accumulated experience by members "as they see fit."

Section Five: Cooperation in Science and Technology

A similar pattern develops in the separate section on cooperation in the sphere of science and technology. After first listing the general approaches to be taken (including the systematic holding of policy consultations, the working out of ten-to-fifteen-year forecasts, joint planning on individual problems by interested countries, and expanded specialist training), a considerable list of "agreed-upon" topics for joint resolution is given, at the end of which it is said that the "interested" countries will conclude agreements or contracts on these subjects during 1971.

"Measures designed to create an international system of scientific and technological information" are also to be taken by interested countries. This system is to be built on the basis of cooperation between national systems and of international information subsystems for industries and for special types of information, and "also on the basis of the activity of the International Scientific and Technological Information Center." Interestingly, nothing further is said about the latter, even though it had often been viewed as a potential headquarters for the exchange of information in this field.

Section Six: Foreign Trade and Pricing

The main point of interest here is the idea of nonquota trade. The idea appears to be to start raising nonquota trade from its *ad hoc* status and to make it into a distinct, respectable category of trade. However, no new mechanism was settled upon for engaging in it. The same general delivery terms as apply in the rest of Comecon trade are to be used, and the prices of goods are still to be negotiated bilaterally on the same (old) principles as the rest of Comecon trade. There is no suggestion that domestic prices should play a greater role in determining "socialist market" prices. However, in 1973 the experience of 1971-72 is to be examined, and this examination is to include the question of the "expediency of implementing" nonquota trade on a multilateral basis. Although no explicit connection is made between this vague formulation and financial reform, the two are obviously closely related (see the discussion of Section Seven, below).

The major question of price formation is handled very briefly—in just two sentences, to the effect that "in the immediate future currently operative principles" will prevail and that a comprehensive study of the question of improving the system of foreign-trade pricing is to be made before the end of 1972. In other words, neither in connection with nonquota trade nor on pricing in general were the members able to come to any agreement.

Other major issues also remain unresolved, notably that of increasing responsibility for fulfillment of delivery commitments and that of improving the servicing of machinery and equipment. In both of these areas, the necessary measures are supposed to be formulated during 1971-72.

Section Seven: Financial Reform

Because of the evident lack of agreement on foreign trade and pricing improvements, particularly in connection with nonquota trade, it would be quite remarkable if any major breakthroughs had been made or foreseen in the financial sphere. They weren't, and they aren't.

Section Seven, on "improving currency and financial relations," begins with a discussion of the role foreseen for the transferable ruble, the "collective currency." The general intent is to make the transferable ruble "fully perform" its functions as a measure of value and as a means of payment and accumulation and to "ensure its actual transferability and the realistic nature of [its] exchange rate and gold content." But the basic idea is that, in accordance with the planned development of Comecon ties, the "enhancement of the role of the . . . transferable ruble must be based on the necessary economic prerequisites and, primarily, on a stable multilateral foreign trade turnover and the accumulation of commodity and currency reserves," Further, the "real commodity coverage" of the transferable ruble is based on the "planned development of the trade turnover of the Comecon countries according to agreed-upon contract prices established on the basis of world prices. . . ." While the transferable ruble must "effectively serve foreign economic ties, providing countries with the opportunity to make economically sound decisions," it is the "planned organization of mutual economic ties" which will "create real conditions for ensuring the stability of the gold content and exchange rate" of the transferable ruble. Thus, in each phrasing, the line of causality runs from the real world of planned economic relations (and Western pricing) to the financial world of the transferable ruble. Although not expressly precluded, there is no suggestion that transferability or multilateralism would be automatic or might play any independent or stimulative role in Comecon economic relations.

To carry out these rather vague objectives, it is provided that a "study of the conditions necessary to ensure the realistic nature of the exchange rate and gold content" of the transferable ruble will be conducted prior to the end of 1973; that measures to extend multilateral transactions in all types of mutual trade ties, including nonquota trade, and to permit multilateral trade balancing are to be formulated and implemented during 1971-73; and that in 1974 the results will be examined and further specific measures outlined. The hope is expressed that, in the long run, the transferable ruble may come to be used in transactions with countries outside the Comecon area.

The question of exchange rates or coefficients is taken up separately from the discussion of the transferable ruble.* Comecon

---

*The term coefficient appears to be used here in the Hungarian sense of setting a rate between a domestic currency and an external measure of value such as the ruble or the dollar for internal

members are to set "economically substantiated and mutually agreed upon ratios against the transferable ruble and against each other, in order to extend cooperation, develop integration, etc., " and "possibly introduce, in the long term, reciprocal convertibility of the transfer ruble and national currencies." During 1971, the "aims, procedures, methods, and terms" for establishing new ratios are to be decided upon; during 1972-74, the ratios will be set; and during 1976-79, the Comecon countries are to study the possibilities of, and to work on, the "creation of the preconditions for introducing a single exchange rate for each country's national currency." The transfer to these single rates is to occur as the "considerable differences in the levels of, and correlations between, wholesale and retail prices in the [Comecon] countries are eliminated," with a decision on the question and the establishment of a deadline for their introduction set for 1980. In all of this, the Comecon countries "will resolve the questions of the relations between domestic wholesale prices and foreign trade prices in accordance with their own potential and conditions [and] will determine independently both the question of whether the [new] ratios will be in the form of an exchange rate or a coefficient, and the methods of utilizing these ratios within the country."

Having been mentioned only in passing in connection with exchange rates and coefficients, as noted above, the convertibility issue is then taken up separately and very briefly. Convertibility will be studied during 1971-72, and the terms and procedure for its implementation are to be jointly formulated during 1973—but not, as specified on some other aspects of the program, necessarily agreed upon. Furthermore, its sphere of application will be "jointly determined, taking into consideration each country's specific conditions." There is no reference here to anything that went before, such as the discussions on nonquota trade, transferability, and multilateralism.

This remarkable insulation appears to stem from the fact that there was still no agreement on what convertibility should mean in the Comecon context. The most tangible and realistic concept of convertibility that anyone had come up with is the rather old notion of disciplinary convertibility (under which, after a certain time or achieving a certain size, balances would become repayable on harder terms, e.g., partially in gold, convertible currencies, or high priority goods). The remark about the possible introduction of "reciprocal convertibility" in the long term in the discussion of

---

calculations. This need not involve the actual exchange of currencies. Hereafter both exchange rates and coefficients are included under "ratios."

exchange rates and coefficients, however, suggests that something else was contemplated, viz., convertibility of balances held in one Comecon currency into another. This could perhaps eventually be applied, on a limited and carefully controlled scale, in nonquota trade—e.g., through the offer of surplus consumer goods by organizations with the right to make direct contacts—but there is no hint in the subsection on convertibility as to what they actually have in mind.

A further possibility is suggested implicitly, however, in the following subsection on improving "currency and financial instruments when implementing measures in the sphere of economic and scientific-technological cooperation." It is said that these improvements are to extend to "transactions in the national currencies [and to] the principles for improving transactions relating to expenditures effected in the Comecon countries' internal prices and rates during the construction of joint projects . . . and the maintenance of international . . . organizations." Measures in these areas are to be formulated and agreed upon during 1971-73, the same period during which convertibility is to be first studied and have its terms and procedure for implementation formulated. Although no explicit connection between the provisions in this subsection and convertibility is made, it would appear that the only really effective way to improve financial arrangements in these areas would be to bypass the cumbersome transferable-ruble accounting system altogether, and to settle such domestic expenditures in domestic currencies. Here, too, a limited and carefully controlled convertibility would have obvious benefits.

The concluding discussions in this section, which cover briefly the two Comecon banks and noncommercial settlements, are unrevealing.

Section Eight: Direct Ties and Joint Organizations

The discussion of direct ties once again reaffirms that interest must be displayed by individual Comecon members before any progress can be made in a particular sphere. Moreover, although there is a general commitment to create the "economic and legal preconditions" for direct ties, each member is in charge of its own domestic affairs in this field. Members can decide which of their organizations have the right to establish direct ties and are only obliged to keep the other members informed. It is said, somewhat obscurely, that direct ties "can be effected on individual initiative and with the agreement of the corresponding organs and organizations having the right to establish such ties." At just what level the initiative can be taken is not clear, but this may represent a (small) victory for those seeking greater flexibility in the development of direct contacts.

Similarly, joint economic organizations are to be founded on the basis of contracts between interested countries and "will not be supranational in nature, or touch on internal planning questions." As indicated by earlier discussions, they are to be of two types: "interstate" and "international." The distinction between them is somewhat blurred, but in general the former are to be relatively high-level coordination organizations while the latter are to involve lower-level units operating in narrower spheres. The interstate organizations are to be contractual arrangements among interested countries "basically financed through dues" and are to have "leading" organs and executive organs. On "key questions," the sphere of which is to be determined "specifically" with the creation of these organizations, unanimity is to prevail within the leading organ. On other questions taken up by the leading organs, the "consent of the interested member countries" is required, with each member having the right to declare an interest in any question. Moreover,

> the lack of interest of a member country of the organization in any specific measure does not prevent the interested countries from implementing measures to which they have agreed. The resolutions do not extend to the countries which have declared their lack of interest in a given question. However, each of these countries can subsequently associate itself with the resolutions adopted by the other countries on terms agreed between them.

Thus, a veto will not be possible, but at the same time, neither is majority rule over the minority.

Although nothing is specified about the decision-making procedures within the executive organ, the participating countries "developing and concretizing the established principles can also agree upon other principles for the adoption of resolutions." This statement appears to suggest the possibility of majority decisions on certain nonkey issues, and it may also allow for a degree of real executive authority, if the participants can agree to it.

The "international" organizations appear to be conceived of as normally narrower in scope and more flexible in principle than "interstate" organizations. Again, key questions are to be decided unanimously within the leading organ, and their sphere is to be decided upon "specifically" when the organizations are founded. On other questions, however, the provisions are less precise than with the interstate organizations, for the contract is to determine the decision-making procedure merely by "proceeding from the principle of observing the interests of the participating parties." Moreover, the executive organ's functions and principles appear to be potentially quite broad, for they "must be such that it can successfully and effectively carry out [its] coordinating and economic activity." These organizations are also expected to operate on a "financially autonomous" basis, i.e., to rely on their own income, where possible, as well as to receive dues when necessary. Such organizations, it is said, might include joint enterprises where "expedient," but here the "organizational forms and functions and all other questions linked with their creation and activity" are left up to the interested parties.

The essentially ad hoc nature of these two types of organization and the lack of provision for any further codification of regulations either for them or for direct ties suggest a continuing impasse in these areas. This impasse evidently was already over a year old, for the final paragraph in this section simply says that the implementation of direct links and the creation of joint organizations will be "guided by the principles and provisions approved by the 24th Comecon session".

Section Nine: Standardization

The final section in Chapter Two enumerates the general goals and some deadlines for standardization in a number of spheres. In broad terms, the objective is to "effect, in the years 1971-1980 and on the basis of methodological principles which are being worked out, the comprehensive standardization of the most important forms of output from raw materials to finished articles," particularly those items involved in cooperation and specialization.

CHAPTER THREE (SECTIONS TEN THROUGH FOURTEEN)

Chapter Three is made up of five sections listing the "basic directions and tasks of the development of cooperation" in the spheres of industry, agriculture and the food industry, transport, construction, and water resources. This chapter is the least interesting, yet probably the most important, part of the program. This seeming paradox stems in considerable part from the fact that the previous chapter, which discussed institutional questions, was so inconclusive. Now the planners and engineers take over. Dealing with familiar and concrete topics, they appear to have made more tangible progress than the reformers since the "summit" launched the integration program.

Nevertheless, these sections are still essentially a catalogue of the areas where agreement has been reached in principle, although the deadlines for the completion of studies, the formulation of proposals, etc., are often included. Sometimes the type, and even the location of a project have been decided upon and are given, but otherwise the countries which have already indicated their interest in the projects are not.

Some of the more significant points of agreement listed in this lengthy chapter are:

In Industry

To formulate, during 1971-73, a forecast of fuel and power needs up to the year 2000, and submit proposals for cooperation among the interested countries;

to examine, during 1973-74, on the basis of proposals drawn up in 1972-73, the possible construction by the interested countries of new intersystem power links;

to conclude, during 1971-73, agreements between interested countries and the USSR on cooperation in creating capacities for the production of certain types of ferroalloys in the USSR;

to formulate, during 1971-73, forecasts of the development of power equipment for 1976-80, taking into consideration the possible construction of certain types of nuclear power stations in the Comecon countries; and

to formulate, during, 1971-73, proposals for cooperation in the production of passenger cars.

In Agriculture

To work out comprehensively, before the end of 1972, a forecast of the development, up to 1985, of demand, production, and sales for selected types of output and for certain sectors of agriculture and the food industry;

to examine, during 1972, the possibility and expediency of implementing joint planning to develop the production and sale of certain types of produce and certain sectors of the food industry; and

to examine, during 1971, the possibility of creating, by the joint efforts of interested countries enterprises for the production of certain products such as enzyme preparations, edible acids, and dyes.

In Transportation

To conclude, in 1972, a multilateral agreement on the introduction of a unified container transport system among the Comecon countries.

CHAPTER FOUR (SECTIONS FIFTEEN THROUGH SEVENTEEN)

The final chapter is relatively short, containing sections on the "legal basis" of cooperation, "organizational questions," and "final provisions." According to Section Fifteen, it has been agreed, among other things, to improve the legal basis of cooperation "by bringing closer together the corresponding national legal norms and also through their unification by the interested countries." It has also been decided to devise "general legal norms and conditions" for implementing cooperation in the various fields, including that of the "legal status on the territories of the Comecon countries of the organizations and enterprises created by the interested countries on a multilateral basis." During 1971-72, the possibility of concluding a multilateral agreement on the legal regulation of joint organizations will be studied. In connection with improving procedures for the settlement of disputes, it is said, rather fuzzily, that the "results of studying the proposal on the creation of a Comecon international arbitration organ will be taken into account," while at the same time coordinated measures will be implemented to improve the operations of existing arbitration organs.

Section Sixteen, on organizational questions, adds little to the vague formulations about Comecon's future role in the introductory section. Comecon is to carry out economic research and engage in consultation on the main, long-term directions of economic policy, and to compile forecasts for interested members. Moreover, "if the need arises, Comecon may show initiative to ensure that the interested states enter into negotiations on the creation of new specialized organizations. . . ." Its other mandates are even vaguer, and simply amount to encouraging Comecon to be as helpful as possible.

The final section sets out the principles under which participation in the various activities of the program is to take place. Participation is to be on a "completely voluntary" basis. Furthermore:

> Every Comecon country has the right to state at any moment its interest in participating in a measure of the comprehensive program in which it has previously refused to participate for one reason or another, on terms to be

agreed upon between the interested countries and the given country.

Nonparticipation by one or several Comecon countries in individual measures of the comprehensive program must not prevent the interested countries from effecting joint cooperation. The nonparticipation of some countries in individual measures must not influence cooperation . . . in other spheres of activity.

Nonparticipants in a particular area, moreover, are to be kept informed of what is going on there by the participants. Non-Comecon countries can participate partially or fully in the implementation of the program—fully if they share the program's aims and principles.

LOOKING FORWARD

The integration program turned out to be much more a schedule for the future than a record of achievement since the summit. Reflecting the fading hopes of reform and the growing acceptance of a step-by-step integration process, particularly after the Twenty-fourth Council session, the program reaffirms principles and procedures and provides a compendium of the spheres and projects toward which cooperative efforts are to be directed. Yet the program's sections tend to read like seventeen separate interim reports drawn up by commissions, each of which has been assigned a narrow field. This evidently is just what they are, and no real attempt appears to have been made to tie them together into anything resembling a single comprehensive concept. This is of course because no such uniform concept of integration, either as an ultimate state or as an ongoing process, could be agreed upon.

The program, moreover, did not take the form of a treaty or other interstate agreement, as some had anticipated it would. Rather than the program itself being approved by state and party organs, the activities of their respective delegations were approved, as were measures deemed necessary for the program's fulfillment. As explained by Hamouz, the program had been approved in a "form which enables all countries to accept it as a binding program under the conditions of their legal system and legal relations, [but] there is no need of a ratification; what matters above all is the implementation."[2]

Yet this implementation will evidently get little help from any rapid evolution of approach to planning co-operation, foreign trade, or financial arrangements. The "new" departures foreseen in planning—forecasting, long-term plan coordination, joint planning, and exchange of experience—represent, to a considerable extent, the extension and formalization of past practices, and the voluntary nature of this planning cooperation is stressed throughout. Joint planning in particular is treated very cautiously, and the Soviet idea of incorporating integration obligations separately into national plans was not adopted. Little was decided on the regulation of direct ties or on the regulation and authority of joint organizations. There was no progress on the price question, and no new framework was established for nonquota trade. In the financial sphere the clearest commitment is to the adjustment of exchange rates or coefficients, but, unless more fundamental steps are taken toward multilateral settlements or convertibility, such realignments will mean little, given the marginal role of such ratios at present. On the questions of both multilateralism and convertibility, however, it is clear that no agreement had been reached since the 1969 summit, and the vague and directionless formulations on these questions in the program indicate that, as so often in the past, they were simply again deferred.

At the same time, Comecon's original principles do not appear to have been further eroded since the Twenty-fourth Council session. The elimination of the veto through the substitution of "voluntaryism" for the original principle of interestedness is formally codified in the final provisions, as well as in Section Eight. There is no specific reference to majority decision-making, but it was evidently not accorded wider scope and is not expected to give way to majority rule. Moreover, there is only a vague commitment to policy coordination in the sphere of economic reforms and no perceptible increase in the authority of Comecon's organs. The program thus leaves plenty of scope for interpreting and reinterpreting both the meaning of integration itself and the means of pursuing it. This process began immediately after the Twenty-fifth Council session—even before the program was published.

NOTES

1. The discussion and quotes in this chapter are based on the "Complex Integration Program" published in Pravda and Neues Deutschland, August 7, 1971.

2. F. Hamouz's press conference as reported by Radio Prague, August 5, 1971.

CHAPTER

9

POSTMORTEMS

After the 25th Council session and its adoption of the integration program the reactions among Comecon's members were mixed. There was some disappointment that so little progress had been made on institutional questions during the more than two years of discussion since the summit, but, in general, interest was directed much less to the program's tentative reform provisions in Chapter Two than to the more tangible cooperation projects listed in Chapter Three and, particularly by the Soviets, to the commitment that the program was felt to represent to the joint search for "socialist" integration.

RUMANIA

At the luncheon following the Twenty-fifth Council session the host, Gheorghe Ceausescu expressed his satisfaction with the successful conclusion of the meeting and said the program provided a good basis for future cooperation.[1] He took the opportunity, however, to note that the endorsement of the program was only a start and that the "means for translating it into life" must be found in the same spirit with which the program had been formulated and adopted. Just how wary the Rumanians were of a change in spirit very quickly became apparent.

Right after the meeting closed the Rumanian media began to use the new Comecon program as the basis for again spelling out their views. Any restriction on national economic policy was rejected, and all the familiar Rumanian reservations on Comecon were reiterated. However, economic cooperation within Comecon was soon again being treated positively—beginning in fact at the height of the subsequent campaign against Rumania's independent foreign policy and her flirtation with China.[2] This suggested that Rumania was once more preparing to move ahead in certain new spheres of economic cooperation within Comecon. Rumania also again used the tactic of acknowledging the newer, more far-reaching concepts such as joint planning and economic policy consultation—to which she was now committed in principle through the program, and then playing down their novelty and significance.[3] Moreover, she did not find, as others were to do, that agreement on the program had implications for political cohesion and stressed the continuing requirement of unanimity in the making of important decisions.

In short, whatever others might think, for Rumania the situation and the issues hadn't changed all that much with the adoption of the integration program, and there was no immediate sign of any modification in her established policy of fighting for principle while cooperating in new projects and in new approaches when she deemed it beneficial.

HUNGARY

Hungary again appeared disappointed at the lack of progress toward institutional reform. On his return from the council session, Premier Fock confirmed that the program agreed upon was not quite as comprehensive a program as many had anticipated the Twenty-fifth Council session would adopt. He reportedly said that things did "not go smoothly" and that a number of questions had still to be solved, including "basic aspects of cooperation and commodity-money relations."[4]

Subsequently there appeared to be a further effort to minimize what had been accomplished and to present the program as inconclusive and open-ended, particularly on the question of reform. In an interview, Peter Valyi, the new Hungarian representative to Comecon (since May, 1971) said, among other things:

> During the next two or three years we will have to face the theoretical clarification of a number of questions and make decisions about concrete forms of integration.
>
> . . . I should say that most of the accepted principles of integration are such that their implementation must take place in the context of bilateral agreements.
>
> . . . Most of the work still lies ahead of us. . . .[5]

In a similar vein, a commentator argued:

> Throughout the program there occurs the frequently mentioned concept of integration. But one will not find anywhere in the program a definition of integration, since the program does not attempt to interpret the idea—presumably because the member countries of Comecon take differing views of it and in some cases even contest its existence and practical expression among the socialist countries. There is room for different interpretations of integration, since it is still a concept which has not been clarified in all respects, even as to the economic processes which result in integration or which could be called integration. Thus it is very difficult to decide at the moment which is more important: the concept, the theoretical interpretation, of integration and the establishment of a common standpoint on this question, or the working out of a program for the practical expression of socialist integration—or, more exactly, for making economic cooperation among the socialist countries more effective. The program does the latter. . . .[6]

The author then asserts that this means that "in form, sphere, and method the possibilities are almost unlimited, and everything depends on how these possibilities will be utilized by the interested socialist countries."

A subsequent article gave perhaps the best indication of Hungary's future tactics.[7] In reviewing the program and the progress in the integration discussions, no grand designs were offered and the tone was accommodating toward the interests of others and toward the program's pragmatic approaches to promoting integration. It was argued, however, that no generally accepted concept of integration had been agreed upon and that the most important result of the discussions was the realization of the critical role of the coordination of the aspects of economic policy which affect international cooperation. In this latter connection the touchy issues of systemic reforms and sovereignty were taken up, but this was done in order to put them in the context of taking others' needs into account and of conducting consultations. A major point here was that in order to coordinate group interests and to find practical solutions a system of compensation was necessary. Because no such system had ever been worked out, it was maintained, opportunities to cooperate were frequently foregone. Therefore, the "most difficult and least attacked" problems of commodity-money relations, socialist preferences, regulated markets, and incentive systems have still to be tackled. In this, moreover, the possibilities of pan-European cooperation and of connections with other integration groups, including the EEC, have to be faced.

Like Rumania, Hungary appeared unwilling to view the program as conclusive or as requiring a fundamental change in her long-range concepts, but it now appeared that Hungary's longer-term institutional reform objectives would have to be pursued in a less direct manner, with the program and the necessity of mutual adjustments to the requirements of integration being taken as the points of departure.

Nevertheless, in the fall of 1971 Hungary again, as at the Tenth Party Congress a year earlier, took steps which could be interpreted as reflecting the need to adjust in practice to the demands of integration.[8] Faced with a number of serious economic problems, including an excessive expansion of investments, Hungary chose to increase direct administrative control over investment and international cooperation by the Central Planning Office and other central organs. While a number of domestic considerations were involved in these decisions, a suspicion was raised that the choosing of more traditional responses at the expense of the reform's principles may have been in part dictated by the need to adapt to general Comecon practice. This was also suggested by the sharp contrast between previous Hungarian statements, including Antal Apro's rather aggressive remarks a year earlier on the success of the new Hungarian system and on the need to exchange reform experience (see page 115), and the remark at this time by Premier Fock that "we shouldn't always be talking about [the new system] and giving the general impression that this is a world-saving idea, that it should be adopted everywhere, etc." Little practical result had come of the accommodation to Polish reform views, and, with formidable economic problems at home and no prospects for the acceptance of her Comecon concepts in the foreseeable future, Hungary was evidently feeling more defensive.

CZECHOSLOVAKIA

In an interview following the Council session Premier Strougal showed Czechoslovakia's by now accustomed enthusiasm, mentioning the program's political significance, the common struggle against imperialism, etc., but he found it difficult to point to anything very tangible on which to base his judgment.[9] In fact he sounded rather like an optimistic Hungarian when he remarked that "because the complex program is not bound to a specific timetable and to specific objectives we, like the other Comecon members, also see the possibility of gradually completing it and making it more concrete on the basis of experience gained, practical activity, and theoretical research." In response to a question on the financial measures included in the program Strougal was vague and unenthusiastic, and he managed not to mention convertibility.

In a press conference Hamouz stressed the importance of planning, maintaining that everyone was agreed about its primary significance.[10] He argued that, while the "program does not force anything on anybody . . . and everyone has the right to seek optimal solutions [for himself]", respect must be shown for the development requirements of others, and "we are embarking on new forms of legal, binding contracts which are to contain provisions concerning sanctions and recourse measures" in case of nonfulfillment. He too noted that the program was subject to further elaboration "on the basis of new findings and requirements."

Thereafter, the political significance of the program and its "open nature" with regard to other countries were major themes, as was the Czechoslovak commitment to integration and to the carrying out of the program. But cooperation with the Soviet Union was still of primary significance. The decisions of the Soviet Twenty-fourth Party Congress were even found by Strougal to be the "main guarantee of implementing the program," while in Pravda the chairman of the planning commission, Vaclav Hula, spoke enthusiastically of joint planning, including that of "entire sectors."[11] He argued that while joint planning was still experimental it promised "considerable positive results, even in the immediate future." Nevertheless, it appeared that a better balance might emerge in the Czechoslovak approach, for it was lamented that the central organs stifled the initiative of the enterprises, and, in express agreement with the program and with Soviet experience, an expansion of direct contacts and of the activities of foreign trade organizations and production associations was called for.[12]

POLAND

The Poles continued to stress the great significance of integration and their full commitment to it, but they did not appear to be very happy with the results of the long search for a better institutional framework and tended to point to how much still had to be done to fulfill the tasks set by the program. In an interview on his return from the session Mieczyslaw Jagielski, the new Polish representative to Comecon (who replaced Jaroszewicz in early 1971 and became planning chief as well in October), spoke of the uniqueness and comprehensiveness of the long-term "action" program which had been unanimously accepted at the meeting, but played down the suggestion that a "new stage" had been reached.[13] He noted the many difficulties involved and the need to develop the methods and mechanisms for carrying out the program. In speaking of "gradually creating more effective goods and money instruments" he mentioned price and exchange rate reform but also managed to avoid convertibility. And, in fact, in an interview, K. Olszewski, the Foreign Trade Minister, saw the question of Western convertibility as unimportant at present.[14] He argued that only after the socialist economies were strong enough "could there be talk about making our currencies internationally convertible," suggesting that Poland had virtually abandoned its idea of convertibility with the West for the time being.

Poland's attitude toward the more practical aspects of the program was mixed. In his speech to the Sejm in October, Jaroszewicz referred to the "now indispensible principle of integration" for solving the problems of development common to all Comecon members and found integration to be a prerequisite to the successful implementation of Polish plans.[15] However, in practice these plans, as was stressed in this speech and elsewhere, increasingly concentrated more on developing relations with East Germany and Czechoslovakia, along with the USSR, than on Comecon as a whole. Earlier differences with Ulbricht and apparent receptivity to the Hungarian interest in forming a reform alliance evidently did not now have much impact on the Gierek regime's drive for rapid, tangible economic improvements through cooperation with the most developed members of Comecon.

BULGARIA

In his toast at the luncheon concluding the Twenty-fifth Council meeting Premier Stanko Todorov called the program an historic document of great political and ideological, as well as economic, significance.[16] This "historic, . . . political, . . . ideological significance" of the new program became standard in Bulgarian commentaries, often being linked to increasing the defensive might of socialism in the struggle with capitalism.

It was even found by one military man that the fulfillment of the integration program was

> most directly related to the military might and combat ability of the fraternal armed forces. The objective laws of the present stage of development in the world socialist system necessitate the close alignment and interconnection of national economies and integration in sociopolitical life in the name of communist goals and ideals, rendering this even more imperative in military-technical cooperation. The defense capability of our countries may be developed and perfected only on the basis of the integrated material and technical bases of Warsaw Pact member states. . . .

> . . . The Bulgarian Communist Party has always been an active advocate of the economic and military integration of socialist countries.[17]

On financial reform Bulgaria maintained her strong reservations. Any form of "free convertibility" at the enterprise level or the creation of foreign exchange markets was rejected, and convertibility was seen to be operating only "within the framework of the state foreign exchange plan on the level of central planning organs."[18]

Despite general enthusiasm, in a widely publicized interview Tano Tsolov showed considerable restraint for a Bulgarian spokesman, and in viewing the present task as one of bringing the integration program to materialization he acknowledged that there would be difficulties.[19]

EAST GERMANY

As one would expect, East Germany made the most of the implications of the integration program for bloc cohesion. Premier Stoph saw it as creating "favorable preconditions for shaping our interstate relations in political, military, cultural and other fields. . . ."[20] In a similar, familiar vein Weiss saw the most important prerequisites to integration as the members' common socioeconomic order, ideology, and aims, and found that the program would strengthen the bloc's defense capacity in the face of the intensified struggle with capitalism.[21] The enthusiasm for bilateral economic cooperation, particularly with the USSR, and for the program's specific provisions was effusive,[22] and an effort was made to demonstrate East Germany's constructive contribution to the working out of the program and its full commitment to the fulfillment of this step of "truly historic importance."[23]

In addition, the East German position on conformity evidently was now to be modified. In an interview in Einheit, Stoph enthusiastically spoke of the "inseparable unity" of politics and economics, the multilateral coordination of foreign policy, and the significance of economic integration for cooperation in "culture, education, sports, tourism, and other areas." He went on to acknowledge, however, that Comecon's members are building socialist society under partially different political and economic conditions and that this led not only to differences in their economic interest in particular questions but also to certain differences in the direction and planning of their economies.[24] This apparently conciliatory gesture toward other East European members, particularly Hungary, may have reflected not only East Germany's perception of the fading of the reform threat, but also the emerging new policies of the Honecker regime.

As reflected in the program, the East Germans had not received Soviet backing for their strict, self-serving concepts of systemic and political conformity, and particularly in the face of the Berlin accord and a deteriorating economic situation—due to a very bad harvest and growing industrial imbalances—it was evidently felt necessary to promote renewed friendships in Eastern Europe more actively. Bilateral economic cooperation was now to be expanded in the avowed interests of socialist integration and the new complex program. Increased cooperativeness and modification of the previous hard line on systemic unformity would seem to be logical policies of a regime whose special status within the bloc was disappearing while the prospects for its international legitimization were improving.

USSR

The Soviet media were by far the most vociferous and enthusiastic about the adoption of the integration program. This was not primarily because of the economic benefits it promised, although these were also seen as significant, but because of the very great importance that the program was to have for the political and ideological future of the communist movement. The new integration program was "imbued with the spirit of socialist internationalism" and was "convincing evidence of the consistent implementation of the decisions of the Twenty-fourth Soviet Party Congress and of the other fraternal party congresses—decisions in which socialist integration is considered to be an enormous force in the creation of the new society and in the whole of mankind's progress."[25] Integration was to be a "law-governed process," and the unanimous adoption of the comprehensive program was viewed as an "important step on the path to implementation of the fraternal parties' common, agreed upon political line."[26]

Whatever objective inadequacies there were in the program or whatever compromises were necessary to reach unanimous agreement, there could be no doubt that the Soviets intended to treat the integration program as a new, firm commitment to the drive for political and ideological, as well as economic, cohesion.

Yet continuity was still of very great significance. The program was found to regard socialist integration as an "objective historical process" and integration as the "logical continuation of the close and all-round" past cooperation.[27] It was found, in addition, that "in the course of working out the comprehensive program the socialist countries have proceeded to the practical realization of many of its provisions."[28]

Discussion of this practical realization focused on the comprehensiveness of the program and on improving planning. While the latter was the "center of gravity" of the development of integration, Comecon's members had "adopted the firm course of developing socialist economic integration in every possible way."[29] Thus even those aspects which had not received high priority in the USSR, such as financial reform and the development of the initiative of enterprises and associations, were duly supported.

However, when financial reforms were being discussed the idea that planning improvements were prerequisites to financial improvements was presented even more sharply than in the program. It was argued, for example, that

> the extensive development of multilateral coordination of plans and of production specialization and cooperation and the improvement of the organization of foreign trade links will create the preconditions for the extension of multilateral accounting and multilateral balancing of payments effected in transferable rubles.[30]

After the program had been digested for a few months, an article devoted to the currency and financial "instruments" of integration spelled out the role that they were expected to play in more detail and with more apparent candor than had been the custom while the program was under negotiation.[31] Financial reform within Comecon was closely linked to planned integration, the idea of mutual advantage, and domestic reforms. It was acknowledged that the "sphere of operation of value levers is considerably broader in the international arena than within the socialist states," but these levers are in no sense to "dictate economic cooperation strategy." They are rather to be better integrated elements in the plan coordination mechanism. In fact, it was found, the transferable ruble already performs the essential functions of a world currency, and the enhancement of its role is primarily a question of improving planning and the price formation system and of fulfilling the other aspects of the program. Here the main thing is to introduce "economically justified" exchange ratios to serve as instruments of planned decision-making. The convertibility issue was then addressed more directly than usual, it being argued that

> under socialist conditions convertibility cannot operate on the basis of free market relations and cannot function in the manner of the so-called freely convertible capitalist currencies. . . . The introduction of currency convertibility presupposes simultaneously solving a number of complex problems . . . problems determined by economic and organizational preconditions chiefly in the sphere of

material production [including] more rapid development of highly efficient industries, . . . deepening production specialization and cooperation, . . . and effecting a repprochement among price-formation principles within [member] countries and improving foreign trade prices.

In all of this the role of the collective currency, the transferable ruble, must be enhanced, for, "as experience has shown, it has helped to resolve a whole series of integration tasks which would have to be resolved through reciprocal convertibility of national currencies if the collective currency did not exist."

In addition, any possibility of convertibility with the West, even for the transferable ruble, which would involve Western currencies in intra-Comecon trade appeared to be ruled out by the Soviet Minister of Finance.[32] Whatever "socialist convertibility" might turn out to mean, the Soviets clearly had no intention of letting it play the significant role that many enthusiasts had foreseen.

The greatest Soviet interest and enthusiasm were reserved for the concrete cooperation tasks, which were reported in detail. Along with joint planning, on which there was renewed stress, and the ambitious plans for increased trade in machinery and equipment between the USSR and Eastern Europe,* the projects listed in the program were seen as the most significant aspect of integration. They were closely linked to a renewed interest in giving integration obligations some sort of priority in national plans, and particularly to coordinating economic systems.[33]

Under party control and sponsorship the technocracy was to discover better ways to coordinate plans and management. There was an "urgent need to determine methodological positions on a number of the major problems of integration [and to create] an integral theory of controlling the processes of socialist integration."[34] The focus of this concern was planning methodology, and the significance of improving national systems of planning and management and of exchanging experience in these spheres was stressed. Cooperation in the computer field was singled out in Kommunist as being of

---

*During the 1971-75 plan total Soviet-East European trade was expected to increase about 50 percent, as compared to a 33-35 percent rise in total Soviet trade, thereby raising Comecon's share from 57 to 63 percent of total Soviet trade. Trade in machinery and equipment between Eastern Europe and the USSR was expected to grow some 80 percent and Soviet deliveries to double.

extremely great importance, for it would ensure the creation of national economic management systems within Comecon which would reach the highest scientific and technological standards.[35] One article even spoke of the need for "reciprocal dove-tailing of forms, methods, and trends of economic reforms in Comecon countries with the object of ensuring their growing conformity to the general tasks of integration [for] the general trends of the reforms are linked with the tasks of integration or subordinated to them."[36]

Thus, while the Soviet position retained a certain eclecticism, enthusiasm for the various aspects of the program varied considerably and the pressure for integration and adjustment to its demands was evidently to be stepped up. Interest was concentrated on improving planning techniques and developing East European participation in the many concrete cooperation schemes contained in the program. Integration obligations were expected to be accorded higher priority than in the past—with or without any formal supranational authority for Comecon. This was to be facilitated by the comprehensive approach which took in the entire production cycle, from forecasting and research to reciprocal deliveries, and which sought out every possible way of developing integration.

TOWARD IMPLEMENTATION

Despite the widely differing interpretations put on the integration program by Comecon's members, the implementation of its provisions, particularly of the concrete cooperation projects listed in Chapter Three, became the focal point of their attention in the latter part of 1971. This orientation toward practical cooperation was reflected, for example, in the September signing by all members but Mongolia of multilateral specialization and cooperation agreements in the automobile, glass, and ceramic industries. These were claimed to be the "first exclusive agreements of this type" by the chairman of the Engineering Commission.[37] This practical concern was also reflected by the apparent concentration on such questions as power supplies and machine building at the executive committee meeting in October.[38]

However, as noted, the authority of Comecon itself to deal with these various issues had not been raised. Although the communiqué did not deal with the question, it was subsequently reported that the Twenty-fifth Council session had "advised" the Comecon countries but instructed" Comecon's agencies to be "guided by" the new program, and at the October executive committee meeting the "recommended . . . instructed" formula was once again used to distinguish between Comecon's authority over its own organs and its lack of authority over member countries.[39]

What had evidently happened, in a compromise analagous to that of 1963, was that efforts to strengthen planning at the central level were to be conducted outside the Comecon hierarchy. After Khrushchev's idea of a united planning organ had been rejected, a bureau of the executive committee on integrated planning problems was established which was made up of deputy state planning chairmen and was supposed to advise the executive committee.[40] While this bureau does not appear to have played a very significant role and evidently lacked any real authority, the (unspoken) idea now appears to be to try again through the establishment of the new committees on planning and on scientific and technological cooperation. These committees, to be made up of the chairmen of the state planning commissions and the heads of the leading scientific and technological organs respectively, are to have a "wider sphere of authority and more complex responsibilities" than the standing commissions.[41] Because of their composition, however, they would appear of necessity to be rather remote from the Comecon secretariat and (while like their predecessor perhaps advising the executive committee) in no real sense subordinate to it. The lack of discussion of the anticipated role of these two new committees, either before or immediately following their establishment at the Twenty-fifth Council session, suggested that their prerogatives were rather ill-defined, and indeed in November it was reported that the regulations concerning these committees had not yet been ratified.[42]

Remarks following the adoption of the program confirmed that the financial reform issue was still open and long-term. It was fully acknowledged that financial problems, including convertibility, had "not yet been dealt with," and that there was "no practical experience" on which to proceed.[43] It was also noted that the program "does not take a stand on whether the existence or nonexistence of convertible currency is a condition for socialist integration" and that the possibilities for extension of monetary relations were quite limited because the interests of members differ.[44] As seen above, a major theme in Eastern Europe, as well as in the USSR, was that financial reform had prerequisites which involved the strengthening of socialist economies and the general fulfillment of the integration program.

These very limited prospects for change in the financial sphere meant that the opportunities for making the investment bank into a real financial institution remained equally limited. In an interview in Pravda shortly before the bank council's fourth session in November (at which Hungary, East Germany, Poland, Rumania, and Czechoslovakia received credit),[45] the bank's chairman, V. Vorobyov, was unable to point to anything tangible in his response to a question on what role the bank played, simply maintaining that its activity was organically connected to other aspects of the integration program.[46] Elsewhere, however, there was less reluctance to admit that the bank had little role to play and had little control over its ruble resources. In fact it was still not very clear what these resources were, because "there was never any uniform understanding about basic capital deposits particularly in regard to the transferable ruble." These deposits, it was noted, were to be made through the older Comecon bank in the form of a promised surplus of high quality goods, but it was still not possible to "measure with accuracy what the deposits cover and what purchases of goods they provide for," nor was it settled how claims on these pledges would be exercised. Bilateral barter was still expected to be the rule, for the bank could not take on commercial functions or "undertake to coordinate the operational plans and commercial arrangements of the interested countries involved in an investment."[47] Moreover, no acceptable methodology had yet been developed for judging credit applications, and in a candid moment it was acknowledged that action on the major credit granted (to Czechoslovakia) at the bank's November council session was simply taken "on the basis of the agreement on specialization and cooperation in truck production."[48] Thus, in practice this fledging investment organization still appeared to be more of a clearing house for joint investment proposals than a "bank."

Rather ironically, the one area where it could look forward to performing some of the functions of a real bank was in the utilization of its convertible currency capital. There reportedly was considerable interest in cooperation with it among Western banks, and optimism was expressed that, as had been hoped from the beginning, the convertible currency portion (30 percent) of the bank's capital would serve to attract Western loans and deposits and to facilitate the floating of bond issues on international markets.[49] This expected involvement in Western capital markets by the new investment bank was but one aspect of the evolving policy toward the West.

OPEN INTEGRATION: A LENINIST MODEL

During the Twenty-fifth Comecon Council session there were two conveniently timed statements which indicated that the recent thrust of bloc thinking on Comecon's role in East-West relations was to continue. At a press conference on the second day of the session Hungarian Foreign Trade Minister Jozsef Biro noted that some European countries were thinking in terms of entering the EEC or receiving preferential treatment from it, and argued that this would lead to a new kind of unity in trade policy which would exclude the socialist countries and have an adverse impact on all-European cooperation. He maintained that the security and welfare of European states could only be promoted by wider European cooperation, not by breaking Europe up into blocs.[50] On the same day Finland, which had been playing a major role in the security conference campaign, announced that it had decided to explore the possibilities of cooperating with Comecon, with the first contacts expected to be made before the end of 1971. This announcement followed exploratory talks between Prime Ministers Ahti Karjalainen and Alexei Kosygin in April, when major agreements on bilateral economic cooperation were signed and the question of Finnish cooperation with the new investment bank reportedly came up.[51]

The communiqué on the Twenty-fifth Council session did not attempt to bridge the awkward gap between what integration is expected to do for the socialist community in its struggle against imperialism and how cooperation with the West is to be to everyone's mutual advantage. It simply treated these two issues separately, claiming on the one hand that integration would

> still further consolidate the political unity and solidarity of the fraternal socialist countries, which have special importance in the struggle against imperialism and its policy of undermining the positions of world socialism . . .

while on the other hand offering to let

> any country that is not a Comecon member . . . participate fully or partially in the implementation of the measures envisaged by the comprehensive program . . .

and promising that Comecon members

> will continue to develop economic, scientific, and technological ties with the developing countries and the developed capitalist states on the basis of peaceful coexistence, equality, mutual advantage, and respect for sovereignty.[52]

The latter sentiments were echoed by the head of the only non-member delegation to the session, Aleksandar Grlickov of Yugoslavia, who felt that the program adopted represented an active approach toward cooperation with other countries and that Comecon was "opening up to a much greater extent" to cooperation with the rest of the world.[53] (Subsequently there were indications that Yugoslavia planned to expand her ties with Comecon, cooperation with the investment bank and with additional permanent commissions being under discussion.)[54]

The program itself did not go into the question of external economic relations or Comecon's prospective role in such relations in any great depth or with much clarity. As noted in Chapter 8, it said that the transferable ruble might come to be used in transactions with countries outside the Comecon area, and, as in the communiqué, it offered to let non-Comecon countries participate in the implementation of the program. The program also claimed that the socialist division of labor would be carried out while taking into consideration the world-wide division of labor, and that relations would continue to be developed with all other countries, irrespective of their social and state systems (although special significance was attached to relations with the developing countries). Then appear two potentially very significant, yet very obscure, sentences, which read:

> The members of Comecon will effect, jointly or individually, measures undertaking to guarantee the cooperation and equal membership of socialist states still discriminated against in international economic and scientific-technological organizations. To this end, the members of Comecon will coordinate their foreign economic policy in the interest of normalizing international trade and economic relations, and above all in the interest of eliminating discrimination in this sphere. (Emphasis added.)

While the circumstances under which this coordination of foreign economic policy is to take place appear to have been deliberately left ambiguous, the basis for a more unified Comecon position on some aspects of economic relations with the West appears to have been laid.

In the first months after the adoption of the integration program East European media did not appear to have moved very far beyond their previous positions on East-West economic relations. The familiar themes of the antiimperialist struggle and the contrast between Comecon and the EEC were constantly reiterated. The Poles suggested, however, that the Soviet agreements with the Benelux countries might be a step toward a new formula for East-West economic cooperation.[55] They also noted, as did the USSR, China's more accommodating attitude toward the EEC, a factor which could perhaps be expected to spur developments in Soviet policy.[56]

The next phase in the bloc campaign for all-European economic cooperation and in their thinking about the role of Comecon in fact soon began to take shape in Soviet media. The Soviets spent much of their time sharpening the image of Comecon integration as a weapon to be used against the imperialists and as a promoter of bloc cohesion. The coordination of Comecon members' activities in the world market was found to be an objective demand of the planned socialist economy and to be "particularly important during integration"—the contrary views of "some economists" being rejected.[57] At the same time the program's respect for "sovereignty and national interests" and its "strictly voluntary" nature were used to distinguish it from capitalist integration, and to support its open character in contrast to closed Western groupings such as the EEC.[58] It was then argued that the Comecon states had never supported exclusive groupings, and the program's provisions for cooperating with all countries were stressed.

These rather predictable arguments were linked to an attempt to build up Comecon and the integration program as models for the rest of the world. It was constantly stressed, beginning with the communiqué on the Twenty-fifth Council session, that the Comecon states had been out-performing the capitalist states economically. In fact, it was found that, particularly in view of the West's financial crisis, the "socialist community is establishing for the whole of mankind the path of development for the material and spiritual forces of society," and the integration program was directly linked to Brezhnev's Twenty-fourth Congress vision of the "people of the world [seeing in socialism] the prototype of the future world society."[59] Comecon had even become

> a kind of international laboratory in which the forms and methods used to achieve economic links among the countries of socialism . . . are not only of domestic importance for those countries themselves but are also of tremendous international importance. . . . Socialist economic integration is a new concept in economic theory. . . . The monopolistic bourgeoisie and its politicians and ideologists are striving by all possible means to discredit socialist economic integration [but they] do not wish to—indeed, cannot—understand that only socialism is destined to develop and to bring to fruition the tendency already apparent under capitalism to create a unified world-wide economy as a whole, regulated according to an over-all plan.[60]

The idea of Comecon integration as the prototype of Lenin's common plan for the world could of course simply be part of the mandatory ideological trappings of the new program. But it appeared also to point to something more tangible. It obviously supported the program's bid to the third world and helped to provide an ideological rationale for the extension of large, Comecon-type projects to the whole of Europe. But most significantly, the extolling of Comecon and the "tremendous international importance" attributed to its forms and methods would also seem to qualify it as the prototype for the permanent regional organization being sought under the aegis of a security conference.

A SUMMING UP

The adoption of the complex program did not end the discussions over integration, and the members of Comecon were soon again voicing their views. Since the summit, however, a certain consensus had emerged over what could be attempted during the first, fifteen-to-twenty-year phase of integration, and as a result, for the foreseeable future the relative significance of the issues had changed. There was now little prospect of integration becoming essentially an economic process based to a large degree on a devolution of decision-making, as many had imagined it might during the preinvasion period of high reform hopes. There was also less prospect of integration becoming a suprastate process, which many in the immediate postinvasion period feared would happen through the introduction of some sort of central planning role for Comecon. This was reflected in the program, where the extreme solutions of a market of supranationalism were rejected.

It was not, however, simply a standoff between liberal reformers and conservative centralists. The former's ranks had been depleted by the loss of Czechoslovakia, and the positions of those remaining had adjusted to the emerging possibilities. The Hungarians and the Poles acknowledged that little institutional reform, particularly in the financial sphere, was yet feasible. They had evidently come to be more concerned with keeping Comecon options open than with actually pushing through much institutional change in the near future, and had gradually shifted the focus of their interest to the more immediate issues involved in improving plan coordination and cooperation.

In Eastern Europe, however, it was not only the reformers whose interest in the economic benefits of integration was still paralleled by a fear of the potential political implications. Rumania of course remained the most wary. Her attitude toward principles, if not her economic circumstances, had changed little, and her effort to prevent expanded economic cooperation from leading to political-ideological concessions was clearly to continue as long as Ceausescu was in power. But even East Germany, which had come to feel that there could be a certain political merit in economic integration and which appeared less truculent under Honecker, did not show much interest in sacrificing sovereignty or economic advantage to socialist international policies in which its own interests might not prevail. As a result, there had been little institutional improvement in Comecon from the centralists' point of view either, and differences over the economic forms and methods of integration and over economic policies and their coordination were destined to continue.

The lack of progress toward any sort of economic solution to the integration question and the agreement to disagree over economic issues and to carry the debate forward enhanced the significance of the political framework within which economic integration was to take place. In Comecon, even more than elsewhere, "integration is a political act,"[61] and in seeking to integrate the Comecon states in the absence of much domestic economic reform or of either a market or a suprastate authority within Comecon, the impetus for economic integration must continue to come from political consensus, which is then translated into action by the party's executive organs, the individual state apparatuses in each country. As Professor Wiles has observed, Comecon has "suffered from being a state and not a party organ. The supreme authority being in each country the party, a truly effective Comecon would be 'supraparty,' not supranational as noncommunists understand the term."[62]

Within Comecon this is well understood, and, as the Soviet Union keeps reminding everyone, for all its inconclusiveness, the complex program does amount to a collective commitment, at both party and state level, to participate in the search for the means to integration. Because of its "voluntary" nature the program's lack of formality does not appear to be of great consequence here, and, as Hamouz suggested, the program's degree of success will be far less a question of the legality behind its vague provisions than of the political will to push them through. The stress on the role of central planning organs in the program and the decision to establish a Comecon planning committee at the Twenty-fifth Council session are therefore significant as manifestations of a joint political commitment to integration.

This commitment is the more crucial because the role of the party in integration, as throughout the economic field, is now generally expected to grow. Most of Eastern Europe, as well as the USSR, has been retreating, in varying degrees from its earlier reform concepts, and has generally come to see more complex, sophisticated planning and the accelerated application of the scientific-technological revolution under close party control, rather than devolution of authority, as the main hope for improving economic performance. At the same time, the growing sense of the complexities of economic processes and relationships and of the potential of modern science and technology, including computers, to help overcome them has led to a considerably more sophisticated understanding of integration than existed when Khrushchev broached his idea of a forced division of labor. In particular, the stress on moving back in the production process to research and development and looking further ahead through forecasting means that nothing so simple as a unified planning organ, dealing essentially with investment and specialization, would solve the problem. The broad scope of the provisions in the complex integration program and the proliferation of multilateral coordinating bodies and agreements dealing with all the many aspects of economic relations reflect this understanding, as does the long struggle over broadening the decision-making powers of quasi-autonomous organizations set up under Comecon auspices. Unwelcome a conclusion as it may be, if the sort of extensive domestic economic reforms being projected in the mid-1960s are generally not to be carried through, then the current approach to institutional reform within Comecon makes considerable sense, the lack of more basic financial reforms in Comecon is of lesser moment, and there is a certain logic in continuing to place the collective will of the parties in charge of integration.

Such logic, particularly from the Soviet perspective, must become overwhelming when, without granting supranational authority to Comecon, socialist integration is to be abetted by expanded economic contacts with the West. The USSR has always had a greater political than economic stake in developing Eastern Europe's economic dependence on its supplies and markets, and if this process must, in the interest of viable East European economies, come to involve more interdependence and multilateralism, the first priority is still the political-ideological framework. One can afford to be somewhat eclectic in form and method—even while stressing planning and centralism—as long as integration is furthered and the chosen economic means do not threaten socialist international ends, for, as was demonstrated by Czechoslovakia and Rumania in 1967-68, the greater danger is that without a political commitment to economic integration bloc cohesion can be even more gravely endangered.

Just after the invasion of Czechoslovakia, as the integration drive was getting under way, it was observed that

> the policy choice facing Moscow in coming years is how to balance the defense of its hegemony in East Europe with the pursuit or exploitation of favorable change in West Europe. The difficulties [during 1964-68] arose in part because the Soviets attempted to treat these two dimensions of policy separately in a period when they became essentially inseparable.[63]

Since then, in large part by Soviet choice, in the economic sphere these two dimensions of policy have become even more inseparable. Its members would appear to have been preparing Comecon for two possible roles in future East-West economic relations: that of representing them in economic dealings with the West, and that of serving as a model for the European regional organization expected to be set up at the security conference. The moves to strengthen Comecon's foreign presence and the suggestions that it might deal with the EEC have helped to prepare the way for the former, while the approval by all Comecon members, including Rumania, of an integration program which explicitly rejects supranationalism has strengthened the credibility of the latter.

Although Comecon's continued inability to speak for its members and its dubious credentials as a successful model make one skeptical, "open integration" and the possibility of wanting to give Comecon some role in East-West economic relations mean that the USSR must strive to build the program's obscure commitment to coordinate foreign economic policy and the "new type" of sovereignty being developed under socialism into a political-ideological framework which will tolerate no violation of socialist international interests. Particularly if troop reductions and formal dissolution of military pacts should become real negotiating points between East and West, bloc cohesion would require that integration and its ideological rationale be expanded to encompass military as well as economic relations. Arguments which relate economic integration to military integration or which seek to codify it into Marxist-Leninist law reflect both this need and the hope that economic integration can come to provide the basis of a broader "socialist" integration process.

NOTES

1. N. Ceausescu's toast, Radio Bucharest, July 29, 1971.

2. Evidently beginning with an article by Gheorghe Badrus in *Scanteia*, August 12, 1971.

3. In particular, Rada Constantinescu in *Scanteia*, August 15, 1971, and *Viata Economica*, 33, August, 1971.

4. On Hungarian television, July 29, 1971, as reported by Associated Press, *International Herald Tribune*, July 30, 1971; remarks reported by Radio Budapest, July 29, 1971.

5. *Tarsadalmi Szemle*, August-September, 1971.

6. Pal Gyulai, editor-in-chief of *Vilaggazdasag*, in *Nemzetkozi Szemle*, October, 1971.

7. J. Szita in *Tarsadalmi Szemle*, November, 1971.

8. Revealed in J. Fock's speech on October 22, 1971, *Nepszabadsag*, October 23, 1971.

9. Lubomir Strougal interview with Jan Lipavsky, *Rude Pravo*, July 31, 1971.

10. F. Hamouz press conference as reported by Radio Prague, August 5, 1971.

11. L. Strougal in Sotsialisticheskaya Industriya (Moscow), November 10, 1971; V. Hula in Pravda, November 17, 1971.

12. F. Hamouz's report to the Federal Assembly, September 29, 1971, Ceteka and Radio Prague, the same day; and Jan Lipavsky in Rude Pravo, September 9, 1971.

13. Interview with Mieczyslaw Jagielski, Trybuna Ludu, July 31, 1971.

14. Svenska Dagbladdet (Stockholm), October 13, 1971.

15. P. Jaroszewicz's speech on October 26, 1971, Trybuna Ludu, October 27, 1971.

16. Toast by Premier Todorov, reported by Agerpres, July 29, 1971.

17. Colonel D. Gospodinov in Narodna Armiya, September 22, 1971.

18. Interview with First Deputy Minister of Finance, D. Bazhdarov, in Otechestven Front, August 15, 1971.

19. T. Tsolov's interview on Bulgarian Television and Radio Sofia, August 10, 1971, published in Rabotnichesko Delo, August 11, 1971.

20. Interview with Premier Stoph, East Berlin Radio, July 29, 1971.

21. Interview with Gerhard Weiss, ADN, August 8, 1971.

22. Herbert Weiz in Pravda, September 25, 1971; Kurt Fichtner in Neues Deutschland, October 12, 1971.

23. Peter Florin in Horizont, 40, October, 1971.

24. Interview with Willi Stoph in Einheit, 9, 1971.

25. Pravda, August 8 and 3, 1971.

26. A. Alecseyev in Pravda, August 13, 1971; Izvestiia, August 10, 1971.

27. Pravda, August 8, 1971; N. Fadeyev in Izvestiia, August 19, 1971.

28. Pravda, August 3, 1971.

29. V. Ladygin in Ekonomiches kaya Gazeta, 38, September, 1971; M. Ivliyev, in Ekonomicheskaya Gazeta, 41, October, 1971.

30. V. Garbuzov in Izvestiia, September 11, 1971.

31. Yu. Konstantinov in Ekonomicheskaya Gazeta, 48, November, 1971.

32. V. Garbuzov in Izvestiia, September 11, 1971.

33. V. Ladygin, op. cit.

34. A. Alekseyev in Pravda, August 13, 1971.

35. O. Chakanov in Kommunist, 13, September, 1971.

36. Yu. Kormnov and B. Dyakin in International Affairs, September, 1971.

37. K. Polacek in Svet Hospodarstvi, November 4, 1971.

38. The communiqué on the Fifty-fifth Executive Committee Session, Pravda, October 15, 1971.

39. Ibid.; V. Karpich in International Affairs, October, 1971.

40. See Michael Kaser, Comecon Integration Problems of the Planned Economies (second edition; London: Oxford University Press, 1967), pp. 111-12.

41. Interview with J. Fock as reported by MTI, July 29, 1971.

42. T. Angelov-Todorov, the Bulgarian deputy secretary of Comecon, in Sotsialisticheskaya Industriya, November 2, 1971.

43. S. Potac, Chairman of the Czechoslovak State Bank, in Svet Hospodarstvi, September 10, 1971.

44. Pal Gyulai, op. cit.

45. Radio Bratislava, November 12, 1971.

46. Interview with V. Vorobyov, Pravda, October 27, 1971.

47. K. Botos in Penzugyi Szemle, August-September, 1971.

48. Interview with the Czechoslovak representative to the Council session, Miroslav Kobl, over Radio Bratislava, November 12, 1971.

49. V. Vorobyov interview in Pravda, October 27, 1971; V. Garbuzov in Izvestiia, September 11, 1971.

50. MTI, July 28, 1971.

51. Statement by Finnish Foreign Trade Minister Olavi Mattila, July 28, 1971; RFE Special/Ridala from Helsinki, July 29, 1971.

52. Communiqué published by Agerpres, July 29, 1971, in Pravda, July 30, 1971.

53. As reported by Tanjug and Radio Belgrade, July 30, 1971.

54. Tanjug, October 14, 1971.

55. W. Kubicki in Zycie Warszawy, August 3, 1971.

56. T. Bartoszewicz in Polityka, August 28, 1971.

57. Yu. Kormnov and B. Dyakin, op. cit.

58. V. Ladygin in Ekonomicheskaya Gazeta, 38, September, 1971.

59. V. Mayevsky in Pravda, September 19, 1971; Pravda August 3, 1971.

60. Pravda, August 13, 1971.

61. P. J. Wiles, Communist International Economics (Oxford: Basil Blackwell, 1969), p. 309.

62. Ibid., p. 314.

63. Fritz Ermarth, "Internationalism, Security, and Legitimacy: The Challenge to Soviet Interests in East Europe, 1964-1968," Memorandum Rm-5909-PF, The RAND Corporation, March, 1969.

APPENDIX

PERMANENT COMECON REPRESENTATIVES: JANUARY, 1968-DECEMBER, 1971 (All Deputy Premiers)

Bulgaria	Tano Tsolov
Czechoslovakia	Otakar Simunek (until April, 1968) Frantisek Hamouz (after April, 1968)
East Germany	Gerhard Weiss
Hungary	Antal Apro (until May, 1971) Peter Valyi (after May, 1971)
Poland	Piotr Jaroszewicz (until early 1971) Mieczyslaw Jagielski (after early 1971)
Rumania	Gheorghe Radulescu
USSR	Mikhail Lesechko
Mongolia	Damdingijn Gombozhav

MAJOR COMMUNIST SOURCES

	Radio	News Service	Party Daily	Other
Bulgaria	Sofia	BTA	Rabotnichesko Delo	Novo Vreme
Czechoslovakia	Prague Bratislava	Ceteka	Rude Pravo	Hospodarske Noviny Planovane Hospodarstvi
East Germany	East Berlin	ADN	Neues Deutschland	Sozialistische Aussenwirtschaft Einheit
Hungary	Budapest	MTI	Nepszabadsag	Magyar Hirlap The New Hungarian Quarterly Kozgazdasagi Szemle
Poland	Warsaw	PAP	Trybuna Ludu	Zycie Warszawy Gospodarka Planova Zycie Gospodarcze
Rumania	Bucharest	Agerpres	Scanteia	Lupta de Clasa Viata Economica
USSR	Moscow	TASS	Pravda	Izvestiia Ekonomicheskaia Gazeta International Affairs Kommunist Voprosy Ekonomiki
Other		Tanjug (Yugoslavia)		World Marxist Review

ABOUT THE AUTHOR

HENRY SCHAEFER has been an economic analyst for Radio Free Europe in Munich since 1967. Previously, he served as a U.S. Naval pilot and as an analyst on communist economic affairs with the U.S. Government. He is a graduate of Yale University and did his post-graduate work at the University of California, Berkeley, and at Columbia University. He has published several articles on Soviet and East European affairs.